P9-EJT-790

DONALD TRUMP *v.* THE UNITED STATES

DONALD TRUMP

v.

THE UNITED STATES

Inside the Struggle to Stop a President

Michael S. Schmidt

RANDOM HOUSE
NEW YORK

2023 Random House Trade Paperback Edition

Published in the United States by Random House, an imprint and division of Penguin Random House LLC, New York.

Random House and the House colophon are registered trademarks of Penguin Random House LLC.

Originally published in hardcover in slightly different form in the United States by Random House, an imprint and division of Penguin Random House LLC, in 2020.

ISBN 978-1-9848-5468-1
Ebook ISBN 978-1-9848-5467-4

Printed in the United States of America on acid-free paper

randomhousebooks.com

1st Printing

Book design by Debbie Glasserman

In memory of my cousin
Marine Corps Lance Cpl. John Taylor Schmidt III.
He was born nineteen days before me.
Like far too many of my generation, he paid the ultimate price on the battlefield in the years after the attacks of September 11, 2001.

Think'st thou that duty shall have dread to speak when power to flattery bows? To plainness honor's bound when majesty falls to folly.

WILLIAM SHAKESPEARE, *KING LEAR*

CONTENTS

PROLOGUE

★ ★ ★ ★ ★

WHEN DONALD J. TRUMP entered the Oval Office as president of the United States on January 20, 2017, he ushered in a new age of American politics. His improbable victory stemmed from an explosive collision of novelties. Trump, a political unicorn, without the experience or comportment of any previous public figure seeking high office, was propelled by a new set of forces that were taking hold inside and outside the country.

These forces had begun swirling during the Obama era, when siloed echo chambers increasingly prevented objective facts from penetrating, hardening partisan lines. Political discourse started to reflect a growing sense of grievance and conspiracy, contributing to an erosion of public trust in established institutions. At the same time, a beleaguered foreign adversary tapped into the very same fissures forming in American society to sow chaos and discord, and to undermine the integrity of the country's democratic institutions. Vladimir Putin's Russia showed that in some ways it knew America better than Americans, using the very hallmarks of democracy—particularly the free flow of information—to launch a wide-ranging attack on the 2016 presidential election, designed to bolster Trump's chances of winning the White House.

Nearly all public figures would reject this domestic divisiveness and foreign disruption. But Trump embraced these dual forces, emerging as both the outgrowth and embodiment of this new political era. His refusal to follow norms or honor tradition became a core feature of his political appeal. Trump weathered a series of campaign crises that would have ended the candidacies of anyone else. Stoking a growing tribalism and resentment among a segment of the electorate that felt ignored during the Obama years, he rode their support to the White House. By all accounts, Trump's ascension to the presidency represented one of the most extraordinary stories in our nation's political history.

But the story of his rise would soon be overshadowed by what happened next. As president, Trump sought to wield power in a way so concerning to those around him—his top aides and officials in the executive branch tasked with implementing the administration's agenda and enforcing the law—that they pursued a path rarely, if ever, seen since the country's founding. Instead of enabling the commander in chief's exercise of power, several sought to thwart it. These individuals undertook a mission to stop a president because they feared he could damage himself, the country, and the presidency.

In this era, with Trump now installed as commander in chief, the traditional checks on presidential power would be largely neutered. No part of the Washington establishment seemed protected from the pull of Trump's demand for loyalty to his party of one. Figures of the Washington establishment were faced with a singular question: Are you with Trump or against him? A professional bureaucracy that had historically operated outside the churn of partisan politics, keeping the gears of government turning across Democratic and Republican administrations, found itself thrust into the post-fact, hyperpartisan energy now emanating from the Oval Office. This phenomenon enveloped Congress. Trump routinely outflanked the Democratic lawmakers investigating him, and Republican leadership became Trump's public defenders. Those charged with "calling balls and strikes," career civil servants and journalists, were now maligned as part of the "Deep State" and deemed "fake news."

The place where this new force had its greatest impact was at the Justice Department and its investigative arm, the Federal Bureau of

Investigation. In the forty years since the Watergate scandal, DOJ and the FBI had evolved to a point where trying to keep the perception of politics out of their work was almost as important as enforcing the law itself. Trump's unrelenting push to use the country's law enforcement department as an appendage of his political and personal empire placed DOJ and the FBI under excruciating pressure. Some officials would seek to mollify Trump with half steps, others would outright refuse to bend, and face the consequences. All would feel the strain of the president's demands.

For much of human history, journalists, authors, and academics have focused on how leaders, like presidents, with the help of their advisers, exert power to shape public policy, and on what that says about them, those whom they led, and the times in which they lived. Trump's exercise of presidential power is, of course, worthy of examination, even more so because he has used his power in unprecedented ways. This book covers that ground.

But, at its heart, this book is not the standard account of presidential power or a chronicle of the cabinet meetings and deliberations that animate an administration's agenda. Rather, this book tells the story of a few individuals who were compelled to confront the most powerful leader in the world, uncertain whether he was acting in the interest of the country, his ego, his family business, or Russia. Through their eyes and ears, we observe an epic struggle to restrain an unbound president.

The Trump presidency is the biggest story of our time—a tall tale of brute political power and the titanic struggle atop the United States government. But it is also the most basic human story about how people, thrust into highly unusual circumstances, reacted when, under great pressure, they saw right before their eyes the president act in ways that deeply unnerved them.

You and I will almost certainly never find ourselves in the position of standing between the most powerful person in the world and the abyss, fighting to stop a president from using his power. But whether dealing with a financial hardship, a setback at work, or even just a problem at home with a child, we have all faced a trying situation in which we thought, maybe, we could overcome a challenge that might ultimately be out of our control. In the clashes between Trump and those seeking to stop him, we see, and perhaps identify with, ordinary people operating under extraordinary pressure, trying to stop something that may ultimately be beyond them.

There were several officials who stood up to Trump that I could have chosen to concentrate on. I ultimately focused on two main ones: former FBI director James B. Comey and former White House counsel Donald F. McGahn II. I chose Comey because, besides Presidents Obama and Trump, I believe Comey made the decisions that had the greatest impact on the country. His significance makes anything that illuminates his decision making essential to history. If you scored the Trump administration, there are probably people—like John Kelly—who did more to stop Trump than McGahn did. But along with serving as a major container of Trump, McGahn did two other things that made him remarkable: He was in charge of Trump's greatest political accomplishment, and he found himself caught up as the chief witness against Trump in an investigation that posed an existential threat to the president. The arc of this book covers how Comey's decisions led directly to McGahn's problems.

For this monumental struggle, I had a front-row seat. This is what I saw.

—Michael S. Schmidt, June 2020

ACT ONE

I

★ ★ ★ ★ ★

RULE OF LAW, RULE OF TRUMP

AUGUST 1, 2018

ONE YEAR, SIX MONTHS, AND TWELVE DAYS INTO THE PRESIDENCY

WASHINGTON, D.C.—Just before 9:30 on a brutally humid summer night in Washington, I was in a dead sprint down Connecticut Avenue toward the White House, chasing after a man who had no idea I was trying to catch him.

The math, I figured, was simple: I had to cover three city blocks in about thirty seconds before the man reached the northwest gate of the White House grounds and passed through security screening into the eighteen-acre headquarters of the United States' executive branch, safely out of reach. I had a fifty-fifty shot of getting to him.

It definitely occurred to me that it was ridiculous that I was running down the street like a cop chasing after a robber while wearing black dress shoes, jeans, and a sport jacket. But we'd long moved beyond normal in the year and a half since Donald J. Trump had been sworn in as president of the United States and we began confronting the daily bewilderment and furor that came with him running the country. What was unfolding before us was more a rolling series of crises than a traditional presidency, and with every twist and turn it became clearer that the Trump era in America would be the story of our lives.

And so I ran in the dark after this man. Since I'd started at *The New York Times* two months out of college as a clerk in the sports department, I had probably done stranger things in pursuit of a story. For one of my first big assignments, I tracked George Steinbrenner, the combustible owner of the New York Yankees, as he left the stadium and headed to the parking lot after games, aiming to capture a complaint about his club that would make a headline the next day. From there, I eventually took on a beat no one else wanted—performance-enhancing drugs—and had been hired as a full-time reporter. After four years, I left sports to spend a year in the *Times*' Baghdad bureau, before being moved to the Washington bureau in 2012. I covered the Secret Service, the FBI, and the Defense Department. But now, having joined a team investigating the Trump White House following the 2016 election, none of my experiences prepared me for the sheer velocity and disorientation of covering this president.

A few months earlier, it had become clear there was an emerging existential threat to Trump's presidency. A team of investigators from a special counsel's office was bearing down on the White House, the president wasn't taking it well, and his volatility itself had become a matter of grave national importance. A president in trouble, whose conduct was so unpredictable, required good sourcing to understand. It pushed us to get better at cultivating and protecting our sources, so I had recently found myself chauffeuring a key witness to the chaos around the Washington metro area. At all hours of the day, I would pick the source up at airports and train stations in my mother's fourteen-year-old Volvo station wagon for secret meetings in the only place where I could have the source's undivided attention and guarantee him that, as we snaked aimlessly through Washington's leafy neighborhoods and talked, no one would see us together or hear what we were saying.

Now, as for the man I was chasing down the street, he had never been a source, but I wanted badly to know everything he knew about President Trump and the inside dynamics of his administration. The man had been in the room for many of the events being investigated by the special counsel, though his significance in the unfolding saga went far beyond just passively witnessing extraordinary, possibly historic, or even criminal events in real time. Based on my reporting, the man two blocks in front of me striding back to the Executive Mansion, Donald F. McGahn II, the White House counsel, was more important to the success and survival of Trump's presidency than anyone else in the West Wing.

McGahn was only really known to those who closely watched the administration and monitored the rising and falling cachet of the people around the mercurial president. From McGahn's perspective, he was there to serve as the most senior lawyer responsible for counseling the president behind closed doors and helping him work the levers of power to achieve his policy goals. But because that president was Trump, this was complicated, and what McGahn actually spent his days doing amounted to trying to fit the square peg of what Trump wanted to do as he worked the levers of power through the round hole of what was legal and ethical. Trump had a profound insensitivity to how his actions would be perceived and was often indifferent to the law and precedent. He routinely staked out positions on issues that violated the law and that ran counter to what career law enforcement, intelligence, military, and economic officials believed was right. Even more mysteriously, at times Trump appeared to favor policies that benefited America's geopolitical adversaries, like Russia, more than the United States.

McGahn was one of the few Trump advisers—or members of the Republican establishment, for that matter—who regularly stood up to the president, telling him when his ideas were harebrained and screaming back at him when he unloaded nasty digs at the senior staff. Their clashes were primal, I had been told, and when they got really bad, Trump would go for what was the ultimate insult in his book, telling McGahn that he "used to be a great lawyer." All of this left McGahn sufficiently scarred, and he had started calling Trump "Kong," "King Kong," or "fucking Kong" behind his back, in honor of the oversized gorilla from film lore who would destroy anything in his way. Despite their penchant for clashes and fireworks, McGahn had actually approved a number of Trump's decisions that ultimately boomeranged devastatingly on the president—including some that led to the appointment of Special Counsel Robert S. Mueller III to investigate ties between Trump and Russia and Russian interference in the 2016 election. More important, McGahn had been a rare guardrail on the president—standing in the way when he sought to fire Mueller. And as much as his attempts to rein Trump in infuriated the president, McGahn was almost singularly responsible for the two greatest political accomplishments of the Trump presidency: stacking the courts with conservative judges and slashing government regulations.

McGahn wasn't just the rare senior Trump staffer with the spine to stand up to him—there was more. I had been told there was a secret about McGahn that had the potential to drive Trump from office. A trusted source had told me that as the special counsel had accelerated the investigation of the president the previous year, McGahn had become convinced that with Trump's fleeting sense of loyalty the president was going to make him a scapegoat. Fearing his own legal exposure, McGahn had begun cooperating with Mueller's investigators far more extensively than the White House and Trump knew. He'd even arranged for nearly a thousand pages of handwritten White House notes to be given to investigators without the president's lawyers or anyone else in the White House knowing—notes that provided a road map for how the president had potentially obstructed justice. By giving Mueller's team such an unfiltered and sweeping view of the inside of Trump's West Wing, McGahn was putting his boss's entire presidency in peril.

Sources told me that in a windowless conference room inside the special counsel's offices on the other side of Washington from the White House, McGahn had spent hours laying out what the president did and said behind closed doors as he sought to maintain control over the Russia investigation. McGahn told the prosecutors about how the president insisted on having a loyalist oversee the investigation. He had told them the true reasons the president had for firing the FBI director, James Comey. He had told them that Trump wanted Mueller out. I had discovered that the cooperation had become so chummy that Mueller's team had begun trying to run McGahn—"run" being a term used to describe how investigators use informants to infiltrate the mob or drug gangs—and tap him for real-time information about what was going on inside the White House.

Despite essentially turning state's evidence against the president,

McGahn stayed in his job as White House counsel, advising on everything from trade policy to national security. A source told me that McGahn believed he needed to try to stop the president from inflicting damage to the office of the president and the country. The source said that McGahn also worried that if he quit, Trump would install one of his crony lawyers from New York who would rubber-stamp whatever the president wanted—lawyers in the mold of Michael Cohen, who functioned more like fixers.

McGahn's own personal and political ambitions complicated his calculations about whether to stay. He was an ardent libertarian who had become convinced that under both Democratic and Republican presidents the government had overreached in nearly every regard—from health care to education to the wars in the Middle East. With a broken Congress, the most effective way to reverse this trend was to stack the federal courts with hard-line judges in the mold of Antonin Scalia and Clarence Thomas. In fact, McGahn had accepted the White House job on the condition that he essentially serve as a committee of one to determine whom Trump would nominate to the federal bench, including district, appeals, and Supreme Court vacancies. Unlike previous administrations that relied on teams of White House and Justice Department officials who spent months if not years carefully deliberating on candidates for judicial nominations, McGahn streamlined the process and ran it out of his office. When he settled on candidates, he would present them to Trump, who would approve the nominations without raising many questions—simple as that. This hastened the pace at which the administration could get nominations to one of McGahn's closest allies in Washington, the Senate majority leader, Mitch McConnell, who would then ram them through the Senate. By the end of the second year in Trump's presidency, this judicial conveyor belt had nominated more judges than any other modern administration had at the same point. McGahn knew that he would never have this power again. The longer he stayed in his position—even if doing so imperiled him legally and politically if he ended up on the wrong side of Kong—the more he would change the courts, cement his legacy, and, perhaps, have the chance to fill another Supreme Court vacancy.

Trump's success at confirming conservative judges had become his political umbilical cord to the base—no matter how unseemly his personal conduct or how bombastic his tweets, the judges were his insurance policy against the growing threats to his presidency. Social conservatives, the largest and most enthusiastic faction of the Republican base, had increasingly seen the courts as their best avenue to enact policies they supported on issues like abortion and gun rights. Trump's transformation of the courts allowed many of these Republicans, who otherwise found Trump revolting, to hold their noses and continue to support him, arguing that a president who wanted to champion their values was more important than one who actually lived by them. The bond between Trump and his voters over judges was vital to his survival—Democrats would need to peel off Republicans in Congress if they ever wanted to drive the president from office.

But could this dynamic really explain why McGahn stayed in the West Wing despite misgivings about the president's conduct? Or was McGahn so alarmed by Trump's behavior that he stayed to do whatever he could to protect the country? By advising Trump while at the same time talking to Mueller's prosecutors, was he ethically compromised? I needed to find out, and the only source who was in a position to answer these things was almost at the northwest gate of the White House.

I had been alerted to McGahn's whereabouts ninety seconds earlier by my editor, Amy Fiscus, who'd called me at my desk as she made her way out of the bureau. Until that point, it had been a typical day in the Trump era. Typical in the sense that it had been upended that afternoon by yet another astonishing development that alone would have been a remarkable moment in any other presidency but would soon be overwritten in our collective consciousness by the next outlandish thing the president did. That day, my colleague Maggie Haberman and I had reported that Trump claimed he still wanted to sit for an interview with the special counsel's office, even though his personal lawyers had told him not to, because they believed he would lie.

We'd filed our story on the development late, around 6:00 p.m., and it would be 8:00 p.m. by the time it was edited and sent up to the *Times*' headquarters in New York, going online and making the first edition of the next day's paper. At that hour, the bureau was finally quiet. The rest of the evening looked to be time to finally catch up on everything that had fallen by the wayside—going through my notebook and emails to take inventory of all the leads for stories I had to follow up on. My high school baseball coach had taught us that we should run out every ground ball because you never knew whether there was a scout in the stands clocking times on how quickly you made it to first base. I had adapted this to work, setting out to run down every lead because you never knew which one would turn out to be the big one. And while a call that Don McGahn had just left a nearby restaurant didn't exactly qualify as a standard lead per se, it was an opportunity to talk to *the* key source in the biggest story in the world.

"He's headed back to the White House," Amy relayed to me, watching him head down the street.

As soon as I'd received Amy's message that McGahn was on the move, I threw on my sport coat and raced to the elevator and out of our building, just three blocks north of the White House. About three hundred feet from the White House, in the middle of Lafayette Park, I could see Secret Service officers, straggling tourists, and protesters scattered on Pennsylvania Avenue in front of the spiked fence. I was running on land that supposedly used to be an actual swamp, and even though it wasn't raining, the humidity and heavy air made it feel as if I were running through water.

A hundred feet away, I saw what looked vaguely like the back of McGahn's head as he took his final steps toward the northwest gate. As I got closer, I had to slow down—the last thing I needed was for the Secret Service officers to think I was a fence jumper or that I meant to assault the White House counsel and apprehend me. About forty feet from the entrance, I reached him.

"Don," I said, out of breath.

He turned around.

He did not look happy to see me, and for a second I tried to see myself through his eyes—winded, sweaty, and frantically chasing him toward the most fortified office building in the world at a full sprint. How had it come to this?

I'll try to explain. By this point, Trump had been president for eighteen months, and by every measure, he was looking increasingly vulnerable politically and legally. To understand where we were in the story of the Trump presidency, how susceptible it was to his impulses, and what might happen next, you had to understand every step that had come before it. Because for as polarizing and destabilizing as his presidency had become, the reality was that a series of highly unusual and combustible events and reactions to those events over the past six years had contributed to the defeat of both Mitt Romney and Hillary Clinton, and had propelled Donald Trump to the White House. The way the events lined up was likely more accident than conspiracy, but whatever it was, the conditions had been created to make this extraordinarily unconventional presidency possible.

The way I had come to see it, it had all started with Mitt Romney and a decision he made on September 11, 2012.

In the eleven years since the attacks on the World Trade Center and the Pentagon, which had put America at war and changed everything about the way we think of ourselves and our relationship to the world, the anniversary of that day had become a solemn occasion. And in election years, that day had unofficially become a twenty-four-hour period when the political battles would be suspended. Whether motivated truly by patriotism or out of fear of appearing crass and callous, politicians had learned to control themselves on that day. Indeed, in 2008, John McCain and Barack Obama had actually visited the site of the Twin Towers together, where they laid roses, bowed their heads in prayer, and met with the family members of victims.

But on September 11 four years later, at 6:54 p.m. eastern daylight time, as Mitt Romney's campaign plane made its way over the southeastern United States, the wire service Agence France-Presse moved an alert, indicating a major breaking news story. One American had been killed and another injured in an attack on the U.S.

consulate in Benghazi, Libya, by "an armed mob protesting over a film they said offended Islam," according to the wire service. And that wasn't all. In Cairo, reports indicated that dozens of protesters had climbed over the walls of the American embassy, torn down the American flag, defaced it, and then raised a black flag that read, "There is no God but Allah and Muhammad is his messenger." Images from the scene showed protesters standing atop the concrete walls that surrounded the facility.

The embassy in Cairo, in an apparent attempt to calm the protesters, had released a statement about the controversial film in question, in effect saying that free speech had its limits. The statement had condemned "the continuing efforts by misguided individuals to hurt the religious feelings of Muslims," and added, "We firmly reject the actions by those who abuse the universal right of free speech to hurt the religious beliefs of others."

Romney campaign aides immediately convened a call to figure out how to respond to the attacks. For the Romney aides on the call, the portrait emerging of American diplomatic outposts overrun by violent Muslims as the Obama administration remained largely silent played directly into the image of how Republicans and the conservative media had long sought to portray the president. Since Obama had first emerged on the national scene in 2004 as a candidate for Senate in Illinois, Republicans saw national security issues as one of his greatest vulnerabilities. But depending on where they stood on the party's political spectrum, Republicans displayed their dissatisfaction differently. At the far end of the party, figures like Sarah Palin and Trump openly questioned Obama's patriotism, with Palin describing Obama as "palling around with terrorists" and Trump falsely suggesting that Obama might have been born outside the United States and therefore was constitutionally prohibited from being president. More sophisticated and moderate Republicans like Romney and his aides portrayed Obama as too eager to apologize for the United States abroad, contending that he failed to support allies like Israel and that he had been soft on dictatorships like Russia, which Romney argued as he campaigned was the greatest geopolitical threat to the United States.

In Obama's first term, he offered a rebuttal by aggressively pursuing terrorists through drone strikes and commando raids. No major terrorist attacks on Americans occurred, and he oversaw the greatest national security accomplishment of the post-9/11 era, the successful mission to kill Osama bin Laden. But now a nasty firefight with jihadis—with American casualties—appeared to provide an opening to counter that narrative. "From the point of view of some on the Romney high command, this was manna from heaven," said Gabriel Schoenfeld, a campaign adviser.

On their call, the aides discussed how the White House's reluctance to issue a statement signaled that Obama, in their view, wanted to pretend the attacks were not terrorism because such an admission would mean admitting that al-Qaeda was still active. The aides kept coming back to words like "feckless," "weak," and "coddling."

Several advisers on the call suggested it might be wise to wait a day, until more complete information could be known about the attacks. But others advocated a more confrontational approach. Stuart Stevens, Romney's chief strategist, and policy adviser Lanhee Chen drafted a statement to be issued in Romney's name. "I'm outraged by the attacks on American diplomatic missions in Libya and Egypt and by the death of an American consulate worker in Benghazi," the statement read. "It's disgraceful that the Obama administration's first response was not to condemn attacks on our diplomatic missions, but to sympathize with those who waged the attacks." Initially, the statement was meant to be embargoed until the next day, but when the campaign received word that a reporter had sent the statement to the White House seeking comment, the embargo was lifted. And so, too, was the informal embargo on campaigning on September 11.

Romney's statement tapped a reservoir of dark energy that had been simmering, first on the margins of right-wing media with the advent in 2007 of Breitbart News, a far-right website trafficking in incendiary commentary, and then brought to a boil—and into the mainstream—by the aggrieved, conspiratorial tone of Fox News and conservative talk radio pundits. Whether he realized it or not, with his Benghazi statement, Romney had sounded a dog whistle to an emergent base of the Republican Party, who were primed by this aggressive style and hypernationalist, even nativist, rhetoric of the far-right media machine. On a primal level, as this version of the story went, the Benghazi attacks were perpetrated by shadowy foreigners who posed a threat to "us," possessed values alien to our own, and could have been thwarted with better fortified walls protecting the besieged American outposts. Had the United States not been so deeply—and wrongly—engaged in global affairs, intervening in conflicts in far-flung countries while ignoring the erosion of life at home, according to this narrative, we could have avoided such violent attacks. Perhaps worst of all in the eyes of this growing faction of right-wing activists, instead of standing strong in the face of violence directed at America, the Obama administration's response was to cower and capitulate. Now the Republicans' so-called mainstream candidate was using his position as the face of the party to throw an accelerant on this smoldering fire in the party.

The Romney campaign was roundly attacked for responding prematurely to a still-unfolding national security crisis, and for doing so on a solemn day of mourning. Even some Republicans said that what Romney had done was "hasty and stupid."

Then, at 7:22 a.m. on September 12, the news got worse for the country, and for Romney. The White House said that the death toll in Benghazi, which had risen to four, included the American ambassador to Libya, J. Christopher Stevens.

In Florida, Romney believed he had been right on the merits to attack Obama but was increasingly nervous about the backlash. He knew he could not afford to fall further behind in the race, and walking back the statement felt like the safest thing to do. On an 8:00 a.m. conference call, he let his frustration be known, criticizing his top aides for botching the response and suggesting they might need to reverse course.

"Guys, we screwed up," he said. "This was a mistake."

It took Romney's advisers some time to convince him that he had to hold the line. In fact, they said, the only option was to double down. Eventually, Romney agreed, even if he was going to have to face more contentious responses from adversaries and key allies.

Around 9:00 a.m., Chen received a call from John McCain, the senior senator from Arizona, who immediately began berating him.

"You guys have got your heads up your asses," McCain told Chen. "What kind of irresponsible operation are you guys running?"

McCain, seventy-six at the time, was a war hero, had run for president twice, and was considered one of the elder statesmen of Washington. He knew when to put politics aside, and in his view this was just such a time. McCain was so concerned by how partisan Romney's initial response had been that he feared it could hurt his chances of winning, and he was desperate to see Obama defeated.

McCain told Chen that Romney had crossed a line, having acted far too hastily and failing to consider the implications of going after a sitting president in the middle of an international crisis. The gambit, McCain said, made Romney appear undisciplined and unpresidential on such an important day.

"Why put out a statement when you don't have all the facts?" McCain asked Chen. "Why talk about this in this sort of way without recognizing there was a whole bunch going on you don't know about?"

Well, in terms of the politics and the norms, McCain was right. The way in which Romney had responded to the attack in Benghazi had damaged his faltering campaign. He would go on to lose to Obama less than two months later. His embrace of the most sinister narrative about the Benghazi attacks wasn't solely to blame, but his legitimization of it would put in motion events that would contribute to the defeat of another establishment politician from a famous political family: Hillary Clinton.

To the Republican base, long suspicious that Obama was not ardent in defense of the country against the threat of radical Islam, Romney's line of attack took root and allowed some middle-of-the-road Republicans to question whether the White House's shifting explanations amounted to fog-of-war confusion or a cover-up. For a year and a half, those suspicions deepened, mixed in with half-truths and elements of dark-web conspiracies, as various Republican-controlled committees investigated the attacks. The pressure from the Tea Party wing of the Republican Party to continue digging became so great that in May 2014, the Speaker of the House, Republican John A. Boehner, appointed a select committee to look into the attacks. Boehner named South Carolina Republican Trey Gowdy as head of the committee. Gowdy, who had been a death penalty prosecutor, knew the strongest cases were built on documents, so that's where he started his work.

He wanted to have a baseline understanding of what the State Department had handed over to the four other committees that had already investigated the Benghazi attacks.

Gowdy would learn that, indeed, the State Department had a tranche of fifteen thousand documents that had never been handed over to Congress because there were thorny questions about whether they contained sensitive information, such as classified materials. In a meeting between State officials and Gowdy's investigators, the investigators said they wanted those documents as soon as possible.

At State, now led by Secretary John F. Kerry, lawyers and document specialists worked furiously to go through the documents so they could be quickly produced to the House, celebrating with whiskey as they were pushed out the door in boxes to Gowdy's committee.

The committee, up and running for two months, had only a few investigators on staff and little work space, so the boxes were taken to a windowless room inside the House visitor's center. One of the investigators parked himself on the floor, opened up one of the boxes, and began going through the papers inside. As they thumbed through the emails, giant stacks of documents began to build up on the floor. The investigators saw that some of the most senior officials, including Clinton's top advisers, had sent messages to someone whose name came up only as "H." Given what was written in the text of the emails, the investigators believed it was likely Clinton herself. Other messages were sent to or from another email: hdr22@clintonmail.com.

The investigators determined that there was little to do about the emails. They assumed that Clinton also had a State Department email account, and that they would soon be receiving documents from that account as well. Maybe, the investigators thought, sometime down the road they could make an issue out of the fact that along with using her government email account she had used a personal one too. It would be a decent political poke in the eye for a potential presidential candidate, they thought. But in the meantime, it would only be a distraction from all the other work they had to do on the investigation, and so the issue was tabled.

Several months later, a source told me that Gowdy's committee had received several emails Clinton had sent from a personal account. I thought this was interesting, and planned to run it down, but like the committee investigators, I assumed she had a government email account as well and had used both. I went about my reporting duties without any urgency on the Clinton lead. I traveled to Afghanistan and Kuwait with the secretary of defense and took on an assignment covering a wedding for the *New York Times* Style section for extra cash. When I did start calling around about Clinton's emails, the reaction from my sources revealed that I had hit on something highly consequential. On March 2, I broke the story that Clinton had relied exclusively on a personal email account when she was secretary of state.

For most politicians, the use of a personal email account wouldn't be a big deal. But the revelation reignited familiar unease about the Clintons among Democrats and fit into the narrative—pushed mercilessly by Clinton's critics—that she and her husband felt they could play by their own rules without consequence.

In the Senate, Republicans asked the inspectors general in the national security world to look into whether she'd sent or received any classified information on her personal account. The lead inspector general, a former FBI agent named I. Charles McCullough, found classified material in Clinton's emails and tried to alert the State Department to the issue. A top State official, Patrick Kennedy, pushed back, and in a move of last resort, McCullough referred the matter to the FBI, which opened an investigation into whether Clinton had mishandled classified information.

On the Right, the matter ignited a feeding frenzy—many Republicans had been obsessed with investigating the Clintons since before the couple left Little Rock.

Additionally, a populist strain had been building in the Republican Party, fueled by anti-immigration, anti-free-trade, and isolationist sentiments. And Trump, a New York real estate developer and reality television star who figured he had little chance of getting elected but could run to remain relevant as a public figure, had actually been weighing in on those issues for many years. Unlike the sixteen other candidates running for the Republican nomination, he had a keen instinct for the building populist wave and intuitively exploited it. As a candidate, Trump was unprincipled—vicious and vulgar, with a proclivity to outdo himself that made him a car wreck the country could not stop watching. He was thin-skinned, but somehow impervious to things that would—and did—destroy more normal candidates. He couldn't take a punch, yet he could survive a beating better than anyone else. Despite making racist and sexist comments that created media firestorms, as well as a steady stream of humiliating disclosures about his personal life and business failures that would have ended the candidacies of traditional politicians, Trump trudged on and won his party's nomination. Around that time, the Russian president, Vladimir Putin, who despised Clinton, accelerated a clandestine effort to meddle in the American presidential election, with the objective of undermining Clinton and weakening her before she took office, as she appeared to be skating to an inevitable victory over Trump. Then, twelve days before the election, the FBI director, Comey—who had held an unusual press conference three months earlier to pronounce that the FBI had failed to find enough evidence to prosecute her but had taken the moment to criticize her conduct—publicly announced that the bureau had to examine new evidence about Clinton's email account. The polls were thrown into disarray, and on Election Day, a total of fewer than eighty thousand votes in three states—Michigan, Wisconsin, and Pennsylvania—swung the Electoral College in Trump's favor, even though Clinton would win the popular vote by a substantial margin.

At the age of seventy, as Trump assumed the presidency, he had no interest in changing the behavior that had shaped and defined his public career over four decades as a Manhattan celebrity. In New York, Trump had lied, cheated, and twisted arms, operating in a world dominated by tabloid coverage and among other similarly ethically unbridled businessmen. The worst consequences he had faced in those circles had been bad press, multiple bankruptcies, and hundreds of civil lawsuits. But in Washington, Trump quickly ran up against forces far more powerful: the Justice Department, the FBI, the national media, the laws of the United States, the politics of Capitol Hill, and foreign adversaries. Instead of adapting, he tried to bend the law and reality in ways no president had ever done before, in effect running the federal government just like the private fiefdom he had operated from the twenty-eighth floor of Trump Tower.

A mere four months into Trump's presidency, his antipathy for rules and his belligerence toward his opponents caught up with him. After the FBI director had publicly announced that the bureau was investigating whether Trump's campaign had worked with Russia to sway the election, Trump fired Comey. It was what his New York playbook called for. But in the objective reality of Washington, it seemed as if the president were brazenly shutting down an investigation that he was the subject of, in plain sight, and the move forced Trump's own political appointees at the Justice Department to appoint Mueller, a former Marine officer and FBI director considered one of the last few public officials trusted by both parties, as a special counsel to take over the investigation. The turn of events cast a suffocating cloud over his presidency just as it began.

Trump had never faced an adversary like Mueller, who quickly assembled a team of the best prosecutors and FBI agents and analysts in the country. Many of them left high-paying law firm jobs or top Justice Department posts to join the investigation for what they regarded as a once-in-a-career opportunity. In New York, Trump had always been able to bluff and bluster his way through all manner of difficulties, but Mueller and his team had immense powers to examine Trump's life in ways that had never been done before.

To anyone paying attention, Trump looked like he was in trouble. But he still didn't seem to get it. Instead of taking a disciplined approach led by experienced Washington white-collar defense lawyers, as Bill Clinton had done when he was under investigation, Trump had initially put together a hodgepodge legal team of undisciplined lawyers and television pundits. In the same way that he'd used the tabloids in New York, he thought he could use his Twitter account to undercut Mueller. Even as he intuitively sensed the danger Mueller posed to him, he still coped with that danger with bravado and arrogance—the same way he'd managed banks, creditors, civil lawsuits, and divorce lawyers throughout his public life. Trump obsessed about the investigation publicly and privately. He vented to friends on the phone, ranted to aides in the West Wing, and tweeted about the "Highly conflicted Bob Mueller & the 17 Angry Democrats." At one point, as the investigation seemed to be intensifying, Trump told McGahn that there was nothing to worry about because if it was zeroing in on him, he would simply settle with Mueller. He would *settle* the case, as if he were negotiating terms in a lawsuit.

Fast-forward a year later, to the summer of 2018, and Trump was still president, still showing his remarkable ability to survive political maelstroms that would have ended the career of nearly any other public official. But Mueller, his team, and now prosecutors in New York who'd started their own additional investigations looked like they were operating like surgeons, slowly dismantling the world around Trump. Mueller and the prosecutors charged the people closest to the president—his confidants, advisers, campaign officials, and even his national security adviser and his personal lawyer—with crimes and moreover negotiated with a good number of them to turn on Trump. Armed with that cooperation, Mueller and the prosecutors were moving to build a series of cases against the president.

Mueller apparently knew a great deal about what had gone on inside the White House as Trump had tried to control, frustrate, and end the Russia investigation. I thought—but was not entirely sure—that one of the main reasons Mueller knew so much was McGahn.

I had actually met the White House counsel once before—in a similar circumstance, in fact—the previous fall. I'd been leaving work one evening when a colleague of mine alerted me that McGahn was eating dinner at BLT Steak, the semi-fancy restaurant next to our office. It seemed like a good opportunity to meet him, so I persuaded the colleague to sit at the restaurant's bar with me and try to snag him for a chat. We sat at the bar for about forty-five minutes until he was done eating—with a friend from his hometown, as it turned out. As they walked out the door, we stopped them and chatted for about twenty minutes. McGahn was relaxed and funny—a talker.

Talkers make promising sources. In the back of my mind ever since, I'd wondered if that encounter could be a precursor to something more. When I wasn't in a rush, I would frequently poke my head into the restaurant on my way home from work or walk through the dining area to see if McGahn was there. But I never caught him after that first encounter, and despite all my interest in talking to him, I'd never made a real effort to reach out to him beyond that. My calculation was that he was far too busy trying to make sure the administration followed the law to talk to reporters on the phone. Plus, McGahn was a longtime Washington elections lawyer who knew dozens of reporters. If he was going to engage with the media, he was likely going to do it with someone he'd known from before he entered the White House—someone he was already comfortable with.

There was another factor, too: McGahn was represented by one of the most sought-after lawyers in Washington, William A. Burck. Along with McGahn, Burck represented a dozen other witnesses in the Mueller investigation, including the president's former chief strategist, Steve Bannon; the former White House chief of staff, Reince Priebus; and Secretary of State Mike Pompeo. Burck no doubt wanted to shield McGahn from Trump and by extension the media. If I called McGahn, he'd likely tell Burck, who would then get irritated with me for trying to engage McGahn directly, and I didn't really need that.

But now we were standing on the street in front of the White House, in what could at least be later justified to Burck as a chance encounter. Catching my breath from my three-block sprint, and unsure whether McGahn remembered me, I introduced myself.

"Mike Schmidt with *The New York Times,*" I said, extending my hand. "I had to run to catch you."

He shook my hand.

"Did you see who I was eating with?" he asked in a way that made me believe it was someone I'd be interested in.

I told him that I hadn't.

Typically, when I would go to meet someone like McGahn, I'd want to make a plan in advance, or talk it through with an editor or fellow reporter, about how best to direct the conversation. But because I had had no idea I would encounter him, none of that preparation had been done. So I fell back on a lesson I was taught early in my career at the *Times* from a veteran reporter: When you're in front of someone who has information, just keep the person talking; you may never get another shot. Plus, by getting out of the way and letting him talk, I could allow myself to think and map out where I wanted to take the conversation.

As we made small talk about West Wing gossip and stories in the news that day, the first questions that came to my mind cut directly to the heart of the story. How much did you really cooperate with Mueller? Why have you continued to work for Trump? Is the power of your job so great that you'll endure working for someone whom I know you despise in order to get your political goals accomplished? Are you Mueller's secret mole in the White House? Those might have been the right questions, but they were far too aggressive and intrusive. Instead, it occurred to me that the safest place to let him go was his greatest accomplishment to date in the White House: his unrelenting drive to stack the courts.

In some ways, McGahn was the typical Washington insider. He had come to Washington in 1995 after law school and built a practice as a Republican elections lawyer, soon becoming a partner at a top-tier firm. In 2008, George W. Bush nominated McGahn to be the chairman of the Federal Election Commission, the agency created in the wake of Watergate to police money in politics. You might think that someone who was at the top of such an agency would use his power to rain down enforcement. But ideologically, McGahn was almost militantly libertarian, and it was at the FEC that his libertarianism found its full expression. He had come to believe that regulatory agencies had accumulated too much power, and so when he joined the commission, he set out to shut it down.

In his five years on the commission, he gutted its ability to enforce election law.

Bob Bauer, who served as Barack Obama's White House counsel and a top Democratic elections lawyer, told me that McGahn was the most consequential commissioner in the history of the FEC. "He brought a discipline to the Republican side and a sort of relentlessness, if you will, to that effort that was unparalleled in the history of the commission," Bauer said.

Even though he was part of the establishment and made more than $1 million a year in his private sector jobs, he still thought of himself as a blue-collar kid from New Jersey and still had nothing good to say about the "elites." He had a penchant for the hair bands of the 1980s, played in a 1980s-style rock band, and even hung out with actual rock stars from the 1980s. He often sported long hair that he had to pull behind his ears, even when he was head of the FEC. While leading the agency, he fought openly with the other commissioners, undoing much of its ability to regulate voting and campaign finance. This won him the deep affection of the top Senate Republican, Mitch McConnell.

During the primaries, as Trump's improbable candidacy continued to defy gravity, McGahn became the Trump campaign's lawyer, making sure he followed campaign finance laws and serving as a bridge between the neophyte candidate and the Republican establishment in Washington. The first time he met his client, Trump asked him how much money he made. When McGahn told him that his going rate was $800 an hour, Trump was impressed, and the deal was done. After Trump won, he had agreed to be White House counsel so that he could transform the federal judiciary for a generation or more. How many times had Trump reminded his adoring supporters that he had given them Neil Gorsuch? And McGahn had also just overseen Trump's nomination of the D.C. Circuit judge Brett Kavanaugh to replace the Supreme Court associate justice Anthony M. Kennedy and was preparing for his confirmation hearings.

I knew McGahn was fond of Kennedy, whose retirement after thirty years on the Court had opened up the spot for Kavanaugh. So I brought up Kennedy, asking him where he'd first come to know him. McGahn said he had met Kennedy at a cocktail party in Washington a couple of years earlier and that they had hit it off. McGahn noted to me that Kennedy always wore a suit, a tie, and a handkerchief in his breast pocket and was a nice combination of classy, charming, and thoughtful. The two had grown so close that McGahn often consulted with Kennedy about different judicial picks, McGahn said.

For all the stress McGahn was presumably under, he seemed at ease. The suit he was wearing was nicer than what most government employees wear, and his tie was still fully done and neatly positioned in the middle of his spread-collar shirt, which looked as if it had just been pressed. His hair was short.

"I heard you got a haircut when Kelly came in," I said.

There had been a rumor that when John Kelly, a four-star general, had become White House chief of staff a year earlier, McGahn had cut his hair in a show of deference to Kelly's military style.

"Not true," McGahn said.

He didn't seem to be in a rush to stop talking to me, so I wasn't in a rush to start turning this into some sort of inquisition. I turned the conversation to show that I knew something about his life. The previous Labor Day, I'd been to McGahn's hometown of Brigantine, New Jersey, a small town on the Jersey shore right outside Atlantic City. Even though you can see the casinos of Atlantic City from there, Brigantine has a small-town feel, with modestly sized houses, many of which are rented throughout the summer to vacationers.

The McGahn family had lived on a street where everyone basically had the same amount of money. The kids whose fathers were doctors or lawyers had lived in houses that were only slightly bigger than the others, and there was a sense there that everyone was on the same level. McGahn told me he really liked Brigantine because there wasn't a rigid class system that was ruled by elites.

"Now, life in Washington—there are elites," he said.

I asked what his parents did. He said that his mother was a nurse and his father was a Treasury agent who did IRS investigations and was also, not for nothing, a well-regarded shot. His father would come home from the practice range with the paper target, one hole in dead center. He had fired six times, hitting the same spot each time. The family claim to fame was that his father had once protected Gerald R. Ford on a postpresidential visit to Cape May, New Jersey.

By now I'd delayed his entrance into the White House for at least half an hour. The sky was a reddish purple, the shade that appears at night when a thunderstorm is about to roll in. My time was short.

"I've probably written more stories about you than anyone else," I said. "I realize we aren't perfect. We don't have badges and guns and the power of subpoena. We don't bat a thousand. But what percent do you think I've gotten right? Have I gotten anything big wrong?"

Until then, the conversation had been cordial and about nothing of consequence. "I never saw anything that was really off," he said. "The biggest thing is that you make things more dramatic."

"That's fair," I said. "People sometimes say that about us, that we overdramatize things; sometimes things can feel more dramatic reading them than living through them. I get it."

It began to drizzle. It was now or never. I had to find out if the information I had received was true. Had McGahn turned on the president? And if so, why?

"You've done a lot of damage to the president and nobody knows it," I said.

McGahn tried to sidestep.

"I told them what happened—don't know if that's damage," he said.

To be perfectly clear, I repeated myself.

"You did a lot of damage to the president. I understand that," I said. I then pointed at McGahn. "You understand that."

I paused. Then I pointed at the West Wing.

"But he doesn't understand that," I said. "You did a lot of damage to the president and only you and I realize it."

"I damaged the office of the president; I damaged the *office,*" he said, in recognition that a White House counsel speaking so freely with investigators was highly unusual. His point was that such a precedent would likely make it harder for future presidents to stop investigators from speaking with White House lawyers. But I thought he was still understating the gravity of what he had done.

There was another pause. Our conversation had quickly turned from personal to professional, from casual to intense. But McGahn wasn't looking for an exit. At least not yet. Instead, he seemed to want to know what I knew.

"That's not it. You damaged *him,* and he doesn't understand that," I said. "It amazes me that he never understood why you really went in there and how extraordinary your cooperation has been."

He again tried to downplay what he had done.

All was quiet for a moment, and then I added, "We're going to have to write this at some point."

McGahn did not like that. The idea of a *New York Times* story chronicling the extent of the White House counsel's cooperation, going so far as to note that the special counsel felt as if he were "running" McGahn, would be devastating for his relationship with this most mercurial president. McGahn hinted at what we both knew: If the president realized the severity of what his own lawyer had done, he could be fired.

I told him that I understood the concerns about his job, but that that would not factor into our decision about whether or when to publish the story.

Just then, sheets of rain. My time was up. In the downpour, we shook hands.

"I'll be in touch," I said, loud enough to cut through the storm.

"This is the last time we ever talk," he responded with a smile as he turned and walked away.

ACT TWO

II

★★★★★

THE INSTITUTIONALIST

JULY 10, 2015

ONE YEAR, SIX MONTHS, AND TEN DAYS BEFORE DONALD TRUMP IS SWORN IN AS PRESIDENT

THE SEVENTH FLOOR OF THE FBI'S HEADQUARTERS IN WASHINGTON, D.C.— On summer Fridays in the mid-2010s, I tried to work from home in my sweats. There was no indication anything would get in the way of that plan on Friday, July 10, 2015, or that the day would be at all eventful, much less consequential. But on that day, as most of the capital was enjoying a long break the week after Independence Day, two things occurred at the FBI's headquarters that would have a profound bearing on the following year's presidential election.

The call from my regular contact at the FBI came in early that morning.

"Just get over here," the voice said in the slightly irritated tone of most FBI agents.

This made no sense.

Just a day earlier, the FBI director, James B. Comey, had held one of his quarterly sit-downs with all the reporters who covered him and the agency to answer our questions about the bureau.

Now he wanted to see us again?

I threw on a sport jacket and hightailed it from my small one-bedroom basement apartment in northwest Washington over to the bureau's headquarters six blocks east of the White House. After passing through the security screening, I was brought up to the same plain room where all of us on the FBI beat sat with Comey around a table at the same time the previous day.

Reporters don't like being kept in the dark. As we waited for Comey to arrive, speculation filled the void.

Maybe the FBI had nabbed a major terrorist? No, we would have definitely heard something about that. Had the bureau discovered that one of its top agents was a spy? Was Comey sick?

Just then, Comey walked in, a grave expression on his face, quickly sat down in front of us, and studied a single sheet of paper.

Over his two years as FBI director, everything had seemed to go right for Comey. His predecessor, Robert S. Mueller III, rarely spoke to the press or connected with agents in the FBI's fifty-six field offices spread out across the country. Instead, Mueller managed the bureau from behind closed doors in Washington, with a reserve that had distinguished his long career in federal law enforcement. As he remade the agency into a counterterrorism fighting force in the aftermath of the September 11, 2001, attacks, Mueller's rigid style left many of the agents, analysts, and other personnel in the bureau feeling chastened and alienated. Members of Congress, tasked with oversight of the bureau, felt similarly miffed by Mueller. Comey had recognized this problem before he became director and brought to the job a personal charisma and communication skills that set him apart, not only from his predecessors at the agency, but from nearly every politician in Washington.

In his first year as director, Comey had gone on a "listening tour." He visited all the field offices, giving a press conference at each stop, and spent hours getting lunch and coffee with lawmakers. Could anyone remember Mueller convening a single press conference, much less fifty-six of them? And since when did the director of the FBI owe anyone public utterances, on any subject, for any reason? Mueller's model had been a posture of complete probity. But although Comey meant to imply no criticism of his predecessor, he was transforming the position of director from that of a sphinx—opaque and silent—into a veritable public figure. In his second year, Comey had begun using the directorship as a bully pulpit of sorts, speaking out about issues that went beyond the day-to-day churn of the bureau's investigations. He had an ease about him in the role, an air that communicated the utter conviction that principle was on his side. For any flaws that Comey might have possessed, he did not seem to suffer much from self-doubt, at least not publicly. In February 2015, he had given an unusually candid speech at Georgetown University about race and policing in which he quoted the Broadway show *Avenue Q,* saying, "Everyone's a bit racist." Comey was widely praised for the speech, including by police commissioners and officers. That reaction stood in stark contrast to how many responded several years earlier when, as attorney general, Eric Holder said that the United States "has proudly thought of itself as an ethnic melting pot" but had been "a nation of cowards" on race.

But in the conference room on the seventh floor of FBI headquarters, Comey sat in front of a group of puzzled reporters, clearly disturbed. Normally comfortable speaking off the cuff, on that day he instead studied that piece of paper in front of him and then read some of it aloud.

"I believe the job of the FBI director is to be as transparent as possible with the American people, because we work for them," Comey said. "As you know, I try hard to explain our work to them, and I am also committed to explaining to them when we make a mistake and what I intend to do about it. I'm here today to talk to you about a mistake, in a matter of heartbreaking importance to all of us."

The mistake, Comey said, related to Dylann Roof, the twenty-one-year-old man who, the previous month, had joined an evening prayer service at the Emanuel AME Church in Charleston, South Carolina, and then proceeded to execute nine Black parishioners with a Glock .45 handgun. Roof had said he committed the massacre in the hopes of starting a race war and that he believed Blacks were violent and had lower IQs than whites.

That morning, Comey said that because of what he described as a terrible breakdown in the FBI's background check system, involving a cascading series of mistakes and bureaucratic miscommunications, Roof had been allowed to purchase the weapon despite an earlier drug arrest that should have disqualified him from gun ownership.

By 2015, mass shootings had become the norm in America. But the murders at Mother Emanuel, as the church is affectionately known, shocked a country that had grown numb to gun violence. Roof had targeted people at their house of worship, hunting them because of their race. The intensity of the grief was a powerful reminder of America's deep and seemingly eternal racial wound. The nine victims were still being mourned in the Charleston community and beyond. In the days following the murders, the immediate survivors of the dead—in an act of grace that stunned the country—had forgiven Roof. And grace was the theme of President Obama's eulogy as he led the country in mourning at the memorial service nine days after the shooting. As he finished speaking, the president broke into song, leading the congregation in "Amazing Grace," a soaring moment of pain and promise that banished cynicism and enshrined the moment in history.

And now, as I sat in FBI headquarters, watching a stricken director and trying to understand the nuances of federal gun laws, I could see something remarkable unfolding before me. The bureau had spent two decades and tens of millions of dollars developing computer systems and training personnel to prevent guns from getting into the hands of murderers. Those efforts had failed monumentally and tragically, and here was the FBI director admitting to the country that it was his agency that had let it happen.

"We are all sick this happened," Comey said. "We wish we could turn back time. From this vantage point, everything seems obvious."

The FBI makes roughly twenty thousand arrests a year, a significant portion of which result in convictions and prison sentences and receive no public attention. But mistakes in cases can leave a lasting stain on the bureau. In the early 1990s, following lengthy standoffs at Ruby Ridge in northern Idaho and Waco, Texas—during which a combined eighty-nine people were killed—the bureau was heavily criticized by the public and its actions were eventually investigated by government officials. After 9/11, government investigators placed significant blame on the FBI for failing to effectively utilize well-placed informants and for neglecting to share intelligence with other agencies that could have thwarted the attacks.

While it was very unusual for the director to make any pronouncement about an ongoing investigation, much less offer a heartbreaking mea culpa, Comey calculated that keeping the details about Roof's gun sale secret could lead to similar negative consequences for himself and for the bureau. Unlike many of his predecessors, Comey believed in getting bad news out early and explaining it thoroughly. Transparency was the greatest disinfectant. Congress and the media became most agitated, and curious, when an official played "hide the ball," seeking to withhold information from the public. If you leveled with them, Comey believed, those charged with oversight typically moved on to another target to scrutinize.

This approach had been hugely beneficial to Comey in his career. In 2004, shortly after he became deputy attorney general under President George W. Bush, he confronted the case of an accused terrorist named Jose Padilla who had been arrested on suspicions that he was plotting a "dirty bomb" attack on American soil. Although he was an American citizen and had been arrested in the United States, Padilla had been treated as an enemy combatant, and the Department of Justice had been holding him under extreme conditions in a military facility for two years, despite having not charged him with a crime. The Padilla case raised all sorts of questions about how long the government can detain an American citizen without affording him his constitutional rights to due process and a speedy trial.

In June 2004, Comey decided to air out those questions, holding a press conference to lay out the facts of the Padilla case. It worked. Questions about the prisoner's detention leveled off in the weeks that followed.

Now, in the case of Dylann Roof, Comey was running the same play. Would it work again?

I rushed out of the briefing and back home, where I quickly pounded out a story that the *Times* posted online. The following day, the *Times* ran the story on the front page under the headline "Background Check Missed Charleston Suspect." There was plenty of reason to be critical of the bureau's grave error, and virtually no media outlet passed on the opportunity to assign blame for the mistakes that had proven catastrophic. But because Comey admitted to the FBI's failure, it was only a one-day story. There would be no high-profile congressional hearings or investigations.

In my decade as a reporter for the *Times,* I had seen my fair share of savvy operators navigate media scrutiny, whether it was Yankees manager Joe Torre or the generals and colonels I had dealt with when in Iraq to cover the last year of the American occupation. But Comey had done something far more extraordinary than bring the media along to his point of view. He had resolved a serious political problem without resorting to classic moves in the Washington PR game—shifting blame, calling names, or diverting attention. Instead, he had simply traded on his reputation for principle and relied on exposing the facts to sunlight. Comey had tamed the political winds of Washington at a time when, unbeknownst to even its shrewdest players and observers, the rules of engagement were beginning to shift.

Comey could not have realized it at the time, but that moment would be the last high point of his professional career. From that point forward, a man who had appeared infallible, with an uncanny ability to steer through political storms, would face the greatest professional test of his life, which would humble him in ways that he could never have imagined as he commanded this impromptu press briefing.

On that same day, July 10, 2015, the seeds of his future and the colossal challenge he would face were being planted just down the hall from him. And it wasn't just Jim Comey's fate that was sealed that day; in a very real sense, the future of the country changed course that day as well. In the FBI's counterintelligence division, which protects the United States against espionage and also leads the bureau's investigations into the mishandling of national security secrets, agents and their supervisors initiated a classified FD-1057; that is, they began a highly sensitive investigation.

> Title: Opening of Full Investigation on a Sensitive Investigative Matter (SIM)
>
> Synopsis: FBIHQ, Counterespionage Section, is opening a full investigation based on specific articulated facts provided by an

> 811 referral from the Inspector General of the Intelligence Community, dated July 6, 2015 regarding the potential compromise of classified information.
>
> This investigation is also designated a Sensitive Investigative Matter (SIM) due to a connection to a current public official, political appointee or candidate.

With this short and cryptic communication, the FBI had opened a criminal investigation into whether the leading Democratic candidate for president, Hillary Clinton, had mishandled classified information during her tenure as secretary of state through her use of a private email account. The investigation would be code-named Midyear Exam.

Hillary Clinton was a singular figure in American politics who just one month earlier had announced her campaign for the presidency. A partisan lightning rod, she was a longtime foil for conservatives, dating back to her husband Bill Clinton's first national campaign in 1992, and ever since then Republicans had made it a mission to demonize Clinton, routinely accusing her of corruption. Those attacks, going back decades, had only hardened the view of Democrats that relentless investigations of Clinton were baseless and purely political.

Comey's deputy director, Mark Giuliano, briefed him on the decision.

"You know you are totally screwed, right?" Giuliano said to Comey, suggesting that regardless of what the investigation revealed, half the country would be enraged.

Dating back to his days as a prosecutor, Comey knew the Clintons well enough to have a realistic view of them. In his view, they were neither the cartoon villains the Republicans made them out to be nor the innocent victims of right-wing conspiracies the Democrats would have you believe. But because those were the only two characterizations on offer in the political culture, Comey also knew that his deputy was right: The alternate realities from which Republicans and Democrats regarded the Clintons meant that no matter how the investigation ended, he and the FBI would come out damaged.

"Yup," Comey said. "Nobody gets out alive."

★★★

JANUARY 23, 2016

363 DAYS BEFORE DONALD TRUMP IS SWORN IN AS PRESIDENT

HUMA ABEDIN AND ANTHONY WEINER'S APARTMENT, MANHATTAN—As Hillary Clinton campaigned in Iowa for the Democratic nomination, facing a surprisingly strong challenge from the Vermont senator Bernie Sanders, a fifteen-year-old girl in North Carolina sent a message to a disgraced former congressman on Twitter. She had read about his public scandals and had become fascinated with him.

"We should skype sometime," the girl said.

"Where do you go to school," said the disgraced politician, Anthony Weiner.

The girl told Weiner the name of her high school—the first of several comments she made to him that clearly showed she was under eighteen.

"You are kinda sorta gorgeous," Weiner said.

She sent him photos and he commented on her physique.

"Your body is pretty insane," Weiner said.

"You really think so?" the girl said.

In the previous five years, Weiner had destroyed his reputation and his political career after he had been repeatedly caught sending sexually explicit messages to women online. His wife, Huma Abedin, had risen to become Hillary Clinton's closest aide. Despite being embarrassed beyond belief by Weiner, Abedin had fought for the marriage and stayed with him. Given the prominence of her job with Clinton, he was potentially a political liability for the Clintons if he ever made a mistake again. But given how he had been humiliated and the fact that Abedin had remained with him, it was hard to fathom he would ever do anything again to embarrass himself, Abedin, or the Clintons.

As the primary crawled along in 2016, Weiner and the teenager continued to talk. The girl asked Weiner what he would do if she was eighteen. Weiner replied with a sexually explicit remark.

By March, contacts between Weiner and the girl had stopped. But evidence of their communications remained stored in the smartphones and other electronic devices they had used to chat with each other. What no one knew at the time was how those text messages would alter Clinton's fate, Comey's career, the FBI's reputation, and the arc of American history.

★ ★ ★

LATE JUNE 2016

SEVEN MONTHS BEFORE DONALD TRUMP IS SWORN IN AS PRESIDENT

THE COMEY HOME, McLEAN, VIRGINIA—For the first two years of Jim's tenure as FBI director, he and Patrice Comey lived apart. During the week, Jim stayed in "dad's bachelor pad"—or "Meadowlands" as the FBI code-named it—a modest, two-story 1950s-era house in McLean, Virginia, with a large kitchen, a small, cozy living room, and four bedrooms upstairs. On the weekends, Jim would fly home to Connecticut, where Patrice had stayed in their hulking seven-bedroom house, with a sprawling backyard, a pool, and a hot tub, as their children finished high school. In 2015, Patrice moved down to live with Jim full-time and they fell into a pattern for spending time together. During the week, they usually had a glass of wine after work (pinot noir in colder weather, sauvignon blanc in the summer). On the weekends, the routine doubled—coffee in the morning (half-and-half and no sugar for both), and then a glass of wine at night. Jim and Patrice usually sat in rocking chairs on the back porch. If the weather was bad, they would sit together and talk in the living room with a flick-on fireplace just inside the front door.

The living room had a dull-looking gray rug, but Patrice had moved in a red loveseat and comfy lounge chair with a white and red floral print to brighten the room.

Their conversations typically centered on one of three topics: their kids, their jobs, and their role as foster parents. With Patrice taking the lead, the Comeys specialized in caring for premature babies, who, because of the trauma of being separated from their birth mothers, constantly need to be held to prevent developmental issues. When the Comeys first welcomed a new baby from a local nursery or neonatal unit, Patrice would put her own life on pause and devote herself entirely to holding and caring for the child for weeks or months until the baby was placed with adoptive parents. At night, the babies would sleep on her chest.

When Jim talked about work, he observed the bright line that separated the most sensitive parts of his job from the rest of his life. It's hard to bifurcate one's life, and have whole swaths of your experience that are off-limits to those you love most. But that's the way it is when you have the kind of job that Jim Comey had. And so when he and Patrice would relax and catch up at the end of the long days, Jim almost always focused on the softer sides of his job, not the ins and outs of high-profile investigations or navigating the complicated politics of the bureau, the Department of Justice, and the White House. He loved to tell stories of how each week he would call FBI employees across the country to give them attaboys.

"It's the director calling," he would say earnestly to start those calls. Often, the employees on the other end of the line thought they were being pranked and would hang up. Jim would then have to call back and say, "No, really, it's the director. I want to tell you what a great job you're doing."

The calls might have felt a bit faux folksy. But they were among dozens of ways that Jim changed things around when he took over the bureau as director. Despite receiving significant blame for the attacks of September 11, 2001, the FBI had largely regained the public's trust. Yet on the inside, it was in bad shape. Not only was morale low and its relationship with Capitol Hill fraying, but the bureau's headquarters—the J. Edgar Hoover Building on Pennsylvania Avenue—was actually falling apart. Days after Comey was sworn in as director in 2013, an employee brought him a piece of the building's yellowed concrete exterior that had fallen off and plunged to the sidewalk.

Telling Comey that the building was literally disintegrating, the employee presented him with the concrete piece, on which he had written in blue felt-tip pen "Director." Jim had noticed a netting that surrounded the top of the FBI building, believing it was some sort of security protection. No, the employee said: The netting was actually there to stop pieces of the building that broke off from braining passersby.

"The net was there to protect the public from us, not the reverse," Jim later said.

Over those glasses of wine, Jim never brought up the Clinton email investigation, and Patrice knew not to ask, even as she could see in the media that pressure was building on the FBI and her husband. In his three decades working in law enforcement, without mentioning a word to her, Jim had indicted celebrities and gangsters, signed off on controversial government surveillance programs designed to catch terrorists, and deployed FBI agents on clandestine missions. Even when he had a showdown a decade earlier with Vice President Dick Cheney and President Bush over a constitutionally dubious eavesdropping tool, and threatened to resign, he said little to his wife. This forced Patrice to go around Jim to his security detail to piece together clues about what her own husband was dealing with as he confronted a crisis in his career.

Despite avoiding the topic of the Clinton investigation, both Jim and Patrice were closely watching it unfold under the same roof but from vastly different vantage points, demonstrating their divergent views of politics. To her, politics was a good thing, a means to promote social progress. A lifelong Democrat, Patrice followed the news of the investigation through the lens of an enthusiastic partisan, rooting for the election of the first woman president. She admired Clinton and hoped that the Democratic candidate would soon be cleared by the investigation and on her way to the White House.

By contrast, to Jim, politics was a danger that could infect anything it touched. He had been paying significant attention to the

Clinton probe, receiving briefs on its progress more than any other in his time at the bureau. But unlike his wife, Jim had studiously avoided any personal, political view of any investigation, especially this one. This was in keeping with his almost obsessive efforts since becoming director to put distance between himself and partisan politics. If the bureau's mission was to follow the facts regardless of politics, then the director needed to take extraordinary steps to embody that ethos. Jim had decided that while he ran the FBI, he would not vote. His concerns about any perception of politics influencing his impartial role atop the bureau ran so deep that Jim—who at six feet eight would have been a strong rebounder—refused to even entertain the idea of playing in Obama's weekend pickup basketball game, which was often held at the gym in the basement of FBI headquarters. In Jim's mind, simply shooting hoops with the president could be viewed as a conflict of interest, undercutting the arm's-length distance between the bureau and the White House that he believed was absolutely crucial to maintain.

Every other week during the investigation, the agents and analysts leading the effort sat down with the director in his conference room and briefed him on the status of their work. By the spring of 2016, this investigative team reported to Comey that unless something changed drastically, it was unlikely the bureau would have enough evidence to charge Clinton with a crime.

Charging a crime is hard enough when facts, motive, and intent are all in alignment and easy to discern, with no vagaries and no controversy. But this investigation came with another complicating factor: It was already highly controversial, because Clinton's use of a personal email account had become a scandal in the media, and she was going to be the Democratic Party's nominee for president. To make a case, the bureau would need to clear an incredibly high bar. Investigators had to answer one main question: Had Clinton been so careless with classified information through her use of a personal email account that she endangered national security?

To do that, they would have to first prove that she had indeed discussed classified matters on her email account. And then they would need to show that she had done it knowingly, essentially declaring to her aides something outlandish: *I know that I should not be discussing these classified matters on my personal email account, but I want to do this anyway.*

The FBI had found more than one hundred instances in which Clinton had received or discussed classified information on the account. But the bureau had no evidence that she had done so for any other reason than she simply did not realize she was sending and receiving classified information. The practice might have been malignant, but the intent was benign.

Another major factor stood in the way of making a case. In 2015, the FBI had found that while he was CIA director, David H. Petraeus, a retired four-star general, had taken classified information home with him, provided it to a lover, and then lied to the FBI about it. Despite protests from Comey that Petraeus should plead guilty to a felony, Attorney General Eric Holder had allowed Petraeus to accept a misdemeanor, essentially a glorified slap on the wrist. If Petraeus's conduct was far worse than Clinton's—and Petraeus was allowed to plead to a misdemeanor—making a felony case against Clinton, a major-party candidate for president, would be all but impossible.

By that June, a year after the investigation began, it was coming to an end, and Jim faced a critical decision about how to proceed. For a director who had developed the habit of explaining privileged decision making about sensitive investigations to the public, the conclusion of the Clinton email investigation could not have come at a more perilous time.

The way Jim thought about this decision was also linked to his growing sense that something serious was ailing the country. He had been FBI director for three years, after being out of government for nearly a decade. Upon his return to Washington, Jim could see that partisan politics had turned so toxic that the parties were dividing not just into separate camps but into separate realities.

He saw it as a virus spreading in the country that was eating away at the truth and infecting even national security and law enforcement decisions with politics. When he went up to Capitol Hill for hearings, right-wing Republicans asked all sorts of questions about issues based on conspiracy theories that had nothing to do with the major national security threats the country faced. The mainstream media paid little attention to these rantings, but these narratives found a home on Fox News, Breitbart News Network, and elsewhere in the conservative media world, where the lawmakers pushing the conspiracy theories were treated as credible and given the platform to reach millions of people with false information that warped their views and programmed their politics. No matter the topic, there was a single theme that drove this rhetoric: The government was a corrupt institution. Instead of advancing the interests of the people, it was actually out to hurt them.

Jim saw a similar, but less virulent, strain of this phenomenon on the Left: Democrats were also capable of disregarding facts when the evidence contradicted their own preferred narratives. Most strikingly, during the Clinton email investigation Comey was scheduled to meet with members of the news media for an on-the-record question-and-answer session. Comey and Attorney General Loretta Lynch knew that he would almost certainly be asked about the Clinton investigation, which had been widely reported on at the time. They agreed that he would have to acknowledge the existence of the investigation. But Lynch insisted that Comey refer to it only as a "matter," not an "investigation." When Comey heard Lynch say that, a strange tingling sensation shot up through his neck. The bureau had a full blown criminal investigation underway. But the Clinton campaign had made up a false narrative that the FBI was not actually conducting an investigation but was doing a "routine security review." He was also troubled by how he believed the Obama administration, hellbent on emptying Guantanamo Bay of enemy combatants, inappropriately pressed the intelligence community to water down the assessments of whether the combatants would pose any threat if released.

"I witnessed brow-beating and shaming of Secretary of Defense Chuck Hagel for his reluctance to clear people for transfer," Jim said to me. "To his credit, he stood tall, but they hated him for it and he left as a result."

In such a toxic atmosphere, in the heart of an election year, how could the FBI bring an end to such a fraught investigation in a way that gave the public confidence that a Justice Department, controlled by a Democratic administration, had made a decision based on the facts and not politics?

Making matters worse in Comey's mind, Attorney General Loretta Lynch and President Barack Obama had said and done things during the investigation that he worried had already created an impression that the fix was in to protect Clinton.

Given this state of affairs, in Comey's mind it was unlikely that Republicans would accept that Democratic political appointees running the Justice Department would have conducted an investigation into their own party's presidential nominee fairly and without political bias.

No FBI director had ever been in the position of closing a highly public—and exceedingly politicized—investigation into the nominee of a major party just months before a presidential election. Comey and his deputies began throwing around ideas on how they could bring the investigation to an end. The traditional ways—like saying nothing or putting out a short statement and leaving it at that—likely wouldn't suffice because of the attention the investigation had received, the strong feelings it had engendered, and the fact that Clinton was highly likely to be the next president.

By the book, the public wasn't entitled to know the machinations of this particular investigation, any more than they were entitled to know the inner workings of any investigation. But because of the politics involved and the high stakes, there was a strong expectation that the outcome of the investigation would indeed be aired publicly.

Comey's deputies started discussing with the Department of Justice how they might best proceed, and the department indicated that Comey's public credibility might be the best tool they had at their disposal for maintaining both the actual independence of the investigation's findings and the appearance of independence to the public. Through the spring of 2016, as those talks progressed, Comey came up with a radical idea, and in a small meeting in April with his closest aides in his conference room he put it on the table: What if he, alone, went out to the lectern and, without telling his bosses at the Justice Department, told the world about why they were closing the investigation without charges? Trust is the coin of the realm, and if the bureau didn't get out in front of this issue, control it as much as it could be controlled, half the country would believe that the fix had always been in, and the credibility of the FBI would take yet another hit. The idea was to kill the potential problem with the facts.

That was Comey's thinking, anyway. His top aides initially disagreed. Sitting to Comey's right at the meeting was the deputy director, Andrew McCabe.

Oh, my God, McCabe thought. *We don't do that. That is* not *what we do.* He looked at Comey and shook his head. "*Ooofff,* I don't know, that seems like really putting us out there," McCabe said.

McCabe reminded Comey that speaking publicly on the case deviated sharply from the bureau's past practices, in which it rarely, if ever, discussed the findings of a case that resulted in no charges.

"That's really abandoning tradition and practice and could set a bad precedent," McCabe said. "I don't know that there's a specific policy about that, but that's not who we are most of the time."

But Comey's idea seemed to take on its own momentum.

In the weeks that followed, he discussed it with a close friend who worked for the Justice Department, to gauge his reaction. Comey told the confidant, Only I have the credibility to do this. Comey said that among his peers in government, he viewed himself as the only one who had the stature, skills, and impartiality to ensure that the results of this investigation would be seen as legitimate to such a balkanized American public.

He could feel it in his body, he said. He knew that this decision would be the most consequential and scrutinized of his life. He would be injecting himself into a presidential election and in the process mortgaging the FBI's credibility. He was sure of what he wanted to do. But he needed to hear from someone who was willing to tell him that his idea was crazy and could see problems that he had failed to consider.

That person was Patrice.

She'll just fricking tell me, he told himself. *I never have to worry with her that she's holding something back because I'm important or because I'm whatever. She doesn't give a rip.*

It was over one of their glasses of wine in late June 2016 that Jim for the first time broached the subject of the investigation with her.

He laid out how, in the final act of the investigation, agents were scheduled that coming Saturday to interview Clinton at FBI headquarters.

"Basically, if she doesn't lie and just tells the truth and admits to the things we know, she won't be charged," Jim told her.

It was the first Patrice had heard from him about how the investigation was likely to end. In the year since the investigation began, Donald Trump had emerged as the Republican Party's presumptive presidential nominee. Trump's rise baffled Patrice, but she did not see him as a serious threat to Clinton. Nevertheless, lifting the cloud of the investigation would ensure an even clearer path for Clinton to defeat Trump.

Jim explained to his wife that he had essentially two options. He could sit back and allow the Department of Justice to take the lead in making the announcement. Or he could take it upon himself to hold a press conference announcing what the investigation found, and essentially clearing the Democratic nominee.

Patrice would give it to him straight. And her response would not make the decision easier.

But then, she had a history of saving him.

Jim and Patrice met in 1980, their junior year at the College of William & Mary. A mutual friend introduced them at a dorm party.

"We sat together on a couch," Jim once remembered. "She let me talk about myself for three hours. Naturally, I walked away deeply in love with her, because she let me talk about myself, a habit which she has since fixed."

After graduation, Jim went to law school at the University of Chicago, and Patrice moved to Sierra Leone for two years to serve in the Peace Corps. She was stationed in a small village in the southern part of the country near the Liberian border. From there, she traveled to remote villages on a 125 cc Yamaha dirt bike to tutor teachers who were taking entrance exams for college and to educate local women about children's health and nutrition.

In the summer of 1983, Jim visited her there. As a treat one night, Patrice arranged for them to stay in a guesthouse atop a remote mountain in the Kambui Hills Forest Reserve.

"We were sitting there watching the sunset, and I turned to her and said, 'What are the symptoms of malaria?'" Jim later recalled.

"I'm not going to tell you, because then you'll get it," Patrice said, assuming he was just imagining things.

Jim said he felt a pain radiating up his spine and that he was getting chills. It was late in the afternoon, it would be dark soon, and help was hours away.

"We gotta get out of here," she said.

Patrice would get them off the mountain on her motorcycle. With Jim fevered and shaking, she told him to sit behind her and hold on no matter what.

"You can't let go! You *can't*!" she hollered as they headed down the switchback dirt roads to the bottom of the mountain.

By the time they arrived at the bottom, it was night out. She drove him to a nearby volunteer's house, where she left him in a bed under a mosquito net. With few lights on the roads, Patrice took off by herself to search for medicine, only to be attacked on the dark road by a pack of wild dogs, crashing her motorcycle trying to avoid them. The dogs circled her, but she somehow managed to get away. Eventually, she found the antimalarial drugs and made it back to Jim, who was by then hallucinating.

The next day, she realized his condition was so serious that she needed to get him to a hospital. She rented a bush taxi, and they climbed in with two other passengers and a live chicken. The taxi got them to the hospital, where Patrice served as his nurse until he was out of danger.

Now, a world later, with the decision about what to do about Clinton's emails hanging in the balance, Patrice thought he was in danger of a much different sort.

"I wish you wouldn't do it," Patrice told her husband.

"I have to," he said.

"This is going to be bad for you," she said.

"This could be very bad for me," he answered. "But how would I make a decision on that basis? There is a whole institution to think of."

The Comeys' glass of wine that June evening had suddenly turned into a taut conversation. The fact that Jim was even talking about this told Patrice that it was a close call, even for him. Why else would he be asking her about it?

She was upset, and he was losing his patience. He paused and told her that if the bureau said nothing about what it had found, that would almost certainly arouse the anger and suspicion of the Republican Congress and that instead of a single painful event he would be hauled before committees on Capitol Hill from then until the election.

"There will be hearings all frickin' summer that are not going to be fair to Hillary Clinton," he told her. "We need to end it, we need to end it credibly, and we need to put it to bed. So rather than have it drip, drip, drip, I can control the story and get it out there in a way that's best for everybody."

Not best for everybody, Patrice thought. They both had their priorities. He said he was concerned about the FBI, and she said she was concerned about him. He understood her position but for once didn't find it very helpful. He was reaching to her for something, but in a way he was already beyond her help.

"Why do you have to step out and get shot?" she pleaded. "Why you?"

Acknowledging the impasse, they both fell silent.

"You're going to get slammed," she finally said.

A few days later, on July 4 weekend, with several of their kids and their significant others coming into town for the holiday, the house seemed more like a hostel than a home. In the room Jim used as an office, his daughter's boyfriend slept on a futon. A blanket was tacked to the frame around the glass doors to the office to keep the sun out. Two of their daughters—and one of their husbands—bunked on air mattresses in the basement. The other children were in bedrooms upstairs. Although Jim was preoccupied with his plans for the following week's press conference, the family still made sure to continue an annual Comey family tradition.

Since the children were young, Jim would assign each family member a section of the Declaration of Independence to read aloud on the Fourth of July.

Patrice would typically read the first paragraph, Jim the last, and the rest would be divided up among the kids. "I thought when the kids started to move out and live on their own, it would fade away, but they were like, 'What, Dad?'" Jim said.

As the kids added partners, they too were assigned sections. Those children who were elsewhere for the holiday would call or use FaceTime.

"What I do is give out these pieces," Jim said. "The new sons-in-law get the crappy pieces."

Through the barbecues and dinners that weekend, Jim closely monitored final tweaks his aides were making to his remarks. He wanted to maintain eye contact with the camera, and so he would memorize the speech. But the house was so crowded that there was no place for him to sit alone to work on it. So, over the weekend, as Americans celebrated the birth of the nation with hot dogs and fireworks, and Clinton headed back onto the campaign trail after being interviewed by FBI agents and federal prosecutors at the bureau's headquarters, Jim took a beach chair and parked himself alone in the driveway. Sitting behind a gate the FBI had installed as a safety measure—in the ten- to fifteen-foot gap between his house and the neighbor's—Jim recited the speech to himself over and over again, practicing for what he thought would be the most important public moment of his life.

How had he gotten to this point, to this feeling that the director of the FBI would personally and publicly need to explain the agency's secret deliberations, in the most high-profile way imaginable? And where had this strange sense of personal destiny come from? From the vantage point of what was to come, Patrice's sense of foreboding was well placed. But from childhood, Comey had been seized with the conviction that the world was a dangerous place and that only principled individuals can make a difference.

Comey grew up in Yonkers, New York, where his grandfather was the police chief. He was late to grow and got bullied a lot, which was a formative experience. Instead of playing sports, he sang in the choir and stocked shelves at the local grocery store. When he was sixteen, he started carrying around a quotation from Ralph

Waldo Emerson in his wallet: "It is easy in the world to live after the world's opinion; it is easy in solitude to live after our own; but the great man is he who in the midst of the crowd keeps with perfect sweetness the independence of solitude."

A kid that earnest and that alone starts looking at the world differently, and Jim developed a code about the proper way that people should be treated. He started questioning his Catholic upbringing and what he perceived as the hierarchical—and often hypocritical—structure of the religion. He would struggle in the years to come with questions about whether God existed. He couldn't bring himself to believe that there is a divine force that plays a role in human history, answers prayers, and intervenes. And he couldn't reconcile the concept of a loving God with reality, given the awfulness and tragedy of so much of human experience. It just wasn't logical.

The parts of Christianity that he didn't have any problem embracing were the teachings of Jesus. Jesus was a radical, and that excited Jim. Not God-made man, but a human, born to a husband and wife, and executed by the government for his radicalism. Jim didn't believe the theology surrounding the biblical Jesus, but he found his call to live for other people to be profound. *Whatsoever you do to the least of my brothers, that you do unto me; love your neighbor as yourself*—those ideas made sense. Jim found them to be wholesome, logical, and important.

So you might say that he approached spirituality like a lawyer. And just as the canon of laws provided a code for how best to treat each other, and influence human behavior, so too did the Bible. It was solid, he thought. You could organize a stable and principled society around those ideas. And without such a robust code for mankind, went Comey's civic theology, we are lost.

I have a very dark view of humans, Jim would come to think. People are capable of so much that is awful and are dominated by biases and insecurities that drive to do awful things, especially in groups. The theologian Reinhold Niebuhr was central to his evolving idea of justice, because Niebuhr argued that to combat the evil in the world, good people needed to actively build and maintain a system to protect themselves from one another. *The best you can hope for in human existence is to achieve something short of love, which is justice.*

Jim thought the law, more than any other profession, had a direct hand in seeking justice, so he chose that path.

As a young lawyer in the U.S. attorney's office in Manhattan—the most prestigious office in the country—he prosecuted mobsters, fraudsters, terrorists, and gangsters from the mid-80s to the early 90s. He loved the work and the meritocratic nature of the office.

"The only relevant question was, 'How good are you at your job?'" Jim recalled. "It was like picking sides for a pickup basketball game; you care only about picking the best squad."

Jim noticed that the higher he rose in the Justice Department, the more he became disillusioned with political appointees above him who often looked at decisions through the lens of what it meant to their party. Whenever they were confronted with a difficult situation, too many political officials' first instinct was to ask, "How does this look?" and "What can be said about this?" Only later would they ask, "What's true?"

As deputy attorney general in the administration of George W. Bush, Comey saw flagrant examples of this impulse up close, which only darkened his view of politics. In the spring of 2004, he was forced to tilt against Vice President Dick Cheney, to prevent the White House from pushing the ailing and hospitalized attorney general, John Ashcroft, to sign off on a legally dubious surveillance program.

And just weeks later came the disgrace of Abu Ghraib, as photographs depicting dehumanizing abuse from the military prison in Iraq were published, sparking a reckoning across the government about the use and definition of torture and whether the CIA's "enhanced interrogation" methods were legal or moral. In spite of his silence, Patrice could tell that the revelations agonized Jim. She confronted him on the issue.

"Torture is wrong," she told him one night that spring. "Don't be the torture guy."

"What?" Jim responded. "You know I can't talk about that stuff."

"I don't want to talk about it," Patrice said. "Just don't be the torture guy."

"Don't be the torture guy" became a refrain in his head. Patrice's warning had a profound effect on Jim and took on a larger significance than even the issue itself: It was a bracing reminder to Jim that people in power simply cannot be counted on to do the right thing, that people in power can seek to justify almost anything, and that power itself can hopelessly distort right from wrong.

In the aftermath of the scandal he stayed at the Justice Department, even though he would later come to question the decision.

"I convinced myself I was protecting the institution and that, without me, it would be worse off," he says of that period. "Of course, that's an easy thing to convince oneself of. I think a factor—maybe unconscious—was my desire to get out of there in a way that wouldn't ruin my employment prospects."

"Don't be the torture guy" also brought home to Jim the extent to which Patrice served as a conscience. Unalloyed and unvarnished, Patrice's appraisal was always there to put him straight. But in the end, Jim alone would step out before the lights.

He had tried to dedicate his life to getting at the truth of disputed matters. And with the Clinton investigation, he was confident that he could prevent a political firestorm by throwing facts at the problem.

"There was going to be a bad fire, and it would hurt the FBI," he says. "That was inevitable. I never doubted it. When you are standing in the middle of hell, there is going to be fire damage."

III

★★★★★

THE POINT OF NO RETURN

JULY 5, 2016

199 DAYS BEFORE DONALD TRUMP IS SWORN IN AS PRESIDENT

BONAPARTE AUDITORIUM, FBI HEADQUARTERS, WASHINGTON, D.C.— Comey picked up the phone in his office that morning and called his boss, Attorney General Loretta Lynch. He told her he was going to hold a press conference. But he refused to say what it was about. She could have ordered him to tell her what he was up to, but she didn't.

Around that time, the FBI alerted the media that the director planned to make a statement at headquarters later that morning, also declining to elaborate on what Comey might be saying. Reporters and photographers rushed over to a small auditorium on the bureau's ground floor.

At home, Patrice had the television on as she anxiously waited.

Early that morning, as Jim was getting ready for the day, she had walked into his closet, examining his ties. "What tie . . . ," she said, deliberating what would look best on television.

They agreed on gold—not red or blue. Best to avoid the gang colors.

At 11:00 a.m., Jim walked out into the small auditorium and began his presentation.

"Get to the point, Jim," Patrice said to herself. "Get to the point."

But he didn't get to the point. In anticipation of the criticism that he was in for, Comey's speech first detailed all the ways in which Clinton had been reckless. Fact upon fact, his presentation was creating the unmistakable impression that the FBI director was building an argument for why the Democratic nominee should be charged with a crime.

"There is evidence to support a conclusion that any reasonable person in Secretary Clinton's position, or in the position of those government employees with whom she was corresponding about these matters, should have known that an unclassified system was no place for that conversation," Comey said about Clinton's use of her personal email system.

Patrice's friends who were also watching at home started sending her text messages.

Is he going to indict her? Oh my god?

"There is evidence that they were extremely careless in their handling of very sensitive, highly classified information," Comey said.

After thirteen minutes, his tone abruptly shifted as he at last got to his point.

"No reasonable prosecutor would bring such a case," Comey said. "No charges are appropriate in this case."

Patrice said to herself, *Jeez, Jim, why did you take so long to say that?*

"If I had led with the exoneration," Comey would say, "nobody would have listened to anything else."

In reaction to the press conference, the Clinton campaign made a strategic decision to embrace the director's conclusions. Although they saw Comey as arrogant and out of line for holding the press conference and criticizing Clinton, they ultimately decided that there was no good reason to pick a fight with the head of the FBI in the middle of a presidential campaign. Instead of litigating that in the media and attacking Jim, they moved on. The rest of the Democratic Party fell into line behind the Clintons.

In fact, many top Democratic leaders praised Jim for how he handled the Clinton investigation.

"This is a great man," the House minority leader, Nancy Pelosi, said about Comey shortly after the press conference. "We are very privileged in our country to have him be the director of the FBI."

Tim Kaine, the Virginia senator Clinton would choose as her

running mate, would say on the campaign trail that Comey displayed the "highest standards of integrity."

One of the few Democrats who went public to criticize Jim was a former Department of Justice spokesman who was known only to Washington insiders. The former spokesman, Matt Miller, took to cable news to say Jim had broken Justice Department rules. Miller said that it was not the department's practice to use the fruits of an investigation to go out and tarnish the reputation of someone who has no ability to defend herself in court. If the department found wrongdoing, it should bring charges; otherwise, it should say nothing. Miller wrote a *Washington Post* op-ed titled "James Comey's Abuse of Power" that claimed that by going public, Comey had set a dangerous precedent.

"Generations of prosecutors and agents have learned to make the right call without holding a self-congratulatory news conference to talk about it," Miller wrote. "Comey just taught them a different lesson."

Fellow Democrats told Miller that they wished they could also speak out, but that they feared doing so because they had their own relationships with the FBI to maintain.

But while Democrats—save for Miller—moved to put the investigation behind them, Republicans—who had been Jim's main concern—dug in. For Republicans to understand Jim's press conference, they needed a bit of intellectual dexterity, but not much. It asked Republicans to understand and appreciate two concepts at the same time: that Clinton might have done something improper related to national security but that she should not be charged with a crime. But that was a level of nuance that much of Washington lately could not accommodate. Because the finding was disagreeable to them, congressional Republicans assumed it was dishonest and called it suspicious. Given Comey's harsh criticism of Clinton, they were enraged at his recommendation that she not be charged. His statements were useful to undermine Clinton, but became a target, too.

What is the difference, they argued, between Comey's "extremely careless" and the "gross negligence" from the criminal statute? His language was proof enough that Clinton was a criminal and that Jim—apparently a Clinton lackey—was covering up her crime.

Two days after the press conference, Jim went up to Capitol Hill to testify before the Republican-controlled House Oversight Committee—a panel dominated by members who had made their bones on Benghazi, often appearing on Fox News to push their latest theory of how Democrats were corrupt. The committee's Republican chairman, Jason Chaffetz, lambasted Jim for deciding there would be "no consequence" for the handling of Clinton's emails.

"I'm here because we're mystified and confused by the fact pattern you laid out and the conclusions that you reached," Chaffetz said. "It seems there are two standards, and there's no consequence for these types of activities and dealing in a careless way with classified information."

Jim tried to explain the nuances of federal prosecutions to thc audience of angry Republicans, who were unmoved.

"We did not find evidence sufficient to establish that she knew she was sending classified information beyond a reasonable doubt, to meet the intent standard," Jim said. "I understand why people are confused by the whole discussion. I get that, but you know what would be a double standard? If she were prosecuted for gross negligence."

In explaining his conclusions, Comey also provided even more sound bites of him criticizing Clinton, which in Washington's vicious cycle made his conclusions that much more assailable.

"She should have known not to send classified information," he said. "That's the definition of negligent. I think she was extremely careless. I think she was negligent. That I could establish. What we can't establish is that she acted with the necessary criminal intent."

Despite the backlash from Republicans, Comey headed into July believing the press conference had been a success. Getting knocked by partisans was far better than if the Department of Justice had sought to end the investigation silently and unaccountably. And any involvement by Loretta Lynch or other top political appointees would have given the chattering class more ammunition to push more mainstream Republicans to go after the Justice Department. So, while it would live on in the conservative media echo chamber, Comey was convinced that it would have only so much appeal and little of the criticism would stick.

"By doing the announcement alone, I was spending some of my credibility and the FBI's to protect both the bureau and all of DOJ," Jim would later say. "I actually think that the goal was achieved, in large part, because the attackers were forced to come through me and focus on the FBI's decision making. There was very little of the 'Loretta Lynch is corrupt' stuff that summer. Instead, they had to say I was wrong and the bureau was wrong, which was harder for them. It meant that I had to spend a lot of time testifying and fighting their bullshit, but it shifted the ground of the battle from political to tactical."

So as July wore on, Jim thought the Clinton matter was behind him and that he could return to regular FBI work, like looking for funding for a new headquarters to replace the collapsing one. On the tactical side, he knew the bureau and the country still had major challenges. The FBI's top priority was thwarting attacks from Islamic-linked terrorists and homegrown violent extremists. A horrific example of that type of violence was still fresh in his mind. Three weeks before the press conference, a twenty-nine-year-old man who had sworn allegiance to the Islamic State had killed forty-nine people at the Pulse nightclub in Florida, marking the deadliest attack on Americans since 9/11. Such mass violence had become sickeningly routine in the United States, and federal law enforcement had been impotent in the face of it. This was the important work that the FBI could now focus on. Comey was confident that he and the FBI could now leave the politics to the politicians, and do just that.

But whatever punches he had taken from the Far Right would be nothing compared with what was awaiting him.

* * *

JULY 27, 2016

177 DAYS BEFORE
DONALD TRUMP IS SWORN IN AS PRESIDENT

TRUMP NATIONAL DORAL MIAMI RESORT IN DORAL, FLORIDA—As most eyes in the political world were on Philadelphia—where Obama was set to cap off the third night of the Democratic National Convention with a much-anticipated speech—Trump gathered reporters and television cameras for a press conference at his golf course in Doral, Florida. It had been less than a week since hacked Democratic National Committee emails had been released, and intelligence officials pointed to Russia as the culprit. And because Trump would be taking questions, the Republican candidate was bound to be asked about the Russian hack. Late in the morning, standing in front of flags of the United States and the State of Florida, and just thirteen minutes into the press conference, Trump addressed himself directly to a foreign adversary in a way that no reputable presidential candidate ever had before.

"Russia, if you're listening, I hope you're able to find the 30,000 emails that are missing," Trump said, referring to those of Hillary Clinton's personal emails that had been deleted. "I think you will probably be rewarded mightily by our press."

He made other comments about Russia that day, too. Some contradicted things he had previously said, like when he said he had "never spoken to" Putin. And some were starkly in opposition to U.S. foreign policy, as when he was "looking at" recognizing the disputed Crimea region as a Russian territory—an act that would, astonishingly, encourage Vladimir Putin's territorial ambitions and reward the menace Moscow posed to its neighbors and to Europe.

But the headline of the day was clear: here was the Republican Party's nominee encouraging—*soliciting*—Moscow's interference in his race against Clinton.

At the bureau, Comey and other top officials were struggling to understand Trump's bizarre overture and were deeply bothered by it. At this level of American politics, such a pronouncement could not simply be dismissed as a joke, as some apologists tried to do. The behavior was so far outside acceptable norms—and was so vexing in its challenge to geopolitical realities—that it commanded the attention of American officials at the highest levels, who were already beginning to see evidence that Putin and his government were up to something that appeared designed to upend the American election. "Russia is a sworn adversary of the United States, committed to degrading our country's power, influence, and reach," Jim would later tell me. "The United States intelligence community, of which the FBI is a part, devotes billions of dollars and countless hours each year to trying to understand and thwart the threat Russia poses. And yet, in the middle of an unprecedented Russian effort to erode the legitimacy of our electoral process, the Republican presidential candidate openly called for their assistance and participation in that electoral process. The conduct is so outrageous that the mind struggles to even categorize it, which is why I suspect so many people underreacted to it at the time, and maybe still do."

What no one knew at the time was just how seriously the Russians had taken Trump. Less than five hours after Trump's comments, that night marked the first time a Russian intelligence unit nicknamed Fancy Bear attempted to infiltrate email accounts used by Clinton's personal office. Russian hackers sent "spear phishing" emails—a common way to infiltrate specific accounts—to fifteen different email addresses associated with Clinton, none of which were publicly searchable. They also attacked seventy-six separate email accounts under the Clinton campaign's domain.

The comment was so outlandish that it was enough, some former FBI officials now acknowledge, for them to open up a counterintelligence investigation into whether Trump was coordinating with a foreign adversary to undermine the United States. But they did not do that because Trump was a major-party candidate and such a move was politically precarious. While the Obama administration was required to investigate any potential election interference, no one in the administration wanted to be seen as interfering in the election themselves. It was an unprecedented and untenable situation. How had it come to this moment? How was it that the Russians were interfering in the election and one of the two major-party candidates was asking them for help? How had the Russians burrowed so deeply inside the American system that they could follow through on Trump's request within five hours? How had the American intelligence community and national security apparatus been caught so flat-footed again—only fifteen years after the tragic failure of imagination in advance of the 9/11 attacks? And how had a foreign adversary undertaken a sprawling campaign to disrupt an election? The failures dated back to the end of the Cold War and included countless decisions taken by Republican and Democratic presidents. I was shocked by Russia's success, dexterity, and understanding of America's vulnerabilities and capacity to exploit them. But I knew from a reporting experience I'd had only three years earlier just how unprepared official Washington was for Russian aggression.

* * *

OCTOBER 16, 2013

THREE YEARS, THREE MONTHS, AND FOUR DAYS BEFORE DONALD TRUMP IS SWORN IN AS PRESIDENT

STETSON'S FAMOUS BAR AND GRILL, NORTHWEST WASHINGTON, D.C.—A month after Comey became the FBI director in 2013, and long before Hillary Clinton's emails ever became a public issue or Donald Trump was considered a serious candidate for president, I took the three-block walk from my apartment to my favorite local bar, Stetson's, for dinner by myself.

Stetson's looks like your typical neighborhood bar that serves burgers and wings and has free popcorn. It's dimly lit and has a long bar down the right-hand side of it with televisions playing sports on the wall and high-top tables on the other side. It became a go-to place for me in large part because there was hardly ever food in my refrigerator to go home to. I liked the bar so much that I had my thirtieth birthday party in a room on its second floor.

I ordered a turkey burger and a beer and watched playoff baseball. It was a Wednesday night and fairly quiet—quiet enough to hear the chatter of the half dozen or so people scattered around me. The folks I could hear the best were a woman and a man in their thirties sitting at the bar, roughly fifteen feet to my right. They looked like a typical young Washington couple. They dressed professionally and acted as if they were dating or married. I overheard the man say something along the lines of *You're never going to believe what happened at work today.*

The man told the woman that a whole kerfuffle had been unfolding between the State Department, the CIA, and the Pentagon over something the Russian government wanted to do. Obviously, I couldn't tune this out, so I started listening while making it appear as if I were just watching the game and eating dinner.

The man told the woman that the Russians have their own GPS-like system called GLONASS. He explained that it is potentially even better than the GPS we have on our phones because it can also determine an individual's exact altitude. He said that feature can be particularly helpful in urban settings because firefighters and paramedics are able to see exactly which floor a fire or ailing person is on.

The Russians, however, had a problem with GLONASS, the man said. They wanted to sell the technology to cell phone companies, but unlike GPS—which is owned by the U.S. government and operated by the U.S. Air Force—the Russian system is not completely functional around the world. For that to happen, the Russians would need to put at least two large monitoring stations equipped with antennas on American soil to achieve full global coverage.

As I sat there, I thought back to the legal training the *Times* had given me over my career. Anything that happens out in public is essentially fair game for us to report on, whether we're seeing a car accident or overhearing a conversation. Knowing that, I took out my phone and, as if I were writing an email, started typing out what the man was saying.

From the sound of it, I guessed that he worked at the State Department. He said that the Russians had found a receptive ear at State, where officials were seeking to improve relations between the United States and Russia, and the officials believed the technology could help first responders. But, the man said, State faced big obstacles. The CIA was all worked up about this and contended that allowing the Russians to put their own monitoring stations on our territory would essentially be giving them a beachhead, and a jump start, on hacking into our infrastructure and other networks.

Analysts working elsewhere in the American government had come to a different conclusion from the CIA, the man said. Those analysts said the CIA's views were shortsighted and simplistic, arguing that the Russians are so good at spying on us that they do not need these antennas to get at what they want in the United States. The man said that the Russians already had the trove of documents that the NSA contractor Edward Snowden had stolen that year from the intelligence community, giving the Russians an even greater advantage in hacking our networks. So, the analysts argued, if allowing the Russians to put these monitoring stations on our land helps our relations, why not allow it?

The couple's conversation finally turned to other matters.

At this point, I had three choices: I could go over, identify myself, and ask some follow-up questions. Or I could tell them I was a reporter and say that I wasn't going to write a story but that they should learn to be more discreet. Or I could say nothing to them. Just eat dinner, pay the check, walk out without saying anything, and then try to get the substance of this rather amazing bar chatter confirmed elsewhere. There was no way I would be able to write a story simply off some random guy I overheard at a bar; accurately reporting such information would require asking questions across the intelligence, diplomatic, and defense communities. I left without saying a word.

In the following weeks, my colleague Eric Schmitt and I pursued the story with our sources—many more of Eric's than mine—across the government. The conflict between the CIA and the other departments and agencies on the topic was real. We were able to confirm much of what I heard at the bar and add several new details, including how the Pentagon had also tried to stop the Russians from putting in the satellite receptors and that some lawmakers—including a lesser-known Republican representative from Alabama named Mike Rogers, who chaired a sleepy House subcommittee on transportation security—had voiced concerns on Capitol Hill. The Obama administration had delayed making a decision on the issue until the Russians provided more information about what they wanted.

A couple of weeks later, Eric and I led the Sunday edition of the *Times* with our story under the headline "A Russian GPS Using U.S. Soil Stirs Spy Fears." I had essentially operated as a spy to report a scoop about espionage games reminiscent of the Cold War, but there was no major outcry from either party about the prospect of the Obama administration allowing the Russians to put two satellite receptors on American soil. A year had passed since Mitt Romney had said at one of the presidential debates with Obama that Russia represented the United States' greatest geopolitical threat. His statements were still being mocked. The Cold War was long over. National security officials in Washington were focused on terrorism, China, and ending the war in Afghanistan. For better or worse, our coverage often focused on the issues the officials running the government believed were most important. At the *Times,* there was no push from our editors to do more. None of our major competitors wrote follow-up pieces.

In the months and years that followed, I rarely returned to the topic of Russia and the potential national security threat it posed. Whenever I did, the stories received little attention. There was enough violence in the United States to keep me occupied. My assignment at the time—covering the FBI—meant I essentially served as the police reporter for the country. Whenever something awful happened somewhere in the nation—like a mass shooting or terrorist attack—editors in New York and Washington would call me and say, "Call the FBI and find out what the hell is going on."

But what I failed to realize—along with James Comey, top intelligence officials, the Obama White House, and everyone else in the media—was that we were living through the country's greatest intelligence failure since 9/11.

Our long-defeated foreign adversary, Russia, had launched one of the most brazen and novel attacks on the United States in history. And we all missed it. The failure to detect this coming attack and defend against it was so great that it would take the intelligence services of the United States two more years to even figure out that America was under attack.

The attack on the 2016 election began in earnest five months after we wrote the story on the Russian GPS system. From a plain-looking building sandwiched in an unglamorous neighborhood in St. Petersburg, Russia, a company—known as the Internet Research Agency, or IRA—devised a canny and comprehensive attack on American society. Masquerading as Americans on social media, the Russians designed a plan to exploit the fissures of American society by polluting the American information ecosystem with unprecedented levels of disinformation, weakening American democracy. The disinformation campaign was only one part of the interference. Starting in 2014, the Russian intelligence services began a hacking campaign that targeted the White House and State Department. But even though the Russians had gone after the biggest targets in Washington, it was hard to get the Obama administration to take these attacks seriously.

When agents briefed senior national security officials about the hack, which they code-named "Raven Rain," the officials pushed back, questioning the agents' evidence. In response, the agents showed the officials copies of White House emails that the bureau had obtained through its own spying on the Russians. Among the emails the Russians had obtained, in fact, were those sent by the president himself.

The White House hack would be one of more than a hundred such hacks that the Russians pulled off in the years leading up to the election. When American departments and agencies belatedly fortified their defenses against these types of intrusions, the Russians moved to the next layer of institutions in Washington: the organizations on the periphery of the government, such as think tanks, and by 2016, political parties, most notably the Democratic National Committee.

The American intelligence community watched these hacks but completely misunderstood them. They perceived them as part of intelligence-gathering operations. All the Russians were doing, the FBI and intelligence community concluded, was looking to learn what was going on behind the scenes. They had no clue that the true intentions were to weaponize the information. By the summer of 2016, the American intelligence community had little to no intelligence that the Russians had launched a disinformation campaign on the United States through fake social media posts and that they planned to deploy the stolen emails. In a classified briefing about Russia, Senate Majority Leader Mitch McConnell fell asleep.

Russia's election meddling would dramatically change American history. Unlike after 9/11—when Congress, with the support of President Bush, appointed a bipartisan panel to study the failures that led to the attacks orchestrated by al-Qaeda—there would be no such commission created to look at the failures that led to the Russian active measures launched by Moscow, aiming to influence the outcome of the American election.

Had counterintelligence investigators scratched under the surface a bit more, they would have discovered long-standing ties between Trump and Russia and Trump's penchant for praising the strongman in Putin, who, with dreams of a resurgent empire, had strangled Russia's brief post–Cold War experiment in democracy.

Trump had a long-standing affinity for Russia, Putin, and his business opportunities there. He first traveled to the Soviet Union in 1987 with his first wife, Ivana—a Russian speaker—to look for sites to build a Trump Tower there. After the fall of the Soviet Union, Trump returned to Russia in 1996 with two American businessmen to again examine sites for Trump buildings. Trump claimed at the time that he would invest $250 million in Russia for real estate projects. But it was a hollow boast; he never invested the money. In 2005, he once again pursued real estate properties in Russia. The following year, Trump arranged for his two oldest children—Ivanka and Don Jr.—to travel to Moscow to scout properties with a Russian American businessman. There, his children toured the Kremlin and sat in Putin's office chair. By 2007, Trump was publicly praising Vladimir Putin.

"Whether you like him or don't like him he's doing a great job," Trump said in an interview on CNN's *Larry King Live*.

At a business conference in Moscow later in 2007, he proclaimed that he would now be selling Trump Vodka in Russia. And in 2008, Trump profited enormously from a real estate deal with a Russian oligarch. He had purchased a waterfront Florida mansion three years earlier for $41.35 million and then—after making few improvements—sold it for $95 million to the oligarch, Dmitry Rybolovlev.

The Trump Organization—through Don Jr.—continued to scout out real estate properties in Moscow and build business ties with Russians. The family was so enthusiastic about their ties to Russia that Don Jr. openly discussed them in 2008 at a conference in New York.

"In terms of high-end product influx into the U.S., Russians make up a pretty disproportionate cross-section of a lot of our assets," Don Jr. said. "Say, in Dubai, and certainly with our project in SoHo, and anywhere in New York. We see a lot of money pouring in from Russia."

The Russians continued to deliver important help to Trump. In 2010, Russia's state-run bank provided key funding for Trump Tower Toronto.

By 2013, the family business had become so closely tied to the Russians that Trump's son Eric openly discussed the subject at the opening of a new Trump golf course just outside Charlotte that August. At the time, the golf industry was in bad shape. The Great Recession had particularly hurt golf; at least one course in the United States was closing every week. Despite that downturn, Trump had invested heavily in the industry. The course in Charlotte was just one of nine others he purchased in the United States, Ireland, and Scotland between 2008 and 2014.

A well-known North Carolina golf writer named Jim Dodson attended an event to mark the opening of the Charlotte course. On the practice range, Trump addressed a group of about fifty people, boasting about how he was "saving" the industry, Dodson said. Dodson and another golf writer were then asked to play with Eric Trump, who had taken over responsibility for the family's golf courses. Several holes in, Dodson casually asked Eric about his father's comments on how he was "saving" golf. Dodson noted that no one else at the time was investing in golf and that it was widely assumed throughout the industry that golf courses would remain profitless for the foreseeable future.

"I simply wondered what banks or investment groups were financing their purchases—which in my experience was the way big-time resort developers operated," Dodson recalled. "I asked him who or what entity was helping to finance the many properties they were reportedly buying up—pointing out that no banks that I knew of were investing in golf these days."

Eric said that they did not need to rely on American banks for their money, explaining they had strong foreign investors who were interested in the game.

"Well, we don't rely on American banks," Eric said, according to Dodson.

Dodson wondered whether it was the Chinese, or maybe the Israelis, who he had been told were bargain hunting for golf courses in the United States. Eric told Dodson that the money had come from Russians who were very interested in American golf.

"We have all the funding we need out of Russia," Eric said, according to Dodson.

Dodson recalled being surprised by the disclosure, because it seemed unusual in the industry. But he said that at the time there was no other reason for the issue to raise a red flag. In the days that followed, Dodson told several of his friends and associates about the conversation. In interviews, the associates confirmed his account to me and another colleague at the *Times*.

(Years later, when Dodson would discuss the conversation publicly, Eric Trump would attack him for it, tweeting, "This story is completely fabricated and just another example of why there is such a deep distrust of the media in our country. #FakeNews.")

In October 2013, as a guest on the *Late Show with David Letterman,* Donald Trump continued to publicly discuss his business dealings with Russia. When Letterman cracked a joke about the Russians being "commies," Trump interjected, previewing what would become a defining feature of his presidency: a reflexive defense of Russia. Trump told Letterman, "They're smart, they're tough, and they're not looking so dumb right now."

Trump also told Letterman that he had met Putin once and that he was a "tough guy."

The following month, Trump traveled to Moscow, where his Miss Universe pageant would be held. He publicly raised the possibility of a budding kinship with Putin, tweeting, "Do you think Putin will be going to The Miss Universe Pageant in November in Moscow? If so, will he become my new best friend?"

The Russians paid Trump $20 million for the event. Putin did not show. In the days after the event, the Russian press reported that Trump was once again considering building a Trump Tower there.

By February 2014, as Trump weighed whether to run for president, his son-in-law, Jared Kushner, and daughter Ivanka traveled to Russia, where the wife of an oligarch close to Putin served as their host. During that trip, Ivanka visited a potential site for a Trump Tower in Moscow. That May, Trump continued to praise Putin and contrast him favorably with President Obama.

"I was in Moscow recently and I spoke, indirectly and directly, with President Putin, who could not have been nicer," Trump said near the end of a speech as he discussed his trip to Russia for the Miss Universe pageant, "but to do well, you have to get the other side to respect you, and he does not respect our president, which is very sad."

A year later, Trump rode down the escalator of his Fifth Avenue skyscraper to announce his intention to run for president of the United States. As he campaigned in the Republican primary, his affection for Russia and Putin was a common refrain.

"They're terrific people," Trump said of the Russians during an interview with the conservative talk radio host Hugh Hewitt in September 2015. "I was with the top-level people, both oligarchs and generals, and top of the government people. I can't go further than that, but I will tell you that I met the top people, and the relationship was extraordinary."

Then, in October 2015, just before he took center stage at the third Republican debate, Trump signed a letter of intent to "facilitate further discussions" about building a Trump Tower in Russia.

At the following debate in November, Trump, in response to a question about handling Russian aggression, suggested that he understood Putin well because the two had gotten to know each other when they were both on a *60 Minutes* episode that aired in September.

"We were stablemates," Trump said. "And we did very well that night."

Trump, in fact, was well over four thousand miles away from Putin during the filming of the interview, so it is unlikely that it led them to know each other much better.

By June 2016, Trump had surrounded himself with a slew of individuals with their own ties to Russia, including one who was already under investigation for being a Russian agent and another being scrutinized by federal authorities for his work for Russian-aligned Ukrainians.

One of Trump's closest national security campaign advisers, the retired lieutenant general Michael T. Flynn, had served as the head of the Defense Intelligence Agency—the arm of the Pentagon that studies foreign countries' military capabilities. Flynn had been fired from the DIA by President Obama in July 2014. At the agency, he had taken a number of suspicious actions. In June 2013, Flynn had scheduled a trip for a team of military personnel to go to Moscow for four days to meet with officers from the GRU, the Russian intelligence agency. He believed that a "leadership development" program would be helpful for both sides.

But the idea of the trip raised concerns in the intelligence community, where officers knew that similar attempts to build bridges with Russian intelligence agencies often resulted in the Russians using the contact as an opportunity to hurt the United States. Still, Flynn took the trip and believed it went so well that several months later he wanted to invite the top Russian intelligence officials to the United States. This time, however, the top American intelligence official, James Clapper, forbade it.

After he was pushed out of his DIA post in 2014, Flynn became an occasional guest on RT, the English-language Russian propaganda outlet. The following year, he took home roughly $45,000 for speaking at RT's anniversary dinner in Moscow. At the gala event, he dined with Vladimir Putin. Also that year, he received $11,250 from Russian companies for speaking engagements in Washington, including one for Kaspersky Lab—a Putin-connected cybersecurity firm. The American intelligence community had known for years that Kaspersky and its antivirus software had been used by Russian intelligence to steal information from Americans.

Trump's personal lawyer and fixer, Michael Cohen, was deeply involved in trying to get the Trump Tower built in Moscow. In January 2016, during the presidential campaign, Cohen sent an email to a spokesman for Putin asking for assistance with the negotiations for the tower, which Cohen believed had stalled.

Then, in March, as the Russians were accelerating their hacking of Democrats, Trump added three people to his campaign who also had significant ties to Russia. Trump had faced questions about his inability to attract established or credible national security officials to support him. So in mid-March he announced that he had formed a foreign policy team. Among the members were George Papadopoulos and Carter Page, both sometime energy consultants.

The same month that his hiring was announced, Papadopoulos traveled to London and met with a Maltese professor who was willing to help connect the Trump aide with people he knew at the Russian Ministry of Foreign Affairs, to establish a channel between the campaign and the Russian government. A Russian woman, who Papadopoulos believed was Putin's niece, also attended the meeting and told Papadopoulos that she, too, could help him build relationships in Moscow.

Page had been on the FBI's radar for several years. In 2013, while working for a private equity firm that invested in energy companies, he had provided Russians whom he later learned were intelligence officers with documents about the American energy sector. By March 2016, counterintelligence agents and prosecutors in New York had decided to open an investigation into whether Page was a Russian asset because of his continued contacts with Russian intelligence officers.

Later that month, Trump held a meeting with his foreign policy team at the not-yet-opened Trump International Hotel in Washington. The closed-door meeting largely served as a means to get some positive publicity, but it was at this meeting that one of those in attendance, Papadopoulos, told Trump that his sources had suggested that Putin desired to meet with Trump and that he could arrange a meeting with the Russian president if Trump wanted to. Trump was indeed interested.

Also in March 2016, the Trump campaign hired Paul Manafort—a veteran Republican strategist who had done work for several previous presidential candidates dating back to Gerald Ford—to devise a convention strategy for the campaign and defend against a potential challenge from within the Republican Party. Trump was the clear leader for the Republican nomination. But there were still widespread misgivings among rank-and-file Republicans who thought Trump not only had no chance of winning but could badly embarrass their party if he were the eventual nominee. Given the shakiness of Trump's support, many of his advisers were concerned he could face a contested convention and needed an experienced delegate wrangler like Manafort.

Manafort—who had for years worked as a political consultant abroad—brought with him considerable baggage, especially when it came to his work in Ukraine and Russia. In 2005, he had written a proposal for a Russian oligarch on how he could help "greatly benefit the Putin government" in the United States and Europe by promoting pro-Russian ideas. In 2006, Manafort received a contract worth $10 million a year from the oligarch Oleg Deripaska, who in the same year was described in a classified State Department cable as "among the 2–3 oligarchs Putin turns to on a regular basis" and "a more-or-less permanent fixture on Putin's trips abroad." But by 2014, the business relationship had Manafort in a vise, with Deripaska having significant leverage, claiming that Manafort owed him $19 million.

Manafort also had a close relationship with a Ukrainian, Konstantin Kilimnik, who the FBI would later conclude had ties to Russian intelligence. Manafort had hired Kilimnik in 2005 to work for him in Kyiv, and the two men had remained close. So close in fact that in May 2016, as Trump was closing in on the Republican nomination, the two met in New York, and Manafort instructed his deputy to share internal polling data and other campaign updates with Kilimnik. Why the Trump campaign's most proprietary data would be shared with a figure who may immediately in turn share it with Moscow remains a mystery.

Never before had an American political campaign been so deeply connected to a foreign power, and never had a foreign power been so vested in the outcome of an American election. The entire Russian election interference campaign represented a giant leap for the Russians and their aggression toward the United States, and demonstrated how the intelligence services had evolved under Putin from the one-dimensional Cold War–style espionage to new and sophisticated electronic active measures. Getting to the bottom of what was going on would test a part of the FBI that rarely received much public scrutiny.

★ ★ ★

JULY 29, 2016

175 DAYS BEFORE DONALD TRUMP IS SWORN IN AS PRESIDENT

THE FBI DIRECTOR'S CONFERENCE ROOM—The bureau's top counterintelligence investigators were gathered to brief Comey on what had quickly become the most sensitive matter any of them had ever been involved in.

His investigators told the director that they had received some alarming intelligence from one of the United States' closest allies, Australia.

Two days earlier, Australia's top diplomat in London had gone to the U.S. embassy there to hand deliver a copy of a classified cable he had sent back to his bosses in Canberra. The cable was mostly blank except for one paragraph that mentioned a Trump campaign adviser named George Papadopoulos. The cable said that Papadopoulos had told the ambassador that the Russians had dirt on Hillary Clinton and had offered to help the campaign by having damaging information released to the public.

The ambassador, Alexander Downer, had learned the information in May while meeting with Papadopoulos at a wine bar in the Kensington neighborhood in London. At first, Downer was unsure what to do with it. But in July, Julian Assange's antisecrecy group, WikiLeaks, had released a trove of emails stolen from the Democratic National Committee right before the party's national convention, creating chaos. It was then that Downer decided he needed to alert the Americans.

The American diplomat who received the cable had shared it

with the CIA station chief Gina Haspel and the FBI agent assigned to the embassy. Haspel had looked at the cable and said it was an issue for the FBI, not the CIA. The FBI agent stationed at the embassy sent it along to Washington.

Now, as Comey was briefed in the seventh-floor conference room at the FBI, he remained impassive, a flat expression on his face. Being told of the cable, he said only, "Say more." But inside, he was roiling.

The investigators said they were opening a counterintelligence investigation into ties between the campaign and Russia. Investigators and analysts had begun looking at public records and bureau files to identify potential links between officials on the campaign and Russia. It was a big and potentially damaging move to open an investigation into an ongoing campaign in the heat of election season, but no one who was briefed at the bureau believed the intelligence they had was anything but sufficient for such an action, and based on the intelligence handed to them by the Australians, it would be irresponsible not to open an investigation. They were potentially defending the future White House from Russian agents, and if they didn't act quickly, they knew there was little chance of stopping them.

Along with their long-standing trust in the Australians, the American investigators took the intelligence seriously because of Trump's own behavior and the strange abundance of Russia-connected campaign staff.

Like the investigators in the room, Comey recognized the perilous path the bureau was heading down and understood that the investigation would have to be handled as sensitively as any other in the bureau's history. Most counterintelligence investigations involved questions of whether an American had been targeted by a foreign adversary. In this case, a foreign adversary had declared war on the election and might now be doing it with the cooperation of the campaign of one of the two major American parties. Whatever the connections were between the campaign and Russia, the bureau would be forced to explain why it had investigated a presidential campaign.

Unlike many criminal investigations—such as the one into Clinton's email server—this was not a look back at some conduct that had occurred several years earlier. This was a potential crime in progress.

"We've just got to make sure we keep this very closely held," Comey told his investigators.

Comey later recalled that the bureau needed to be careful "because if they're involved we don't want to alert them, and if they're not involved it would be an incredible smear" to the campaign. It was an almost impossible needle to thread, but the investigators knew what Comey meant. They would investigate but had to do so without making overt moves—investigative actions that could tip off Russia or Trump or lead to it being publicly reported that the FBI had an investigation under way. That meant no interviews could be conducted, because whoever was questioned would know what the bureau was up to. That also meant no search warrants; FBI agents busting down the door of Trump Tower would be a certain tip-off.

That Sunday, the bureau officially opened the investigation, code-naming it Crossfire Hurricane. The following day, counterintelligence investigators flew to London to interview the Australian ambassador about his interactions with Papadopoulos. In the opening weeks of the investigation, the bureau, one by one, opened cases on Papadopoulos, Page, Manafort, and Flynn.

Trying to ensure the investigation would remain secret, the FBI turned to using confidential informants. This tactic would allow the bureau to have people it controlled interact directly with campaign officials to see whether any of them would divulge more information about their links to Russia. In the weeks that followed, the bureau tasked four confidential sources; two of the sources failed to secure a meeting, but the other two were able to provide the FBI with a valuable understanding of their targets. One of the informants, Stefan Halper—a University of Cambridge professor—met with Page, Papadopoulos, and Sam Clovis, the former co-chairman of Trump's campaign. Another informant was able to meet with Papadopoulos several times (all after he left the Trump campaign in October 2016).

The bureau also took another highly unusual step. In August, the intelligence community was scheduled to brief the presidential campaigns on threats to the country. The Office of the Director of National Intelligence took the lead in setting up the Trump campaign briefing but invited the FBI to give a ten-minute rundown on the potential national security threat posed by foreign intelligence agencies. Wanting to see the campaign's reaction to the briefings on Russia or whether anyone—particularly Flynn—said anything unusual, the bureau sent its supervisory agent in charge of investigating the Trump campaign to give the briefing.

As fraught as they were, especially when they involved politicians, counterintelligence investigations—and the agents who worked on them—were Comey's favorites. The cases were like puzzles, and the challenge of solving them attracted agents who were thoughtful, open-minded, worldly, and patient. But these types of investigations were almost always more difficult than other criminal cases and came with more political complications. The investigations almost always included a foreign adversary targeting Americans or institutions and the reliance on spying tools and confidential sources feeding information. Foreign adversaries had tools and abilities that run-of-the-mill gang members, drug dealers, and fraudsters could only dream of. Making it even more complicated, those Americans who were targeted by these adversaries often had no idea that they were being worked over by a spy. "In an organized crime case you're never investigating someone who doesn't know they are hooked up and working for the Gambinos," Comey later told me. "In a counterintelligence investigation you may have a sophisticated person and they're sleeping with someone who is really a foreign agent. It just adds layers of complexity, and to my mind those are the most interesting and hardest cases to deal with."

But with their reliance on sources, these investigations are often complicated. And this counterintelligence investigation was happening almost in the immediate aftermath of one of the largest breaches of U.S. national security in history. That investigation had dramatically demonstrated how quickly these investigations can go off the rails. In order to better understand the forces at work in 2016, I reported more deeply into the previously unknown bizarre investigative turns that the FBI took in the wake of the Edward Snowden case in 2013.

In the spring of 2013, the United States faced one of its most significant espionage challenges in years—this time from an American. In May of that year, a young contractor named Edward Snowden who had been working at a National Security Agency facility in Hawaii suddenly stopped showing up to work. Soon, he materialized in Hong Kong, set to leak and publicize a massive trove of classified documents he had taken from NSA computers. Snowden's leaks about widespread surveillance of Americans swept the globe and rattled the intelligence community. In June, the Department of Justice indicted him on espionage charges.

By August, articles about Snowden's documents were still being published, and he had obtained asylum in, of all places, Russia. President Obama grew frustrated with the chaos Snowden had created and looked for someone to solve the situation. The president turned to his FBI director at the time, Robert Mueller, hoping he might be able to find a way to get Snowden back. But Mueller showed little interest in the project. He had already been at the helm of the FBI for longer than his ten-year term, and he expressed his displeasure to top bureau officials about having to deal with Snowden. Still, he followed Obama's orders. Mueller began calling the head of Russia's Federal Security Service, better known as the FSB, to negotiate the return of Snowden so he could be prosecuted.

For twenty-nine straight days, Mueller called the head of the FSB, often getting nothing of value from the interactions. One of the few things the Russians did hand over was Snowden's email address so the authorities could contact him and try to persuade him to return home. The Russians, in a rare moment of candor, also told the FBI they had tried to get Snowden to take drugs and sleep with women—two strategies used by governments to gain leverage on potential sources. But Snowden showed no interest in their ploys.

To gain an upper hand on communicating with Snowden, the bureau brought in its behavioral science team from Quantico to work on coming up with ways they should converse with him in emails. The bureau struck up an unproductive correspondence with Snowden. There was no way Snowden was heading back without an absolute assurance that he would not be prosecuted—something Mueller and the FBI could not offer. Snowden did show the bureau he had a sense of humor, at the end of 2013 emailing the FBI a Christmas card.

In the middle of the Snowden investigation in 2013, Comey replaced Mueller as FBI director. The bureau had done forensics on everything Snowden touched and might have stolen from the NSA, but as the media published pieces based on those stolen documents in 2013, some stories appeared to have relied on documents to which Snowden had no access. The prospect that there might be a "second Snowden" emerged inside the bureau.

By revealing himself, Snowden had given the intelligence community a chance to determine what might become public and change their programs to ensure they continued to function. But the idea that a different—and anonymous—person might also be leaking classified documents from the intelligence community terrified law enforcement officials more than what Snowden had already done. Snowden put a face and a name to his offenses. A phantom would make putting countermeasures in place harder, if not impossible.

By late 2013, the FBI's Washington field office heard from an informant who claimed that he knew a man in Germany who had access to a trove of NSA documents and might leak them.

Maybe the bureau had found their "second Snowden." The FBI opened a new investigation, code-named Fellow Traveler.

The informant had an unusual background. He was a lawyer based in Europe who also did lobbying work in Washington for Middle Eastern countries. Not all the details of what then unfolded between the informant and the FBI are known, but the tale demonstrates the odd nature of counterintelligence and espionage work and the willingness of investigators to stick with a potential source, even when the source waffles or misleads them.

The informant told his bureau handler—a counterintelligence

specialist—that he wanted to help the FBI stop the man in Germany from leaking the documents. The informant agreed to lure the man to a meeting in Bruges—a small port city in northern Belgium known for its medieval architecture—while bureau agents secretly watched. They would meet at a small bar named Café Rose Red. The bureau would be able to listen in and then apprehend the man with the documents.

But what the FBI failed to realize at the time was that the informant was slyly playing another side in a high-stakes game at the intersection of espionage and journalism. Even as the informant promised to help the FBI find the would-be leaker, he was in contact with a veteran national security reporter for *The New York Times* named James Risen. The informant told Risen, who wrote about government spying, that he could help the *Times* obtain documents from the source revealing abuses of American surveillance authority.

The informant's double game meant telling the FBI that Risen also planned to travel to Bruges around the same time in the hopes of obtaining the leaked documents. The involvement of Risen bothered the FBI for many reasons. The bureau believed that if Risen booked travel to Europe, the operation might be detected by foreign intelligence services and become enmeshed in compromise; foreign spies would almost certainly follow Risen, see whom he met with, and potentially approach the source or hack the source's devices to obtain the documents.

The informant told the bureau that it should stop Risen from traveling, adding that if the bureau could buy him twenty-four hours, he could meet with the source before Risen got there.

"That's all we need," the informant told his FBI handler.

The FBI is governed by strict guidelines on what it can do in regard to journalists, and the agent told the informant there was no way the bureau could interfere with an American journalist's travel.

"Unfortunately, with the way things are, for us to impede the free movement of a citizen-journalist is absolutely beyond the pale," the agent told the informant.

If Risen insisted on coming to Europe, the informant suggested he would have his assistant trick the reporter. The assistant could drive Risen to the potential meeting, but the car would break down. That wasn't going to work for the FBI, either.

"That is a good tool at a tactical level," the FBI handler told the informant. "But that doesn't save us from the wrath of the attorney general and headquarters. If he shows up in country, all hell is going to break loose."

In his conversations with his FBI handler, the informant acknowledged that he was misleading Risen. "Everything about my relationship with Jim has become a lie," the informant told his FBI handler in one conversation. "It takes just one stick to fall down, and I am afraid the house collapses on me."

Despite the back-and-forth about Risen, the bureau decided to move forward with its plan to have the informant meet the source. The FBI's Washington field office deployed an entire squad to Bruges and sent a supervisor to oversee the operation—a level of engagement unheard of for the bureau in a foreign country.

The plan turned into a debacle. The source never arrived at the café, and the informant ended up getting drunk while waiting for him. When higher-ups at the bureau learned what had happened, they grew furious that an entire team had been sent to Belgium based on information from a man with little track record as a source who was also known to be double-crossing a reporter on the same matter.

The entire episode flummoxed agents. Some thought the informant might be working alongside Risen on some scheme, while others, such as the informant's handler, still believed that he was legitimately trying to help the FBI.

At that point, and with that level of confusion, one might surmise that the agency, lesson learned, would cut its losses and sever ties with the informant. But that's not at all what happened, and more often than not this is the rule of counterintelligence investigations, not the exception. In the case of the hunt for the "second Snowden," the FBI persisted with the informant, even after the initial disaster, in an increasingly bizarre cascade of events, which culminated in the informant first offering to install spyware on Risen's computer (under the presumed suspicion that the reporter was already in possession of the intelligence files) for the FBI and then, perhaps even more improbably, claiming to have stolen the files off Risen's computer in a visit to his home.

For the FBI, the prospect of knowing what was on Risen's computer was enticing indeed. Risen had been one of the great intelligence reporters of his generation and persistently a thorn in the side of the government, because he often published stories that exposed surveillance overreach. In fact, at the time, the Justice Department and Risen were in a legal fight about whether he needed to comply with a subpoena to testify before a grand jury about one of his sources. Despite the informant's offer, the bureau refused to go along with that plan.

But then, in 2014, Risen invited the informant to his house in Maryland. The informant later said that while at the house he secretly copied a trove of documents from Risen's home computer onto a thumb drive. Whatever was on the thumb drive, and whatever the informant's motive for supposedly boosting the files from Risen's computer, he did hand over a thumb drive to his FBI handler.

The handler, uncertain about what to do, left the drive on a desk and declined to process it as evidence. The informant, growing frustrated by the delay, called a member of Congress, who then called the top brass of the FBI, who were now learning for the first time that some of their agents had materials that had been stolen from a *New York Times* reporter.

It is not clear if the informant actually stole the files or if he made up that part of the story, and if so, for what reason—a bizarre attempt to frame Risen? But the simple fact that FBI agents had accepted potentially stolen documents from a journalist ignited a tempest at senior levels of the nation's intelligence community.

The episode came at a politically inopportune moment for the Obama administration, which was under intense pressure to stop what had become a crackdown on journalists and their sources. Along with fighting Risen in court, the Justice Department faced bipartisan criticism for secretly seizing phone records from the Associated Press and searching the emails of a Fox News journalist, whom prosecutors described as a potential criminal conspirator for asking questions about national security. In response to the uproar over the targeting of journalists, the then attorney general, Eric

Holder, issued new rules making it harder for investigators to seize records from members of the media.

And now this new quagmire. Senior officials across the government met to discuss what to do with the informant and the thumb drive. The officials considered whether the informant should be charged for hacking Risen's computer. To even consider making that type of case, the FBI would have to examine the contents of a journalist's hard drive, which had proven to be almost impossible in other cases. A related but far more heated debate erupted about whether to just look at what was on the thumb drive to see if Risen had the intelligence documents; even though the FBI had taken the most criticism within the government about how the drive was obtained, the bureau still wanted to access the files. A top FBI investigator eventually approached the attorney general with a plan. In a written document, the bureau explained how it proposed to analyze the contents of the flash drive. Putting it in writing—memorializing it, for future reference—angered Holder, who, when he saw the document, cursed and stormed out of the meeting.

It is still unclear what, if anything, the informant accessed from Risen's computer, because the flash drive still sits untouched in a safe at the FBI's Washington field office. The Justice Department briefly looked into whether the informant had broken the Computer Fraud and Abuse Act. But the FBI ultimately concluded that the informant had likely made up the story about the source in Germany with the supposed NSA documents. The FBI severed its relationship with the informant and later told members of the intelligence community to stay away from him.

The FBI would discipline the two agents who worked directly on the investigation. The handler was reassigned to counterterrorism, and his supervisor left the bureau. The victims of the theft—*The New York Times* and Risen—were never informed about the incident.

And the moral of this story for the FBI, as it embarked on a labyrinthine counterintelligence investigation of a presidential campaign at the fiery peak of an election season, was this: These sorts of investigations are hard to do under the best of circumstances and can often go disastrously wrong.

★★★

AUGUST 11, 2016

162 DAYS BEFORE
DONALD TRUMP IS SWORN IN AS PRESIDENT

GASTON COUNTY, NORTH CAROLINA—A new political news site, Washington Babylon, needed something to draw readers in. So, the head of the site turned to a friend of his, a woman who had grabbed headlines in the political press for her role in the dramatic downfall of Congressman Anthony Weiner.

The woman, Sydney Leathers, reviewed a new documentary called *Weiner,* which followed the former politician's scandal-ridden mayoral campaign, giving it "two thumbs-down."

A reporter at the *Daily Mail,* Alana Goodman, quickly saw a passage eleven paragraphs into the review that seemed more important than the rest. Leathers had written, "I am certain his behavior continues to this day because a woman who claims to be one of his current sexting partners has reached out to me for advice."

If true, confirmation of a new Weiner scandal would be tabloid gold.

Looking to report the news before anyone else jumped on it, Goodman contacted Leathers to see if she had more information about the woman who was messaging with Weiner. Leathers said she had the information but was unwilling to share it with her.

For Goodman, the lead appeared dead.

But weeks later, an agent representing Leathers reached out to the reporter. For several thousand dollars, the agent agreed to give Goodman the name of the woman with whom Weiner was corresponding.

To Goodman's surprise, Weiner's latest target wasn't even of age; she was a fifteen-year-old girl in North Carolina.

There was no good way to approach such a young girl. This left Goodman with a reportorial choice. She could work the phones and try to reach the girl to get her to divulge her story. But that could be complicated in any situation, especially with a fifteen-year-old. Or she could jump on a plane down to North Carolina and try to land the story in person.

Goodman decided to fly to North Carolina and, without any notice, make the approach cold. But not wanting to blindside the girl at school or show up at her house without warning, Goodman decided it would be best to first talk to her father, who is a lawyer. Goodman went to his office to broach the idea of speaking with his daughter.

Most fathers would probably not react well to such an overture. But when Goodman talked to the father, he calmly said he knew about the messages and was unsure how to best handle the situation. The father said he was willing to talk to his daughter; he just needed to wait until later in the day because she was still at school. Goodman indicated that the *Daily Mail* was willing to pay for the story and protect the girl's identity.

After speaking with her father, the girl agreed to talk with Goodman and share all of the screenshots and messages she had from Weiner, and she also committed to sit for an on-camera interview. In exchange, the *Daily Mail* paid her $30,000.

That evening, in a bland conference room at a nearby cheap hotel, the girl and her father sat for interviews.

On September 20, the *Daily Mail* published the girl's allegations in a twenty-two-hundred-word story—along with a number of embedded screenshots of the inappropriate conversations and photos that were exchanged—under the headline "EXCLUSIVE: Anthony Weiner Carried On a Months-Long Online Sexual Relationship with a Troubled 15-Year-Old Girl Telling Her She Made Him 'Hard,' Asking Her to Dress Up in 'School-Girl' Outfits and Pressing Her to Engage in 'Rape Fantasies.'"

Once the story was up, it took less than a day for federal investigators in New York to subpoena Weiner's records to determine whether he had violated the law by exchanging sexual messages and photos with a child. Four days later, the FBI used a search warrant to seize Weiner's phone, iPad, and laptop.

FBI investigators examined the electronics. On the laptop, they found more than 300,000 emails, including many that had been sent or received from the domains @clintonemail.com and @clintonfoundation.org. The analysts could see that there was at least one BlackBerry message between Clinton and Abedin.

On September 28, realizing the significance of the discovery, the case agent notified his superior, who later that day had a secure videoconference with the deputy FBI director, Andrew McCabe, and nearly forty other senior bureau officials, to discuss the findings.

In the course of the Clinton email investigation, the FBI had failed to find emails from the first two months of her time as secretary of state, when Clinton had primarily used a BlackBerry to communicate with her staff. Investigators had speculated that the first two months would have been a key period for evidence, theorizing that if there was a smoking-gun email that showed Clinton acknowledging that she knew she was circumventing normal email channels and potentially handling classified information, it would have been in her first few months at State, when she was establishing systems and deciding how best to communicate.

Suddenly, as a result of Anthony Weiner's very public and ongoing self-destruction, the FBI had in its possession an extraordinary cache of possibly new evidence in a case that Jim Comey had closed three months before. But immediate action did not come from the discovery. For reasons that have never been explained, the computer and its contents somehow fell off the radar for senior officials at FBI headquarters in New York and Washington.

Comey would later ascribe the oversight to the Russia investigation, which had taken over the agency's attention that summer following the closing of the Clinton email case. But in mid-October, three weeks after FBI leadership first learned about the laptop, a senior Justice Department official named George Toscas asked them about what had happened to the emails one day after an unrelated meeting. That incidental question brought the issue back to life, and FBI leadership held a conference call with their colleagues in New York on October 26, along with attorneys from the Southern District of New York's U.S. attorney's office.

The agents and lawyers on the call determined that if they wanted to look at the emails, they would need an expanded search warrant from the court. At 5:20 a.m. the following day, McCabe emailed

Comey to ask "if you have any space on your calendar," hoping to discuss what to do with Weiner's laptop.

★ ★ ★

OCTOBER 20, 2016

NINETY-TWO DAYS BEFORE DONALD TRUMP IS SWORN IN AS PRESIDENT

THE DEPARTMENT OF JUSTICE—The Russia investigation created a once-in-a-generation challenge for Comey and the bureau as they sought to understand how a foreign adversary had launched such a wide-ranging attack on the United States. But there was a particularly frustrating aspect to the investigation that I would discover in the reporting for this book. Many details have not been reported anywhere before. Not only did top bureau officials feel as if they were fighting the Russians—they also felt as if they were fighting their own government. The contours of the Russian attack were coming roughly into focus, but the Americans were so unprepared for Putin's aggression that they didn't even know what to do with the evidence of it once it was in their possession.

The American intelligence community had unique insight into what the Russians had stolen from the United States during a hacking campaign that began in 2014 and resulted in breaches of servers at the White House, the State Department, and nongovernmental institutions like the Democratic National Committee. Dutch intelligence—an agency allied with the Americans—had gained extraordinary access to the networks of a top hacking unit for the SVR, the Russian intelligence agency that is the modern-day KGB. The group—known as Cozy Bear—was one of the most notorious Russian hacking teams and had first breached the DNC systems a year before the election. Along with gaining access to their networks, the Dutch could see precisely what the Russians had stolen from American computers.

Once the Dutch understood just how valuable the information they were receiving was, they began to share it with the Americans, handing over several flash drives to the FBI containing tens of thousands of pages of documents stolen from American institutions. The FBI had long been searching for ways to understand the Russians' cyberaggression. Now, by seeing precisely what the Russians had chosen to steal, they had a vast evidentiary record to analyze and could have a chance to establish methods and motives.

But the materials also created an incredibly serious legal question about the separation of powers in the U.S. government. Among the trove were documents stolen from Congress, the White House, and other government agencies. These documents were crime-scene evidence. But they were also the privileged communications of officials who were not known to have done anything wrong. Should the bureau be allowed to rummage around in the documents from another branch of government if there was no evidence that those officials broke the law? Was it right for the FBI to be looking through and assessing the messages sent by the top advisers to the president and other executive branch leaders?

Bureau officials initially determined that it was probably safest for an American analyst to work with the Dutch to index the recovered documents, giving the FBI only the broad strokes about their contents. Few details are known about how the FBI, Department of Justice, CIA, and White House handled the drives or what was on them. People familiar with their contents said that among them were emails that had been sent and received by President Obama. In May 2016, at least six months after receiving the drives from the Dutch, the bureau completed a memo about what material had been stolen. That August, Attorney General Lynch met with FBI officials to hear their argument for why they wanted full access to the drives.

"Why shouldn't we know what the Russians know?" one senior American official said. "The FBI said, 'Fuck no, we should be able to look at it. What's the privilege?'"

It seemed simple to the investigating agents. The Russians were looking at the documents and might even eventually make them public, in which case they would no longer be considered secrets. And if they were able to access the documents, the bureau believed it could be of great benefit—possibly even allowing them to map out the Russians' hacking playbook, or at least understand their strategies.

In mid-October, Andrew McCabe, the deputy FBI director, and his top aide, Lisa Page, wanted approval to look at the materials but were facing strong opposition from Deputy Attorney General Sally Yates, according to FBI text messages that have never been previously revealed. Three and a half weeks before Election Day, McCabe and Page discussed their need to get the CIA's deputy director, David S. Cohen, on their side to help win over the Justice Department and White House, according to the text messages.

"It would be very very helpful to get DDCIA to clarify that they DO want the content," Page wrote in a text message, using the acronym for Cohen's position.

"The DAG continues to use that as an excuse," Page said, referring to Yates.

"We will very much need to get Cohen's view before we meet with her," Page said. "Better, have him weigh in with her before the meeting. We need to speak with one voice, if that is in fact the case."

"I will reach out to David," McCabe responded.

Page said that she had asked a top FBI counterintelligence analyst to put together a memo about everything the bureau's cyber division knew about the drives. A meeting was scheduled at the Justice Department for October 20, between McCabe, Cohen, Yates, and the White House counsel, Neil Eggleston. But in that meeting Eggleston refused to give them the authority to examine the flash drives.

As Election Day neared, the FBI had the contents of what had been stolen but was forbidden to look at them. When the Republicans on Capitol Hill later found out about the thumb drives, their conditioning led them to one conclusion: Surely they must contain the thirty thousand emails Clinton had deleted.

★ ★ ★

OCTOBER 27, 2016

EIGHTY-FIVE DAYS BEFORE DONALD TRUMP IS SWORN IN AS PRESIDENT

THE COMEY HOME, McLEAN, VIRGINIA—After her husband's July press conference, the response had surprised Patrice. She knew that Jim would be criticized. But it was the fervor and tenor of the criticism that stood out. He ignored the press and public opinion for a living. But Patrice read everything, from the damning op-ed by the former Justice Department official to all the comments sections, too, which is never a good idea. Maybe it was just the heat of an election year, she thought. Whatever it was, as the fall approached, the intensity had dissipated, and the focus shifted to the increasingly bizarre national election.

But, on a Thursday evening, just twelve days before the election, the issue that had created so much consternation in the summer came back. That evening, shortly after Jim got home from work, he and Patrice were alone in the kitchen when he told her that earlier that day he had been briefed by his deputies that agents investigating the disgraced former House member Anthony Weiner had made a startling discovery. Weiner was under a criminal investigation for sending explicit messages to a teenage girl over the internet, and on the devices he used to communicate with the girl, investigators had found an enormous number of Clinton's emails, including some that the bureau investigators thought they had not found during the original email investigation, which had been closed several months earlier. Complicating things even further, the investigators could not just look at the emails to ensure they contained no classified information. They would need to go to court to get a warrant.

There were less than two weeks to go before the presidential election, and now the Clinton email investigation that Comey had taken the rare step of personally and publicly closing in July was about to roar back to life.

"It's a shitshow," he told Patrice. "They told me that there's thousands of emails."

It would fall to the director to make the final decision about what to do. Making it all the more complicated, he reminded Patrice that he would have to tell Congress. Over the summer he had pledged that if there were new developments in the email case, he would notify the leadership and pertinent committees.

This was a nightmare. And between Jim and Patrice, the looming dilemma would precipitate a kitchen conversation that would be a déjà vu reprise of their talk in late June, but this time the gravity of the moment multiplied a hundredfold as they alone peered into what this could lead to for the country.

Of course Comey was talking to Patrice about it. And of course she was aghast—aghast that her husband and the country were in this position, and aghast that the renewal of the investigation just as the country was turning to decide what America would be for the next four years could hurt Clinton and help get Trump elected. As upset as she was getting, she knew that making a direct appeal to her husband about Clinton's political fate would be a losing argument, and so she shied away from mentioning Clinton's name as she pleaded with Jim.

"You can't do this this close to the election. You can't do this to a candidate," she said.

She peppered Jim with questions.

"What the hell are Hillary Clinton's emails doing on Anthony Weiner's laptop? How is Huma Abedin that incompetent with emails? Why is this coming out now?"

She asked why the FBI couldn't just go get the warrant without having to tell Congress.

"If we get the warrant, it will leak," he said.

If that occurred, he said, it would look as if the bureau had reopened the investigation and hidden it from Congress, after pledging transparency. That would compound the disaster.

"What is our relationship with Congress if we're going to lie to them and not say something?" he asked.

Patrice understood that logic. But she could not get past the fact that this could be severely damaging to Clinton and that her husband was again going to become a target—a target in a far bigger way than in the aftermath of the press conference. She believed Trump had proven throughout the campaign why he was an existential threat to the country. Everything needed to be done to ensure he never set foot in the White House. If the FBI decided it had to charge Clinton after the election, Patrice was fine with that—so long as Trump wasn't president.

"It's too close to the election. It's too close to the election," she said. "Don't you understand that?"

This irritated Comey. The timing had nothing to do with it. The FBI director was not supposed to factor partisan politics into his decision making. If it had been any time of year, he would have told Congress. He could not hide it from them now. Comey's dilemma was actually not without precedent.

Four days before the 1992 presidential election, with Bill Clinton challenging President George H. W. Bush, a debate raged back in Washington in the office of the independent counsel overseeing the Iran-contra investigation. The prosecutor leading that office, Lawrence E. Walsh, faced a legal deadline. A judge said that Walsh had until October 30 to refile an indictment against Caspar Weinberger, the secretary of defense under Reagan. Walsh and his team contended that Weinberger had obstructed their investigation when he had made false statements to investigators and hidden notes from them.

Walsh, who had inflicted more political damage on Reagan and his allies, like Bush, than anyone else in Washington during his six-year investigation, had decamped to his personal office in Oklahoma City, where he lived, to write the final report that examined whether the Reagan administration sought to sell arms to Iran and illegally funneled the proceeds to fund a rebel army in its fight against the government in Nicaragua—after Congress had expressly forbidden funding the contras. Two days before the deadline, Walsh's staff faxed him a copy of the draft indictment. It included several direct quotations from Weinberger's notes that had never been made public before. One of the quotations implicated Bush in the scandal, saying that he had "favored" the sale of weapons in exchange for American hostages. This revelation was significant because Bush had claimed for years that he was not fully aware of the discussions surrounding the deal. He had famously claimed he was out of the loop.

Back in Washington, two of the more junior members of the prosecutorial team were alarmed when they saw that the quotation about Bush was set to be included in the indictment. With the election just days away, they believed it could be a move that could potentially influence public opinion in the critical days before a presidential election. And they thought such an aggressive move on the eve of the election would likely anger Bush and might even lead him to retaliate by pardoning Weinberger.

The junior prosecutors voiced their concerns to Walsh's deputies. One of the deputies said that they could give no consideration to the timing of the upcoming election because of a Justice Department policy that barred prosecutors from making prosecutorial decisions based on the political calendar. And in any case, Walsh didn't want to water down the indictment, because the substance of Weinberger's damning quotation had already been made public during congressional testimony years earlier. "Nobody believes Bush when he says that," Walsh said on the phone, referring to Bush's claims of ignorance about the deal.

So, four days before the election, on the afternoon of Friday, October 30, 1992, the independent counsel's office filed the indictment in federal court. It was an incredible boon for Bill Clinton, who immediately moved to capitalize on Walsh's action, holding a news conference to accuse Bush of diminishing "the credibility of the presidency."

The indictment changed the messaging of the race profoundly in the closing days of the campaign. Four days later, Clinton won 370 electoral votes.

"Probably cost me the election," Bush said in the aftermath. He said he viewed the whole thing as a "big witch hunt."

Bush talked to Attorney General William P. Barr—the young lawyer Bush had appointed a year earlier—about dismissing Walsh.

But he held off, and at the urging of members of Congress he asked the head of the Justice Department's criminal division, Robert Mueller, to look into whether Walsh had been politically motivated to file the indictment. No evidence of that ever surfaced.

Years later, Walsh acknowledged that the timing of the indictment might well have turned the election.

At home, Jim laid out to Patrice how to him there was only one choice: disclosure. He would at least be transparent and honest and show that politics had not factored into the decision.

"What is the alternative?" he asked Patrice.

He answered the question for himself.

"The alternative is a fucking disaster," he said, explaining how the bureau would be accused of having covered up for a newly elected president Clinton.

Patrice believed that her husband wanted Attorney General Lynch to tell him not to send a letter to Congress, thereby relieving him of the burden of the decision. But she knew that was unlikely.

"But why do you have to keep stepping out front?" she asked.

The melding of her concerns as an American and a wife made for an extraordinary moment. The presidency was supposed to be in the bag for Clinton, she thought. The election, to Patrice, was supposed to be a formality, one where voters would denounce Trump and forever shun his brand of politics—"Trumpism"—from the civic life of America. Could her husband—someone she believed was a pillar of honesty and transparency in Washington—really be put in a position to alter the course of history like that?

"This is going to be awful for you," she said. "You just can't do it."

"Tricey, that's not helping me," he said. *"That's not helping me."*

If nothing else, talking to Patrice disabused Jim of any notion that this was going to be anything but awful. And as a small grace, that gave him a sense of liberation.

"I am screwed no matter what happens," he told Patrice. "If I disclose this, I'm screwed. If I don't disclose this, I'm screwed. And so it's freeing in a way."

In the hours after telling Patrice, Jim gave himself pep talks.

Look, you don't want to be anything else, he told himself. *You're not going to go anywhere else, you have more money than you ever imagined, and you have a ten-year term—so what?*

The next morning, Comey sent a letter to select members of Congress notifying them of the situation; it immediately leaked, and the firestorm was just as Patrice expected—with Republicans reigniting their insistence that Clinton was a criminal all along and Democrats attacking Comey for abusing his power and inserting himself into a presidential election.

After seeing Comey reopen the Clinton email investigation, a former British intelligence Russia specialist named Christopher Steele was worried that the FBI director might be working to help boost Trump's odds of getting elected. The firm Steele worked for had been investigating the Republican nominee for a succession of clients—and since Trump had won the nomination, for the law firm that represented Clinton's campaign. He was alarmed at what he had found concerning the myriad ways that Trump was potentially compromised by his indebtedness to the Russians and had managed to share his findings with the FBI. With the election just over a week away and the bureau unlikely to make any public statements about their investigation of the Trump campaign before it was time to vote, he decided to go public himself.

Steele reached out to David Corn—a reporter for *Mother Jones*—and told him he had provided the FBI with a dossier of memos that tried to prove that Russia had been supporting Trump and cultivating him as an asset for years. On October 31, Corn's story, citing Steele as "a former senior intelligence officer for a Western country who specialized in Russian counterintelligence," was the first piece on the public record discussing Steele's dossier.

The next day, when approached by the bureau about the story, Steele admitted that he was Corn's source. Because it is frowned upon for an FBI source to talk to the media about their interactions, Steele's relationship with the bureau had to be cut off.

Just a day or two before the election, Comey received an unusual message from a friend of his. It turned out his friend had heard from one of Hillary Clinton's close allies who was looking to pass along an assurance to the FBI director. Comey's friend said the message came from the Democratic candidate herself. She apparently wanted to make it clear that Jim would not have opponents in the White House when she was president. Comey felt that the message reflected a confidence from the Clinton camp that she was going to win.

The message left Comey relieved, and hopeful that when Clinton became president there may not be an all-out war between the FBI and her White House.

IV

★ ★ ★ ★ ★

"OH, GOD"

NOVEMBER 8, 2016

SEVENTY-THREE DAYS BEFORE
DONALD TRUMP IS SWORN IN AS PRESIDENT

McLEAN, VIRGINIA—On Election Day, Jim would not vote. Long before the issues with Clinton arose, he had decided he would not vote as FBI director. It was important, he thought, not to take sides but rather to simply live with equanimity in the world that the voters chose.

Patrice, on the other hand, was excited to vote. She had waited decades to vote for a woman presidential candidate, and her eyes brimmed with tears as she selected Clinton.

She remembered a lifetime of conversations with other women about how they never thought they would see a woman president. A book club she had been part of had read Susan Faludi's *Backlash,* published in 1991, about ways in which popular media narratives stunted the feminist movement. When her club met, Patrice remembered saying to the group that "every kind of man" would be president before a woman got elected.

She had voted for Clinton eight years earlier, during the 2008 primary, but Clinton failed to reach the general election. By 2016, another eight years after her prediction, it seemed as if she might finally be proved wrong. She couldn't wait for that to happen.

Patrice returned home nervous but excited for the results to come in. She kept a close eye on *The New York Times* online app containing a presidential forecasting needle that started the day predicting Clinton had an 82 percent chance of winning. That evening, she watched the coverage with their youngest daughter. She texted their other children to see what they were thinking. Jim puttered about the house, watching little. He assumed that Clinton would win, and he found punditry and cable news off-putting. He had also been making a concerted effort for the months leading up to the election to stay as uninformed as possible about the presidential horse race.

After the Associated Press called Florida for Trump at 10:50 p.m., Jim went to bed, still thinking Clinton would win. At 2:30 a.m., when the AP called the race for Donald Trump, Patrice cried on the phone with her daughters, not giving voice to what she feared: that their father might be blamed for Trump's election.

Patrice finally went upstairs to their dark bedroom and woke up her husband to tell him the news. Jim sat right up.

"Oh, God," he said.

Oh, God, Oh God, Jim thought to himself. *Did we contribute to this? Is this something I did?*

He immediately started convincing himself that this was not his or the FBI's fault. To reduce the pain that came with that notion, he tried to convince himself of things he knew were likely untrue.

Maybe the office will change him, Jim told himself.

He also couldn't help but think about what his next four-plus years were going to be like. He had no idea what was in store for him or the FBI. It did not cross his mind that his job might be in jeopardy.

To cope, the brain is wired to rationalize the irrational. Comey knew that was exactly what he was doing. Telling himself that the majesty of the office of the presidency would sand down Trump's crass edges was more of a silent prayer than a prediction. But it was one he clung to that early morning as he lay in his bed contemplating the reality of a Trump presidency, next to a distraught Patrice. He was also convinced of his own power to be one of the people who could, at least in law enforcement matters, lead the president away from the darkness of his sometimes xenophobic and uninformed campaign persona and toward the light of something resembling more traditional presidential conduct. Comey didn't yet know that Trump would wield some of his darkest visions of vengeance and retribution and character assassination against him. But even if he had known, he might have been sanguine about it. He had stared down political ruin during the Bush years. But after the Bush administration he had faced the very real prospect of leaving Patrice a widow. And that experience had led him to become FBI director. If he could survive looking death directly in the eye, why couldn't he survive Trump?

★ ★ ★

AUGUST 2006

TEN YEARS, FIVE MONTHS BEFORE DONALD TRUMP IS SWORN IN AS PRESIDENT

RECOVERY ROOM AT THE JOHNS HOPKINS HOSPITAL, BALTIMORE—Jim's decision to leave the Justice Department early in Bush's second term and become the top lawyer at Lockheed Martin had an enormously positive impact on his family. Not only was Dad no longer working in such a stressful job, but he was now making more money than the family could ever have imagined, relieving the tremendous financial stress the Comeys had been under for years.

When his signing bonus landed from Lockheed Martin, Jim worried the bank would file a suspicious activity report on him. Overnight, he went from being unable to pay one month of his daughter's college tuition to being able to write a check for the entire thing. His time in government was over; life was good.

Then one day, a little less than a year after leaving the Justice Department, Jim noticed that he had passed some blood in his stool and made an appointment with his doctor to have it checked out. Within days, he was told that he had an advanced form of colon cancer.

To those with the misfortune of such a diagnosis, the prognosis is bleak: Among cancer patients the rule of thumb is stage 3, you're in trouble; stage 4, you're dead. When cancer cells are found in the lymph nodes, that means they have left the point of origin and the cancer is on its way to another organ. That's stage 3. Sometimes the difference between the two diagnoses can be a matter of days. Jim's cancer was detected at stage 3, and if he was going to stop it from becoming a terminal metastatic disease, the treatment would have to be quick and harsh. Jim would undergo radiation, several rounds of chemotherapy, a surgery that rewired his digestive system and left him with an ostomy bag. A port was installed in his chest for all the chemotherapy drugs to flow into his system. It was a desperate race to kill the cancer before it killed him. Complications from that treatment led him to be hospitalized twice—one time for an abscess that formed in his stomach and the other for a blood clot found in a lung.

Patrice lied to Jim, telling him that his hair was not thinning. They tried to maintain some sense of normalcy, and he and Patrice continued coaching one of their daughter's basketball teams. He tried to work through it, but serious illness is its own full-time job. And after months of being terribly sick, he was weak and frail, and he began to assume that he was going to die.

Jim and Patrice put their wills in order and talked about writing letters or taping videos to show to their kids after he passed. Every family birthday or holiday was treated as if it would be his last. But he didn't die from his cancer. And in the oddest of serendipities, it was his surrender to that fate that would lead to his appointment to be director of the FBI.

In November 2006, the Democrats won control of Congress and by the following January began investigating the Bush administration, including a scandal involving the firing of several U.S. attorneys. Few people had a closer view of the Justice Department under Bush than Comey, the former second-in-command. That spring, the top staffer on the Senate Judiciary Committee, which was now controlled by Senator Chuck Schumer of New York, reached out to see whether he would answer their questions about the scandal. Comey knew the staffer, Preet Bharara, who had worked for him at the U.S. attorney's office in New York, and he agreed to testify. In the course of their conversations in the week before the testimony, Comey told Bharara about something unrelated to the U.S. attorneys' firing scandal. Comey described in detail Dick Cheney's attempt in March 2004 to go around him to get a hospitalized and incapacitated attorney general, John Ashcroft, to reauthorize a surveillance program that Comey had concluded was illegal.

The story and its dramatic details stunned Bharara. If Comey was willing to share the story publicly, it would provide conclusive firsthand evidence from inside the administration of the extent of what Bush, Cheney, and their deputies had been willing to do in the name of executive power. Bharara asked Comey whether he would testify publicly about what he had told him privately.

Comey had a choice to make about how he would testify. He could answer questions minimally, offering the senators no more than what was necessary to be truthful. Or he could testify expansively and tell Congress of his experience fully and completely.

Depleted from cancer and wary that it would return, Comey thought it likely that he would die in the coming months or, if he was lucky, in a year or two. This hearing could be the last time he would ever speak publicly. So he entertained the expansive approach. He could be unrestrained and lay out the scene that unfolded in Ashcroft's hospital room three years prior in all of its dramatic detail.

I feel like my life is ending, Comey thought. *So, if I'm going to tell the story, I should tell the whole story.*

"The shorter-term perspective allows you to think of things in a bigger way," Comey would say later. "I would have testified anyway and answered the questions. But there was an end-of-life feeling that made it easier to tell the story. I wasn't thinking about how will this affect my future."

In the days before the hearing, Bharara told only Schumer about the new revelation. They both wanted to surprise viewers with the shocking new testimony and make it impossible for the White House to block it.

On May 15, 2007, Comey walked into the hearing room. Two years had passed since he had left government. In that time, he had seldom been seen in public. To nearly everyone in the room and watching on television, he was a former deputy attorney general reemerging to testify as Democrats amped up their scrutiny of the Bush administration. But physically and emotionally, Comey was in a different place. He was still hooked up to the ostomy bag. His chest was starting to develop scar tissue around the area where the pump had been removed just a few months earlier. The blood clots had permanently damaged the vascular system in his leg, and he would from then on wear a compression sleeve to prevent further clotting. The chemo had left him with no feeling in the tips of his fingers or the bottoms of his feet. His hair was still thin, and he looked pale.

Damaged as he was, Comey put on a show.

He walked the Senate Judiciary Committee, and the public, through the ugly details of the March 2004 hospital exchange. He described how the White House had tried to undermine the Justice Department and the lengths he had to go to—including the never-before-discussed race to the hospital bed of John Ashcroft—to stop Cheney, White House chief of staff Andrew Card, and White House counsel Alberto Gonzales.

"It was only a matter of minutes that the door opened and in walked Mr. Gonzales, carrying an envelope, and Mr. Card," Jim said. "They came over and stood by the bed. They greeted the attorney general very briefly. And then Mr. Gonzales began to discuss why they were there, to seek his approval for a matter, and explained what the matter was. . . . I was angry. I thought I just witnessed an effort to take advantage of a very sick man, who did not have the powers of the attorney general because they had been transferred to me."

The testimony made enormous news and fed a growing narrative that the Bush administration had expanded and abused its executive power in the years after the attacks of September 11, 2001.

The testimony had dramatically changed how Comey was viewed in Washington. Instead of being branded as a senior official in the Bush Justice Department at a time when legally dubious practices occurred, Jim had put immense distance between himself and the Bush administration. Some Democrats even considered him a whistleblower.

If his bitter resignation from the Bush Justice Department in 2005 hadn't signaled that his career in government was over, the Senate testimony that day in 2007 certainly had. He had publicly turned on a Republican administration. Democrats might have looked at him more favorably, but he was still not a Democrat and would almost certainly not be considered for a top position if Democrats reclaimed the White House. But six years later, in a Rose Garden ceremony to announce Comey's nomination to be director of the FBI, the president cited the showdown over the surveillance program, saying Comey had joined Mueller in "standing up for what he believed was right."

"He was prepared to give up a job he loved," Obama said, "rather than be part of something he felt was fundamentally wrong."

A cardinal rule of American politics was that if you expose the truth of your opponent's flaws more than they expose yours, then, armed with the facts, the voters will make the right decision. You win. And if you have the benefit of your opponent's ample public record that helps you make the case that they are a racist or a misogynist—all the better. You win.

For Democrats in 2016, this conventional wisdom was turned upside down. Trump's victory marked the most shocking presidential election result since Harry S. Truman beat Thomas E. Dewey in 1948. And it left Democrats more enraged than they had been even after a thirty-six-day recount led to George W. Bush winning the 2000 election. But Trump's win did more than put Democrats on the losing side of a presidential election. It fundamentally undermined their view of politics and the country. In Trump's case, on Election Day the country knew that he had discussed grabbing women by their genitals, had filed for bankruptcy six times, lied almost daily about many aspects of his own life and business, and conducted himself like no other modern presidential candidate as he made racist comments on the campaign trail and even attacked the family of an American service member who died in Iraq. And despite the voters knowing all of that, he still won.

It wasn't as if Trump had beaten someone who, like himself, had no government experience. He had beaten Hillary Clinton, the person Democrats believed was probably more qualified to be president than any other modern candidate. Democrats thought she had embarrassed Trump in the debates and were confounded that he had even remained in the race after the *Access Hollywood* video came out. On top of that, the Republican establishment that Democrats had faced off against over the past two decades had shunned Trump. The Bush family had signaled they had no interest in supporting him, and Mitt Romney had given a speech during the campaign calling him "a phony, a fraud."

"His promises are as worthless as a degree from Trump University," Romney said.

For Democrats, there was also the way Trump had beaten Clinton. From the day Trump declared his candidacy, he turned dog whistles on issues like immigration into bullhorn moments and tapped into Americans' nativist sentiments. Democrats asked themselves, how could anyone get away with this? Making it all the more confounding, Trump won in a way that ran directly against what the Republican Party had concluded was its only path forward. An autopsy the party did on itself after Romney's 2012 loss said that Republicans needed to broaden their support and appeal to minorities. To do that, they needed to tack to the center on immigration. Instead, Trump had run to the far right on the issue.

The blast radius of blame from the Clintons and the Democratic Party spared no one. Clinton and her supporters pinned her loss on the far-left wing of the Democratic Party controlled by Bernie Sanders, Russia's election meddling, and a hostile media (particularly the *Times* and my coverage of emails). But no one received harsher treatment for her defeat than Comey. His decision to reopen the investigation into her emails had come so close to the election that it was almost a given that it had a measurable—and perhaps decisive—effect on the outcome. It was the quintessential October surprise, resurrecting her most damaging issue just as voters were making their final decisions. It was simple: To Clinton and her supporters, had Comey not sent the letter to Congress, Trump would never have won.

Trump's victory also changed Democrats' view of the July press conference. Now the press conference, when coupled with Comey's decision in October to reopen the email investigation, was seen by Democrats as a one-two punch that sabotaged her campaign.

One top Democrat, Representative Jerrold Nadler of New York, said that there should be dire consequences for Comey: Obama should fire him.

"What Jim Comey did was so highly improper and wrong," Nadler said shortly after the election in a television interview on CNN. "From the very beginning in July, he was putting his thumb on the scale right then."

Speaking as though he were describing a third world country where sinister groups like the military, the police, and security services fight for power, Nadler referred to the FBI as a police agency.

"And it's unforgivable for a police agency to opine, frankly, publicly about legal conduct," Nadler said. "The president ought to fire Comey immediately, and he ought to initiate an investigation."

As the political ground under Comey shifted, the perception of his conduct from the law enforcement establishment and watchdogs who scrutinized the bureau changed. The inspector general for the Justice Department, who had declined to open an inquiry into the press conference in its aftermath, announced that he would be examining how Comey had handled the entire email investigation.

Ever since the angst of July had been compounded by the horror of October, Patrice had started to keep a mental list of the people she had thought were friends, only to have even some long friendships wrecked by a national election. It was not a short list. Harsh judgments and harsher criticism are facts of public life, but for Patrice this was beyond her understanding. After the election, though, singling out individuals would be impossible; her estrangement list would have to be expanded to include half the country. But was it her husband's fault that Clinton had set up her private server and discussed classified matters in her messages? Was it his fault that Clinton was not the greatest at connecting with Americans? Was it his fault she didn't campaign in a swing state like Wisconsin in the final days of the campaign?

In the weeks that followed, the press flayed Comey. He eagerly wanted to tell his side of the story. But he felt unsure of when he should do it and whether to do it in public. He could have held one of his quarterly meetings with reporters. But that might cause too much of a stir. He could do it during testimony before a House or

Senate committee. But there was no hearing coming up on the calendar. As Comey waited for the right moment, he went up to Capitol Hill to meet privately with senators, including the top Democrat on the Judiciary Committee, Dianne Feinstein of California. Comey believed that behind closed doors he could walk lawmakers through his decision making. In an intimate setting, Comey believed, he could make them see how he had had no choice but to go public. He explained to the senators that his conundrum had been between speaking and concealing. If it ever came out that the FBI kept the investigation secret, Comey said, the bureau would have been accused of covering up for Clinton to ensure her victory, inflicting grave damage on the bureau's reputation and credibility. Comey believed the lawmakers had heard him, giving him the sense that maybe, if he ever had to face them in a public setting, their criticism would be more muted.

More uncertainty existed about what a Trump presidency would look like than any other winning candidate in American history. Many of the same commentators, reporters, and politicos who discounted Trump's chances of winning now believed that he would temper his behavior because he was going to become president. But despite his giving a traditionally gracious speech the night of his victory, the transition ushered in an even more outlandish version of Trump. The tweeting and unpredictability that dominated the presidential campaign now embodied the person who would lead the country and the team that assembled around him. He fired the head of his transition team. He had unstaffed calls with foreign leaders, on unsecured phones. And he held reality-television-style auditions for cabinet positions. The anger on the Left grew more intense. It boiled over as evidence emerged about Russia's efforts to aid Trump in the election and questions arose about whether Trump and Putin had colluded.

Trump, who had celebrated Comey's independence for holding the press conference and reopening the email investigation, was becoming more and more agitated with the media coverage of Russia's election meddling and refused to accept the mounting evidence that Putin had thrown his weight behind his candidacy.

"Can you imagine if the election results were the opposite and

WE tried to play the Russia/CIA card," Trump tweeted. "It would be called conspiracy theory!"

Trump then ratcheted up his skepticism of Russia's meddling.

"If Russia, or some other entity, was hacking, why did the White House wait so long to act? Why did they only complain after Hillary lost?" Trump tweeted.

With all the vitriol being directed at Comey by Democrats, a subtle shift occurred as the goat became the last line of defense. As angry as the Democrats were with Comey, Trump was becoming a bigger threat and needed to be stopped. And now the characteristics that Democrats hated in Comey, like his independence and ego, became assets for them. For reasons that were largely political, the only institution that might be able to credibly investigate Trump was Comey's FBI. The election of Trump had ushered in a rarity in Washington: unified government. For only four of the previous sixty years, Republicans had controlled the presidency and both houses of Congress and had a conservative advantage on the Supreme Court. They now had that again. If Trump wanted, he could pressure House and Senate Republicans to hold back on investigating his administration, campaign, or Russia's election meddling, potentially jeopardizing bipartisan oversight. And, as president, Trump could replace nearly everyone in the executive branch. That meant Trump could have pretty much whomever he wanted as attorney general. But out of everyone in the executive branch, Comey had a special status designed to protect his job. When the bureau's first director, J. Edgar Hoover, died in 1972, after serving in his post for forty-eight years, Congress made it law that every director would be appointed to a fixed ten-year term. Hoover amassed far too much power over his time. The new ten-year term would insulate FBI directors from politics, because they knew they could make tough decisions without fear of being fired. Many legal minds said that the fixed term was unconstitutional, because the president had the authority to replace anyone he wanted in the executive branch. But the post-Watergate norm that law enforcement needed to be kept at arm's length from politics stopped nearly all presidents from dismissing their FBI directors. Comey had already displayed his independent streak. While Democrats blamed him for Trump's election, they knew he had not done it as part of a plot to get Trump elected. They hoped serving as a check on the new president would appeal to his interest in rewriting his own narrative.

First, Comey needed to meet the president-elect.

* * *

JANUARY 5, 2017

FIFTEEN DAYS BEFORE DONALD TRUMP IS SWORN IN AS PRESIDENT

THE WHITE HOUSE—The election meddling so alarmed Obama that in the days after Trump won, he ordered the intelligence community to conduct a formal assessment to determine who had been behind it. Eight weeks later—a remarkably short time for such a weighty report—the heads of the FBI, CIA, and NSA, and James Clapper, the director of national intelligence, completed the report, briefed Obama on it, and prepared to release an unclassified version to the public. In an Oval Office meeting with Obama, Comey and the other intelligence chiefs detailed their sourcing methods and laid out their conclusions: The Russians had meddled in the 2016 election to damage Clinton, benefit Trump, and undermine Americans' faith in democratic processes. Most significantly, Putin approved and directed the complex operation.

The document's conclusion—which would be present in the unclassified report the next day but would not include sensitive sourcing methods—would have an enormous impact on how the public saw the incoming president. The Obama administration intelligence officials saw it as their job to conduct an intelligence review of the greatest attack ever on an American election—a review that the incoming administration might never perform. But for Trump, it would be seen as bitter Democrats using the power of the intelligence community to tar him before he even set foot in the White House. While the intelligence report did not determine whether the Trump campaign had coordinated efforts with the Russians, the finding that Putin had tried to get him elected gave Democrats enough to cast doubt on the legitimacy of his presidency. And for the media, it set up a once-in-a-generation story that combined celebrity, politics, and espionage: A reality television star, unmoored from the norms observed by his predecessors and with a penchant for crudeness, might have become president because a defeated foreign adversary put him there.

Given how this intelligence document would shape the perception of Trump's presidency, it is important to understand how it was created and what it was based on. The intelligence chiefs based their conclusions on the U.S. government's best intelligence. Intelligence is different from evidence. It is not meant to be seen in shades of black and white or used at a criminal trial. But it is essential to give American officials the best possible understanding of dynamic and changing events across the world.

The intelligence agencies attach confidence levels to their conclusions to assess how probable they believe it is that they have accurately captured the truth. These designations can be more important than the actual intelligence. For example, an agency can hear that a foreign adversary has new nuclear weapon capabilities. But if a "low confidence" designation is attached to the intelligence, it means it's essentially worthless.

For Russia's election meddling, the CIA and the FBI determined that they had "high confidence" in the report's central conclusions. The NSA reported only "moderate confidence."

The differing confidence levels appear to have come down to the intelligence community's sourcing inside the Kremlin. Because the information came largely from a human source cultivated by the CIA, the NSA—which was, for much of the run-up to the election, kept in the dark about the source—approached the information with additional skepticism.

The legendary *Washington Post* reporter Bob Woodward reported in his book *Fear* that the central conclusions were based on six human sources who had been providing the Americans with accurate information for years. However, only two of them were "solid." One of those sources, Woodward wrote, was offered exfiltration out of Russia in the waning days of the Obama administration because the CIA had serious concerns about the source's safety. However, the source declined to leave, fearing the ramifications for his family.

Since then, it has been reported that the source had been uniquely important in identifying Putin's direct role in the plot and effort to get Trump elected. The source had been offering accurate intelligence to the Americans for decades, rising from a role as a mid-level official to a top-level aide with access to Putin and knowledge of the inner workings of the Kremlin. Although he was not in Putin's tight inner circle, he was around the Russian president regularly—even close enough to take pictures of his desk. Information from the source had been handled in the most secretive way possible: The CIA kept it out of the president's daily briefing and instead passed it along to the White House in a sealed envelope to limit the number of eyes on it.

In early 2017, the CIA had grown particularly concerned about the source's safety, including the possibility that he would be assassinated, after it was reported in the American media that the intelligence community had moles in the Russian government. This created angst at the CIA, where officials already questioned his trustworthiness, believing his unwillingness to leave might be a sign that he was working as a double agent for the Russians and had fed bad information to the agency. The CIA launched a review of his career to see whether the information he had passed along over the years had been reliable. Analysts concluded he had been truly helpful. But even when the source passed that review, some CIA agents and analysts still had doubts.

Months into the Trump presidency, the source would eventually be persuaded by the CIA to leave Russia and live in the United States. His departure left a major blind spot in the Kremlin for Western intelligence, who were almost certain that the Russians would be back for more, seeking to undermine the American 2018 midterms as well as the 2020 presidential election.

In reporting for this book, I learned more about the intelligence collection for the assessment. According to a former top government official, the CIA had at least one other source in Putin's orbit who provided information that the intelligence community relied on to reach its conclusion about Putin's role in the election interference. On top of that human source, the intelligence community had some form of electronic surveillance that they believed buttressed the validity of their sources and of the report. The assessment was regarded as solid and authoritative. No such review had ever been undertaken so quickly before, and its speed was due to the emergency that it confirmed: The United States had been attacked. And the United States was vulnerable to more attacks.

Comey was pretty sure this was going to be his last time in the Oval Office with President Obama. There was a bowl in the Oval Office filled with apples, part of the health consciousness that Michelle Obama had brought to the White House. He wondered, will fresh fruit be a thing in the next administration?

As he walked out, he casually took one of the apples from the bowl, later sharing it with his daughter that night at home. That apple was a witness to one of the most important intelligence briefings in American history.

* * *

JANUARY 6, 2017

FOURTEEN DAYS BEFORE DONALD TRUMP IS SWORN IN AS PRESIDENT

A CONFERENCE ROOM ON THE FOURTEENTH FLOOR OF TRUMP TOWER—If Obama was going to be briefed, then the incoming president needed to be briefed, too. A day after the Oval Office meeting, the intel heads traveled to Trump Tower in Manhattan, the same place where Russian operatives promising dirt on Clinton had met with Don Jr., Paul Manafort, and Jared Kushner seven months earlier.

It would be Comey's first meeting with Trump. The encounter would be momentous. Since the election, Trump had openly questioned the news reports that Russia had actually been behind the hacking, saying it could have been China or "some guy in his home in New Jersey." Now the intelligence chiefs had to tell the incoming president why he was wrong. Moreover, Comey knew that four of Trump's associates—including one who ended up sitting next to him at the briefing, Michael Flynn—were under investigation for their ties to Russia. Trump had already shown how sensitive he was about losing the popular vote, and Comey planned to take the lead on briefing the president-elect, one-on-one, on another personally sensitive subject: the Steele dossier.

There was an added urgency to the briefing. The intel chiefs had been told that Carl Bernstein, the veteran Watergate reporter for *The Washington Post* who now worked as an analyst for CNN, had a copy of the dossier and planned to publish it. If CNN said that the intelligence community had the dossier but had kept it secret from Trump, Comey thought it could deepen his suspicion that there was a "Deep State" aligned against him.

Comey was already learning how erratic Trump could be and was unsure he could trust his response to the briefing. In anticipation of discussing highly sensitive material with the president-elect, he thought there was a good chance he might need to document his side of the meeting to create a record. Complicating matters further, everything he would be discussing with Trump would be classified, so he wouldn't be able to record his impressions on an unsecure laptop. He asked one of his aides to bring along a computer that was approved for the transfer of classified material. It was something he had never done as FBI director. It was something he had never even contemplated as necessary.

Comey initially thought that Trump would come to the FBI's field office in Manhattan to receive the briefing, because it involved the most highly classified information and Comey believed that the proper place to discuss such matters would be in a secured government facility, where it's harder for adversaries to eavesdrop. But Trump's aides balked at that suggestion and insisted on meeting at Trump Tower, and a small conference room on the fourteenth floor was agreed to. It's unclear if the FBI or the intelligence agencies swept the room for bugs or did anything to secure the space. In Trumpian fashion, a makeshift secured facility was created. A thick dark gold curtain was hung over a large glass wall that faced a hallway. The curtain was slightly too long and bent at the floor. There were eight chairs around the table and a row of chairs in front of the curtain, where incoming CIA director Mike Pompeo, spokesman Sean Spicer, and other aides sat. Trump arrived ten minutes later and sat at the conference table with Reince Priebus, Mike Pence, and Flynn.

The Trump team's reaction to the briefing on the Russian interference bothered Comey. Instead of asking questions about how the attack was orchestrated or how another one could be prevented in the future, they tried to figure out how to spin the assessment to falsely claim to the public that the intelligence community had concluded that Russian interference played no role in the election result. The report had made no such determination.

When Trump was informed about the sources the intelligence community had relied upon within the Russian government, he told the intelligence chiefs that he was skeptical of their trustworthiness.

"I don't believe in human sources," Trump said. "These are people who have sold their souls and sold out their country. I don't trust human intelligence and these spies."

After the briefing, Comey pulled Trump aside in the conference room for his one-on-one about the dossier. The FBI director told Trump about the specific allegation in the dossier that, in 2013, Trump had prostitutes urinate on a bed in the Ritz-Carlton in Moscow that Obama had slept on, and that the Russians had video footage of it.

Trump fixated on the prostitutes and appeared defensive. To put Trump at ease, Comey told him that he was not under investigation.

Trump's behavior in their first encounter showed Comey several things. The incoming president seemed to have no interest in evidence that Russia, a foreign adversary, had meddled in the election. Trump was incredibly defensive about the issue of prostitutes. And he acted as arrogant and blustery as he had on television. In his years working in the Bush and Obama administrations, Comey had never before felt the need to protect himself by writing contemporaneous memos to document what he had witnessed or done. But Trump had so unnerved him that he thought he had to do it now. Someday the details of the meeting might come out, and he feared Trump wouldn't tell the truth. As his armored sports utility vehicle pulled away from Trump Tower, Comey began typing out a memo on the laptop.

"I was honestly concerned he might lie about the nature of our meeting, so I thought it important to document," Comey said. "I knew there might come a day where I might need a record to defend not just myself but the FBI and our integrity."

In the months that followed, Trump obsessed about the dossier to Comey and with aides, and in public. A week later, FBI agents would interview the primary subsource relied upon for the dossier. The subsource would tell the FBI that the allegation about Trump and prostitutes was, like much of the dossier, "rumor and speculation." But inside the FBI, for reasons that still remain unclear, Comey was apparently not told of the interview. And so as Trump complained about the dossier and the Russia investigation that spring, Comey would not know about the doubt that had been cast on some of the dossier's most salacious allegations. The FBI would become increasingly convinced as it continued to investigate the dossier that some of its information had been planted, as part of a Russian disinformation campaign. But years would pass before Trump would be told about this.

When Comey returned home, he didn't tell Patrice that he'd written the memo. But she knew her husband well enough to pick up that something had gone awry. He was not angry but quiet—the same way he'd retreated into himself at the height of the battles between the Justice Department and Cheney over torture and surveillance during the Bush administration.

Going forward, Comey's demeanor would be different whenever Trump came up. Before, when Trump did or said something ridiculous, Comey could just make a joke. But it wasn't funny anymore.

What Patrice didn't know was that her husband's demeanor belied problems that Patrice never could have fathomed. He had just learned something highly classified that raised questions about whether one of the people closest to the president had been working secretly with the Kremlin: the incoming national security adviser, Michael Flynn.

The problem was directly tied to Obama's decision to impose sanctions on Russia for Putin's election meddling. Curiously, Putin had chosen not to retaliate, and Trump had publicly praised the Russian leader's decision as "very smart." The White House, meanwhile, had tasked the intelligence community with finding out why Putin had reacted this way.

Intelligence analysts—including those at the FBI—sifted through the mountains of wiretaps and source reporting they collected on a daily basis. As part of that process, in early January they reviewed wiretaps on the Russian ambassador to the United States, Sergey Kislyak. The wiretaps revealed that Kislyak had spoken to Flynn five times on the day the sanctions were announced. On the calls, Flynn had told Kislyak not to overreact to the new sanctions, suggesting the Trump administration might offer the Russians more leniency when they were in power—in spite of Moscow's attack on the American electoral process. This left Comey and his team flummoxed and even more suspicious of the links between Trump and Russia. Why would Flynn, a retired Army general who had served as the military's top intelligence official, offer that kind of assurance to a foreign adversary, especially when he certainly knew that the Americans would be listening? The FBI, which was already investigating Flynn, now expanded its investigation to take an even deeper look at him.

Now Comey had to grapple with the possibility that the incoming president's national security adviser was in cahoots with the Russians. Comey briefed the Justice Department and the Office of the Director of National Intelligence, telling them that it was up to them whether to brief the White House, and a briefing was scheduled in the days that followed.

Then, on January 12, the *Washington Post* columnist David Ignatius wrote a column questioning the Obama administration's delay on addressing Russia's hacking. In the column, Ignatius, citing a senior U.S. government official, said that Flynn had spoken with the Russian ambassador several times on the day Obama announced the sanctions.

"Holy shit, that's a FISA leak; that doesn't happen," Comey said to aides. Someone had leaked the contents of Flynn's wiretap, which are considered the most tightly held forms of intelligence.

Comey thought to himself: *I hope political people who are about to leave the administration are not freaking out about Trump becoming president and doing something improper.*

The Ignatius column prompted immediate questions about Flynn's contacts with the ambassador. Contact is one thing, but was Flynn undermining current U.S. foreign policy? In televised interviews, Pence and the incoming chief of staff, Priebus, insisted Flynn had not discussed sanctions on the calls. To Comey, either they were all conspiring together to cover up Flynn's discussions with an ambassador for a country that had just sought to tip the election for Trump, or, more likely, Flynn had lied to the incoming vice president and chief of staff.

Both were bad.

Comey and Sally Yates, the deputy attorney general, along with other top Justice Department and FBI officials, began debating what to do. Yates wanted to warn the incoming administration that their national security adviser might have lied to the vice president. She claimed that Flynn could be blackmailed by the Russians, who knew Flynn had lied. Comey did not believe it was his responsibility to police lying in Trump's inner circle; that could be a never-ending task. And Comey thought the chances the Russians would use the call as *kompromat* were overblown. Most important, he wanted the FBI to get to the bottom of Flynn's relationship with Kislyak. Why had they talked with such frequency, and why had Flynn lied about discussing sanctions relief with the Russian ambassador? If the bureau engaged the Trump transition team, Flynn would almost certainly find out that the agency was scrutinizing his conduct and might take additional measures to mask his contacts and destroy evidence.

With Inauguration Day approaching, Patrice Comey and her daughters planned to attend what would be a massive Women's March on the National Mall the next day to protest Trump and his treatment of women and to sound an alarm at the sudden and shocking turn the country had taken. Patrice wanted to check with her husband before they went, because they could be photographed there and word might get out that the FBI director's entire family was protesting the new president.

Comey told her they should go.

"Don't get arrested," he said.

ACT THREE

V

★ ★ ★ ★ ★

THE ROAD TO MUELLER

JANUARY 20, 2017

INAUGURATION DAY

THE OVAL OFFICE—Five hours after being sworn in as the forty-fifth president of the United States, Donald J. Trump bounded into the Oval Office for the first time as commander in chief. With the solemn and historic transfer of power completed, a signature of America's constitutional democracy, Trump now crossed the threshold of the most storied office in the world, as its occupant for the next four years. The energy from his inaugural address, and from the validation of his dramatic electoral victory, brought a certain buoyancy to Trump in his first moments behind the Resolute desk. Some of his children and many of his former campaign aides, now thrust into high-level positions within the new administration, surrounded him. This array of confidants and officials was a diverse and poorly organized group who brought to the White House little government experience and a dizzying collection of political viewpoints and agendas. Now, tasked with translating the slogans from the rollicking campaign into a coherent governing agenda, they faced the daunting challenge of coordinating the launch of a new administration.

The Trump campaign had indeed been unlike any other in American political history. Every element of the effort to win the White House had been unconventional: It featured a meager and constantly shifting organizational structure, embraced messaging that frequently pushed into taboo territory, and took on a tone seemingly antithetical to the serious and sober nature of serving in the highest office in the country. In the end, the Trump campaign, in its road-show quality, had reflected the character of the candidate.

But this was the moment—Trump's first time walking into the Oval Office as president—when everything was supposed to change. Few things hold such a place in the collective American imagination as the power of the presidency. Runners-up fade with time, but presidents assume a sort of immortality. Surely the weight of history and the sense of majesty the office conjures would be the antidote to the lack of discipline and seriousness reflected in the Trump campaign and in the candidate himself. Or so went the story that Jim and Patrice Comey, establishment Republicans, the Washington elite, and many voters told themselves. The accuracy of this theory would be tested when Trump and his team first assembled in the space from which every U.S. president since John Adams had wielded power.

Throughout his life, Trump had been a man whose identity was uniquely tied to buildings. He measured success in the size of the skyscrapers that bore his name. Through the scale of these buildings, Trump had built his personal brand and public persona. He projected an image of himself as a master builder, and in the reflection of his projects Trump saw himself as the rich and powerful figure he constantly strove to become. Now, a question hung over the moment:

Would the man make the office, or would the office remake the man?

As it turned out, Trump had already begun redecorating the Oval Office in his signature style before he ever set foot inside as president. Obama's crimson drapes had been replaced with golden ones the new president had picked, adding an immediate Trumpian touch. Photos of Trump's parents were arranged on a desk in the back of the room. And the desk that Obama had occupied just hours before was completely bare, except for two landline phones, a coaster, and a small box with a red button atop that Trump could hit when he wanted a Diet Coke brought to him.

What else could Trump ask for?

Entering into the Oval Office for the first time as president, Trump could have focused on the history that had been made in that illustrious space, or on the possibilities for what his own administration might now achieve there. Instead, he immediately fixated on one thing: the lighting.

In all of the buildings Trump had erected—in New York, Chicago, Las Vegas, and overseas—he always paid special attention to the lighting. He knew that a dim and shadowy setting would never make a good impression. And now he could tell that the Oval Office lights—which project up toward the ceiling and, just as important, are indirect and remain concealed, almost magically producing exceptional brightness—would create optimal conditions for the cameras taking pictures of him, making a dramatic backdrop to document his new life as the most powerful person in the world. For a man who had never served in government, and for whom so much of existence was being seen through the lens of a camera, Trump now sought to create in the Oval Office a stage set reminiscent of the famous, stark, and imposing boardroom of *The Apprentice*. Except here, the power was not a fantasy.

This attention to the aesthetics of the Oval Office above all else began to answer the question of whether the grandeur and gravity of the presidency would transform Trump. Because rather than investing him with a newfound sense of sobriety and seriousness of purpose, stepping into the West Wing for the first time as president had in fact magnified Trump's constant focus on the superficial. It appeared to those who knew him that entering the White House hadn't so much changed Trump as it had supercharged his innate attraction to the shiny trappings of wealth and power.

What Trump needed to grasp in that moment was that the city that surrounded this new set in Washington was far different from New York. For his entire life in New York City, Trump had lied and arm-twisted his way through everything, operating in worlds dominated by tabloid coverage and businessmen a lot like himself who were brash, uncompromising, and ethically unbridled. The worst consequences he faced there for his misdeeds were bad press stories in the tabloids and civil lawsuits. But in Washington, the actors were more skilled, and the consequences were exponentially greater. Partisans, media, and officials from the law enforcement, military, and intelligence communities, and even foreign adversaries, played a sophisticated game of shivving at a far higher level, constantly calling fouls on each other for breaking a group of written and unwritten rules. In Washington, things like conflicts of interest, keeping a distance between politics and law enforcement, and even the appearance of improprieties that Trump had never given a moment's thought were all serious matters.

At the most basic level, because Trump now headed the executive branch, he found himself closer to the law than any other person in the country. He had never shown great care or appreciation for nuance. Now everything he did—whether it was tweet, privately complain, or sign an executive order—would be seen through the prism of the law. If he made a real mistake, he would be labeled a criminal.

A friend who spoke with Trump the day after his inauguration said that Trump not only had failed to grasp the new realities and sensibilities of Washington but also had entered into "another dimension of reality." The toys of the White House, the friend said, had turned Trump into a child who sounded as if he had just opened his birthday presents.

"I have the best toys, you won't believe the toys, and I have the best Secret Service, they will kill anybody and follow you around everywhere—there's nothing like them," Trump told the friend.

"I got the sense," the friend said, "that he came into this place and was completely oblivious to what he was walking into and was completely mesmerized by this new world he was in, and for the first time realized just how powerful he was going to be."

For Trump's entire life he had wanted to create his own reality, the friend said. But often, he ran up against others—people on the street, other businessmen, and the media—who reminded him of his standing as an outsider from Queens. But as he had skated along in the business world, he always had the ability to put things into perspective.

"He was in on the joke," the friend said. "He was P. T. Barnum and he let you know from time to time he was in on the joke."

Now, behind the walls of the White House, the friend sensed

that Trump believed he could finally live in his version of reality and that no one was going to get in his way. With the symbols of ultimate power at his disposal, people would finally have to take him seriously.

"Behind the White House wall and gates he was completely protected," the friend said. "Now he was surrounded by sycophants, and nobody around him would be honest with him. On January 20 he finally walked into a building where he could say whatever he wanted to say, and believe whatever he wanted to believe, and live in this alternate reality."

Even after he had taken over his father's real estate business, Trump still felt like a kid from the outer boroughs who was looked down upon by those he saw as members of the elite class. Even when he expanded his business and created a worldwide brand, the titans of New York real estate still thought of him as an act without real substance. But now, just months before he turned seventy-one, Trump had reached the pinnacle of American life. He was the president of the United States; no one, not even his doubters, had a more powerful job.

But Trump's expectations for how the world would now see him were setting him up for a huge disappointment.

After first walking into the Oval Office and noticing the light, Trump posed for photos with his children behind the Resolute desk. His aides congregated behind him for what would be his first event at the White House: the signing of a largely symbolic executive order to signal his intentions to attempt a rollback of Obamacare and eliminate federal regulations generally.

Standing behind Trump in the room were the people who were supposed to be guiding his presidency. One of them was a family member, his son-in-law, Jared Kushner. Presidents had long been expected to turn to the best and the brightest in any given field and bring them into the executive branch, shunning nepotism and favoring experts. Trump, however, had no such compunction regarding the practice and eagerly installed members of his family in positions of great power like his daughter Ivanka and Kushner, who had ill-defined roles. On the organizational chart, the two highest-ranking White House officials were supposed to be the chief of staff,

Reince Priebus, and the chief strategist, Steve Bannon. None of them had worked in government before, let alone the White House.

While the title of chief of staff belonged to Priebus, many of those who worked directly for him believed Kushner was the true chief of staff. Priebus acted as if he had little power, especially to say no to bad ideas. He seemed more comfortable in a glorified communications director role. He had his office set up with so many televisions hung on the wall that White House staffers joked that it looked like a Buffalo Wild Wings sports bar. Bannon, the chief strategist, came to the White House with all sorts of self-confidence and gusto and a slew of executive orders of questionable legality that he wanted to rush in to have Trump sign. But he had no idea how the government functioned.

However, two aides in the room did have extensive experience working in the executive branch. One was Flynn. The other was a longtime Washington lawyer named Don McGahn.

McGahn had been the lawyer for Trump's campaign and had maintained a far lower profile than the Bannons and Kushners of Trump's world. Throughout the race, he was more of a voice on the other end of the phone from Trump than someone who traveled with him; McGahn would update him on the nitty-gritty matters of a campaign, like fundraising numbers, and it was McGahn who would see to it that Trump would be on the ballot in all fifty states. Even during the transition, the two had spent little time together. McGahn largely stayed in Washington. He fought recount efforts in the few states where Hillary Clinton or Jill Stein supporters had challenged the vote. He hired lawyers to work under him at the White House, and he closed up his private law practice.

Although Trump and McGahn had known each other for only a year and a half, the two had developed a decent relationship. They found each other funny. Now that they were both in the White House, McGahn would see Trump just about every day. White House counsels are typically charged with attending meetings with the president and other top aides to offer advice on the legal restrictions that may arise in the process of everyday governing. They have a hand in questions of ethics, pardons, executive orders, and a slew of different topics. But more than any other White House counsel in recent history, McGahn—whose high-level experience was largely in the realm of campaign law—had a more defined role. Sure, he would have to commit time to many of the same things past White House lawyers had done. But he was given additional responsibility. Taking advantage of Trump's lack of core political beliefs, McGahn—in the process of signing on as the White House's chief lawyer—had the president grant him extraordinary latitude in the appointment of judges. As a staunch libertarian, McGahn had long dreamed of a judiciary that worked to limit the reach of government. ("I enjoy liberty," McGahn once said in an interview. "I don't like the government.") With the okay from Trump, he could nominate scores of judges to lifetime appointments who were all far more conservative than the judges who had been appointed during the Obama and Bush administrations, changing the courts for decades. In fact, McGahn was so singularly focused on the appointment and confirmation of judges that he had a memo drawn up that had a day-by-day and even hour-by-hour schedule of the plan to announce and confirm Trump's first Supreme Court pick.

McGahn knew he was receiving a once-in-a-never-again opportunity. In another Republican administration he would have been passed up for the job in favor of someone who had an Ivy League degree and perhaps even prior experience in a White House or the Justice Department. But now McGahn would have the sole power to present judicial options to Trump. No other White House had operated in a similar manner. And with a Republican Senate and an open seat on the Supreme Court, the arrangement gave McGahn an extraordinary power.

In the Oval Office on Inauguration Day, McGahn could tell that little work had been done during the transition to establish an agenda and that no one on the leadership team had any real idea what their roles were or, for that matter, what the administration's plans were for its first several days. To McGahn, the assembled group of staff and family felt like a group of people who had decided on a whim to run the country, without putting any time or planning into learning what that actually entailed.

"It was a pickup game of basketball with some people who

maybe you think are smart or have talent or whatever but they had never played on a court before, had never played as a team, weren't going to work as a team, and have a coach who has never coached before and had no real interest in coaching," said one aide.

And something seemed off about the president. Aides noticed that amid the feeling of joy and disbelief that suffused the White House, a darkness had quickly set in with Trump himself.

Trump said nothing about how he was feeling. It was Trump, after all; we may never know what he was feeling. The aides thought there could be two reasons for why the president acted upset. One sense was that Trump, now the most powerful man in the world, was finally feeling the weight of the office. He had been taken with the idea of being president, but now what?

Presidential historians have written for generations about how "the office" had changed presidents once they'd actually assumed the job and confronted the realities, responsibilities, and limitations of their position on the world stage, where the implications of any action they took could alter history. Maybe this scared Trump.

But maybe his emotions were shallower than that. After all, among the reasons Trump had looked forward to his inauguration was that he thought being the forty-fifth president of the United States meant at last he would be accorded the respect from the media he felt he deserved. Yet within hours of taking the oath of office on the Capitol steps, he was seeing media reports highlighting how many more people had attended Obama's first inaugural than his.

On the campaign trail, Trump had flung vicious attacks at the other Republicans seeking the nomination and Clinton. They hit him back with damaging disclosure after damaging disclosure. But Trump survived them all. The rhythms and pace of campaigning had been perfect for him. He jumped from city to city on his own plane. At each stop he fed off the crowd. He lived in the spotlight and thrived on the constant motion and media attention and constant sense of embattlement. Even when the polls had been heading south, aides had rarely seen Trump lash out angrily or grow depressed. While he was someone who struggled to take criticism, running against Clinton not only gave him a foil, it also gave him an outlet for his insecurities.

"On the campaign, he was the one hurting others," said one aide. "He had an enemy. As long as he's hurting them more, he can take the incoming."

But now Clinton was gone, and all the attention would be cast directly on him. By achieving the presidency, he would now breathe the rarefied air of a historic figure, and would now be measured against the likes of Washington and Lincoln. Bluster is fine in real estate and reality TV, but now it would be much harder to trash-talk his way out of his problems. Along with being upset with the media's coverage of crowd sizes, Trump grew angry that Obama had received such a warm send-off that afternoon from television commentators when he departed the Capitol in a helicopter after the inaugural ceremony. To Trump it was as if the media were mourning Obama's leaving and dreading his own ascendancy.

"All of a sudden he's president, and he took it pretty hard," said one aide. "All sorts of people who couldn't believe he was elected were saying horrible things about him."

His ego aside, Trump's ignorance of how government worked could be a profound liability. To McGahn, a best-case scenario would be for Trump to emulate Ronald Reagan. Enjoy the trappings and ceremonial roles of the presidency and let aides like him ruthlessly execute his agenda. McGahn had seen the reporting that the FBI was investigating links between the campaign and Russia. He thought it was all bullshit. Whatever it was, the campaign and its lawyers could handle any questions that came up. It wouldn't be anything serious that the White House would have to handle. He could focus on just the judges.

What McGahn did not realize was that a freight train was steaming toward the White House. Jim Comey and the FBI were closely watching Trump's public behavior and the chaos that enveloped him. They were prepared to act in a way that would spark a series of events that would drastically change the trajectory of the presidency and McGahn's life. For any White House, facing off with an adversarial FBI would be a complex, and even crippling, challenge. But for a White House that had little idea how to govern, dealing with the investigation in an organized, effective way would be virtually impossible. It would all happen so quickly that by the twenty-sixth day of the presidency, Trump would have done enough to create an existential threat to his presidency that would potentially define his term in office. More than that, the impending clash would create an unprecedented level of chaos at the highest levels of the American government, a chaos that in many ways would redefine Washington.

It would put Trump on a collision course with himself, the establishment, the FBI, and the Justice Department. Standing between Trump and the abyss would be Comey and McGahn. As the presidency got under way, McGahn thought everything would be fine.

But he might have known better. His own family's history should have taught him that being Donald Trump's lawyer was never that simple.

* * *

1980

ATLANTIC CITY, NEW JERSEY—Paddy McGahn was the most prominent lawyer and fixer in the newest industry in town. If you wanted to make it in casinos in Atlantic City, you had to see Paddy McGahn. As a young man, Paddy had spent three brutal months deployed on the front lines of the Korean War as a Marine platoon leader. A bullet struck him in the back of the head. A grenade went off in front of him, sending shrapnel flying into his face. Another explosion left fragments of metal lodged in his spine. His injuries were so severe that he lost some use of his right arm and would only ever be able to greet people with his left hand. The military awarded him the Navy Cross and three Purple Hearts for valor.

Despite the strain of the tour, Paddy returned home to Atlantic City after the war just as outgoing, aggressive, and ambitious as he had been before he left for Korea. But he needed a job. He felt endlessly proud to be a Marine—even keeping his military-style crew cut—and believed he could channel that energy into helping his hometown by getting involved in politics. His mother suggested he meet with the notorious South Jersey Republican political boss who ran Atlantic City, Hap Farley. Republican bosses had controlled the city's public offices, and the locals were convinced that the power structure would never change. Bribes, backroom deals, and nearly unanimous Republican support made Farley the ultimate decision maker when it came to any government post or consequential policy decision. (Decades later, the book and HBO series *Boardwalk Empire* would evoke the bare-knuckle thuggery and horse-trading that dominated Atlantic City politics.)

There was another reason it made sense for Paddy to meet with the boss: Farley was close to the McGahns, even serving as a pallbearer at the funeral for Paddy's father—an Irish immigrant who came through Ellis Island and went on to run a popular pub in downtown Atlantic City. Paddy believed that Farley would give him a low-level post so he could begin to work his way up the machine's ladder.

But when Paddy met up with Farley, their exchange went badly. Instead of finding Paddy a position, Farley suggested that he look for work out of state if he wanted a start in politics. Paddy felt rejected and, according to family lore, went down to city hall that very day to change his political affiliation from Republican to Democrat.

He also decided to finish getting the law degree he had started before the war. After graduation, he opened his own small law office in Atlantic City. Operating as a Democrat in a Republican town would be a challenge. But over the next decade, Paddy relied on charm and a whatever-it-takes mindset to deepen his ties with local officials. Along the way, he became a prominent lawyer specializing in working the wheels of the local bureaucracy, claiming that his connections went "all the way to heaven."

As Paddy built up his legal practice, he watched Atlantic City continue its decline. Situated on a small swath of land that occupies just 3 miles of New Jersey's 130-mile coastline, Atlantic City is about an hour's drive southeast of Philadelphia and two and a half hours from Manhattan. It started as a spa and wellness retreat in the late nineteenth century. A railroad line that ran into the middle of the town from Philadelphia helped turn it into an easy weekend getaway for upper-middle-class city dwellers. With a boardwalk along the water and a government willing—even eager—to ignore the law to lure visitors, the city quickly grew to prominence, and fancy hotels sprouted up on the water. By the 1920s, gambling, drinking, and prostitution were freely available along the boardwalk, and local authorities would raise the drawbridge at night, a signal to law enforcement on mainland New Jersey to mind its own business. The Miss America pageant got its start there, and entertainers like Harry Houdini and W. C. Fields worked the boardwalk.

With so much money streaming in from tourists, there was little incentive for locals to build a self-sustaining economy. That thinking would backfire profoundly as the advent of the automobile allowed Americans to visit any beach—not just those they could reach by train. The interest in Atlantic City waned even more dramatically after World War II, when affordable air travel brought Florida and the Caribbean within reach. As a last-ditch effort to turn things around, Atlantic City spent $600,000 of its taxpayers' money to lure the Democratic Party to host its 1964 presidential convention there, hoping to spark some national interest and media coverage. But that gambit backfired after the media's attention was instead drawn to the city's collapsing economy and dilapidated facilities.

By the late 1960s, Paddy and his brother Joe decided they needed to do something to return Atlantic City to its glory days. Paddy still resented Farley and the corrupt Republican political bosses he felt had held the city back by coddling their cronies. The first order of business would be shaking up the establishment.

Joe was a promising political candidate. The valedictorian of his college class, he went on to serve as an Army surgeon during World War II, then returned home to become the main obstetrician in Atlantic City; few babies were born in town that he had not delivered. He spent a few years as a councilman and mayor of an Atlantic City suburb, and now—with Paddy serving as his campaign manager and behind-the-scenes fixer—he planned to challenge Farley for his state senate seat in the 1971 election.

With Joe as the front man and Paddy as the muscle working behind the scenes, the two brothers ran a campaign in South Jersey aimed at convincing voters that Farley and his Republican Party were corrupt and had to be thrown out. The campaign worked. Joe won overwhelmingly, and from his first days in office he and a young Democratic assemblyman from the area who had also just been elected fixated on the one thing they believed could bring back Atlantic City: legalized casino gambling. Joe and the assemblyman—a Yale-educated reformer named Steven Perskie—thought they could create Las Vegas on the East Coast, providing the region with a massive new industry to create jobs and return Atlantic City to its former self. To legalize gambling, Joe and Perskie needed to persuade the state legislature to pass a massive piece of legislation, a project that would take several years. They got a boost in that effort from Resorts International, a former paint company that had refashioned itself as a hotel and gambling enterprise that wanted to build one of the first casinos in Atlantic City. Resorts had hired Paddy to help grease the skids locally.

The push eventually worked. In 1976, the state legislature legalized gambling. Across the top of the front page of *The Press of Atlantic City,* the headline read, "CITY REBORN: Casinos, New Charter Win." Joe's legacy as one of the godfathers of legalized gambling in Atlantic City had been cemented, and anyone paying attention knew that Paddy was now a player as well.

Joe eventually faded from political life after a series of electoral setbacks, but Paddy's career thrived as the gambling industry the brothers helped start began minting money. Local officials feared a rush of companies would allow the Las Vegas mob to muscle its way into Atlantic City, so for the first year of legalized gambling, Resorts was the only company licensed to operate a casino. It raked in piles of cash, and patrons would line up for hours around the casino waiting to get in. The lines would get so long and slot machines were so novel and enticing that some gamblers were even known to urinate on themselves rather than lose their place in line.

Clients lined up at Paddy's door, too. In the legal profession, if you're one of the few lawyers who understands a new and important part of the law, you can become indispensable. Paddy was the lead lawyer for Resorts, making him essentially the first local attorney to learn how the New Jersey gaming industry would operate. His knowledge made him a must-hire for the next wave of casino owners targeting Atlantic City and for anyone else who needed a lawyer to navigate local politics and secure the proper licenses. Among those who noticed Paddy's emerging importance in Atlantic City was a young New York real estate developer looking to cash in on the gambling industry.

Donald J. Trump's career as a real estate developer was on the ascent in the late 1970s. He had successfully developed the Grand Hyatt in midtown Manhattan in a partnership with Chicago's Pritzker family, but he was eager to set out on his own. He had heard about the success of Resorts and the Atlantic City gold rush and wanted a piece of the action for himself. He knew nothing about the casino, hotel, or entertainment businesses, but he had a strong nose for fast cash and celebrity, and Atlantic City had plenty of both.

Trump eventually built his first casino, the Trump Plaza, at the foot of the Atlantic City Expressway—the main gateway into town and a location that turned the property into a cash cow.

In February 1982, when Trump couldn't get the city council's approval to expand the Plaza's footprint, he turned to Paddy McGahn. Trump wanted to build a bridge connecting his casino to a parking garage on an adjacent street, and Paddy went to work on the local officials, helping push the approval through by purchasing air rights over the road. There was nothing wrong with selling the air rights; such deals happen between developers and cities all the time. But this deal was sketchy. The air rights were worth tens if not hundreds of thousands of dollars given the property values in the area. But in a move that smacked of Atlantic City's old-school cronyism, Paddy arranged for Trump to purchase them for just $100—fleecing taxpayers of money they should have received for the sale.

The deal elated Trump, who gave Paddy more and more business. Paddy also fit the model of the type of lawyer Trump liked to rely on: scrappy, street-smart, willing to bend the rules, and presiding over a small firm that was highly dependent on his business. The more beholden Paddy became to Trump, the more willing he was to push boundaries to keep Trump happy (and the more susceptible he became to Trump's refusals to pay his entire legal bill—a common danger for anyone who did business with the young tycoon). Still, Paddy continued to work for Trump for years in a relationship that was mutually beneficial.

Paddy also knew how to hide things and how to make problems go away.

In 1982, Trump wanted to buy a property adjacent to the Plaza. But it was owned by the sons of high-ranking Philadelphia mobsters, and Trump wanted to conceal his name from the deal—not because he was concerned about dealing with mobsters (he had done so willingly in the past), but because he was worried they'd raise their price if they knew he was the buyer. So Paddy arranged for the land to be sold to his secretary, who then had the property transferred to Trump. Through the 1980s, as Trump expanded his Atlantic City operations, it seemed as if Paddy could do no wrong, and Trump openly boasted about his work. He was even so appreciative of his lawyer's efforts that he named a bar in the Taj Mahal, his doomed mega casino, Paddy's Saloon.

When three of Trump's top casino executives were killed in a helicopter crash on their way to Atlantic City in 1989, Paddy handled the legal fallout. He also kept a secret for Trump, who had lied to the media by claiming he narrowly missed flying on the ill-fated helicopter. Paddy knew Trump was lying because he had been with him in a scheduled meeting at the time of the crash.

Even as Paddy grew older, and Trump's businesses began to spiral toward bankruptcy, the developer didn't tire of his fixer. Shortly after the helicopter crash, the president of the Plaza went to Trump to complain about the high fees ($150,000 to $200,000 per month) that Paddy was charging. Trump shooed one of his deputies, Jack O'Donnell, away.

"Jack, I'm 13 and 0 with this guy," Trump said, as O'Donnell later recounted in his book *Trumped!* "What do you want me to do? He gets things done in this town."

But by the early 1990s, Trump's luster was gone and his businesses were failing. He had overexpanded, larded his operations with debt, and found it difficult to make money in a business that should have been a cash register. He had little understanding of what made the business work and spent too much time glad-handing high rollers and putting on boxing matches, instead of tending to the more mundane things like slot machines, where all the money was to be made. He was also overextended in other ways and about to slip into a series of corporate bankruptcies in New York and Atlantic City that would put him on the cusp of personal bankruptcy.

After a fresh group of casino executives began eyeballing Paddy's bills, they complained about him to Trump. For example, they said, Paddy had charged Trump for 23.75 hours of work on a single day and 24.75 hours for another day of work. This time, Trump listened. He stopped paying Paddy's bills, even as he kept him working full-time. Then Trump sued him.

Paddy jumped into the litigation with gusto, certain he would win because he had the records and a good explanation for why he had billed so much. When asked in depositions about his bills, Paddy explained that he needed a second lawyer to shadow him at every meeting. He needed a shadow, he testified, because Trump lied so much. Paddy described Trump as an "expert at interpreting things"—meaning that Trump's account of events and reality had little to do with each other. The legal brawl didn't officially conclude until Paddy died in 2000, taking to his grave the claim that Trump still owed him about $1 million in back legal fees.

Paddy, who kept his Marine haircut until he died, was buried in Arlington National Cemetery with a twenty-one-gun salute. One of his nephews, a young elections lawyer, drove down to the burial from the Republican National Convention in Philadelphia. Don McGahn had seen his uncle only a few times in the past decade and a half because a family dispute about an Atlantic City property deal had divided the family, but he knew about his uncle's experience with Trump.

In the decade and a half that followed, Don rose to become one of the more prominent election lawyers in Washington. By the 2016 cycle, he had become convinced the only way to beat Hillary Clinton was to eschew the self-examination that the Republican Party had undertaken following Mitt Romney's loss in 2012—the so-called autopsy that had advocated an aggressive outreach to minorities and an embrace of immigration—and instead run to the far right. When Trump first hired Don McGahn to work for his campaign, McGahn did not mention his uncle's ties to the candidate. McGahn had a sense of what had happened between the two but was unsure whether to bring it up.

"There's three sides to every story: There's one side, the other side, and somewhere between is the truth," McGahn would later say. "My instinct was that the conflict was not so much personal with Trump. And that's a different generation, a different time, and I'm a different guy."

* * *

JANUARY 24, 2017

113 DAYS UNTIL THE APPOINTMENT OF SPECIAL COUNSEL ROBERT S. MUELLER III

FBI DIRECTOR'S CONFERENCE ROOM—"Let's take a cold shot at him," Comey told the counterintelligence agents and senior bureau officials assembled around him.

His agents had briefed Comey on how they wanted to interview Flynn. For the past several weeks, the investigators had scoured his phone records, examined his contacts, and sifted through intelligence. They had found little that gave them greater insight into why the incoming vice president and chief of staff were falsely claiming that Flynn had never talked to the Russian ambassador about sanctions.

Now, the investigators told the director, they wanted to speak with Flynn, and Comey had to make a decision.

Giving the go-ahead to interview Flynn was the easy part for Comey. It was the logical next step for the investigators. When a bureau investigation hit a dead end as this one had, they typically moved to interview their subject, because it was seen as their last chance to learn something. For all the powers the FBI had amassed over its nearly century-long history, it was in interviews where the agents most often turned up the keys that unlocked the mysteries they sought to solve. The bureau's interviews came with an added layer of leverage over the person they were speaking to: Making false statements to a federal agent is a felony. If interviewees lie, they can be prosecuted.

While green-lighting the interview made sense, determining how to do it was far more complicated. It was just the fourth day of the Trump administration. Speculation swirled about ties between Trump, his associates, and the Russians. The most powerful law enforcement agency in the country—led by the only high-level official in the entire government whom the president supposedly could not replace—had an open investigation into the campaign of the new president. And now that agency wanted to interview one of the people closest to the president about Russia.

The FBI, the White House, and the Department of Justice had a long-standing protocol for when the bureau wanted to interview someone in the White House. The bureau did not just send its agents over to the executive mansion whenever they wanted to question someone. Such a move would be seen as far too aggressive, especially for an agency that, after all, was part of the executive branch and worked for the president. Under protocols, the FBI would contact the Justice Department, which would tell the White House counsel's office whom the bureau wanted to speak with and what they wanted to question them about. Parameters were set for the interview and the administration official would be accompanied by a lawyer from the counsel's office and sometimes a personal lawyer. This ensured the FBI did not rummage around the White House. In rare cases, it was done less formally, and top FBI officials would call a very senior official at the White House—like the chief of staff—and say that they needed to have agents come over to speak with someone for an investigation or give them what's called a "defensive briefing," which is essentially a tutorial on how to ensure they are not targeted by a foreign adversary trying to spy on them.

But Comey and his counterintelligence agents now wanted to throw those protocols out the window and do something different. The bureau likes to conduct "cold interviews," where witnesses have little time to prepare and no lawyer is present. In those settings, interviewees tend to be the most forthcoming. If the Justice Department called the White House counsel's office and said that agents wanted to question Flynn about his ties to Russia, all sorts of red flags would go up. The White House would likely delay, if not altogether block, an interview. But maybe, if someone senior from the bureau called over to Flynn, he would agree to quietly sit down with them.

In his career, Comey had never so aggressively worked around the protocol. But to him, the question of whether the national security adviser—the top foreign policy aide to the president—could be in cahoots with a foreign adversary that had just launched the most audacious attack on the United States' democracy ever was so troubling that it justified abandoning the protocols. And the four-day-old Trump administration had acted in a way that made it a sitting duck. Comey was ready to pounce. The director had a sense of the chaos in the new White House and was concerned about the false and misleading statements, the bizarre lies about inaugural crowd sizes.

Comey knew he could not have gotten away with circumventing the White House counsel in a functioning, more organized White House, such as the two previous ones. But he had never faced a problem like this, where he couldn't trust that the White House wasn't working with the country that had just attacked the American elections. No FBI director had ever faced that problem.

Comey asked his deputy, Andrew McCabe, who had known the retired general from their days working on counterterrorism together, to call Flynn and say the bureau wanted to question him about the calls. McCabe told Flynn he could have a lawyer present. But if Flynn wanted a lawyer, they would have to go through the hassle of running everything through the Justice Department. Flynn said there would be no need for that. The FBI, Flynn added, already knew what he had said on the calls, telling McCabe he assumed the bureau had been listening in.

Comey determined he needed to defy normal operating procedures even further. For the previous couple of weeks, he and acting attorney general Sally Yates had been going back and forth about what to do. Instead of conferring with her about this move—by far the most important one the bureau would make in the investigation—he decided to make the decision to send in the agents on his own, without telling her.

"If it takes us in a bad direction, it will immediately be attacked as an Obama holdover trying to get the Trump administration," Comey recalled.

So, as the agents headed over to the White House for the interview, Comey called Yates, who happened to be conferring with her staff about whom she should reach out to at the White House to alert them to the problems with Flynn.

Comey told her what he had set in motion.

Yates erupted in anger. She thought they had been working together on this, and again here was Comey, just as he had done in the July Clinton email press conference, freelancing whatever he thought was right without consulting his bosses.

She told Comey that she wanted to be briefed right after the agents returned.

As Yates chewed out Comey, the agents arrived at the White House. To ensure no one else figured out what they were up to, an FBI agent who had been detailed to the White House quietly signed the agents in, allowing them to get on the grounds without having to go through formal channels.

Flynn met the agents in the West Wing and seemed completely at ease, giving them a quick tour as he ushered them to his office down the hall from the president. On their way, they passed the Oval Office, where they could see Trump telling movers where they should place the room's new art. Flynn did not introduce the agents to the president but told them that Trump had a real eye for decorating.

In Flynn's office, the agents spoke to him for an hour about his contacts with the ambassador, then returned to the FBI, where they immediately briefed Comey and other senior FBI officials in his conference room. The agents said that Flynn repeatedly lied to them, saying that he had not discussed sanctions with the ambassador. Flynn claimed that all he had talked about was setting up a call between Trump and Putin.

The statements from Flynn about the ambassador perplexed the agents, who had even used some of the same language in their questioning of Flynn as he had on one of the calls with the ambassador in hopes of prompting his memory. The agents said Flynn didn't seem to be in a rush or have any idea that he was under investigation. He did not display any of the signs agents are taught to look for in someone who is lying, like sweating or looking away. Either he was a great liar, had some cognitive issue, or truly believed he was telling the truth. Even though they all knew he was lying, the agents said, he somehow seemed credible. Adding to the peculiarity, on three separate occasions in the span of the interview, Flynn looked out a window into midday brightness and said, "What a beautiful black sky."

Investigating the campaign of the president was going to be an enormous challenge for Comey. Now the national security adviser had broken the law and lied about his contacts with the foreign adversary that had meddled in the election to help Trump win. Had Flynn explained it all away as a miscommunication or told the FBI that he had lied to the vice president and the public to conceal the fact that he had talked to Kislyak, the bureau would likely have closed the investigation. But he didn't. He lied to the FBI, and lies suggest cover-ups. Now, the relationship between Trump, his associates, and the Russians appeared even more suspicious.

Comey tried to come up with an explanation. What did Flynn have to gain from lying? Flynn said himself he knew the government was listening in, so why the heck did he think he could get away with it?

Flynn's lies reminded Comey of two of the most high-profile cases he had been involved in during his career. When he was the U.S. attorney in Manhattan, his office indicted the home merchandising personality and executive Martha Stewart for making false statements to federal agents about whether she used insider information to profit on a stock sale. And when he served as the deputy attorney general, he oversaw the investigation into Vice President Cheney's chief of staff, I. Lewis "Scooter" Libby, for lying to federal authorities about whether he had discussed the identity of an undercover CIA agent with reporters. Both Stewart and Libby were convicted. But the government and Comey never got a real answer for why they had lied—something Comey had always remembered.

Plenty of lies make no sense, and we never get an answer for them, Comey would say later. "People sometimes lie for reasons that have nothing to do with the investigation. They lie because they think things will go away. I thought that Martha lied because she thought it would just go away."

For the FBI director, the Trump administration had gotten off to a very troubling start. They were less than a week in. Trump had shown that he would continue his behavior from the campaign. The national security adviser had broken the law and lied about Russia, and the bureau had no idea why.

How could it get worse?

★★★

JANUARY 26, 2017

111 DAYS UNTIL THE APPOINTMENT OF SPECIAL COUNSEL ROBERT S. MUELLER III

McGAHN'S OFFICE ON THE SECOND FLOOR OF THE WEST WING—One of McGahn's most critical tasks during the transition was writing a detailed fifteen-page memo that laid out an hour-by-hour chronology about how the administration should roll out its Supreme Court nomination, to fill the vacancy left by Antonin Scalia's death. Politically, it was the most important thing Trump could do, McGahn thought, because it signaled to his base that he would be true to his word and install hardened conservatives who shared their views on abortion and immigration. The opportunity to appoint an associate justice so soon in the administration would be a statement of principle and a marker to the base that had put Trump in office. To ensure the base heard this message and received this gift without any distraction, McGahn believed the entire administration should be disciplined and coordinated and not do anything that would steal attention from their nominee until the Senate had held its hearings and taken its vote.

But by the sixth day of the administration, it was clear no one was in charge and no one was following that plan. Behind the scenes, Steve Bannon and Stephen Miller were pushing a travel ban by executive order that concentrated on closing travel from predominantly Muslim countries, a measure that McGahn knew was legally dubious. In a normal White House, the counsel's office would be central to planning such a profound action, but not in this White House. McGahn seemed to have no control at all over stopping it. And by angrily fixating on the inaugural crowd size, the president and press shop had ensured that that story had dominated the first week of the presidency.

The acting attorney general, Yates, shattered any remaining notion that McGahn would be able to focus on the Supreme Court nomination on Thursday morning, January 26, when she called McGahn with an urgent matter to discuss. She wanted to see him in person. The counsel's office was a secure space, impervious to electronic monitoring, so they agreed to meet later that morning there, in McGahn's office, where they could discuss classified information.

At 11:00 a.m., Yates, accompanied by one of the Justice Department's top national security officials, walked into McGahn's office and sat down; the door was closed, and she got straight to the point. She laid out what the FBI knew about the calls between Flynn and the Russian ambassador and how the sanctions imposed by President Obama had been discussed. Yates said the fact that they talked about sanctions was significant, because Vice President Pence, Chief of Staff Priebus, and Press Secretary Spicer had said publicly that Flynn had not discussed sanctions with the ambassador. Yates said this raised two concerns. It was likely that the national security adviser had lied to the vice president. Plus, the Russians almost certainly knew that Flynn had lied, supplying them the ammunition for blackmail.

Yates had even more details that made the whole situation worse: Two days earlier, FBI agents had been in the West Wing to interview Flynn. The FBI was investigating the new national security adviser. That information was grave enough; Yates would say nothing further about what he might have told the agents. McGahn struggled to comprehend the implications. But here, on the sixth day of the new administration, the acting attorney general, who had run the day-to-day operations at the Justice Department under the previous president, was in his office telling him that he had a problem that posed a grave national security risk to the United States. Whether either Yates or McGahn realized it at the time, there could be no more profound picture of the clash of cultures between the incoming and the outgoing administrations, or between the political poles in America. From the perspective of Obamaworld, Flynn had just demonstrated his disloyalty to the United States and should be fired immediately and face legal sanction. To Trumpworld, Yates was a symbol of the elites whom they had defeated in the campaign but who still wanted to destroy them. To them, she was the hand of the Obama administration reaching into Trump's presidency to take out Trump's top surrogate, the lock-her-up guy, and McGahn didn't know what to do.

Coming into the administration, McGahn recognized that as White House counsel he would have a hand in all executive branch issues, ranging from basic employment contracts to complex trade negotiations. There was no way he could be an expert in all subjects. He was cognizant that national security would be a potential soft spot because in a career in elections law he had rarely dealt with classified information before. But now, six days into the administration, at a time when McGahn wanted to be almost singularly focused on the nomination of Neil Gorsuch to the Supreme Court, the acting attorney general had presented him with an extraordinary national security problem.

McGahn had spent very little time with Flynn during the campaign. Flynn seemed like a nice guy. But he had taken to Trump's vicious brand of politics a bit too much for McGahn's taste—even leading the Republican convention crowd in a chant of "Lock her up!" about jailing Hillary Clinton, which just seemed reckless and bizarre. But Trump had rewarded the reckless and the bizarre with significant jobs in his administration. Flynn was Exhibit A of how the shortcomings of the campaign had bled into the White House. To McGahn, it signaled a larger problem: Like attracts like. Because Trump had himself behaved so recklessly during the race—and few thought he could win—he struggled to attract established and respected Republican politicians and policy aides to work for him. Yes, Trump had captured lightning in a bottle, but the world of Washington was still unsure whether he had wholly captured the

Republican Party or whether mainstream conservatives, who had their careers to think of, would sit out this presidency and return when a more traditional Republican ran the country.

So after Trump won, those who had been early supporters were in line to get key spots in the administration. At the top of the list was Jeff Sessions, an immigration hard-liner who had been the only senator to endorse Trump before he clinched the Republican nomination, and Flynn, a three-star general whom Obama had fired for incompetence. Rewarding supporters for their loyalty was fine to McGahn, who had benefited from this himself. But the U.S. government should attract the top talent in the world, and there were processes in place to make sure that it did. None of that mattered to Trump, who was so impulsive and so mistrustful of expertise that he made McGahn nervous, because critically important jobs seemed to be doled out to those whose only qualification was loyalty. In the early stages of the transition, Ivanka had told Flynn he could have any job he wanted in the administration. The job of national security adviser was among the most critical ones for a president, because that official needed to take the interests of the diplomatic, military, intelligence, and law enforcement communities and distill it into a coherent strategy for the country. This would be an especially critical post for an administration being led by a president who had never worked in government. Having Flynn in that position would be of great benefit for Ivanka and Kushner, who wanted to have free rein to dabble in whatever policy they wished and would have fewer roadblocks and no questions asked with a compliant Flynn in place. When Flynn took the unusual step of calling the Russian ambassador just as Obama was implementing the sanctions during the transition, several of the top transition officials—including Bannon, Priebus, and Spicer—had been included on an email in advance of the call. But no one had thought to tell McGahn, or ask whether it would be a prudent move, or whether there might be legal complications to consider. At the time, after all, there were three weeks remaining in the Obama presidency, and the foreign policy of Barack Obama was still the official policy of the United States. Now McGahn was learning about the call from the acting attorney general left over from the Obama administration.

McGahn respected Yates's record as a prosecutor, and she had developed a far better reputation inside the Justice Department than Loretta Lynch, whom the Trump team saw as weak and political. But he had a natural mistrust of Yates. She was a high-ranking remnant of the government under Obama—the same government Republicans had long criticized and Trump had repeatedly demonized during his campaign. Of Trump's top aides, few felt as strongly as McGahn when it came to government overreach. And as McGahn saw it, the Obama-era governing class—led in part by Yates—held exactly the kind of elitist, overly powerful, and rights-infringing ideology that he so despised.

It was a strange dance that Yates and McGahn were doing. He wasn't entirely sure what she was suggesting he should do about Flynn, and there was only so much she could tell him. He pressed Yates again about what Flynn said to the FBI, but all she would say, elliptically, was that Flynn had told the agents what he had told Pence and Spicer. Yates said nothing specific about whether she or the FBI believed that Flynn had committed the federal crime of lying to the agents.

That led McGahn to make a wrong assumption, one that would later be seen as a sign of his inexperience. He thought that if Flynn had lied to the agents and broke the law, Yates almost certainly would have had to tell him.

McGahn asked Yates what they should do.

"Should we fire Flynn?" McGahn said.

"That's not my call," Yates responded.

McGahn then made another mistake.

Instead of pressing Yates for more details, he asked few other follow-ups, leaving him with only a loose grasp of the facts when he would need to explain this to Trump later in the afternoon. He would later admit to colleagues that he had mishandled the situation.

"There's no way I should have allowed her to leave this shit burger on me," he would say. "I should have said, 'Sally, you're the acting attorney general and you're not leaving my office until you give me some counsel on what to do, and you know a hell of a lot more than I do because you're overseeing the FBI.'"

McGahn found another way to complicate the situation.

The moment called for someone to dive headfirst into the problem, figure out what Flynn had done and said, and push for immediate action. Instead of doing that himself, McGahn asked John Eisenberg, the top lawyer for the National Security Council, to look into it. McGahn had not gone to an Ivy League law school and, despite his contempt for elites, had undue regard for those who had. Eisenberg had one of the greatest pedigrees in the White House—Yale Law, Supreme Court clerkship—and seemed like the perfect person for the assignment. Eisenberg—who became known as Johnny Mumbles for how he spoke—had served as a top national security lawyer at the Justice Department under George W. Bush and was considered one of Washington's smartest legal brains. But what McGahn failed to realize was that Eisenberg was much more of a thinker than a doer. And, instead of jumping in to wrestle the problem to the ground, he would have a plodding approach in the days that followed that only made the situation worse.

Despite not having all the facts, McGahn did recognize the severity of the situation and wanted to tell Trump immediately. But earlier that day, Trump had traveled to a Republican Party retreat in Philadelphia, and the Flynn issue was too sensitive and confusing to speak with the president about over the phone. Whatever was going on, Flynn was a potential bad apple, and as the White House's top lawyer it was McGahn's job to keep Flynn away from the president.

At 4:00 p.m., Trump returned to the White House, and McGahn went to the Oval Office to brief him.

McGahn tried to explain what Yates had said.

Trump looked confused.

The bottom line, McGahn said, was "he's gotta go."

Trump had no government experience but did have a finely honed instinct for PR. Firing your national security adviser on the sixth day of your administration for his suspicious ties to the Russian ambassador would create terrible press.

The president called in Priebus and Bannon to tell them about what had happened.

How the heck can these guys help the situation? McGahn wondered.

McGahn struggled to answer many of their questions, including whether Trump would be jeopardizing an ongoing investigation if he fired Flynn. Flynn could be erratic, and Trump had already grown increasingly irritated with him. Obama had warned Trump in a meeting after the election about bringing the former general into the administration. Flynn's son had been fired from Trump's transition team after spreading a debunked conspiracy theory called Pizzagate, which alleged Hillary Clinton was at the center of a secret pedophile ring run out of a D.C. pizza parlor.

"Not again, this guy, this stuff," Trump said.

But Trump wanted to avoid the negative coverage. McGahn did not have enough answers to their questions to yet justify firing Flynn. And he didn't have the answers, because he hadn't asked Yates the right questions. They were in some trouble, but so far the trouble was still shadows dancing on a wall. They needed a clearer picture—McGahn would need to meet with her again, to get her to be more forthcoming. In the meantime, the president's main concern was that everyone remain quiet about the matter.

No one said anything about telling the vice president that the Justice Department and FBI had figured out that the national security adviser lied to him and might be compromised by the Russians.

★ ★ ★

JANUARY 27, 2017

110 DAYS UNTIL THE APPOINTMENT OF SPECIAL COUNSEL ROBERT S. MUELLER III

MCGAHN'S OFFICE ON THE SECOND FLOOR OF THE WEST WING—The following morning, McGahn tried to correct some of his mistakes of the previous day and get to the bottom of what Yates was saying. He arranged to have another meeting in the hopes that she would provide more information and help clarify the situation. That afternoon, when she returned to the White House, he asked her if Flynn was being investigated.

Yates wouldn't answer the question.

What the fuck, McGahn thought. How was it that the acting attorney general, who reported to the president, could refuse to be forthcoming about any matter? The attorney general worked for the president of the United States but concealed information from the White House? For the Obama holdovers at the Justice Department, McGahn's reaction and the White House's response in the coming days would show how inexperienced the incoming Trump administration was, and just how unfamiliar they were with how the Department of Justice functioned.

"Why does it matter to DOJ if one White House official lies to another White House official?" McGahn asked Yates, she later recalled.

She answered carefully.

"The misrepresentations were getting more and more specific, as—as they were coming out," Yates said, describing how the varying accounts of Flynn's conversation with Kislyak were at odds with what the FBI knew to be true. "Every time that happened, it increased the compromise, and to state the obvious, you don't want your national security adviser compromised by the Russians."

McGahn asked Yates if the White House could potentially disrupt an ongoing investigation if they chose to fire Flynn. Yates said the Department of Justice was fine with the White House taking whatever action it felt necessary.

"You know it wouldn't really be fair of us to tell you this and then expect you to sit on your hands," Yates said.

That day, Eisenberg briefed McGahn on his initial legal analysis. He told McGahn that Flynn might have criminal exposure for making false statements to federal officials.

Around the same time that Yates went back to the White House, Trump called Comey at his office. McGahn had warned Trump against having direct contact with the FBI director, but Trump ignored him.

The FBI director was at his desk eating lunch when the call came in. In his three years working for Obama, he had never spoken to him on the phone, let alone received a call from the president out of the blue.

But here was Trump on the line.

The president asked Comey if he wanted to come over for dinner that night.

To Comey, the overture sounded ominous.

"The head of the FBI could not be put into the position of meeting and chatting privately with the president of the United States—especially after an election like 2016," Comey would later say. "The very notion would compromise the bureau's hard-won integrity and independence. My fear was that Trump expected exactly that."

In an instant, Comey tried to rationalize the invitation, ascribe a benign motive to the president's invitation. Certainly, Trump had to recognize the problem with having a private meeting one-on-one with Comey. It must be a group dinner, he thought.

The FBI director could have said no. But he reasoned that it was the seventh day of the administration. Saying no might create unnecessary tension.

"Of course, sir," Comey said, accepting the invitation.

Comey hung up the phone with Trump and called Patrice. They had a date scheduled that night—Thai food. That needed to be put off, he said. "Sorry, Tricey," he said. "I'll make it up to you."

That afternoon, Trump signed a ban on travel from seven Muslim-majority countries at a ceremony at the Pentagon. It would take only a day for a federal judge to rule parts of it unconstitutional.

At 6:20 p.m., Comey's two-car motorcade of black sports utility vehicles arrived at the White House. He was brought up to the Green Room on the first floor—an austere room with green silk walls used for small events and meetings. Thomas Jefferson ate dinner in the room. Morticians embalmed Lincoln's eleven-year-old son in it. Eleanor Roosevelt greeted the pilot Amelia Earhart there after she became the first woman to fly across the Atlantic Ocean.

Comey entered to see the table was set for only two people.

Oh, shit, he thought.

Trump arrived on time at 6:30 p.m. They sat down and dinner began.

Perhaps not surprisingly, the president dominated the conversation. To Comey, it was "conversation as jigsaw puzzle," where

Trump would never stick with one topic or engage in lengthy exchanges, instead flipping around between a multitude of unrelated subjects and returning to earlier ones for no apparent reason. As they were served courses of salad, shrimp scampi, chicken Parmesan, and vanilla ice cream, Trump gave Comey a tour of his mind, expounding on his appreciation of the White House's luxuries, his media savvy, his son's height, his understanding of the Clinton email investigation, and even the sexual assault allegations against him. He never really asked Comey a question or gave him much room to speak. He just didn't seem interested.

What Trump was interested in was whether Comey wanted to keep his job. Several times he asked Comey what he wanted to do. It was a strange line of questions to ask a man with a ten-year appointment—so designed to be beyond the reach of politics. Trump's intimation surprised Comey, because he already had the job and it was widely accepted that he would be there for the foreseeable future. By the third time he asked the question, it was becoming clear to Comey that Trump was trying, not so subtly, to signal that his job might be in jeopardy.

"I need loyalty," Trump told him.

Comey ignored the comment.

He had thought during the transition that Trump might simply need to be taught how the government worked. Now, as he sat alone with the president in the Green Room, Comey started to realize that Trump didn't need to be taught, nor did he have any interest in learning how to do things the right way. Trump knew exactly what he was doing; he just wanted to do things his own way and now had the power to do that.

During Comey's time in government, he had been struck by the reality that the conduct of the institutions—which can seem from the outside to be massive and monolithic—was actually entirely dependent on the conduct and character of individuals. There was a president, his top few aides, and the leaders of Congress. If they went along with something, good or bad, that was it; their acts would be the acts of the United States. The direction of the country really turned much more on what those few leaders were like as people than he had ever imagined.

After becoming FBI director, Comey told his predecessor, Robert Mueller, that he was surprised by how much power and autonomy came with leading the agency. The bureau's agents, analysts, and professional staff revered the role of the director and would go along with what Comey said, and the Department of Justice had little ability to see what Comey was doing or manage it.

"Now you see why the character of the person in that job matters so much," Mueller had told him.

Seven months earlier, Comey had held an unusual press conference to put distance between the FBI and politics and then in October reopened the investigation in a desperate bid to protect the bureau's credibility. He had been blamed for electing the man who now sat across from him, and had tried to convince himself that with adult supervision even this White House might be able to govern in a way that was akin to other presidencies. But here, now, the president of the United States was leaning on him for a commitment of loyalty—not to the institution of the presidency, he feared, but to Trump himself. His biggest concerns about who Trump was and how he would behave as president were coming true. And, to his astonishment, he now had real doubts about whether the president was acting in the country's best interest. Was Trump just out for himself? His cronies? The Russians?

Trump wouldn't let it go. He brought up loyalty again. Comey still could not come up with a good way of responding, but felt the need to say something.

"You will always get honesty from me," Comey said.

"That's what I want, honest loyalty," Trump responded, studying Comey's face to see if he agreed with his framing.

"You will get that from me," Comey said, looking to end the conversation.

Comey got home that night with the same quiet demeanor that Patrice had noticed following the initial Trump Tower meeting.

"He asked for my loyalty," Comey said.

"What is that?" Patrice responded.

The two found a giggle in something Trump had said at the end of the meal. The president said that the entire Comey family should come over to the White House for dinner or a tour. Comey wouldn't play basketball with Barack Obama for fear of what it might look like. It wasn't that hard to understand: The FBI director should not be the president's buddy. In response to Trump's overture, Comey had said nothing.

The next day, Comey sat down to write up a memo about his dinner with Trump. He took four pages to lay out all of the details he could remember, ensuring there would be a contemporaneous account of Trump's request for loyalty.

"The conversation, which was pleasant at all times, was chaotic, with topics touched, left, then returned to later, making it very difficult to recount in linear fashion," Comey wrote. "Normally I can recall the pieces of a conversation and the order of discussion with high confidence. Here, given the nature of it, there is a distinct possibility that, while I have the substance right, the order was slightly different."

A week had passed since Trump became president. The FBI was investigating the president's campaign. The national security adviser had lied to the FBI. The president had asked the FBI director for his loyalty. The FBI director was keeping memos on every major interaction he had with a president whom he did not trust. And Comey felt like he was a man alone, with no one else in the government there to help.

★ ★ ★

FEBRUARY 8, 2017

NINETY-EIGHT DAYS UNTIL THE APPOINTMENT OF SPECIAL COUNSEL ROBERT S. MUELLER III

RICHARD BLUMENTHAL'S SENATE OFFICE, WASHINGTON, D.C.—Despite the turbulence created by Trump, the travel ban, and Flynn, the Gorsuch nomination remained on track. McGahn made it known to everyone in the White House that this project was his baby and nothing would get in the way of moving along the nomination. All McGahn and everyone else had to do was follow the memo he had written that laid out the schedule and plan they needed to follow.

Trump had announced the nomination in the East Room in the second week of the administration. Now it fell to McGahn to usher Gorsuch through his confirmation process.

Eight days after the nomination, Gorsuch met with Senator Richard Blumenthal of Connecticut—a top Democrat on the Judiciary Committee. The meeting seemed to go fine. Afterward, Blumenthal went to reporters to share some of the notable remarks the Supreme Court nominee had made. Days earlier, a federal judge in Washington State had temporarily blocked the travel ban nationwide, and Trump broke a long-standing norm and responded by tweeting that the opinion of the "so-called judge" was "ridiculous and will be overturned." Blumenthal said that Gorsuch had described Trump's attack on the federal judge as "disheartening" and "demoralizing."

The comments pitted Trump and his nominee against each other. In a move meant to win the news cycle, Trump then publicly called Blumenthal a liar, accusing him of fabricating the account of the meeting. But Trump's attack was discredited after a White House aide working on Gorsuch's nomination confirmed the remarks. Privately, Trump fumed. To him, the world was a series of quid pro quo arrangements, and the relationship at hand demanded absolute loyalty from his nominee. How could Gorsuch—a man he had less than two weeks before nominated to a lifetime appointment on the nation's highest court—criticize him like that?

Around the time Gorsuch sat down with Blumenthal, Comey arrived at the White House for his first face-to-face meeting with the new White House chief of staff, Reince Priebus. He was confronting the reality that he did not trust the president. But Comey was not ready to let Trump destroy the FBI's independence. If Trump was uncontrollable, the next best option was to hopefully train those around the president.

When Comey entered the White House, he headed to the reception area inside the front door to the West Wing, where a Marine stands when the president is in the Oval Office working. That day, the Marine was there.

Comey sat quietly in a chair on the side of the room near a receptionist. He wanted to avoid seeing Trump, figuring nothing good could come of that. As he waited for Priebus, someone else he wanted to avoid walked out of the vice president's office.

Holy shit, it's Flynn, Comey thought to himself.

Flynn walked directly toward him.

Comey stood up, and they shook hands. Then it got worse: Flynn sat down next to him.

What if Flynn asks about the investigation? Comey thought to himself. He tried to make small talk.

All Flynn wanted to talk about was how much sleep he was getting, when he was waking up, and how, in his new job, he was finding it hard to carve out time to work out. This was easy: Comey loved talking sleep and work-life balance. He rattled off a list of ways that he learned when he was deputy attorney general to remain rested and in shape despite the stress of the job.

Blessedly, the small talk was cut short, because Comey was summoned into Priebus's office.

Having avoided a confrontation with Flynn, Comey now had to deal with a chief of staff who seemed to have little handle on his job. Priebus asked him about the Steele dossier. Comey said that much of it was consistent with other intelligence the government had and that it was important for Trump to know what was out there about him.

"Is this a private conversation?" Priebus asked Comey.

Comey said it was.

"Do you have a FISA order on Mike Flynn?" Priebus asked, using the acronym for a government wiretap.

Comey saw this as a time for a teachable moment, and paused. He said he would answer the question: No, there was not a wiretap on Flynn. But he also laid out the protocols for contacts between the White House and the FBI, telling Priebus that going forward, this was the type of question that the Justice Department should only be answering in direct communication with the White House counsel's office. Comey talking about the contact policy was rich. Just two weeks earlier he had flagrantly disregarded that very policy and sent his FBI agents into the White House to interview Flynn.

Priebus then brought up the dinner Comey and Trump had just had, adding that Trump had told him Comey was interested in staying on. Comey repeated what he told Trump, adding that there would be no need for an announcement. Priebus seemed confused about how the FBI director's tenure functioned. Comey explained that although the president could fire him at any time, he had been appointed to a ten-year term.

After twenty minutes or so, Priebus stood to usher Comey out. A few more steps and the FBI director would avoid Trump and make a clean getaway. And in any case, presidents are normally so scheduled that impromptu meetings are almost unheard of. But as Priebus and Comey passed the open door of the Oval Office, Priebus motioned for Comey to say hello to the president, who was meeting with Sean Spicer. After quick introductions, Comey took a seat across from Trump, and the two began to talk about several different topics Trump was unhappy about, including Hillary Clinton, leaks, and the Steele dossier. Trump brought up his recent interview with the Fox News host Bill O'Reilly. He was upset that O'Reilly had questioned Trump's respect for Putin and described the Russian president as a "killer," to which Trump responded by saying, "There are a lot of killers; we've got a lot of killers." Comey was learning that Trump had basically two modes of communication: He was expert in attacking, and he was constantly seeking affirmation. Clearly, he was looking for Comey to affirm his realpolitik, everybody-is-ruthless theory of world leaders, but no such affirmation would be forthcoming. Comey told Trump he disagreed that there was a comparison between the United States and Russia when it comes to political killings. That brought the conversation to an abrupt end, and Comey left.

For Comey, the experience only deepened the mystery of Trump's motivations and actions regarding Putin. American intelligence had come to the shattering consensus that the Russian president had directed a comprehensive campaign of cyberattacks on the American elections, and not only did Trump seem blithely unconcerned about that, but he was for some reason ardently defending Putin. Not only publicly, but privately as well. "I thought there was something weird, there were a number of possibilities, but something weird that led him to speak about Russia and Putin in the way he did, including in private," Comey would later say. "That ate at me."

That evening, as Comey wrote the third in what was quickly becoming a series of memos to document his short meeting with Trump, Priebus called McGahn at home. The chief of staff wanted to warn McGahn about something Trump was saying.

"He wants to pull the Gorsuch nomination," Priebus told McGahn.

McGahn was flabbergasted.

Why was Trump behaving this way? The presidency was not painting by numbers, but McGahn had a plan, and all Trump had to do was follow it. So what if Gorsuch said something that walked up to the line of being mildly critical? Gorsuch was exactly the person they needed on the Supreme Court. And, as a judge, he was allowed to do and say whatever he wanted. Pulling the nomination would be devastating to those voters who were able to look past Trump's personal behavior and outlandish style because they believed he shared their values. It was the Supreme Court that had gotten Trump elected. Without Scalia's open seat, Trump might not have won. And now he was going to turn his back on those people? And look hopelessly mercurial and petty in the process?

Trump was so thin-skinned that McGahn believed that not only might he pull the nomination but, for being Gorsuch's champion, McGahn himself might get fired, too. From Priebus's call, the only thing that was clear was that no one knew what would happen with the nomination. Not surprisingly with Trump, there were several potential wild cards. The president had started talking about Rudolph Giuliani as an option. During the transition, the investment banker and Trump supporter Anthony Scaramucci had talked to the Fox News legal analyst Andrew Napolitano about a spot on the Supreme Court.

In the White House the following day, McGahn made it known across the staff that he opposed any effort to withdraw Gorsuch's nomination or otherwise undermine his confirmation. However, he avoided making a direct appeal to Trump, instead discussing his frustration with others in the West Wing.

Later that day, as a sign of support—a signal that not everyone in the White House was abandoning him—McGahn gave Gorsuch a call. He told the nominee what Trump had been saying. Gorsuch didn't blink, wouldn't be backing down from his statement to Senator Blumenthal, and insisted that he would defend the role of the judiciary over and over, regardless of whether it created a problem with Trump. McGahn told Gorsuch he was glad to hear that. If it came down to it, he replied, he would quit before going along with a withdrawal of the nomination.

Shortly after the call, McGahn had one of his deputies draft a one-sentence resignation letter for him. After just over two weeks on the job—among the most sought-after legal positions in the entire government—McGahn was ready to leave, if it came to that. Nominating judges was why he had taken the job. He was told this was going to be his turf, entirely. If Gorsuch was out, so was he.

Over the coming weeks, Trump became distracted by other matters and ended up sticking with his nominee. On April 7, 2017, the Senate would confirm Gorsuch as the 113th justice of the Supreme Court, installing a 5–4 conservative majority after fifteen months of an evenly split court. When McGahn had written his memo months earlier, he had predicted that Gorsuch would be confirmed between April 3 and April 7. Soon after, McGahn gifted the new justice a memento: the resignation letter he had drafted when Gorsuch's nomination seemed in doubt.

★ ★ ★

FEBRUARY 10, 2017

NINETY-SIX DAYS UNTIL THE APPOINTMENT OF SPECIAL COUNSEL ROBERT S. MUELLER III

THE SITUATION ROOM—In the two weeks that had passed since the Justice Department warned the White House about Flynn, the national security adviser—potentially compromised by the foreign adversary that had just meddled in the election—had been allowed to remain in his post, because the White House mishandled the matter in nearly every way possible. There was apparent inertia and distraction: The White House counsel's office, which had initially been skeptical of how the Justice Department described Flynn's calls and was apparently busy dealing with the fallout of the travel ban and the Gorsuch nomination, took days to read the transcripts of the calls between Flynn and the Russian ambassador.

There was bad timing: On January 30, Trump had fired Acting Attorney General Sally Yates, the main point of contact on the Flynn matter, for her refusal to defend Trump's travel ban on constitutional grounds.

There was deceit: Even though McGahn, Trump, Priebus, and Bannon knew that Flynn had almost certainly lied to Vice President Pence, they held back from telling Pence anything about what they had learned. And Flynn had lied to fellow White House officials, saying that the FBI had told him during his interview that the investigation into him had been closed.

There were things that were inexplicable. Given everything he already knew about Flynn's conduct, on Saturday Trump had allowed Flynn to sit in on an Oval Office call that he took with Putin. This not only invited more questions about the true nature of Trump's relationship with Russia; it also raised the question: Was Trump disturbed about the Flynn affair because his national security adviser now posed a threat to American national security, or was he disturbed by the Flynn affair because it posed a public relations problem?

Even though Trump's reality television persona fired people with bravado, not only did Trump the president not enjoy the prospect of firing people, but he would come to rely on others to do it for him—a pattern that would become more tumultuous in the coming months. And in the case of Flynn, an inertia had set in at the White House. It would take an external factor to force Trump to actually do something about his troublesome national security adviser.

The delay in doing something about Flynn only agitated the

departed members of the Obama administration and those in the know about the calls at the Justice Department, FBI, and intelligence community. Two weeks after Yates's warning, *The Washington Post,* citing "current and former U.S. officials," reported that Flynn had in fact spoken about sanctions with the Russian ambassador on December 29, the day they had been imposed. In the article, the spokesman for the National Security Council contradicted Flynn's previous denials, saying that "while [Flynn] had no recollection of discussing sanctions, he couldn't be certain that the topic never came up."

That disclosure finally forced McGahn and Priebus to act and particularly aggravated Pence, who was left looking as if he were either part of some sort of conspiracy or hopelessly out of the loop. That Friday, February 10, they all gathered in the Situation Room to read the call transcript for themselves, after which McGahn and Priebus determined that Flynn had to be fired and told Trump. But Trump, who was preparing for a weekend meeting with the Japanese prime minister, Shinzo Abe, at Mar-a-Lago, said that it could wait until after he returned.

So, Flynn, known to the vice president, the chief of staff, the White House counsel, and the rest of the country to be a liar and potentially compromised, continued that weekend as national security adviser, heavily involved in the country's most sensitive matters. On Saturday night in Florida, Trump was having dinner at Mar-a-Lago with Abe and aides—including Flynn—when word reached them that North Korea had launched a ballistic missile off its eastern coast and into the ocean. Rather than head to a secure area to deal with a response, Trump—with Flynn alongside him—insisted he could handle the matter right from his dinner table while fielding ad hoc advice from his foreign counterpart. Guests dining at neighboring tables easily listened in on the conversation and debate.

Meanwhile, Trump continued to lie about Flynn. On Air Force One, he popped his head into the press cabin. Reporters asked him about the *Post* story on Flynn. Trump claimed not to know anything about the reports.

"I don't know about that, I haven't seen it," Trump said. "What report is that? I haven't seen that. I'll look into that."

★ ★ ★

FEBRUARY 13, 2017

NINETY-THREE DAYS UNTIL THE APPOINTMENT OF SPECIAL COUNSEL ROBERT S. MUELLER III

OVAL OFFICE—With Trump and his top aides back in Washington after the weekend at Mar-a-Lago, Flynn continued to be involved in foreign policy matters. He attended a working lunch held with the Canadian prime minister, Justin Trudeau. And the White House continued to put out misleading information on Flynn's situation.

On MSNBC, Kellyanne Conway, a top aide to the president and his former campaign manager, was asked whether Flynn might be leaving the White House in the wake of the *Washington Post* story. Conway insisted that "General Flynn does enjoy the full confidence of the president."

But even as Conway made those statements, Trump and his aides debated what to do about Flynn. The consensus, again, was that he had to go. It's unclear what happened next or whether that message was relayed to Flynn. What is known is that a little after 10:00 p.m., Flynn arrived at the Oval Office with Trump, Pence, and Priebus there waiting for him, each knowing that it would be his final moment as national security adviser. Flynn had a signed copy of his resignation in hand. Trump shook Flynn's hand, gave him a hug, and told him, "We'll give you a good recommendation. You're a good guy. We'll take care of you."

★ ★ ★

FEBRUARY 14, 2017

NINETY-TWO DAYS UNTIL THE APPOINTMENT OF SPECIAL COUNSEL ROBERT S. MUELLER III

JAMES S. BRADY PRESS BRIEFING ROOM, WEST WING—Flynn was gone, but the White House still had to explain what had happened—a task McGahn knew would be a difficult one for an administration that had no discernible communications strategy in place and had already so publicly struggled with the truth.

With headlines of the departure dominating the news the next day, all of Trump's aides knew the daily press briefing would be a bombardment of questions about Flynn. To prepare Spicer for the 1:15 p.m. briefing, McGahn decided he had to intervene, to help ensure the press secretary avoided misleading the public. McGahn spent the morning in Spicer's office, walking him through the background of the White House's work—or lack thereof—on the Flynn investigation.

Then, in the Oval Office, the pair had a larger meeting with Trump, Priebus, Bannon, Hope Hicks, and Conway to talk more generally about what should be said. Trump didn't sit back as messaging was discussed. In going over the coverage, Priebus informed the president that House Speaker Paul Ryan had praised the president for being the person to request that Flynn resign.

"That sounds better," Trump said. "Say that."

Spicer, searching for the truth, asked the president if that was accurate.

"Say that I asked for his resignation," Trump replied.

It was unclear to those in the room what the truth was.

Spicer entered the briefing with a joke, attempting to liven up the mood.

"Good afternoon. Happy Valentine's Day," he said. "I can sense the love in the room."

Once Spicer began answering questions about Flynn, lawyers from McGahn's office closely listened in, wanting to hear Spicer stick to the facts, just as McGahn had briefed him.

But under pressure, Spicer came apart. In the course of the forty-five-minute briefing, the press secretary essentially discarded the notes that McGahn offered him, instead delivering a multitude of false statements to the press. McGahn and his office counted fourteen lies or mischaracterizations in Spicer's remarks about how the White House handled the Flynn matter, spinning a narrative that made the administration appear far more on top of the situation than it had been.

What the hell? McGahn thought. Had Trump gotten to Spicer after their meeting to direct him off the talking points he had approved?

McGahn confronted Spicer in front of several other White House officials after the briefing to lay out the misstatements.

Despite the upbraiding, Spicer would do nothing to correct the record.

McGahn and the lawyers in the counsel's office were frustrated by Spicer's performance and alarmed at what such a performance augured for the White House's ability to communicate accurate information to the world. The national security adviser had been fired for his contacts with the Russians. It was not entirely clear what Trump knew about these contacts, the vice president had been kept in the dark about the entire matter, and the administration had lied along the way. Then after Flynn's dismissal, it gave an inaccurate on-the-record briefing to reporters from the White House lectern. Someday, someone might have to explain all this. So McGahn and the lawyers took the ultimate move to protect themselves. They compiled an eight-page memo marked "Confidential" and "Attorney Work Client Product." It was addressed to "FILE," and it outlined and recounted the timeline of the Flynn affair and how the counsel's office had handled it and included a two-page appendix that listed all of Spicer's misstatements in the press conference.

The press had already determined Spicer was a liar. Now that same conclusion would be memorialized in a secret White House document, which ended with a stark pronouncement about how McGahn and his team viewed the entire episode.

"The White House Counsel's office remains concerned that Spicer's inaccurate briefing remains the definitive public account by the White House of the events surrounding Flynn's resignation. As noted above, and in Appendix A, Spicer's remarks misstate the record and mischaracterize the legal process and legal conclusions of the White House counsel's office in important respects."

Don McGahn had been Trump's White House counsel for twenty-six days. From a completely different vantage point from the FBI director, he could see how Trump and the administration had been staggered and undisciplined from the outset. Much more than

Trump, McGahn was a committed conservative who relished the policy goals that the administration might be able to achieve. But he also had an obligation to the law and the Constitution. The Constitution required constancy, not chaos. McGahn had already written one resignation letter and at least one memo to the file to protect himself. He was alert to trouble, and his wariness at the outset of the administration was similar to Comey's. But for McGahn, the warnings hit even closer to home. Not a month in yet, and he was already creating a record with the Flynn memo, the same kind of thing his uncle Paddy had done in Atlantic City decades earlier to protect himself from Donald Trump.

At 4:15 p.m., as the lawyers in McGahn's office began putting the memo together in the wake of Spicer's briefing, Comey and other top intelligence officials walked into the Oval Office to give Trump his first briefing on terrorist threats to the country.

Sitting in one of six chairs in front of the Resolute desk, Comey laid out some fairly dire ways terrorists wanted to kill Americans.

Trump said little and seemed uninterested. After the briefing, Trump asked everyone, except for Comey, to clear the room.

Kushner lingered, apparently realizing that Comey being alone with Trump could be problematic.

But Trump insisted everyone leave.

"I knew whatever we were going to talk about was going to be really important," Comey would say later. "I was so focused on trying to remember every word because I knew whatever we were going to talk about was something I would need to remember. So I was looking at his mouth, literally trying to remember every word."

Trump started by saying he wanted to talk about Mike Flynn, who Trump said "hadn't done anything wrong" on his calls with the Russian ambassador. Trump said he was a good guy but had to be let go because he lied to the vice president. The president's comment about Pence was particularly amusing because Trump, Priebus, McGahn, and Bannon had kept it from Pence for two weeks that Flynn had lied to him.

The president then brought up that afternoon's briefing by

Spicer—the same briefing the counsel's office was now dissecting because it was riddled with inaccuracies. Trump praised Spicer for how he had handled it, saying the White House spokesman had done a great job explaining the Flynn matter. Trump's train of thought then hopped over to leaks, and he complained about recent ones that disclosed his calls with foreign leaders. He lightly touched the classified phone on his desk, saying he had made the calls on "this beautiful phone." He then brought it back to Flynn, saying that he had done nothing wrong on his calls but that leaks about the contacts were terrible.

Comey tried to jump into the conversation to say that indeed the leaks were awful.

Priebus then opened the door to try to end the meeting. But Trump said he needed more time with Comey. Priebus closed the door, and Trump began talking again about Flynn. Trump said he was a good guy who had been through a lot. He said Flynn had been wrong to mislead the vice president but did nothing wrong on the call.

"I hope you can see your way clear to letting this go, to letting Flynn go," Trump said. "He is a good guy. I hope you can let this go."

Oh fuck, Comey thought to himself. Trump's overtures in the early days of the administration about loyalty and his job had been inappropriate. But now Trump was walking up to—and maybe over—the line of obstructing justice. Had the president of the United States just broken the law in front of his FBI director?

In response to Trump, Comey said only, "I agree he is a good guy."

Trump brought up leakers again and then ended the conversation.

It was Valentine's Day. Comey and Patrice ordered takeout and ate at home. He wouldn't share much of what had happened that day, though. He saved that for the memo he wrote later that evening to document the meeting. On the twenty-sixth day of the administration, just as McGahn had felt compelled to do, Comey sat at his desk and wrote the story of an astonishing event in a presidency not yet a month old. He had evidence that, at the least, strongly raised the question of whether the president of the United States had broken the law. If that was ever disclosed, it would have a devastating if not catastrophic impact on Trump. Now Comey had to figure out what to do with it and ensure that the president's wishes about Flynn were ignored. The Flynn investigation would continue.

* * *

MARCH 2, 2017

SEVENTY-SIX DAYS UNTIL THE APPOINTMENT OF SPECIAL COUNSEL ROBERT S. MUELLER III

MCGAHN'S OFFICE ON THE SECOND FLOOR OF THE WEST WING—In Oval Office meetings with aides in his first month and a half as president, it was plain to McGahn that Trump was ignorant of the government's most basic functions.

Trump believed that the president could do whatever the president wanted, and he had no grasp of the concept that the founders had set up the government for the three branches to share power. While there were certain executive actions Trump could take unilaterally, he often needed to work with Congress, and the courts had the power to curtail executive actions they saw as illegal.

McGahn and other aides would explain this to the president, who often grew irritated and angry when told the bounds of his powers.

"Let's just do it and if someone wants to sue us, they can," Trump would say when told he could not do something on his own.

Not surprisingly, Trump struggled with the next level of understanding how Washington worked. He had no grasp for how senators could block legislation through the filibuster and that the filibuster could be ended through a cloture vote. He said he did not understand how he could appoint certain officials to cabinet posts during a Senate recess—a move that allowed the appointees to serve in that position but for a fixed amount of time.

He didn't know that the Justice Department was meant to be independent of politics and political considerations. He didn't know that presidents didn't get to decide who and what gets investigated. And he failed to grasp what the FBI was investigating, what it meant to his administration and campaign, and that no matter how much he wanted it to, the investigation would likely not go away. In a sign of Trump's ignorance, in the aftermath of the Flynn firing, Trump and Kushner told confidants they believed that with Flynn gone, they had put the entire Russia question behind them. McGahn, meanwhile, remained skeptical of what the FBI was truly up to but hoped that whatever it was, it would not interfere with the Gorsuch nomination.

Two weeks after the Flynn firing, with the Gorsuch nomination appearing on track, Russia reared its head again for the Trump administration when *The Washington Post* reported that the intelligence community had evidence that the attorney general, Jeff Sessions, had had at least two meetings during the campaign with the Russian ambassador—the same guy Mike Flynn had spoken to about Obama's sanctions. On the heels of the Flynn dismissal, the Russia story suddenly had new legs.

Trump, who was traveling that day to give a speech aboard the aircraft carrier *Gerald R. Ford,* called McGahn. The president was furious. He was so angry that those in the room with McGahn could hear Trump yelling on the phone. Despite the president's indifference to the ways of Washington, he routinely showed McGahn the ability to cut directly to the nut of a problem. Trump recognized the issue with the stories about Sessions. During the attorney general's confirmation hearing two months earlier, Sessions said under oath that he hadn't spoken to any Russians during the campaign. Now, in the wake of the *Post* story, paranoid Democrats and much of the media were looking at the new headlines as evidence that Russian agents were running the country. There were calls from the Left for Sessions to recuse himself from overseeing the FBI investigation into the campaign's ties to Russia. How, Democrats asked, could Sessions oversee an investigation into conduct that he had participated in?

The story came with an added factor that infuriated Trump: It overshadowed some of the only decent headlines he had received since becoming president. Two days earlier, he had given a relatively well-reviewed first address to a joint session of Congress. The reactions were so positive that even a liberal commentator on CNN, Van Jones, said that Trump "became President of the United States in that moment, period."

Sessions had now washed away those stories.

The prospect of someone who might not be completely loyal to Trump overseeing the Russia investigation set Trump off. McGahn had never seen the president that angry. The anger seemed so potent that McGahn was baffled. In the midst of his fit, Trump told McGahn that he needed to stop Sessions from recusing himself. It was an outlandish request, because it cut to the heart of the actual issue of recusal. Only someone with Trump's disdain for norms and the law would be able to ask such a thing. Trump's campaign was under investigation. He was now demanding that one of his closest political allies remain in charge of that investigation—an investigation that could be an existential threat to his presidency.

But that is where McGahn found himself. He tried to appease the president and called Sessions, exposing himself to potential criminality for the first time as Trump's lawyer.

Where Trump was bellicose, McGahn was tactful. Instead of the president's sledgehammer argument that he needed someone loyal to him to oversee the investigation, McGahn made the nuanced suggestion that Sessions put off the recusal until there was an actual decision he needed to make in the Russia investigation. McGahn reasoned that despite the political pressure, the simple act of recusal wouldn't make the problems with his testimony go away.

McGahn spent the rest of the day working the phones in his office, talking to Sessions again, Sessions's chief of staff, Sessions's lawyer, Chuck Cooper, and the Senate majority leader, Mitch McConnell. As much as Trump's anger focused McGahn's attention, it completely rattled Priebus, who spent the entire day going up and down the stairs to McGahn's office to ask him whether he had fixed the problem yet.

What Sessions failed to tell McGahn was that weeks earlier he had already made the decision to recuse himself from all matters related to the 2016 campaign but had dragged his heels to formalize it. Now—thanks to *The Washington Post*—the decision had to be made public. That afternoon, in a nationally televised press conference, Sessions announced his recusal. The announcement caught Trump by surprise. Afterward, McGahn told the lawyers in his office to ensure that no White House officials contact Sessions about the investigation, and he further ensured that that move would be memorialized, telling his chief of staff, Annie Donaldson, who jotted it down in her legal pad, "There should be no comms. . . . No contact with Sessions." McGahn, like his uncle, was taking yet another move to back up his work. He would now have contemporaneous notes to show what he had told his client.

★ ★ ★

MARCH 3, 2017

SEVENTY-FIVE DAYS UNTIL THE APPOINTMENT OF SPECIAL COUNSEL ROBERT S. MUELLER III

OVAL OFFICE—McGahn was learning on the job the rhythms of Trump's anger and how much of it was driven by media coverage. The Sessions recusal only set off more headlines about Russia. The following day, Trump called a meeting in the Oval Office with all of the West Wing senior staff.

The meeting quickly turned into a screaming match.

Trump, infuriated that his original travel ban had been blocked by the courts, put much of the blame on McGahn.

"This is bullshit," Trump yelled. "I don't want a fucking watered-down version."

"I don't have a lawyer!" he screamed at McGahn. "Where's my Roy Cohn?" Cohn, of course, had been Trump's longtime New York lawyer who had been dead for decades but was still considered among the more unethical lawyers in American history.

The president said he needed someone like Cohn, a winner and a fixer—unrestrained by morals, rules, or shame. Someone who got things done the way you get things done in New York. Despite everything that had gone on the previous day, Trump once again told McGahn to talk to Sessions about, now, "unrecusing."

McGahn, showing an increasing willingness to push back at the president, said no, explaining the decision had already been made.

From there, in front of more than a dozen aides, Trump openly revealed his remarkable, and cynical, perspective of how the Justice Department operated and his expansive view of how he believed he should be able to use the department to protect himself and go after his enemies. He said he needed an attorney general like Obama had in Eric Holder, or John F. Kennedy had in Robert F. Kennedy.

"You're telling me that Bobby and Jack didn't talk about investigations? Or Obama didn't tell Eric Holder who to investigate?" Trump said.

Trump then leveled what to him was as brutal an insult as could be delivered. He said Sessions was weak. Bannon, also in the meeting, pushed back on Trump, reminding the president that the recusal should not be a surprise, because they had discussed before he was sworn in that the attorney general would not—under Justice Department rules—be able to oversee investigations related to the election.

The showdown in the Oval Office became so animated that a CNN cameraman who was posted out on the South Lawn as the media waited for Trump to get on Marine One to begin his trip to Mar-a-Lago captured an image of Bannon yelling. Trump was so angry that he kicked Priebus and Bannon off the flight to Florida, stranding them at the White House as he left in a rage.

Within hours, stories laying out what had happened in the Oval Office were leaked to the press. The stories all highlighted Trump's explosive anger, and several accounts identified Priebus as a central target of the president. Priebus had become White House chief of staff by having a well-honed instinct for self-preservation and would spend the next several hours calling reporters to insist that the president's ire had been directed at McGahn. Priebus's decision to focus on how he was portrayed in the media said a lot about how the young Trump administration functioned. The administration faced court fights over the president's travel ban. There were thousands of open positions in the executive branch to fill. Accusations of Russian collusion swirled. Yet there was the chief of staff, spinning himself out of a mess. It was an impressive level of dysfunction for an administration not yet two months old.

* * *

MARCH 4, 2017

SEVENTY-FOUR DAYS UNTIL THE APPOINTMENT OF SPECIAL COUNSEL ROBERT S. MUELLER III

MAR-A-LAGO, PALM BEACH, FLORIDA—The Sessions recusal sent Trump spiraling. The morning after the Oval Office blowup, Trump put out a series of tweets claiming that Obama and the FBI had illegally wiretapped Trump Tower during the campaign.

For McGahn, the tweets fit a familiar pattern with Trump: An issue (like Sessions and recusal) would enrage him, and a series of tweets afterward would be connected to that rage, even as they often made the situation worse.

But there was another big issue that McGahn had to deal with. The courts had stepped in to rule that the original travel ban—which McGahn's office had, under pressure, approved—was illegal. Since then, a revised ban had been produced, but Trump was refusing to sign it.

In the hopes of persuading the president, McGahn, Sessions, and other aides flew down to Mar-a-Lago to get Trump to sign the revised travel ban. That evening, they dined with Trump over steaks at Mar-a-Lago to make their case about why he needed to sign it. Trump said he did not want to water it down, even though it had been deemed illegal. Even amid the arguing, despite Trump being so irate a day earlier, at dinner that night at Mar-a-Lago, he was jovial—a reminder of how Trump had been during the campaign.

Still, on the subject of recusal, Trump had kept up his efforts to pressure Sessions. When McGahn wasn't looking, he confronted Sessions at Mar-a-Lago directly that evening, telling him to unrecuse himself. The president again brought up Holder and Kennedy. Sessions believed that Trump was afraid that without him overseeing the investigation, it could balloon and undermine his presidency.

Meanwhile, amid all the turmoil, Trump's top strategist thought that there was some news coming out that would help the administration. That weekend, as the White House sought to play up the notion that the intelligence community had run amok, Bannon told others that something damaging would be made public that Monday about the Deep State. Bannon said that you would know it when you saw it.

That Tuesday—a day later than Bannon said the surprise would arrive—WikiLeaks published its first trove of stolen CIA documents, part of a larger tranche that it called Vault 7. Within the thousands of pages of secret documents were several road maps for how the agency could use flaws in software to break into various internet-connected devices like cell phones, computers, and televisions. It was one of the largest-ever leaks of CIA documents, and prosecutors later described its damage to the CIA's intelligence-gathering efforts as "catastrophic."

The top strategist to the president of the United States seemed to have prior knowledge that Julian Assange's operation, notorious for obtaining and dumping highly sensitive government documents onto the internet, would be exposing the intelligence-gathering methods of the agencies of the American government. This was extraordinary, not least for the fact that Assange himself was still holed up in the Ecuadorian embassy in London, evading extradition to the United States to face charges for his role in publishing stolen documents from the Iraq War in the Chelsea Manning case.

In the month leading up to the dump, WikiLeaks had repeatedly teased an upcoming release of documents. But the group said nothing about its timing, raising the question, how did Bannon know when the materials were going to come out? Whatever Bannon knew, one of the people closest to the president was giddy that secrets from the American intelligence community were about to be made public. Those types of disclosures almost always damaged the United States' ability to collect intelligence and protect the country. No matter—Bannon saw it as a way to advance Trump's narrative.

The following day, as McGahn headed back to Washington from Mar-a-Lago, things got worse.

The FBI, McGahn learned, wanted emails from the government entity that had overseen the transition. The bureau was looking for evidence in the messages related to Flynn's foreign contacts. This showed that the investigation of Flynn was alive and well and contradicted Flynn's contention shortly before he was fired that the bureau had closed the investigation. For McGahn it was a bastardized way for the executive branch to function.

If there was wrongdoing to investigate, so be it. But at the least the White House counsel should be notified and kept abreast of what was going on and what documents investigators wanted to see. This was a backdoor way, McGahn thought, for the FBI to rummage through their communications—communications that White House lawyers felt were privileged.

That Sunday night, I broke a story that said, in response to Trump's tweets, senior Justice Department officials had denied a request by Comey to put out a statement saying that the tweets were false. The decision had angered Comey and his deputies, who believed that Trump's disinformation needed to be knocked down. The story panicked Sessions and his chief of staff, Jody Hunt, who were already convinced that Sessions could be fired at any time. In the days that followed, Sessions had the United States attorney in Connecticut, John Durham, open a leak investigation into Comey. The handling of the investigation in the weeks that followed unnerved career officials in the deputy attorney general's office. In a highly unusual move, Sessions's office—not the deputy attorney general's office, which runs the day-to-day operations of the department—would oversee the investigations. The Trump administration was less than two months old and the attorney general was already investigating the FBI director.

★★★

MARCH 15, 2017

SIXTY-THREE DAYS UNTIL THE APPOINTMENT OF SPECIAL COUNSEL ROBERT S. MUELLER III

A CLASSIFIED BRIEFING ROOM, CAPITOL HILL—In the days and weeks after Trump's meeting with Comey in the Oval Office on February 14, Comey and his aides debated what to do. The president of the United States had asked him to end an investigation, not based on the facts of the matter, but because Flynn was a "good guy." And, of course, there is no such thing as a casual request from a president. Obstruction of justice is a criminal offense. When the president intervenes directly in an investigation, is that obstruction of justice? Most people generally assume that people obstruct justice in secret and are careful to conceal their crime. If there was confusion at the bureau over what to make of this, it was because of the brazenness of the president's behavior: He unabashedly asked the country's top law enforcement officer, during an ongoing investigation, to look the other way. "Let it go," he had said. But Comey was afraid to open an investigation into Trump, especially when he had no allies at the Justice Department. He was sick of being the lone ranger and needed an ally. But help was on the way.

Trump had nominated a longtime federal prosecutor from Baltimore named Rod J. Rosenstein to run the day-to-day operations of the Justice Department and be the deputy attorney general. Rosenstein had a reputation as a rule-of-law investigator who avoided partisanship. Before this promotion, he had been the longest-tenured U.S. attorney in the country, having first been appointed to his position in 2005 by President Bush and then remaining in that post throughout the entire Obama administration. Rosenstein's longevity bothered Comey a bit, because he wondered what types of concessions he had made to be such a "survivor" under both Republicans and Democrats in the Justice Department. Rosenstein probably would not have been Comey's first choice for the position, but considering Comey's view of Trump's inability to recruit "good people," Rosenstein represented a substantial improvement from the norm. Comey thought that Rosenstein might provide cover as he confronted a president who probably did not like him, and a president with little understanding that law enforcement and politics don't mix.

"As soon as Rod gets here, we're going to be okay," Comey told Patrice. "Rod knows the system. He's been an AUSA, he knows the FBI's role, and so we are so much better off with someone like that than a politician who doesn't understand. Rod will protect us, Rod will wall us off, Rod will be the buffer."

But there was a problem with Rosenstein's nomination. The Republican chairman of the Senate Judiciary Committee, which was overseeing his confirmation, refused to hold a vote on Rosenstein's nomination until Comey briefed the committee on the details of the Russia investigation. The Justice Department told Comey to do the briefing, believing it was his only way to get Rosenstein on board. In March Comey privately briefed the committee leadership as well as the "Gang of Eight" from the House and Senate Intelligence Committees on the Trump associates who were under investigation.

Although Comey's briefings were supposed to be classified, the media quickly found out about the briefing and reported that it had happened, but due to the sensitive information that Comey had shared with the members, the stories contained few details. Trump saw media speculation about what the meeting could have been about and began to agitate for McGahn to figure out what Comey was up to.

Trump wanted to know as much as possible and was fixated on whether he was personally under investigation. McGahn took the president's direction and tried to use some of his old contacts to gain visibility on the investigations that were becoming something of an obsession for the president. McGahn was irritated; Comey, remember, was an employee of the executive branch, and here he was telling members of Congress about the investigation and keeping the White House in the dark. Neither the president nor his White House counsel believed it should work that way.

McGahn had been around Washington for two decades and had

represented hundreds of Republican members of Congress, so he had relationships with dozens of powerful operators. That Thursday, McGahn called one of them: Senator Richard Burr, the chairman of the Senate Intelligence Committee, who had been in the Gang of Eight briefing. Lawmakers and their allies and friends often shared gossip. But what occurred on the call was highly unusual. The information that Burr had received in the briefing had been classified, but Burr didn't hesitate to share it all with McGahn. He secretly told McGahn that there were five Trump associates who were under investigation, including Flynn, Manafort, Carter Page, George Papadopoulos, and Roger Stone. A U.S. senator had just informed the White House of the people in the president's orbit who were under investigation by the FBI.

★ ★ ★

MARCH 20, 2017

FIFTY-EIGHT DAYS UNTIL THE APPOINTMENT OF SPECIAL COUNSEL ROBERT S. MUELLER III

OVAL OFFICE—As part of his efforts to appease Congress and move along the Rosenstein nomination, Comey also testified publicly before the House Intelligence Committee, revealing that the FBI was investigating ties between the Trump camp and Russia. That disclosure and his refusal to say whether Trump was under investigation set off the president all over again. Trump had already thought that Comey was acting almost like his own branch of government and had made too many of his own headlines while leaking to the media. The testimony triggered extensive coverage that certainly made it seem like the president was under investigation.

From the Oval Office, the president berated McGahn, pushing him to call the Justice Department to find out why Comey refused to say he was not under investigation. McGahn relented, calling Acting Deputy Attorney General Dana Boente to try to get more information. Boente replied that putting out a statement specifically saying that Trump was not under investigation was a bad idea because of the perception it would create, calling into question whether the president was picking at an investigation that involved his own associates.

Trump continued to go after McGahn viciously, in any number of ways, from there. While most televisions were tuned to the Comey testimony, on the other side of the Capitol that day, in the Senate, Neal Gorsuch's confirmation hearing had begun in the Judiciary Committee. Trump watched some of that hearing and saw McGahn sitting behind the nominee. Trump told McGahn he couldn't go back the next day, because he needed to get to the bottom of the Russia investigation.

Never one to be discreet with his displeasure, Trump began in the days after the hearing to talk openly in the Oval Office about getting rid of Comey. The talk became ranting, which alarmed the president's aides, who believed that dismissing the FBI director would be a grave mistake. Those fears led at least one White House official to take extreme measures to protect Trump from himself.

At one point, Trump spoke directly with one of McGahn's deputies about his frustration with Comey. Uttam Dhillon was a longtime Washington lawyer who had worked under Comey when Comey was the deputy attorney general a decade earlier in the Bush administration. Dhillon heard the president out and then told him that in order to dismiss the FBI director, he would need to show cause, and further, if he wanted to fire Comey, he should wait until after the Justice Department's inspector general had completed its ongoing investigation into Comey's handling of the Clinton email matter. Afterward, Dhillon went to junior lawyers in the White House counsel's office and asked them to produce a memo about whether the president needed cause to dismiss the FBI director. Contrary to what Dhillon had told the president, the research showed that the president in fact did not need cause to do so. He could fire the FBI director for any reason or no reason at all. But Dhillon was so concerned about the possibility that Trump might actually fire Comey during an ongoing investigation into Trump's associates that he never went back to the president to correct the record. He decided it was better to let the commander in chief remain misinformed about his own legal authorities.

★★★

MARCH 30, 2017

FORTY-EIGHT DAYS UNTIL THE APPOINTMENT OF SPECIAL COUNSEL ROBERT S. MUELLER III

THE FBI DIRECTOR'S OFFICE AT BUREAU HEADQUARTERS, WASHINGTON, D.C.—Comey's disclosure about the investigation into Trump's campaign, coupled with how he had let the question dangle about whether Trump himself was under investigation, gave momentum to Democratic attacks on the president and legitimized their questions about his credibility. Was there fire to go with all that smoke? Trump watched the cable networks go into overdrive on the Russia question. Leading the charge was Congressman Adam Schiff of California, the top Democrat on the House Intelligence Committee, who regularly appeared on television to stoke questions about connections between the Trump campaign and the Russians.

"I can't go into the particulars, but there is more than circumstantial evidence now," Schiff said in an interview with Chuck Todd on MSNBC.

"You have seen direct evidence of collusion?" Todd asked.

"I don't want to go into specifics, but I will say that there is evidence that is not circumstantial, and is very much worthy of investigation," Schiff said.

The coverage—and the prospect that Trump himself might be under investigation—enraged Trump. He had made his closest political ally, Jeff Sessions, the attorney general, and Sessions had recused himself from the investigation. Comey had rebuffed Trump's overtures for loyalty, ignored the president's request to stop investigating Flynn, and, most important, refused to say publicly what he had told Trump in private: that the president was not under investigation.

McGahn knew firsthand that Trump's frustrations were building but warned the president against having any further contact with Comey. But Trump did not care about such sensitivities and had been listening less and less to McGahn, whom he blamed for his inability to stop Sessions from removing himself from any matters related to the Russia investigation. Wasn't it the attorney general's job to protect the president?

Ten days after Comey testified, Trump again took matters into his own hands and called the FBI director. The president believed that he was his own best advocate as well as being the world's best salesman. He had won an improbable election. How could winning over Comey be harder than that?

Comey had adopted a strategy of avoidance for dealing with Trump. The less he talked to him, the less likely the president was to say or ask him to do something improper. If Comey kept his head down, maybe Trump would learn to leave him alone.

But at 8:13 a.m. on Thursday, March 30, here was Trump again on the line. An operator for the secure switchboard at the White House—known by the code name Royal Crown—connected the president with Comey, who was in his office at the FBI.

Trump started the call by talking about the metric most important to the president: media attention. The president noted that Comey had recently received more press than the president himself.

"I hate it," Comey replied.

Trump then brought up what bothered him: He was president, he had a country to take hold of, and the Russia investigation was making that difficult. A recent House vote on repealing Obamacare had failed, Trump said, because of the cloud hanging over his presidency.

Trump reiterated that he had nothing to hide about his connections to Russia, adding that he had a letter from the largest law firm in Washington stating that he had no business ties to the country. And he complained again about the Steele dossier, saying that the accusations in it were so tawdry that he was personally hurt and was looking for revenge.

"Can you imagine me, hookers? I have a beautiful wife and it has been very painful," Trump told Comey.

Trump claimed he was bringing a personal lawsuit against the British former spy who wrote the dossier, Christopher Steele.

The president then reeled off a list of denials to specific intelligence contained in the dossier—including the allegation that Trump had had prostitutes urinate on a bed Obama slept in in the Ritz-Carlton in Moscow. It was clear to Comey that the dossier was still lodged under Trump's skin. The president said that when he traveled to Russia in 2013 for the Miss Universe pageant, he assumed that he had been recorded in his hotel room. Others on the trip would attest that he had done nothing wrong, he said.

Comey was still being kept in the dark by his underlings at the bureau about how the FBI had been told by the dossier's main subsource a month and a half earlier about how much of it was rumor. The FBI director explained to Trump that the bureau was running down the leads about the dossier as quickly as possible and that if it looked as if Trump were interfering with that work, it could undermine the integrity of the bureau's investigation.

Trump agreed and then showed Comey another one of his insecurities: the perception that he was in Putin's pocket. Trump boasted about how he was actually a problem for Russia because he wanted to increase American oil production and update America's forty-year-old nuclear weapons stock.

Comey could hardly believe what he was hearing. In short order, the president had held forth about hookers, the attractiveness of his wife, and suing a British spy. But Trump was just getting started. Now he wanted to get back to what was truly bothering him: Comey's disclosure of the investigation ten days earlier. Trump simply couldn't understand why he would do that.

Comey responded in a measured voice, saying that he had not volunteered the information.

Trump wanted to know who was behind it. Instead of asking about a rival Democrat, he asked about an ally. Was it the Republican chairman of the House Intelligence Committee, Devin Nunes?

Comey said it had been all of the congressional leadership, particularly the Senate Republicans, and singled out Chuck Grassley, the Republican chairman of the Senate Judiciary Committee, who had been holding up Rosenstein's nomination to be the deputy attorney general until he got the information he wanted on the Russia investigation.

Trump was on a mission, and it didn't seem as if he would relent anytime soon. Comey needed to deflect and buy some time. He tried to reassure the president by saying that the bureau was not investigating him and that he had made that clear to members of Congress in his briefings.

Trump immediately seized on this, telling Comey that he wanted that information made public. With Trump seeing his best opportunity in his presidency to change the narrative, he mentioned to Comey several more times how great it would be to get it out there that he was not under investigation.

"I'll see what I can do," Comey said.

But even before Comey hung up the phone, he knew he wouldn't be able to do what Trump had asked. Investigations are not siloed, static events—investigators follow the facts where they lead, and an investigation of one figure can easily lead to the investigation of another. And so Comey wanted to avoid saying publicly that Trump was not under investigation. In addition to the many practical reasons, such a pronouncement would have made it look as if he were taking an action to please the president. No FBI director wants to be put in that position. And while it was true at that precise moment that Trump was not under investigation, Comey was not convinced that would be the case for long. Comey planned to confer with Rosenstein after he was confirmed, in order to determine whether to move forward with opening such an investigation. If Comey were to come out publicly and say Trump was not under investigation, and then he did come under scrutiny, Comey might have to correct the public record and explain the discrepancy. Given his experience with the Clinton investigation, Comey understood better than any other American the problems created by weighing in about whether a high-profile politician was, or was not, under investigation.

To try to stall Trump, Comey did the same thing McGahn had done ten days earlier: he called the acting deputy attorney general, Dana Boente. Comey told Boente about his conversation with Trump and asked for his guidance on what to do.

But Boente, whom Comey saw as genial but unwilling to take a tough stance on any issue that might run up against the president, offered Comey no guidance on the call, and they would never talk about the matter again. Comey decided against following up with

Trump in the days after the call, hoping the president would get the hint and go away or become distracted by something else.

★ ★ ★

APRIL 11, 2017

THIRTY-SIX DAYS UNTIL THE APPOINTMENT OF SPECIAL COUNSEL ROBERT S. MUELLER III

THE FBI DIRECTOR'S OFFICE, WASHINGTON, D.C.—No such luck.

Despite being told by McGahn to stop calling Comey, Trump called the director again twelve days later.

Comey missed the call. At 8:26 a.m., Comey called him back.

"What did you do with my request?" Trump said.

"I passed it on to the acting deputy AG," Comey said.

"Who is that?" Trump said.

"Dana Boente," Comey said. "I haven't heard back from him."

Trump was growing more agitated because Democrats were using the questions about his ties to Russia to weaken him politically. Trump proclaimed to Comey that the Russia questions were all part of the Democrats' made-up arguments to excuse Clinton's loss.

The president went on again about why he needed the word to get out that he was not under investigation, saying it was interfering with his ability to do his job, particularly on the world stage.

Comey's tactics on the previous call had only stalled the president, but they had not deterred him. Now he was on the phone again, asking for the same thing. Comey tried a different approach: teaching the president what is appropriate contact between the president, the White House, and the FBI.

Comey reminded Trump that requests from the White House about the FBI's work were supposed to go through the Justice Department and that Comey wanted to follow that process. The FBI director was seeking to do two things: First, by holding back on saying no to Trump's request, Comey hoped to avoid seeming openly defiant—anything to avoid conflict and confrontation with the president. Second, by redirecting him to the Department of

Justice, Comey wanted Trump to learn that he needed to make his case to officials at the department, not to him.

It was another extraordinary moment in government in the time of Trump: The FBI director, an appointee who works at the pleasure of the president, was telling the president how the executive branch should function.

"Maybe I'll just have Don McGahn call over there," Trump told Comey about the Justice Department.

"Sir, that's exactly what you should do—exactly how it should work, you should have the White House counsel call the leadership of the Department of Justice, and that's the way it should work," Comey said.

Then the president tipped his hand, reminding Comey of their dinner at the White House in the first week of the administration, when Trump had asked for Comey's loyalty and intimated that his job might be in jeopardy.

"Because I have been very loyal to you, very loyal, we had that thing, you know," Trump said.

With his bracing tendency to say the subtext out loud, Trump had just made a mistake. The comment affirmed Comey's belief that with his ingratiation campaign Trump had sinister motives and was scheming to steer the FBI away from legitimate investigations that could hurt him. In response to Trump's comment he said nothing, just repeating that all requests from the White House should go through the Justice Department.

Trump ended the four-minute call by telling Comey he was doing a great job.

Hours later in the Oval Office with McGahn, Trump seemed to relish announcing that he had called Comey twice in the past two weeks about the Russia investigation. Trump proudly told McGahn that Comey was willing to put out a statement that he was not under investigation if Boente approved it.

McGahn had warned Trump against talking to Comey. But now that Trump had done so twice, McGahn figured the best way to contain and pacify Trump was to contact Boente and ask whether he and Comey were actually considering putting out such a statement, as Trump had claimed.

The acting deputy attorney general told McGahn it was a bad idea. The political flames around the Russia investigation were just too hot. Boente said if he put out a statement, it could create the appearance of a conflict, and there might be calls for a special counsel to be appointed.

And nobody wanted that.

★ ★ ★

MAY 3, 2017

FOURTEEN DAYS UNTIL THE APPOINTMENT OF SPECIAL COUNSEL ROBERT S. MUELLER III

SENATE JUDICIARY COMMITTEE ROOM—Seven months had passed since Comey had reopened the Clinton email investigation just eleven days before the election. But he still had not answered questions about it publicly. The day had come for that. On May 3, he would testify before the Senate Judiciary Committee. While the occasion was supposed to be a routine oversight hearing, everyone knew it would be about emails and the Russia investigation. And McGahn knew that Trump would be closely monitoring Comey's statements about whether he was under investigation.

From the outset of the hearing, Comey found himself on the defensive and under harsh questioning from the Democrats, particularly Senator Dianne Feinstein, who channeled the anger of the Left at Comey. Comey thought she was deliberately ignoring everything they discussed at their private meeting during the transition to perform for the cameras. Feinstein accused Comey of taking a huge gamble by sending the letter to Congress about reopening the investigation of Clinton without knowing if the Weiner laptop actually contained anything new, which, it had turned out, it didn't.

She said the episode had damaged the reputation of the bureau, and she demanded to know why his treatment of the Clinton investigation had been so "dramatically different" from his treatment of the investigation into links between the Trump campaign and Russia, which had been ongoing and which Comey had kept secret.

Comey was as practiced in public testimony as any official in Washington and prided himself on his ability to stay cool under questioning. But for the first time in his career, he became unglued. He raised his voice, waved his hands, and grimaced. In his raw state, he answered questions bluntly and spoke personally about his decision to reopen the Clinton email investigation.

"It makes me mildly nauseous to think that we might have had some impact on the election," he told the committee. "But honestly, it wouldn't change the decision."

In the exchange with lawmakers, Comey was asked directly if Trump was under investigation. "So potentially, the president of the United States could be a target of your ongoing investigation into the Trump campaign's involvement with Russian interference in our election, correct?" asked Richard Blumenthal, the Democratic senator from Connecticut.

"I just worry—I don't want to answer that, that, that seems to be unfair speculation," Comey answered. "We will follow the evidence, we'll try and find as much as we can and we'll follow the evidence wherever it leads."

Patrice watched the hearing from home, surprised to hear her husband had actually admitted to being "mildly nauseous" that his actions might have had an impact on the election. While it might offend Trump, she knew it to be true.

That night, Patrice mentioned the comment. "You know he might interpret that as you being nauseous that he became president, right?"

"Ooh, he's not going to like that," Comey agreed.

That afternoon, McGahn told Trump—while he was meeting with Attorney General Sessions in the Oval Office—how Comey had refused to answer a question about whether the president was under investigation. Trump erupted in anger, pinning the blame directly on Sessions, who was conveniently sitting just feet away.

"This is terrible, Jeff," Trump said. "It's all because you recused. Kennedy appointed his brother. Obama appointed Holder. I appointed you and you recused yourself. You left me on an island. I can't do anything."

Sessions tried again to explain why he had been required to recuse himself from the investigation, and to deflect some of Trump's unbridled rage, he changed the topic to the FBI and suggested the time might have come to make a change in the bureau's leadership.

It did nothing to blunt Trump's attack on Sessions, but the beleaguered attorney general had just unwittingly endorsed a notion that the president had already been mulling for days.

★★★

MAY 4, 2017

THIRTEEN DAYS UNTIL THE APPOINTMENT OF SPECIAL COUNSEL ROBERT S. MUELLER III

OVAL OFFICE—In the days that followed, Trump continued to obsess about Comey as cable news played the "mildly nauseous" clip relentlessly, transforming it into a signal event of the Trump presidency. The president brought up the FBI director more than a dozen times over the course of meetings in the Oval Office.

"He told me three times that I wasn't under investigation," Trump told Steve Bannon. "He's a showboater. He's a grandstander. I don't know any Russians. There was no collusion."

Bannon strongly cautioned Trump against firing Comey, saying it wouldn't end the Russia inquiry. "You can fire the FBI director, but you can't fire the FBI," Bannon said.

That afternoon, House Republicans changed the news when they voted to pass legislation that repealed significant parts of Obamacare. Although the bill had still not been passed in the Senate, the president—lacking any major legislative achievements despite Republicans controlling Congress—wanted to celebrate it. So he held a victory ceremony in the Rose Garden, the type of event presidents usually hold when a bill has actually passed and is being signed into law.

Later that day, Trump boarded Air Force One for New York to meet with the Australian prime minister at an event on the *Intrepid* aircraft carrier on Manhattan's West Side. At 11:00 that night, Trump arrived by helicopter at his golf club in Bedminster, New Jersey, with a small number of his advisers—Ivanka, Kushner, Stephen Miller. McGahn, not currently a member of the true inner circle, was back home in Washington. Trump was scheduled to golf that Friday at his club with Greg Norman, the legendary Australian golfer. But it rained and instead of blowing off steam on the course, Trump stewed inside the club about Comey and the Russia investigation. That afternoon, he sat and watched all of Comey's testimony from earlier in the week. The combination of the rain and the testimony would turn combustible.

Comey's disclosures to Congress about the Russia investigation loosened the logjam around Rosenstein's nomination. Still, Senate Republicans would take another month to confirm him. Finally, in early May, Comey was alone in the deputy attorney general's austere office with the newly sworn in man whom he was counting on to be the bulwark between the FBI and the White House—an able partner in investigating the president of the United States for obstructing justice.

Rosenstein had invited Comey back to the office—an office he had occupied a dozen years earlier—after the pair and their aides had the first of what were scheduled to be biweekly meetings between the deputy attorney general and the FBI director.

"What do you think of the old place?" Rosenstein said.

Rosenstein, in a dark club chair with a high back, sat across from Comey, who was on a large tan couch. Comey had originally planned to bring up the meeting with the president on February 14, when he had asked him to end the Flynn investigation. But he hesitated. Rosenstein was still getting up to speed, and he had a lot to sort out about the Russia investigation. Comey only mentioned that he had a "weird" one-on-one meeting with Trump in the Oval Office. There was no need to rush into a discussion about whether to open an investigation into the president. Comey couldn't have known at the time what a fateful mistake he was making.

Instead of discussing the president, the two men talked about work-life balance, sleeping habits, and an oddly elaborate alternating sandwich schedule that Comey used to plan his lunches when he was deputy attorney general.

Because Comey did not seem to have any pressing issues to talk to Rosenstein about, after just a few minutes the deputy attorney general—with a slew of posts to fill and the Trump administration already in court fighting to defend its travel ban—said that he had to go.

The two men parted ways, not having discussed how the FBI director had evidence to open a criminal investigation on the president of the United States. Heading into the coming week, Rosenstein would have no understanding of what had gone on between Trump and Comey.

As Rosenstein rushed to his next meeting, he mentioned to one of his top aides how it seemed that Comey did not like Trump and how Comey thought Trump was weird. For Rosenstein, it was yet another sign of a troubling relationship brewing between the Justice Department, the White House, and the FBI. The FBI director did not think highly of the president. The attorney general did not think highly of the FBI director. And Rosenstein had just been briefed that the inspector general for the Justice Department was going to find that Comey had acted improperly in his handling of the Clinton email investigation.

But that evening, Comey returned home with newfound confidence in Rosenstein, telling Patrice that Rosenstein could be an important force for good. Patrice felt relieved that Rosenstein had finally arrived. Maybe now, she thought, Jim's life would be a bit easier.

★★★

MAY 5, 2017

TWELVE DAYS UNTIL THE APPOINTMENT OF SPECIAL COUNSEL ROBERT S. MUELLER III

AN APARTMENT IN NORTHWEST WASHINGTON, D.C.—Cinco de Mayo fell on a Friday in 2017, allowing for extra-hard partying because most people didn't have work the next day. That Friday night I was invited to a Make Margaritas Great Again party being held by a brash lawyer in the White House counsel's office at a duplex in Washington.

It was the end of a tough stretch. During the transition, I had been named to a team of reporters who were supposed to do investigative work on the Trump administration. I had to balance that assignment with a project I had begun before the election: examining whether the Fox News host Bill O'Reilly had sexually harassed women with whom he worked. Our story had run in April, and later that month O'Reilly had been fired. While that was behind us, it had taken a lot out of me, and that Friday night I did not particularly feel like going to a party.

But a friend who had also been invited had persuaded me to come along, telling me that influential people whom I would find interesting would be there. At the party were a bunch of young Republicans who had joined the administration as White House lawyers working for McGahn or senior officials at the Justice Department. Everyone seemed to know each other, but I barely recognized any of them. This was—as my friend said it would be—a target-rich environment to meet people who could be great sources. But I can be shy at times in large groups of people I don't know, and amid the shouts from drinking games, I spent much of the night on the apartment's back porch talking with the few people I knew while drinking Coke Zeros. I left early, headed straight home, and went to bed, completely missing a moment that foreshadowed perhaps the most important decision Trump would make in his presidency.

That weekend, the friend who had persuaded me to tag along called to report what he described as a curious interaction at the party after I left. The friend said a senior Justice Department official who worked directly for Attorney General Jeff Sessions had been openly asking those at the party whether they had any dirt on Comey. My friend heard the official say that Sessions wanted one bad story a day on Comey in the media, in an apparent effort to undercut his credibility. Now, my friend is a measured guy who is not one to twist the facts to make himself seem more important, which is a common practice in Washington. Nevertheless, I thought the story was ridiculous. Why would Sessions want to get rid of

Comey? Sessions and Trump had been the ones to praise Comey when he reopened the email investigation just before the election. In what I can only describe as one of the more naive thoughts I have ever had, I was convinced Sessions and Trump would be concerned that it would be, for lack of a better term, intellectually dishonest to get rid of Comey, after having lavished so much praise on him for reopening the email investigation on the brink of the election. Making the story even less credible in my mind, Comey was the one conducting the investigation into links between the Trump campaign and Russia. If the president fired him, it would obviously look as if the White House were trying to obstruct the investigation. And the political blowback, so early in an administration, would be devastating.

So I found the tip absurd. Still, I was learning—barely more than three months into the administration, and along with the rest of the country—just how unpredictable Trump could be. The only predictable pattern so far was that his lack of discipline led him to repeatedly undercut himself, his agenda, and his own officials at almost every turn. As it became clear in those early days that this was how Trump was going to operate, I reexamined my presumptions about what the president might or might not do under the pressure of the Russia investigation and the other burdens of his office.

Given the high stakes, I had adopted what I called the "FBI post-9/11 mindset" to tips. In the aftermath of the attacks of September 11, 2001, Robert S. Mueller III, then the FBI director, had made it a rule that every terrorism tip would be logged and run down. Even the most outlandish ones—like people who reported seeing Osama bin Laden walking around midtown Manhattan. By sussing out every tip, counterterrorism agents hoped to ensure that absolutely nothing got by them. And so I thought that if I did the same with Trump, I would lessen my chances of getting beaten on major stories. So I entered every lead I heard in my notebook, however crazy it might have seemed.

Based on the report from my friend at the party, what I wrote in my notebook on May 9 was this: "Sessions out to get Comey." I wasn't even sure where to turn to try to get it confirmed. Although Trump often tripped over himself, if he and the attorney general were plotting against Comey, they or their aides were not going to tell me. And they certainly wouldn't tell anyone at the FBI, who would be likely to let Comey know and would perhaps even be motivated to tell me or another reporter in the hopes of bringing attention to it and stopping Trump.

But there was one person who might be able to help me. I had known Dan Richman, a Columbia Law School professor, from my days working as a sportswriter at the *Times* a decade earlier. We had first met when I was trying to learn how to cover the federal investigation of sports, mainly the BALCO inquiry into performance-enhancing drugs for athletes. My editor at the time, whose only knowledge of federal investigations came from writing headlines at the *Daily News* about mobsters, told me to call one of the local law schools to find "one of those professors to explain this shit to us—you know, one of those guys who wants to get quoted."

I soon found Richman, a professor who taught federal criminal law. He had impressive credentials. He had clerked for the Supreme Court justice Thurgood Marshall before becoming a federal prosecutor in New York, where he locked up violent criminals and organized crime figures under U.S. attorneys like Rudy Giuliani. Beyond his impressive talents and accomplishments, he did one of the most important things anyone can do for a reporter: He always answered the phone. It turned out he was more interested in explaining than actually being quoted in the paper, and, generously, he became my tutor in federal investigations, patiently walking me through how prosecutors thought about their cases and how things like grand juries and plea agreements functioned. He was not a partisan. He always just gave me the facts on how the criminal justice system worked. I needed so much help that I spent hours on the phone with him, and we developed such a close relationship that I occasionally joined him and his wife, Alex, for dinner in their Brooklyn Heights neighborhood. One time, I even brought my then girlfriend with me.

When Richman served as a prosecutor at the U.S. attorney's office in Manhattan, he'd worked alongside dozens of ambitious young lawyers who would go on to climb the rungs of the Justice Department in Washington. One of those prosecutors was a lanky young lawyer named Jim Comey. Although Comey comes across as at ease in public settings, he's a fairly introverted guy who likes to spend hours alone reading. He has few close friends, but in the years after he left the office in Manhattan, Richman and Comey had grown close. They were intellectual equals. But where Comey can come across like a savvy, seasoned politician, Richman—with thick glasses and endless enthusiasm to talk about issues like sentencing guidelines and plea agreements—decamped to academia to teach. After becoming FBI director, Comey had hired Richman to work as a special consultant to deal with new and abstruse legal issues, like encryption, that require extraordinary brainpower.

I reached out to Richman.

"You got a sec?" I wrote in an email the next Monday.

"On Amtrak on way to D.C. Call my cell—not in quiet car," he responded.

I called Richman and told him what I had heard. He, too, said it made no sense. He followed with a comment about how he had recently been with Rosenstein's staff and it had gone swimmingly.

Another useless tip, I thought.

But I recorded my exchange with Richman in my notebook, just in case. And I told Matt Apuzzo, the seasoned law enforcement reporter who sat next to me, what I had heard. Apuzzo also thought it made no sense, but he said it might be worth making some calls. I considered calling two senior officials I knew at the FBI but decided it would be wrong for me to get people spun up about something I did not really believe to be true. There was enough chaos in the air.

* * *

MAY 8, 2017

NINE DAYS UNTIL THE APPOINTMENT OF SPECIAL COUNSEL ROBERT S. MUELLER III

OVAL OFFICE—McGahn drove to work that Monday morning figuring it would be a normal day—at least normal for the Trump White House. But shortly after arriving in the West Wing, he was told that

Trump wanted to have a meeting in the Oval Office with him and his other top aides immediately.

That weekend—with just Miller, Hicks, Ivanka, and Kushner—Trump had decided, without consulting his White House counsel or any other lawyer, to fire the FBI director. Bizarrely, he had Miller, who has no legal training, draft a termination letter to send to Comey. In the Oval Office, Miller handed out copies of the letter. Among those in the room who were learning about the firing for the first time was the late arriving vice president.

McGahn had been through this drill before, when Trump had declared that he was pulling the Gorsuch nomination, only to later forget about it. But this seemed serious. McGahn knew that Trump had become increasingly agitated at the FBI director, especially after his March testimony. As Trump read aloud from the letter to the assembled aides, McGahn became increasingly alarmed. Trump had done a lot of complaining, but he had never gone so far as to actually draft a letter. And the letter was filled with all sorts of claims that McGahn knew would be problematic.

Along with handing out the letter, Miller gave the group copies of a memo he had written for the president based on internet research he had done. By then, McGahn had been joined by his deputy counsel, Uttam Dhillon. Miller handed Dhillon a copy of the memo, which said that Trump did not need cause to fire Comey. Dhillon had told the president just the opposite in March and now hoped that Trump would not single him out for abuse in front of the vice president, McGahn, and other aides. Reading the memo, Dhillon said nothing as Trump pointed to it as evidence that he could act as he wished.

McGahn had actually come to agree with Trump that Comey had to go. To McGahn, Comey acted as if he answered to no one. McGahn thought the FBI was unnecessarily delaying background checks for security clearances, and in his new perch in the White House he had learned about a wide range of areas—like domestic intelligence—that the bureau was involved in that he believed made it clear that the FBI had overstepped its prerogatives and assumed too much power. He also genuinely believed that Comey had made a mess of the Clinton email investigation.

But McGahn also knew that the way Trump was impulsively moving to fire Comey was reckless and could end in disaster. In the middle of an investigation, it would look terrible. Why, he thought, were they taking such an unnecessary step, when the whole town was so jacked up about this Russia investigation? There would be no way to avoid the appearance that the president was using his power to eliminate a threat to himself. And since when did the president of the United States get his legal advice on such a critical decision from an aide—who was not a lawyer—who had done his research on the internet? It struck him again the extent to which he was surrounded by hotheads and amateurs.

McGahn took a copy of Miller's letter back to his office. As he reviewed it closely, he became even more troubled. It read like a rant from a stump speech, railing openly about the Russia investigation and the Clinton email investigation and deriding Comey's deputy director, Andrew McCabe. Paranoid and angry, the letter read as if it had been dictated directly from Trump's id.

> Dear Director Comey, While I greatly appreciate your informing me, on three separate occasions, that I am not under investigation concerning the fabricated and politically-motivated allegations of a Trump-Russia relationship with respect to the 2016 Presidential Election, please be informed that I, along with members of both political parties and, most importantly, the American Public, have lost faith in you as the Director of the FBI and you are hereby terminated.

The letter explicitly criticized Comey for politicizing the FBI and allowing McCabe to be involved in the Clinton investigation:

> The FBI must not be a political organization, but you have totally politicized it—something that should never have been allowed to happen. Few events have represented a more profound breach of public trust than your decision to allow the Clinton email investigation to be overseen by deputy FBI director Andrew McCabe, whose wife Jill McCabe received approximately $700,000 in

> campaign donations steered to her by a top Clinton surrogate. . . . Your job is to look for corruption—at a minimum, McCabe should not have been allowed to work on this matter.

The instant Miller handed out copies of the letter in the Oval Office, McGahn realized it was the kind of document that should have originated in the counsel's office. But he was still formulating a strategy on how to protect Trump from the fallout from the firing and had yet to seize control of the process. So, back in his office, McGahn marked it up, highlighting several sections that he believed needed to be removed, and gave the changes to Miller.

The editing process bought McGahn some valuable time that he used to come up with a way of trying to slow down the president. McGahn spoke with Trump, telling him that it was essential that he first consult with Sessions and Rosenstein, because Comey reported directly to them.

Sessions had a prescheduled lunch with McGahn that Monday. McGahn had an aide call Rosenstein and summon him to the White House. The aide told Rosenstein only that McGahn wanted to see him immediately. The deputy attorney general rushed over. In McGahn's office, Sessions, Rosenstein, and McGahn ordered sandwiches from the White House mess and sat to discuss the firing.

Accounts differ as to what transpired over lunch. One account has McGahn hoping that Sessions and Rosenstein would say that they opposed the firing, and would then try to block it. The other has McGahn representing to Sessions and Rosenstein that the firing was a fait accompli. Whatever the case, McGahn was surprised by how Sessions and, especially, Rosenstein seemed eager to fire Comey.

For McGahn, Rosenstein's endorsement of the move was key to assuring him there would never be any legitimate claim that in axing Comey, Trump was trying to obstruct an investigation. Because of Sessions's recusal, Rosenstein was now the top Justice Department official overseeing the Russia investigation and any other investigation that might involve Trump, his family, or anyone else in the president's orbit. Surely, McGahn assumed, Rosenstein had by that point been briefed on everything the FBI was investigating. If any of the investigations even remotely touched Trump, McGahn believed, Rosenstein would signal that a dismissal was not prudent. Not only was Rosenstein not signaling there was a problem, but he seemed enthusiastic about ousting Comey.

McGahn told Sessions and Rosenstein there was an issue: The letter Trump wanted to send was incendiary and vengeful. By itself, it could have tremendous unintended consequences for the White House. As they ate, Priebus came into McGahn's office several times. The White House chief of staff appeared frantic and sweaty. His eyes were bloodshot. Trump wanted the firing done that day, and Priebus, always trying to please Trump, wanted to know how they could make that happen. Desperate to slow the train down, McGahn tried to brush off Priebus.

Later that afternoon, Sessions, Rosenstein, McGahn, Pence, Priebus, and Dhillon met with Trump. The meeting marked Rosenstein's first time in the Oval Office as deputy attorney general. The president spent much of the meeting talking about his grievances with Comey and at one point called out for his assistant to bring him a copy of the Miller letter and handed it to Rosenstein, who immediately read it and thought that it was just as problematic as McGahn had described, particularly because it started with a reference to the Russia investigation. Such a mention could obviously raise questions about Trump's true motives for firing the FBI director. On its face, after all, characterizing the agency's investigation into his campaign as "the fabricated and politically-motivated allegations of a Trump-Russia relationship with respect to the 2016 Presidential Election" and then proceeding to fire the man overseeing the said investigation in the same paragraph could obviously be interpreted as an open admission by the president that he was purposely obstructing justice.

Rosenstein told the president that the letter was better without that passage.

There are differing accounts of what happened next. Some say Trump suggested that Rosenstein write a new memo laying out why he believed Comey should be fired. Others say Rosenstein, wanting to please Trump, offered on his own to write a memo rationalizing the dismissal. Whatever the case, Trump said Sessions would then write a letter to the president recommending the firing.

McGahn greeted this arrangement with some relief. At least the Justice Department would be providing a more cogent public rationale for what would surely be a controversial move. It was bad enough that that draft even existed. Rosenstein's memo would focus in particular on Comey's handling of the Clinton email investigation, which was clearly safer terrain. After all, both Democrats and Republicans had a beef with Comey's handling of the Clinton email investigation.

In the meeting, McGahn and Dhillon also tried to appeal to Trump to take a lighter touch overall, saying that Trump should offer Comey the chance to resign. Trump, reflexively, refused to go along with that. In fact, simply firing Comey was not enough. Several of the aides arrayed before him were struck that they were not so much seeing a president changing the management at the top law enforcement agency in the country. Rather, this was a vivid demonstration of Trump's primal need to dominate and publicly humiliate a vanquished foe. Trump wanted to put it in Comey's face. Shows of public virtue bothered the president, and Comey was a Boy Scout. Trump wanted to show Comey that he was the more powerful man and wanted to do it in the most humiliating way possible. Comey was out of town visiting FBI field offices, making the firing logistically more difficult.

What could be more humiliating than finding out that you've been fired by watching it on the news, far from home?

* * *

MAY 9, 2017

EIGHT DAYS UNTIL THE APPOINTMENT OF SPECIAL COUNSEL ROBERT S. MUELLER III

CONFERENCE ROOM, FBI FIELD OFFICE, LOS ANGELES—As Rosenstein's memo and Sessions's letter arrived at the White House the following morning, Comey began his day in Jacksonville, Florida, where he spoke at a law enforcement leadership conference. He then boarded the FBI's jet and flew across the country to Los Angeles, where he had scheduled a visit to the field office there.

Around 2:00 p.m. West Coast time, Comey began addressing a group of support staff in a large room.

On the other side of the country, in northern Virginia, Patrice was having happy hour at a friend's house.

She received a text from a friend.

"Is it true?"

Patrice had no idea what the friend was talking about.

She then received a flurry of other texts from other friends, asking if it was true what they were saying about Comey.

Patrice called her husband.

"What is happening?" Patrice asked.

By that point, Comey had seen his firing already being discussed on cable television, but he had not heard from anyone in Washington. "I don't know what's going on," he told Patrice. "I'll call you back."

As Patrice waited, Comey walked into a small room with his aides and called FBI headquarters, where his assistant, dumbstruck, said that a termination letter had just been delivered to her. Trump's body man had handed it to her at the front door of the bureau on Pennsylvania Avenue. She would scan it and email it to Comey.

Comey called Patrice back.

"I'm fired," he said. "And I don't know how I am getting back home."

She had known her husband was under a lot of pressure from the White House and that some of his recent actions, like his testimony the week prior, had angered Trump. But she was not at all prepared for him to get fired. Their family had packed up and reset their entire lives and careers in Washington specifically for this job. Now, less than halfway through his ten-year term as director, this was how they were being repaid.

This was seismic news. Patrice tried to make sense of the firing as she watched the breathless cable coverage. The anchors and reporters kept referring to a letter from Rosenstein that had established the legal basis for Trump's dismissal of her husband. *How could that be?* Patrice thought. Rosenstein was supposed to be a life preserver. Now he had become part of the plot to oust her husband?

"I thought Rod was our savior," Patrice said. "But Rod must have been a very dishonest person."

From Los Angeles, Comey sent a volley of texts to friends, family, and anyone who would listen.

"What a world," Comey wrote. "No call from anyone. I found out while addressing my employees here in LA. There were TVs on in the back and I could see the crawl saying I had been fired. They put it out and then had someone hand deliver a letter an hour later to fbi HQ. Classy."

"I was talking to my troops in LA office and I saw the headline flash on TVs at back of room," Comey wrote in another text. "I laughed because I assumed it was a prank and said it was very funny. My staff then start scrambling around and said I should step into a side office. Before I did I shook the hands of the support employees I was addressing. Went into side office and confirmed it was true (although still no calls of any kind). By this point much of LA office had gathered where I had just been speaking to support employees. I came out and told them I was very sad to leave them but I am sad because of the values this place represents and they must uphold those values. . . . Then I left."

"I'm with my peeps (former peeps)," Comey wrote in another. "They are broken up and I'm sitting with them like a wake. Trying to figure out how to get back to home. May hitchhike."

"Started in Jacksonville talking to cops. Was gonna end day here talking to 500 minority potential applicants. Was gonna do it anyway but just reconsidered. I'm gonna fly back on fbi plane and then drift into retirement 😊🍸"

"I almost kept the diversity event appointment because I really do care but I don't want to make it a media circus."

"Dunno," Comey replied in a text when asked why he was fired. "Not for the reasons stated."

Comey's motorcade, with a police escort, left the field office in Los Angeles and headed to LAX. But it being L.A., a news helicopter followed him, and the footage was televised live, like the slow O. J. Simpson freeway chase two decades earlier. When Comey arrived at the airport, he shook the hands of the police officers who escorted him. He quickly climbed eleven steps into the FBI's G5 jet, ducking his head one last time as he entered the plane to avoid hitting it. Comey sat in the seat reserved for the director. Once he was in the air, he opened a bottle of red wine and received a phone call from the secretary of homeland security, the former general John Kelly. Comey and Kelly had gotten to know each other during meetings at the White House in the first few months of the administration, and Kelly had grown fond of Comey, believing he was a fair and independent voice. Kelly was emotional and said he was sickened by Trump's move and that he didn't want to work for dishonorable people and was himself prepared to resign. Comey told Kelly not to do that. The administration needed any good people who were willing to serve.

Comey landed at Reagan National Airport at 1:24 a.m. and still had things he needed to collect from FBI headquarters, but because he was no longer an employee, he would not be allowed into the building, so he went home instead.

Comey walked into his house through the back porch. Patrice was there to meet him. He had tears in his eyes. The two embraced.

In the days that followed, his things were boxed up and sent to him. Nearly all of his personal items showed up. But one that never arrived was a memento that had been a steady reminder of the work ahead necessary to fix the FBI: the broken piece of the building, with "Director" written in blue felt marker.

That was literally government property. It would remain at the FBI.

But the most important keepsakes Comey had from his time as director were the memos he had written about his interactions with Trump. The former FBI director knew how damaging they could be to the president, because he believed they were evidence of Trump's efforts to interfere with the Russia investigation. Comey had wanted to share them with Rosenstein before he was fired. Now, to Comey, Rosenstein—rather than being a rampart to insulate an independent FBI from the White House—had become a tool of the president's obstruction campaign. In the wake of Rosenstein's betrayal, Comey had a growing fear that no one in the Justice Department would be able to stand up to the president's forceful demands that the FBI back off the Russia investigation. Although Comey was out of government, the most fateful decision of his career still lay ahead of him.

When the news broke shortly before 6:00 p.m. eastern that Comey had been fired, I was standing in the greenroom at MSNBC's studios in Washington preparing to go on Chris Matthews's show. I was hit by a wave of regret for not more aggressively pursuing the information from the Cinco de Mayo party. Sessions had been out to get Comey, after all. But there was not much I could do about it now. I called Richman and was the first to break the news to him. Sounding depressed, he said he wasn't surprised and quickly hung up the phone. The producers asked me to stay around to talk about the firing on the air, but I knew I had to rush back to the newsroom. On such a big story, there is nowhere reporters would rather be than with their colleagues. By the time I got back to the *Times* bureau, chaos had set in. Usually when there's a big breaking news story, you can feel the adrenaline pulsating in your fingers. That energy was certainly there, joined by a sense that this was a truly game-changing event and that we were headed into a darker and more troubling phase of Trump's three-and-a-half-month-old presidency. At his desk, Apuzzo had his shirtsleeves rolled up and was writing the main story of the firing. Sweating and screaming like an emergency room doctor, he pounded away at his keyboard.

When big stories happen, two things almost always occur: The bureau orders massive amounts of food for us to eat on deadline, and reporters who often know little about the event that has occurred come out of the woodwork to gorge on the spread and try to get bylines. In the scrum of assignments, I was stuck working with two veteran reporters, and I ended up with the third byline on a story about how Comey's firing had led lawmakers—including Republicans like John McCain—to call for an independent investigator to look into Russia's meddling in the election. After we had all finished filing our stories, I went downstairs to the street to have a cigarette with my colleagues. It was clear that the firing would have enormous implications—some that we couldn't yet imagine. What did the story really mean? In the middle of our conversation, my phone rang, a call from New York. It was Matt Purdy, one of the top deputies to the executive editor, Dean Baquet. I had worked closely with Purdy on the stories my colleague Emily Steel and I had done on Bill O'Reilly. Emily and I had been chasing some other threads from that story, but the message from Purdy was clear: The Russia investigation was now a five-alarm story, and we had to get to the bottom of why Trump had fired Comey.

Late that evening or sometime the following day, as Washington was still absorbing the jolt of Comey's firing, a trusted source told me that what had gone on between Trump and Comey was "wild." But the source refused to say more. I was unsure what any of this meant. But I trusted the source and realized I had to do everything to go after the story, including taking a new approach to my relationship with one of the most valuable and trusted people I'd relied upon during my career: Richman. He had served as a tutor, but now I needed him as a source.

I could tell from our conversations that he was angry about the firing and that he knew more than he was sharing. He had been through a grueling six months. The previous October, he had been one of the few people to publicly stand up for Comey after he'd reopened the Clinton email investigation, even going on PBS to awkwardly defend his old friend. Richman loyally stood by Comey to me in private, too, even when I had a sneaking suspicion that he really believed that Comey might have gone too far. We should all be so lucky to have a friend like that.

The notion that Comey had helped get someone like Trump elected bothered Richman endlessly. In the wake of the firing, Richman seemed more depressed, losing faith in a government he had spent his life studying, working for, and believing in.

In our initial conversations after Comey's firing, he remained unwilling to disclose anything of his private conversations with

Comey. But I couldn't afford to respect the unofficial lines I'd drawn around our relationship. The stakes were too high. I didn't know what had gone on between Trump and Comey before Comey's firing, but I had a feeling that Richman did and I desperately needed him to share it with me. It was too important for him not to.

I started calling him every few hours, telling him what I was hearing from other sources and interspersing questions that I thought could elicit clues about what he knew. It was a process of elimination. If something was flat wrong, he would usually say so. I noted the awkward pauses in our conversations after I floated new information or theories, a sign that seemed to indicate that I was getting warmer. I was taking notes during our lengthy conversations, scribbling as many notes interpreting his nonanswers as his answers. In subsequent conversations, it was those things I would start with. In that way and little by little, I began to assemble the puzzle of what had happened between Comey and Trump. I took what I could glean from him, talked to other sources, and then would come back to him within hours with new details and added clarity that showed him he wasn't the only one talking to me about this stunning turn of events.

I came to a pretty clear understanding through this process that Trump and Comey had had a one-on-one dinner at the White House sometime early in the administration and that Trump had asked Comey for something. I did not yet know what it was.

That Wednesday, with the fury from Comey's firing still building, I went back to Richman one last time and told him I was going to write about the dinner and that he had to level with me.

He did.

The story I wrote following that conversation began like this:

> Only seven days after Donald J. Trump was sworn in as president, James B. Comey has told associates, the F.B.I. director was summoned to the White House for a one-on-one dinner with the new commander in chief.
>
> The conversation that night in January, Mr. Comey now believes, was a harbinger of his downfall this week as head of the

> F.B.I., according to two people who have heard his account of the dinner.
>
> As they ate, the president and Mr. Comey made small talk about the election and the crowd sizes at Mr. Trump's rallies. The president then turned the conversation to whether Mr. Comey would pledge his loyalty to him.
>
> Mr. Comey described details of his refusal to pledge his loyalty to Mr. Trump to several people close to him on the condition that they not discuss it publicly while he was F.B.I. director. But now that Mr. Comey has been fired, they felt free to discuss it on the condition of anonymity.

The following morning, Trump responded to the story with a tweet implying it was false and that he had recordings of their conversation: "James Comey better hope that there are no 'tapes' of our conversations before he starts leaking to the press!"

The story was solid and provided the first real insight into the relationship between the two men leading up to Comey's firing. Trump went nuts about the reporting, but the article was far from conclusive, as it led to more questions than answers. It also left plenty of room for Trump's defenders to argue that the president was just trying to feel out one of the most important members of the executive branch—one who had plenty of critics in the Democratic Party.

It didn't make sense that Trump would have fired Comey in May over one awkward dinner in January. The two had interacted many times after that, and those meetings remained a mystery. But Trump had already amply demonstrated that he was unwilling or unable to change as president to adapt to Washington's norms. If he had leaned on Comey for loyalty in his first week as president, then the relationship had been fraught from the start. The White House must have known that axing Comey was going to be an earthquake, but they did it anyway. Trump must not have gotten the personal loyalty he demanded. There had to be more to the story. Richman and the other sources I was speaking to signaled that was the case. So I returned to the methodical work of going back and forth between Richman and others, tracking the holes in the conversations, and then working to fill them with other sources and subsequent conversations with Richman himself. I pushed them all more aggressively than I'd ever pushed for anything before. Six days after Comey was fired, finding out what had happened had taken on the air of an emergency.

As I was flailing around with a lot of leads but nothing solid enough to put in the paper, I sent Richman an email, not quite letting on how desperate I was.

> DANNY:
>
> so here's the deal ..
>
> i tried to leave you alone yesterday, as i know what a long and tiring and trying week it's been.
>
> but we're moving forward with something.
>
> it seems like there's a lot of funky shit that went on between trump and comey, especially in the first two months of trump's time in office
>
> what i also know—and this is not just from you—is about a weird meeting in the oval office between comey, trump, sessions and pence. trump kicks the other two out the room and then quizzes comey about leaks. comey didn't like this and said to sessions afterwards you can't leave me in the oval office alone with trump. not sure what sessions said to comey.

In caps, for emphasis, I asked a series of questions. Among them was this:

> DID FLYNN COME UP?

I hit send and had a sinking feeling that if my email didn't crack him open, I'd be at a dead end. That's the worst feeling for a reporter. Richman never replied to the email, leaving me to believe maybe there was nothing there or, worse, that there was and we may never learn what it is.

What I did not know was that weekend, at his home in Virginia, Comey woke up in the middle of the night with an idea. He always slept through the night. But now he lay awake in bed with a realization that if Trump—as he had hinted at in his tweets after the loyalty dinner story—had indeed installed a recording system in the White House as Nixon had fifty years earlier, then their conversations were recorded. If those recordings could get into the hands of federal investigators, there may be evidence that proved beyond a reasonable doubt that Trump had obstructed justice in several ways.

★★★

MAY 15, 2017

TWO DAYS UNTIL THE APPOINTMENT OF SPECIAL COUNSEL ROBERT S. MUELLER III

NEW YORK TIMES WASHINGTON BUREAU—The story about the loyalty dinner had made it easier for us to forget the harsh reality that had set in around us at the *Times.* As we covered the biggest political and national security story of our lives, we were lagging behind our rivals at *The Washington Post.*

There's no exact scoring system in journalism. But one way to measure our work is to focus not just on how interesting the information we uncover is but also on how much it affects perception and policy.

And by that measure, despite our successes, the *Post* was clearly ahead.

Early in the transition, the *Post* had seized the moment and over the next few months had broken the stories that led to Flynn's resignation and Sessions's recusal. Every scoop the *Post* got gnawed at us just as losses will for a sports team. In our heads, there was even more pressure on us because the *Times*' executive editor, Dean Baquet, was longtime "frenemies" with the *Post*'s editor, Marty Baron. The two had come to know and respect each other in the late 1990s as colleagues at *The New York Times*. Dean wanted nothing more than to beat Marty and vice versa, especially on the biggest story of their respective tenures leading their newspapers.

Though my story put us back on the board, that Monday, the reality that the *Post* was ahead was once again brought home dramatically when they broke a story that Trump had disclosed highly sensitive intelligence to the Russian foreign minister and ambassador in an Oval Office meeting on the day after he had fired Comey. In fact, the president had bragged to Sergey Lavrov and Sergey Kislyak that the firing would now lift the cloud of the Russia investigation. The story confirmed many of the biggest fears about Trump: At worst, he was a Manchurian candidate, rewarding an adversary that had just attacked our democracy to help make him president by giving them closely guarded national security secrets. At best, he was a novice president learning on the job.

Either way, the presidency was in disarray, and bizarrely, the president's loyalties seemed unclear.

We scrambled to confirm the story while our editors assured New York we had the situation under control (even though we probably did not). That night I went to talk to the *Times*' Washington bureau chief, Elisabeth Bumiller. A palpable fear was setting in that the Trump story was really getting away from us, and we had quietly begun to point fingers at each other about whose fault it was. Bumiller was a former reporter who made her name as a White House and Pentagon correspondent in the years after the 9/11 attacks, at one point spending weeks with women soldiers on the front lines of the war in Afghanistan. As bureau chief, she had grown into a commanding leader of our ever-expanding bureau in the Trump era. She had an uncanny knack for charming sources and reporters alike, even as she struck fear into anyone who might disappoint her. Her reporting career had begun at *The Washington Post,* and as much as Dean wanted to beat the *Post,* I think Elisabeth wanted it even more.

I walked up to where she was standing at her computer in front of the long series of desks the bureau's editors operate from. I knew she was looking for a story that we could use to strike back at the *Post.* The bureau editors did not know the extent to which I had been chasing leads about what had gone on between Comey and Trump. I told her that if I made some progress overnight, I might be able to write the next day about a series of memos that Comey was said to have written contemporaneously as he had interactions with Trump. As described to me, it was as if the encounters had so disturbed Comey that he felt he had to create a record, memorializing what had happened. While "contemporaneous memos" sounded secret and sexy, the truth was that I didn't really know what they were about. She looked over her reading glasses at me with a sort of puzzled *So what? Why are you bothering me?* look.

She said, "Okay," and went back to editing.

As I walked home that night to my small basement apartment, twenty minutes north of our bureau, I thought about how everything was going wrong. It was the biggest story I had ever covered, and we were in danger of being overshadowed again by the *Post,* just as four decades earlier the *Times* had started way behind on the Watergate story. The legacy of Watergate still hangs over much of what goes on in Washington. Many veteran editors lived through it, and unfolding scandals are measured against it. Bob Woodward is held up as a lion of journalism. Most of all, nobody wants to get beaten on covering a scandal, let alone one that could rival Watergate.

Overnight, I pushed my sources for more information on the Comey memos but came up with little. Still, I left my apartment early the next morning determined to push the story along enough to write something. It was a sunny morning, and Washington's humid summer had not yet set in. And as I walked to work, I got word that I needed to call Dan Richman.

After receiving that message, I hopped in a cab to the office and called Richman as soon as I got to my desk. He said he was at the gym and would have to call me when he got home and had a chance to look at his email. The information he had, I thought, couldn't be that urgent if he was not rushing home from the gym. (In all my years talking to Richman, he had never talked about going to the gym. But there was nothing I could do; I had no choice but to wait.)

Journalists get a lot of practice in waiting, but that doesn't make it any easier. Sitting around while you are expecting to get information that you know could be promising is one of the more excruciating experiences a reporter can go through. It's all but impossible to do any other work. So that morning, I just sat there staring at my two computer screens. I didn't tell any of my colleagues what was going on, because, well, I didn't know what I was—or wasn't—about to learn.

After an hour, Richman, home from the gym, finally called me back. He said he'd received an email from Comey with a memo in it that Richman had never seen before. Richman said he had been instructed by Comey to read it to me. I opened up a window in my computer and prepared to type. There was a moment of silence, and then Richman, who I could tell was quickly scanning the memo, let out a nervous laugh. He started to read the memo, line by line, and I began to type.

The memo began with details including where Comey sat during a threat briefing that he and other senior intelligence officials gave to Trump in the Oval Office on February 14. It ended with a description of Comey's running into Secretary of Homeland Security John Kelly on his way out of the West Wing to his awaiting security detail. In between, there were revelations that I thought might change the trajectory of the Trump presidency because they described what might have been the crime of obstruction of justice.

The memo described how at the end of the threat briefing Trump cleared the Oval Office of everyone—including Comey's boss, Attorney General Sessions—to speak one-on-one with Comey. The president had the door to the Oval Office closed. He then brought up Mike Flynn, the former national security adviser who had resigned the previous day after questions arose about his contacts with the Russian ambassador.

"Flynn is a good guy, and has been through a lot," Trump said to Comey, according to the memo. "He misled the vice president but he didn't do anything wrong in the call."

Then Trump asked Comey to end the investigation.

"I hope you can see your way clear to letting this go, to letting Flynn go. He is a good guy. I hope you can let this go."

Richman read the entire document to me in mostly the same

tone, and neither of us discussed the potential damage that the Flynn conversation could do to the president or the risk to Comey of having his contemporaneous account of the Oval Office meeting made public. We both understood.

When I hung up, I should have felt exhilarated. Instead I was nervous. This story would open a new frontier in the reporting on the Trump presidency and would plunge a White House that hadn't been stable on its best day into crisis.

I walked three desks over to my editor, Mazzetti, and told him that we needed to talk. We went into the closest private area there was, the bureau's lactation room, and I told him what I had just learned. A huge smile came over Mazzetti's face. He asked me why I looked so nervous and told me to start writing.

A few minutes later, I was back at my desk, working on a Google Doc with Mazzetti reading behind me from his desk. We soon pulled Bumiller into her office and told her what we had. There was so much going on in the Trump era that Bumiller had taken to writing down everything—even the most mundane stories or bureau issues—on a white legal pad. As we described to her what we knew, she wrote down what I was saying. She realized the gravity of the story and told us to finish it immediately. She then called Matt Purdy, Dean's trusted deputy, and read him the notes from her legal pad. As Mazzetti edited the story, I sat down with the other members of our Russia team to tell them what I had learned. As word spread through the office, I called my parents, who were traveling in France, to tell them what was about to happen, because I did not want them to be blindsided by the news. My father, a New York liberal who was deeply skeptical of the government, did not sound surprised.

At 3:05 p.m., I sent an email to the president's top aide, Hope Hicks, under the subject line "urgent." I laid out what we knew and asked whether the president had any comment.

I didn't hear anything for half an hour and sent her another email.

"Just want to make sure you got this," I wrote.

I still didn't hear anything. At 3:56 p.m., I sent another email, this time copying several other members of the White House press office.

"Folks, we sent this email to Hope about an hour ago. We need a response by 430 pm, at which time we plan to publish. Thank you."

Inside the bureau, pressure was building on me to just post the story, because we couldn't risk being beaten. The editors were getting anxious. Would the White House try to upend us by giving the story to someone else? Sometimes this happens, when the subject of an article wants to both punish you and try to deflect the negative impact of an impending story by handing the details over to a more forgiving news outlet. What if Fox or Breitbart got this and tried to spin an article on Comey writing secret memos? Why should we give the White House—which had failed to tell the truth about so many important matters—more time to respond? What were they going to say that would change our view of the story?

I pushed back on the editors, telling them it was far too big a story to either rush it or publish it without giving the White House a chance to respond.

I couldn't help remembering a mistake I had made while covering the Clinton email affair, also writing in a hurry. Due to my haste, I had made a small error—the difference between a "national security referral" and a "criminal referral"—and the Clintons drove a Mack truck through the opening I gave them. I was wrong, and I was savaged for it. The problem was that we had been moving too quickly, and I hadn't taken the time to clarify which kind of referral it was with the intelligence community inspector general before the *Times* published the story. I was determined not to make such a mistake again.

At 4:07 p.m., Sarah Huckabee Sanders, then the deputy White House spokeswoman, responded to me.

"What's your number? Will call you."

When she called, I told her that we really needed to get a response quickly. She said, in her thick Arkansas accent, that she knew nothing about the February 14 meeting but would try to get something soon. From the tone of her voice she seemed to appreciate the gravity of the story. Even though we were dealing with such a contentious topic, she could not have been more pleasant.

When I relayed this to the editors, they told me to call the White House back and say they had five minutes or we would publish. Between the top editors at the *Times* and the top staff at the White House, I was in a vise. When I called Sanders back, she pleaded for twenty minutes. I said okay. I knew my editors would be upset, but I also knew that we had to get a response from the White House.

At 5:17 p.m., she finally sent me a statement with a flat denial.

> While the President has repeatedly expressed his view that General Flynn is a decent man who served and protected our country, the President has never asked Mr. Comey or anyone else to end any investigation, including any investigation involving General Flynn. The President has the utmost respect for our law enforcement agencies, and all investigations. This is not a truthful or accurate portrayal of the conversation between the President and Mr. Comey.

More than a dozen reporters and editors had congregated around my desk. In my cubicle stood Bumiller, Mazzetti, Apuzzo, and another top editor in the bureau, Bill Hamilton. They watched over my shoulder as I took the statement out of my email and pasted it into the story. They then rushed over to their desks to publish it.

The story was posted, and I have little recollection of exactly what happened next. I do know that I went on television that afternoon, and then again that night, I couldn't sleep, and I just stayed up watching *Top Gun,* mouthing the words to the movie. That day or the next I dropped my phone and the screen shattered. I wanted to get the screen fixed, but I was too concerned about turning the phone off when Washington was vibrating with such important news and a presidency suddenly seemed in peril. By the time I got a new screen a week later, I had pulled a couple of pieces of glass out of my hands. It was the closest I had ever come to playing hurt in my career.

* * *

MAY 16, 2017

ONE DAY UNTIL THE APPOINTMENT OF SPECIAL COUNSEL ROBERT S. MUELLER III

DEPUTY ATTORNEY GENERAL'S OFFICE—The firing, the White House's misleading statements to the media about it, and Trump's erratic behavior set off a once-in-a-generation confrontation between the FBI and the Justice Department about the future of the Trump presidency.

On Tuesday afternoon, May 16, the acting FBI director, Andrew McCabe, walked by himself from the bureau across the street to the Justice Department to meet with Rosenstein and two of his aides. McCabe, who had been thrust into leading a grieving bureau in the aftermath of the firing, needed to brief Rosenstein on a momentous and historic decision that the FBI had unilaterally made the previous evening.

Inside the deputy attorney general's office, Rosenstein sat in the club chair, with McCabe on the large couch. McCabe told Rosenstein that the bureau had opened an investigation into whether the president was a Russian agent and whether Trump had obstructed justice. The bureau, McCabe said, had also opened an investigation into whether Sessions had lied to Congress about his contacts with the Russian ambassador—an investigation that McCabe and Comey believed the department had been dragging its heels on for weeks.

To McCabe, Rosenstein did not look surprised. Four days earlier, he and McCabe had discussed how they were both suspicious about Trump's true intentions in firing Comey.

In McCabe's account of the meeting, he told Rosenstein that the obstruction investigation was opened based on a series of actions Trump had taken dating back to the first week of his presidency, when the president appeared to have begun an effort to win over Comey. McCabe said that Trump had asked Comey for his loyalty and then asked him to end the Flynn investigation. When it became clear that Comey would not go along with what Trump wanted, the president fired him. Trump had then given an interview with NBC's Lester Holt in which he said on national television that the Russia investigation had been a factor in his decision to fire Comey. McCabe said that Comey had documented his interactions with Trump in a series of contemporaneous memos that he wrote to file, telling Rosenstein that the memos were being kept in a safe at the FBI where few officials had access to them. The meeting marked the first time that Rosenstein had heard the details of what had gone on between Trump and Comey, solving the mystery that Comey had hinted at when the two men had met alone in his office ten days earlier.

Rosenstein asked McCabe to describe what the Russia part of the Trump investigation entailed.

McCabe explained to Rosenstein that it was a counterintelligence investigation that would examine the president's ties to Russia, and determine whether Trump posed a national security threat to the United States. McCabe told him that the FBI had opened an investigation the previous year—the one code-named Crossfire Hurricane—into whether the Trump campaign had worked with the Russian government to interfere in the election. As part of that investigation, the bureau had closely examined the ties between a handful of campaign officials and Russia. Nearly a year into that investigation, they had found no real evidence of such collusion. But during the campaign—and more intensely after he became president—Trump had publicly ridiculed the investigation, shown an odd proclivity toward Russia despite its attack on the election, and privately made a series of requests to Comey that appeared designed to curtail the investigation. As a result, bureau investigators had questions about whether Trump's ties to Russia posed a counterintelligence threat. And now, in firing Comey, Trump may have broken the law by obstructing justice. The fact that Trump was willing to, at the least, walk up to the line of criminality to upend the Russia investigation led counterintelligence investigators to believe they had grounds to open an investigation into whether the president was a Russian agent.

Rosenstein could have ordered McCabe to close the investigation or not proceed with anything until he received notice from him. But he didn't.

Not only had McCabe taken the bold step of opening an investigation of the president, but he was using this information as leverage on Rosenstein. To ensure the independence of the investigation, McCabe believed that Rosenstein needed to appoint a special counsel. The investigation into whether the president was a Russian agent, and had broken the law, would be one of the most consequential—and politically toxic—in the bureau's history. Trump appeared determined to quash any investigation into himself or his allies, and could appoint a crony as FBI director. McCabe told Rosenstein that if a special counsel had been appointed in the Clinton investigation, the FBI would have come out of it far less tarnished. The politics of investigating the president's ties to Russia would be orders of magnitude more problematic for the FBI, and the bureau needed the protection of a special counsel to insulate its work.

One of Rosenstein's aides, Jim Crowell, sitting next to McCabe on the same oversized leather couch, agreed with McCabe. "I think the director makes a good point, and you should consider it," Crowell said.

Rosenstein seemed receptive but unconvinced. He agreed with McCabe that the unanswered questions that loomed around Trump had to be investigated, and he understood the FBI would run into trouble during that process. But he wasn't ready to publicly appoint an investigator to look into it. What Rosenstein held back from telling McCabe was that four days earlier, he had asked the former FBI director, Robert S. Mueller III, whether he would be interested in taking on the role of special counsel. Mueller said that he may consider it if he could remain at his law firm—a condition Rosenstein saw as a deal breaker.

To McCabe, Rosenstein's concerns did not seem to be about the FBI's decision to open counterintelligence and criminal investigations on Trump and the attorney general; McCabe thought Rosenstein was unnerved by Trump. Rosenstein often portrayed himself as just a country lawyer who, armed with the Constitution and a good sense of right or wrong, could bring justice to the world. But the torrent of the Trump presidency, foreign interference in the election, and the resulting political fallout was a more noxious mix than anything he had confronted in his career, and it appeared to have frightened him.

Rosenstein told McCabe what had happened on the day of Comey's firing. Rosenstein said that it was clear to him that Trump had already made the decision to fire Comey before he had arrived at the White House. Given how the White House had lied when it said that it was Rosenstein's recommendation to fire Comey, Rosenstein said that he felt he could trust no one at the White House.

"You can't believe what it's like over there," Rosenstein said.

The two men had met twice since Comey had been fired. McCabe believed that Rosenstein had been disingenuous about the role he had played in helping Trump dismiss Comey, but despite these misgivings, McCabe still saw Rosenstein as the bureau's best bet out of all the senior officials at the department. In their discussions, Rosenstein had grown emotional, acknowledging that he was struggling to deal with the stress of the firing, the cameras parked outside of his house, and his inability to sleep. Now, in their third meeting, Rosenstein appeared to be in even worse shape. Again he became emotional; his voice cracked as he jumped from topic to topic. At times he spoke frenetically. At others he seemed solemn. At one point his eyes welled up with tears and he became so overcome that he had to step into the small half bathroom in his office to compose himself and blow his nose.

Rosenstein's struggle to meet the moment had not surprised McCabe. In Rosenstein's four weeks on the job, something about him had appeared off—erratic. In some of the morning briefings on threats to the country, Rosenstein would walk in, take a seat, clasp his hands in his lap, stare down for the entire time, and leave without saying anything or opening his briefing book. In other briefings, he dominated the meetings and spoke more than anyone else.

Rosenstein said that he was afraid to appoint a special counsel, because it would confirm to Trump that he was under investigation, and likely compel the president to fire him. Instead, what if he wore a wire to record his conversations with the president? He thought it was the best way to learn Trump's true intentions for why he had fired Comey.

"I could record the President," Rosenstein said. "I could wear a recording device. They wouldn't even know it was there. I never get searched, no one ever searches me."

Rosenstein's proposal to wear a wire marked the second time that McCabe had heard him propose the idea. In their meeting four days earlier, the deputy attorney general had also brought up the possibility as they discussed their suspicions about Trump's true intentions for removing the FBI director.

As the lead investigative unit for the Department of Justice, the FBI had a long-standing reputation for having a bias toward taking the most aggressive investigative measures and has been known to chafe at being held back by the department's prosecutors, who are generally known to be cautious. Less than a week earlier, Rosenstein had worked in concert with Trump to fire Comey. But now here was the deputy attorney general—an experienced prosecutor—proposing that he himself use one of the most powerful tools the bureau had at its disposal to investigate the president. McCabe was taken aback by the idea and said he would talk to his investigators about Rosenstein's suggestion.

Rosenstein believed that there was no good way of conducting a counterintelligence investigation into the president. And if they in fact found that the president was compromised, what could they do? The president had the authority to set the country's national security priorities. As he searched for a solution, Rosenstein could only come up with one idea: the Twenty-fifth Amendment. Ratified into the Constitution in 1967, the amendment provides that a vice president, together with a majority of cabinet members, can remove a president who is "unable to discharge the powers and duties of his office." Rosenstein told McCabe that he had done the math and figured they would need six more cabinet members—along with Sessions and Department of Homeland Security Secretary John Kelly, who he intimated might be on board—to secure the majority necessary to remove Trump from office.

"Who would support such a thing?" Rosenstein asked, hoping

that McCabe or his aides might have ideas of cabinet members who may be willing to take out the president if needed. No one in the room said a word.

"Sessions? I think he's a good guy," Rosenstein said, suggesting that he believed the attorney general would be on board. "I don't know him that well, but he seems like a good guy so far. Kelly too," he continued.

McCabe found it unlikely that Rosenstein had ever actually spoken to either Sessions or Kelly about such a move. But to McCabe it was clear that this wasn't a joke, and that made McCabe uncomfortable. The FBI, he believed, should never be part of a conversation about ways to remove the president.

McCabe understood why Rosenstein thought he was going to get fired if he appointed a special counsel, but that was not his concern. This may be the biggest decision that either of them would be involved in in their careers, and they needed to get it right. McCabe was losing his patience with Rosenstein, and he believed that he was acting cowardly. He immediately thought back to the Saturday Night Massacre, when in 1973 the Justice Department's top two officials famously resigned in protest of President Richard Nixon's decision to fire the special prosecutor who was investigating him. Didn't Rosenstein understand that it was better to stand up for what is right and sacrifice your career than sink to the level of Nixon?

No matter how convincing McCabe believed his arguments to be, he could see that he wasn't getting through to Rosenstein. So he went for the next move he could make that he believed would put even more pressure on Rosenstein to appoint a special counsel. McCabe said he planned on going up to Capitol Hill the following day to brief the Gang of Eight about the investigations the bureau had opened and answer any questions the lawmakers had. In telling Rosenstein what he planned to do, McCabe believed he was pressing on an area where he had extensive experience but Rosenstein had little. McCabe had been a senior FBI official for several years, often going up to brief lawmakers on sensitive national security threats. Since graduating from Harvard Law School, Rosenstein had spent his entire career in the Justice Department. While that gave him extensive government experience, he had been the U.S. attorney in Baltimore, one of the mid-tier offices that was often passed over for the most serious, complex, and politically difficult cases. Rosenstein had told McCabe early in his tenure that he knew little about dealing with "the legislature," talking as if Washington were some sort of glorified state capital and affirming to McCabe that he really didn't know his way around.

McCabe believed that he had to inform Congress about such a politically sensitive investigation, as he needed to explain to those who conducted oversight of the bureau and Justice Department what the investigators were doing examining the president and the attorney general.

In another sense, his decision to tell Congress showed how the invisible hand of James Comey was still directing the bureau. When Comey had briefed Congress in March in the hopes of breaking the logjam on Rosenstein's confirmation, he had told lawmakers that he would inform them of any major investigative steps the bureau was taking. Obviously, investigating the president and the attorney general crossed that threshold, and McCabe believed that he had an obligation to inform Congress.

Rosenstein pushed back against McCabe. He believed that the Justice Department and FBI provided far too much information to Congress and worried that McCabe was taking a page from Comey's playbook and acting on his own.

McCabe thought Rosenstein's position was naive and demonstrated a "field guy" mentality, which is a derisive way a senior law enforcement official in Washington refers to an investigator with no experience navigating the political headwinds inside the Beltway. McCabe said he was going to the Hill to brief Congress, with or without him.

"If the bureau is briefing Congress on sensitive matters, I want to be there," Rosenstein said.

"That's great," McCabe said. "But you should know that they are going to turn to you after I finish talking and they are going to grill you on whether or not you've appointed a special counsel and if not, why not."

The meeting ended with Rosenstein still undecided about whether to appoint a special counsel, and with McCabe gone,

Rosenstein turned to his aides, baffled, asking whether McCabe even had the authority to open investigations into Trump and Sessions without consulting with the Justice Department. "How can he do that?" Rosenstein asked. "That doesn't seem right to me that he can do it, to open an investigation on the president and it's a fait accompli."

Rosenstein added darkly, "He is scheming against me."

The aides told Rosenstein that any director or acting director of the FBI did in fact have the power to open an investigation on just about whomever he wanted to. Although the FBI was a subordinate organization, the Justice Department couldn't end an investigation like this one without significant paperwork that would force the department to explain why the investigation was being closed.

To Rosenstein, McCabe had conflicts that were potentially clouding his judgment. Trump had berated him and his wife at campaign rallies and on Twitter for taking money from a Clinton ally, helping to sully McCabe's public image and his standing within the bureau. Trump had then fired his boss, someone for whom McCabe had great respect. And now McCabe had put the president under criminal and counterintelligence investigations.

Once McCabe returned to the FBI, he gathered several of the bureau's top lawyers and told them about what had just transpired. Not only had the deputy attorney general suggested that cabinet secretaries might mount a campaign to invoke a constitutional provision to oust the president from office, but Rosenstein had personally volunteered to wear a wire to gather damaging information on Trump for the obstruction investigation. McCabe said that in the discussion, one of Rosenstein's aides had said, "I fear for the republic," and someone in the meeting said that Trump "was not fit to be president." The bureau lawyers were shocked by Rosenstein's proposal and cautioned strongly against him or anyone else wearing a wire—meaning that the FBI thought it was a bad idea to deploy the most invasive possible technique for evidence gathering against the president of the United States as a first resort. Trump might be out of control, but Rosenstein's suggestion was out of line, FBI officials believed.

A second meeting was scheduled for that evening at 7:00 p.m. in

Rosenstein's office to further discuss the appointment of a special counsel.

McCabe and his top aide, Lisa Page, returned to the Justice Department for the meeting. Rosenstein had spoken so quickly in the earlier meeting that McCabe needed someone there with him to take notes and be a witness. Since they were a few minutes early, they ran into a man just departing Rosenstein's office: Jim Cole, a former deputy attorney general under President Obama. With Mueller seemingly off the list to be special counsel because he wanted to remain at his law firm, Rosenstein had begun considering other possibilities, including Cole, a lifelong Democrat, who was known for his big ego, hard-charging nature, and prickliness. If Cole became the special counsel, the investigation would likely head in a fairly aggressive direction.

Rosenstein and his deputies crammed into his office, along with McCabe and Page. To McCabe, Rosenstein seemed even more out of sorts than in the morning. Again, he spoke frenetically, not finishing a point before jumping to the next. He repeated how he was dragged into writing the memo justifying Comey's firing. He again said that he could wear a wire into the White House, to learn Trump's true intentions. He again brought up the Twenty-fifth Amendment and talked about what it would take to whip the eight necessary cabinet members needed for the removal of the president.

Straining coherence, he had some in the room struggling to understand what he was talking about. Finally calming himself, Rosenstein acknowledged that he understood McCabe's thinking on appointing a special counsel, but he again said that he believed such an appointment would lead Trump to fire him.

"It's better to have a DAG than no DAG," Rosenstein said, using the acronym for his position as deputy attorney general.

To several people in the room, it appeared to be dawning on Rosenstein that Trump might be corrupt, or potentially even a Russian agent, and that extreme action might need to be taken to disrupt the situation and remove the president. But first things first. Only Rosenstein could appoint a special counsel—that was the purpose of this meeting. What did he intend to do?

It was hard to say, and to the officials in the meeting it was also becoming increasingly clear that the one man in the room with the authority to act did not fully understand the weight of the moment or the power dynamics of Washington or his inability to tame the fury that Comey's firing had ignited. Rosenstein said that he was prepared to deal with any blowback from Congress, adding that he had a good relationship with Schumer. At least one person in the room shot a look at one of Rosenstein's aides, as if to say, *What the fuck is he talking about, is he insane?*

Rosenstein then pivoted to throwing out names of well-known former senior Justice Department officials, seeming to propose them for special counsel or FBI director.

"Jim Cole?" he said. "Alice Fisher? Mark Filip?"

He then suggested that Trump wanted John Kelly to run both the Department of Homeland Security and the FBI.

"That's impossible," McCabe said. "No one could do both of those jobs at the same time."

Rosenstein agreed with McCabe, saying that the idea of putting Kelly at the FBI was designed to stymie its abilities to investigate Trump's associates and their ties to Russia. Under Trump's tortured logic, if Kelly was forced to straddle two jobs he would not have enough time to dedicate to the bureau, making it more difficult for investigators.

"It's a strategy for disruption," Rosenstein said.

This, Rosenstein said, was one of the central reasons why appointing a special counsel may not be such a good idea.

"If I put the special counsel in, then I could get dumped, and then I'm not here to be able to exert some control over who they select as FBI director," Rosenstein said. "They're trying to put someone in who will disrupt the FBI, not someone who will lead it independently."

The meeting broke up without a decision made on the appointment of a special counsel, and with McCabe genuinely concerned about how Rosenstein would handle the situation or whether he was capable of even doing so, especially in his current state.

After the meeting, Rosenstein figured he probably had less than twenty-four hours to decide what to do. The congressional leaders were surely going to ask about a special counsel in the Gang of Eight briefing the next day, so he had to come up with a yes or no answer before then. In the week since Rosenstein went along with Trump's plan to fire Comey without objection—and had written a memo that had become the White House's official rationalization for the move—the FBI had opened an investigation into whether Trump had obstructed justice and was a Russian agent. Rosenstein had learned that he had little control over the FBI.

He went back to Mueller and asked him whether he would take the job and leave his law firm. Mueller agreed. Earlier that day, before his meetings with McCabe, Rosenstein had met in the Oval Office with the president and Mueller, who had been called to the White House to discuss the director's job, the qualities that the job demands, and who might be a suitable successor to Comey. No former Justice Department official in Washington had a better reputation as a nonpartisan straight shooter than Mueller. He was one of the few people who had the experience working at the top of the Justice Department, an understanding of how counterintelligence investigations operated, the stature to offer the investigation legitimacy, and the kind of reputation that came without political baggage. On top of that, Mueller was a Republican.

The decision to appoint Mueller would be portrayed in the media as a response to Trump's behavior. Indeed, that was a factor for Rosenstein. But he had another major reason for his decision: He believed he had lost control of McCabe and the FBI, because they had moved ahead on their own and opened investigations on Trump and Sessions. Rosenstein was convinced that the FBI's leadership was pursuing a vendetta to avenge the firing of Comey. If Rosenstein had his way, he would have removed the FBI from the investigation entirely. But that would be nearly impossible. On simpler cases in the past where the FBI had a potential conflict, another law enforcement agency—like the Drug Enforcement Administration or the Bureau of Alcohol, Tobacco, and Firearms—would be brought in. But those specialized agencies had little experience in investigating foreign interference, as Russia had done in the election, or a complicated question of criminal law, like whether the president had obstructed justice. But with the appointment of Mueller, the investigation would now be housed under Rosenstein's roof. The FBI agents on the investigation would report directly to Mueller, not to McCabe.

In appointing Mueller, Rosenstein had several goals, which would later be important when assessing the success or failure of Mueller's investigation. Rosenstein wanted someone to provide clarity on what the Russians had done to interfere in the 2016 election. Trump was already publicly sowing doubt as to whether Russia had been behind the information warfare and election meddling, and the media was already pushing the notion that Trump and his campaign had been working with the Russians. Rosenstein felt that a full accounting of the Russian active measures and a determination of whether Trump's campaign had cooperated in the Russian effort were the only ways to put the questions about the 2016 election to rest.

Rosenstein was leveraging Mueller's credibility to ensure that even amid the rabid climate of Trump's presidency, the investigation would be done in a way that produced results that would be accepted as legitimate and beyond the reach of politics. As much as anyone could in Washington, Mueller had a reputation as an incorruptible and nonpartisan figure. He could be trusted to assemble and lead a team that could not be accused of allowing politics or the perception of them to become a factor.

Mueller was also a forceful speaker, and would present a credible public face for the investigation. Few American officials had testified before Congress more than Mueller. As FBI director, he had been required to testify at least two times a quarter. Over his four decades at the Justice Department, he had testified at hearings a staggering eighty-eight times.

The following afternoon, interviews for the job of FBI director continued in the Oval Office. McCabe came in for his interview with Trump, Pence, Sessions, and McGahn. It's unclear why McCabe had even been put on the list, but in the course of the interview he said nothing to Trump and Sessions about how he had opened criminal investigations into their activities just a day and a half earlier.

Afterward, McCabe received a call from Rosenstein. "Hey, I'm sorry I couldn't be there for the interview," Rosenstein said. "I had to get this thing finished up before the brief. I just wanted to let you know I've appointed Robert Mueller."

The news was a huge relief for McCabe. For more than a week he had believed the most important thing he had to do was convince Rosenstein to appoint a special counsel to oversee the Russia investigation. Now, eight days after the Comey firing, it had finally happened.

"It was the most enormous exhale of my life," McCabe said. "I had been holding my breath since the evening of May 9," he added, referring to the night that Comey was fired.

McCabe then headed directly to Capitol Hill to brief the Gang of Eight. As Rosenstein was making his way to Capitol Hill for the same briefing, he also called McGahn.

After McCabe left the Oval Office, the FBI director candidate interviews continued. Throughout the interviews, McGahn had wondered, Where is Rosenstein? He was meant to be there and was conspicuously absent. Shortly before 5:00 p.m., as the former Connecticut senator Joseph Lieberman interviewed to be director, a staffer came in and handed McGahn a message. It said: Call Rosenstein. McGahn didn't think much of it. Maybe Rosenstein was sick. So a couple of minutes later, McGahn quietly stepped out and ducked into an alcove to return the call.

"I've appointed a special counsel," Rosenstein said. "This is to just pick up where the investigation left off after Comey."

McGahn didn't say anything, but he was intently listening. He knew he would have to explain this to the president in just a moment.

"This is not about you; it's not about me," Rosenstein said. "It's not about people involved in the decision. It's in part about firing Comey, but more broadly it's about Russia."

Rosenstein said he had appointed Mueller, to keep the investigation away from McCabe.

McGahn was baffled. Ten days earlier, Rosenstein appeared to be leading the charge for firing Comey. Now he was appointing a special counsel who would, among other things, be examining the firing of Comey?

As McGahn returned to the Oval Office, Lieberman was still being interviewed. He said nothing about what Rosenstein had told him, but he couldn't hide the distress on his face. At least one person in the room could tell that McGahn had just learned something terrible.

Sessions received a similar message and stepped out to call Rosenstein. When he returned, he locked eyes with McGahn. The interview with Lieberman ended, and McGahn told the president that he and Sessions needed to talk to him before any more interviews, or anything else, could happen. They closed the door to the Oval Office and sat down in front of Trump's desk.

The attorney general tried to take the lead.

"Uh, uh, Mr. President," Sessions stammered. "Uh, the deputy attorney general, uh, has, uh . . ."

Trump shot McGahn a look, *What is this guy talking about?*

McGahn interrupted, slapping his hands down on the Resolute desk. "He's trying to tell you that Rod just appointed a special prosecutor," he said.

It took a few seconds for Trump to absorb this news.

And then he unleashed a torrent. Neither McGahn nor Sessions even had seen Trump—or perhaps any other person—as enraged as the president was in that moment.

Trump's tirade, filled with "motherfuckers" and "you fucking idiots," was remarkable for several reasons, chiefly its duration. And the focus of his most withering attack was Sessions.

"It's your fucking fault!" Trump said to Sessions.

The president knew that a special counsel was a legitimate threat to his presidency and if Sessions hadn't recused himself, Rosenstein would never have had the power to do this. In the president's eyes, Sessions had abandoned him. He had been disloyal.

In the moment, Sessions appeared physically shaken. But Trump did not relent.

"You're *weak*," Trump sneered. "You should *fucking* resign."

Sessions's eyes welled with tears.

"Oh my God," Trump said. "This is terrible. This is the end of my presidency. I'm fucked."

"How could you let this happen, Jeff?" Trump said. "You were supposed to protect me. Everyone tells me if you get one of these independent counsels it ruins your presidency. It takes years and years and I won't be able to do anything. This is the worst thing that ever happened to me."

Ashen and emotional, Sessions said that he would quit. Pence asked to have a moment alone with Trump and Sessions. Then Sessions left the Oval Office. As the attorney general headed for his waiting motorcade, McGahn raced to find Priebus. By the time he reached him, he was out of breath and red in the face.

"We've got a problem," he told Priebus.

"What?" Priebus said.

"We just got a special counsel, and Sessions just resigned," McGahn told him.

"What the hell are you talking about?" Priebus said. "That can't happen."

Priebus and Pence ran to try to stop Sessions from leaving the White House grounds. They reached his motorcade in the White House parking lot and banged on his armored sports utility vehicle. The door opened, and Priebus got in.

"Jeff, what's going on?" Priebus said.

Sessions said he was going to resign.

"You cannot resign. It's not possible. We are going to talk about this right now," Priebus said.

Priebus brought Sessions into his office with Pence and Bannon. Their urgent appeal brought Sessions back from the brink—briefly. He would not be resigning just yet.

But the following morning, Sessions submitted his letter of resignation to Trump in person. The president, perhaps calmed and understanding the implications of his attorney general quitting amid the Mueller appointment, wouldn't accept his resignation. But he did slip the letter into his pocket, giving him something to hold over his attorney general, something that he could use at any point.

Meanwhile that afternoon, on Capitol Hill, the Gang of Eight assembled around a conference table, Democrats on one side, Republicans on the other. McCabe and Rosenstein next to each other. McCabe went first. "As Jim Comey assured you, we'd keep you up to date with the significant developments in this Russia case," McCabe told the lawmakers. "I'm here today to give you an update as to where we are."

While McCabe talked, Senate minority leader Chuck Schumer stared at him while nodding and chewing on his glasses. McConnell, looking dumbstruck, said nothing. To McCabe, the lawmakers seemed somber and resigned.

The only question came from the Speaker of the House, Paul Ryan, who asked McCabe what kind of investigation they had opened on Trump. McCabe laid out how the bureau had opened a two-pronged investigation into the president—one that would look at whether Trump was a counterintelligence threat, and the other that would examine whether he had obstructed justice.

Rosenstein then took over.

"In light of these developments, I've decided to appoint a special counsel," Rosenstein said. "I've appointed Robert Mueller to serve in that capacity."

Lawmakers had many questions for Rosenstein. How long would an investigation like this last? Could Mueller be fired?

That afternoon, I returned to the Washington bureau after a lunch meeting. There was a big commotion around the desk. The Justice Department was about to announce that Mueller had been appointed as a special counsel.

The story I had filed the day before had resulted, in part, in the appointment of a special counsel to investigate the president of the United States. A presidency founded in chaos was now in crisis. The following day, McCabe briefed Mueller and his newly forming team. He felt confident that Mueller would be a great steward of the investigations the bureau had begun. In the days that followed, a public narrative would take hold that Mueller—one of the heroes in the wake of 9/11—had come to investigate Trump's ties to Russia. Whatever he found, Democrats and Republicans said, they would accept his findings, as there was no one who had a better reputation.

★★★

MAY 21, 2017

ONE YEAR, TEN MONTHS, AND TWENTY-EIGHT DAYS UNTIL THE RELEASE OF THE MUELLER REPORT

DEPUTY ATTORNEY GENERAL'S OFFICE—The weekend after his appointment, Mueller sought to fully understand his directives, and began to put together a team of prosecutors. That Sunday, he met with Rosenstein and McCabe to discuss the investigation.

Like brawlers who could not stop going after each other, McCabe and Rosenstein began arguing in front of Mueller. McCabe told Rosenstein that he needed to recuse himself from the investigation, due to his role in firing Comey.

Rosenstein shot back, saying that McCabe was the one who needed to recuse himself, because his wife had accepted money from a Clinton ally for her political campaign, Trump had repeatedly attacked him, and now he was out to avenge Comey's firing.

McCabe, angered by Rosenstein's comments, got up and left the meeting.

Once Rosenstein and Mueller were alone, the special counsel tried to find a middle ground by saying he would still bring FBI agents onto his team but that they would report directly to him, not McCabe.

"You don't need to do anything more; no recusal will be needed," Mueller said, about McCabe. "I will make clear with the agents that they report up through me and not through their chain of command."

The matter of Rosenstein himself was a bit more complicated. Mueller told the deputy attorney general that his team would need to interview him to evaluate whether or not Rosenstein was likely to be a key witness against the president. Following that interview, Rosenstein—who had the ultimate authority to decide if he remained in charge of the investigation—could then make a call on his own recusal.

Two days later, investigators interviewed Rosenstein at the Justice Department, and the silence from Mueller's team that followed told him that there would be no need to recuse himself from his role in overseeing the investigation. Legal experts on television raised questions about Rosenstein's conflict, and Democrats pushed only lightly on the issue, as they now saw Rosenstein—because of his appointment of Mueller—as a potential ally.

In reporting for this book, I learned that Rosenstein's primary reason for remaining in charge of the investigation was his contention that no one had ever told him that the firing of Comey was designed to interfere with the Russia investigation, nor did he believe that Comey's dismissal ultimately had any impact on the investigation.

Secondarily, Rosenstein ascribed a sense of duty to his decision.

"It would be cowardly to recuse without any need," Rosenstein would later say. "Everybody could find a reason so they did not have to deal with it."

ACT FOUR

VI

"HE'S SAYING SOME CRAZY SHIT"

MAY 23, 2017

ONE YEAR, TEN MONTHS, AND TWENTY-SIX DAYS UNTIL THE RELEASE OF THE MUELLER REPORT

McGAHN'S OFFICE ON THE SECOND FLOOR OF THE WEST WING—"I'm not your man," McGahn told the president over the phone.

Six days had passed since Mueller had been appointed as special counsel. Now the president was on the phone from Air Force One, on his first trip to the Middle East, and he had just told McGahn that he wanted him to call the Justice Department and have Mueller removed. Fired.

Trump already had a fairly elaborate three-pronged argument for why Mueller needed to go, including a frivolous contention that the two had once had a dispute about membership fees at Trump National Golf Club in Sterling, Virginia, and so he couldn't possibly investigate the president fairly.

The president's near-immediate impulse to fire yet another figure who was leading an investigation into his conduct and that of his administration was obviously reckless and an extraordinarily bad idea. If the uproar over Comey's firing had rocked the White House, this would raze it. McGahn tried to reason with the president, telling him why he believed he shouldn't try to do it and why the White House counsel wouldn't be going off that particular cliff with Trump if he decided to fire Mueller anyway.

"We'll look like we're still trying to meddle in the investigation," McGahn told the president. "I'm not the right lawyer to do that."

McGahn said that if the president believed the conflicts were such a problem, then Trump's personal lawyer Marc Kasowitz—who was handling everything ranging from defending the president in sexual misconduct lawsuits to the new Mueller investigation—should send a letter to the Department of Justice laying out the conflicts.

"You need your own lawyer. I'm in-house counsel to the White House," McGahn said, explaining the difference between serving as Trump's personal lawyer and being the top lawyer for the executive branch.

Trump did not say what prompted the call. But he had closely watched the media coverage back home during his trip, and earlier that day new signs emerged that Mueller was moving forward with the investigation when the media reported that the Justice Department's ethics officials had cleared Mueller to oversee it.

For McGahn, the Trump presidency had been a string of public embarrassments dominated by Russia, Flynn, Sessions, Comey, Mueller, and Trump's anger about them all. Instead of allowing accomplishments like the judges to stand alone and building on them, Trump spent his private and public time stewing and complaining, creating endless distractions.

Two days after Mueller's appointment, Trump had boarded Air Force One and flown to Riyadh, Saudi Arabia, to begin a nine-day trip through the Middle East and Europe. It was his first time traveling abroad as president, and coming as it did on the heels of a disastrous week, to Trump's aides and the media it seemed inevitable that the trip, too, would be a disaster. But to their surprise, Trump became captivated by the pageantry with which he was greeted, and the gifts lavished on him, and found his footing, carrying out the trip largely in line with the norms set out by his predecessors. In Saudi Arabia, the royal family appealed almost perfectly to Trump's desire to be flattered and treated like a king. They projected Trump's face across five stories of the Ritz-Carlton hotel, where the president was staying. They danced with him at an opulent welcoming ceremony. And they gave him at least eighty-three different gifts before he departed, including a robe lined with cheetah fur and a portrait of himself.

Trump's aides considered the trip a success, largely because he simply had made no major gaffes.

But privately throughout the trip, when Trump was in his plane's cabin, his limousine, or his hotel room, he continued to rage about Mueller. And unknown to McGahn, who had remained back in Washington, Trump had taken Sessions's resignation letter with him on the trip. On the flight from Riyadh to Tel Aviv, Trump had decided to take it out of his pocket while meeting with advisers in his cabin. The president passed it around and asked whether he should accept the attorney general's resignation.

Although he was reluctant to say anything to Trump about it, Priebus thought it was unseemly that the president was being so indelicate with Sessions's resignation letter. Moreover, he was gravely concerned that by advertising his deliberations about whether to fire Sessions so indiscreetly, the president would use the precariousness of Sessions's position to grab the "DOJ by the throat," in order to get whatever he wanted out of Sessions. In a rare attempt by the chief of staff to contain the president, Priebus raised the issue with Trump, inquiring about the letter, in the hopes Trump would give it to him so it could be sent back to Sessions. In response, Trump lied to Priebus. Inexplicably, even though he had passed the letter around moments earlier, he said he had left it in the residence at the White House.

Until this point, McGahn had been willing to go along with Trump's haphazard presidency, largely because he now had more power than he ever could have imagined. There were dozens of open spots in the federal judiciary, and he had the power to influence Trump to make the kinds of appointments that would reshape the country for decades. It was real power, not the showy displays of power that transfixed Trump.

And while Trump had done a lot to inflict damage on his own presidency, McGahn viewed much of the disapproval of Trump's early weeks in office as elites hyperventilating. He was president and had been exceptionally clear about his priorities before the election. And so in McGahn's view, the president had the legal authority to execute actions like the Muslim ban, even while conceding that its rollout had been a disaster. So what if Democrats and the Washington establishment hated it? They were never going to like Trump.

But Trump's desire to fire Mueller as if he were just another political appointee unnerved McGahn. Why was Trump continuing to behave this way? Did he have something to hide? Why did he insist on undermining himself? Why couldn't he just play president?

Trump seemed to think that the appointment of a special counsel—and not just any special counsel, but Mueller—could be tweeted away, avoided, or ignored. It was the worst nonlethal threat a presidency could face. To survive, the conventional wisdom held that he would need to change his behavior. Similar prosecutors who looked into past administrations—Lawrence Walsh, Ken Starr, and Pat Fitzgerald—had turned those White Houses—which were far more capable and professional than Trump's—upside down. Those investigations had flipped aides on each other, and on the president. The investigators got their hands on internal notes, memos, and phone records, wreaking havoc on administrations for years. For McGahn, Trump's move to fire Mueller, combined with the chaotic White House being run by Priebus and Bannon, had brought the presidency to a breaking point. If McGahn had Mueller removed, the investigation of the president would almost certainly widen, and McGahn would be seen as a potential co-conspirator in the president's obstruction. Representing the president had become a hazard for McGahn, and he needed to start thinking about what else he needed to do to protect himself.

He studied the actions of past White House counsels, how they acted in crises and where they had gotten themselves into trouble. He saw that on multiple occasions White House lawyers had jeopardized themselves and their careers by sticking by and enabling their presidents when instead they had a legal and ethical obligation to push back. Two former lawyers—Clinton's first White House counsel, Bernard Nussbaum, and Nixon's third White House counsel, John Dean—were prime examples of people who got caught up in protecting their bosses. Nussbaum found himself in the crossfire of partisan fights on Capitol Hill when House Republicans attacked him as a way of undermining Clinton. He was never criminally charged, but the Republicans accused him of obstructing justice by hiding documents from the FBI. Dean faced something far more significant: criminal problems. In an effort to shield Nixon from the Watergate scandal, Dean paid off the arrested burglars and limited the scope of the government's investigation, and later pleaded guilty to obstructing justice. Now, right before his eyes, McGahn saw himself getting pulled into the same trap. The president wanted to fire the independent investigator who was looking into serious questions about the president's own potentially illegal behavior. By doing so, Trump would certainly be increasing his criminal exposure. And if he followed Trump's directives, it might not be long before McGahn found himself in the same place as Nussbaum (smeared) or Dean (convicted). Over and over again, McGahn told himself he would not turn out like them. No one could afford to be accused of breaking the law. But McGahn, at forty-eight, was not some old Washington hand who could recede into retirement if he got into trouble. He had a reputation to defend and the rest of his career ahead of him, and he needed to be able to make money for at least the next two decades to support his wife and two young children. Abetting criminal activity, destroying his good name, maybe losing his law license—that would be catastrophic.

To avoid that fate, he needed help. Holding back Trump on his own was proving far too difficult and dangerous. Trump's aides were bunched and balkanized, and so he had few allies and was unsure of whom he could trust. He was one of the few on the inside who knew exactly what had gone on and how it would look from the perspective of an investigator like Mueller and his team of prosecutors. Someone had to look over his shoulder, counsel him, and, above all else, keep him out of legal trouble.

The president's lawyer needed his own lawyer.

Two days after Mueller was appointed to take over the investigation of the president, McGahn had met in his office with one of the top white-collar defense lawyers in Washington. The lawyer, Bill Burck, represented prominent clients in dicey circumstances, like FIFA—the international soccer organization that the Justice Department had investigated for corruption—and he checked another two critical boxes for McGahn: He was a Republican, and he had experience working in a White House under siege, because he had also been a top lawyer in the last years of the George W. Bush administration.

McGahn had asked Burck to come into the White House to be the lawyer dedicated to dealing with the Mueller investigation, but Burck had brushed him off. He loved being a private lawyer, traveling the world, and dealing directly with big-time clients—Middle Eastern oil moguls, Fortune 500 companies, and NFL teams—facing complex, serious problems. He made millions of dollars a year, and he and his wife, who had three young kids, lived in a nice neighborhood in Bethesda, Maryland, and had just spent a fortune buying the house next door, knocking it down, and building a beautiful extension onto their home. Burck now had a huge mortgage and couldn't work for government pay. Besides, he had joined the country club down the street and wanted to spend his free time becoming a respectable golfer. A White House job doesn't really allow for that.

"No, never, not a chance," Burck said. "I'm not anywhere close to leaving the private sector and coming in the government. I just can't do it."

What the two men did not discuss was that while they were both Republicans, they essentially had diametrically opposed allegiances and views. Burck's mother was Jamaican, and he had seen enough of Trump's behavior to believe that he was a racist. And he thought that the president could even be a danger to the country. Burck was a Bush Republican and wanted nothing to do with Trump. As a private lawyer, he still maintained a close relationship with George W. Bush and represented him and his presidential library on issues related to the papers from his administration. Burck had been an early supporter of Jeb Bush's presidential bid, donating $2,700—the maximum an individual could give—to his campaign, and an additional $25,000 to a political action committee supporting Bush's candidacy. Whereas McGahn had strong ideological beliefs, Burck was more pragmatic. He thought Trump was destroying the Republican Party, but he declined to publicly become a never-Trumper—why piss off potential paying clients?

McGahn had been appointed to the Federal Election Commission in 2008 by Bush. But he had come to believe that the Bush-era policies of intervention abroad, excessive government spending, and overzealous surveillance had infringed on individual liberties and set the country on a downward trajectory. The middle class was in trouble, and McGahn thought the idea that a so-called establishment Republican like Jeb Bush could beat Clinton was preposterous. For the Republicans to win, they would always need to draw sharp contrasts, and that meant the conservative party had to be conservative and run to the far right. And so while during the Republican primaries McGahn actually thought Trump could win, he'd also decided to represent Trump during the campaign because he thought Trump could help knock Bush out of the race.

In the days after Burck rejected McGahn's offer, McGahn kept on calling him for advice, asking questions about how a White House should position itself to deal with dueling congressional and special counsel investigations. Burck loved being a resource and came to like McGahn. More and more, McGahn would open up to him: *The president is behaving erratically,* he would say, *and you'll never believe what is going on here.* But because they had no professional relationship, McGahn didn't confide too deeply in Burck about what Trump was doing or saying.

Now, as McGahn was facing Trump's attempts to fire Mueller, he came back to Burck with an idea. What if McGahn hired Burck to represent him and the other lawyers in the counsel's office? McGahn told Burck that the lawyers might need someone to represent them if someday they had to answer questions about the Comey firing.

Bingo. That was an arrangement that would work for Burck. It gave him a piece of the action without having to deal with, or defend, Trump himself. Burck dived right in. To fully understand what had occurred around the Comey firing, McGahn and Burck agreed that it would make sense for Burck to come in and conduct an internal investigation of sorts, interviewing McGahn and the handful of other White House lawyers who had knowledge of the firing.

In late May, Burck spent a day in the West Wing and Eisenhower Executive Office Building interviewing the lawyers—without anyone else in the White House knowing. And what he discovered was of great comfort to McGahn. Burck learned that shortly before Trump fired Comey, he'd been warned by McGahn and Dhillon that there could be dire consequences for removing the FBI director.

"If you fire Comey," the lawyers had told Trump, "you're buying yourself a special counsel."

In Burck's view, that statement alone would make building an obstruction of justice case around Comey's dismissal much more difficult. Criminal obstruction of justice hinges on proving that someone had corrupt intent. If Trump knew that firing Comey would only make the investigation worse, how was that obstruction? And best of all to Burck, his clients in the White House counsel's office had done the right thing and dispensed sound legal advice to their client the president, whether he had chosen to follow it or not.

Burck thought that Mueller must instead be training his sights on Flynn's firing, the allegations of collusion with the Russians, or even Trump's finances—none of which concerned McGahn's criminal exposure.

There were other promising signs for McGahn and the White House, Burck reported. During McGahn's discussions with Rosenstein after Mueller's appointment, McGahn had asked the deputy attorney general whether he—McGahn—might need to recuse himself from dealing with the investigation due to his role in the Comey firing. Rosenstein had replied that neither of them had done anything wrong in the firing of Comey, and so no, there would be no need for McGahn to recuse himself. McGahn had also told Burck that Rosenstein's phrasing had left him with the impression that Mueller wouldn't really be focusing his investigation on obstruction of justice.

All good signs, Burck said. If McGahn himself were vulnerable in any way, Rosenstein would almost certainly have told him to take no role in representing the White House on matters regarding the investigation. And in any case, it was Rosenstein who had written the memo that Trump had used as the legal rationale to dismiss the FBI director, and he had also appointed Mueller, and he wasn't recusing himself from overseeing the investigation. If there was a serious obstruction investigation, Rosenstein would at the very least be a witness and would almost certainly not be able to continue in that role.

As the fifth month of the Trump presidency began, in his first official act representing the White House counsel and his staff, Burck had come to believe it was likely that the president and his aides were safe on the obstruction issue. But then, a legal opinion is only as good as the information available to the lawyer producing it. What Burck didn't know is that there was a lot McGahn hadn't told him, particularly that the president had begun a vigorous campaign to fire Mueller and potentially end his investigation. It was not a minor omission. When Burck did learn about Trump's push to fire Mueller, it would utterly change his previously sunny appraisal of the danger his client might face. In fact, the detail that McGahn had neglected to tell Burck would shape the rest of their relationship and bind them together for the next twenty-three months in a way that neither man could have foreseen.

★ ★ ★

JUNE 15, 2017

ONE YEAR, TEN MONTHS, AND THREE DAYS UNTIL THE RELEASE OF THE MUELLER REPORT

THE McGAHN HOME, ALEXANDRIA, VIRGINIA—The twin pressures on McGahn—navigating a poorly run White House and stopping a president from hurting himself—were becoming unbearable. Although McGahn had told Trump that he would not ask for Mueller to be removed, the president continued to badger him on the subject. Late on June 14, *The Washington Post* reported a nightmare scenario for Trump: In spite of the hopeful signs from Rosenstein, Mueller's team was indeed investigating whether Trump had obstructed justice. And of course, as McGahn was by now painfully aware, with this president every day was another opportunity to obstruct justice.

McGahn looked at the story and wondered, Why had Rosenstein given him the impression that Mueller was not seriously looking at obstruction of justice? But McGahn had a more pressing issue. An angry Trump was steaming toward him. That night, Trump called McGahn at home to complain and rage about Mueller, Sessions's recusal, and McGahn's inability to solve it all.

"Where are my fucking lawyers? All I have is Mr. Magoo, Mr. Peepers, and you," Trump said to McGahn, referring to Sessions as Mr. Magoo, the hapless cartoon character from the 1950s, and Rosenstein as Mr. Peepers, the main character in a 1950s sitcom about a dorky teacher.

The call so bothered McGahn that he called Burck, bringing his lawyer in for the first time on Trump's maniacal desire to rid himself of the Mueller investigation.

"I have a real fucking problem," McGahn told him. "I don't want to speak out of school, but he's saying some crazy shit."

"You can't fire Mueller," Burck told McGahn.

The following evening should have been one of celebration for both McGahn and the administration: Neil Gorsuch was receiving his commission, a ceremony of sorts for his induction onto the Supreme Court. For McGahn, it was a short but bright moment of glory. Every day in the White House had been far worse than he could have imagined, but helping to shepherd Gorsuch through the nomination and confirmation process to a lifetime appointment was the most significant accomplishment of McGahn's life, so for him the event was a moment of true celebration. It also reminded McGahn of the scores of additional federal court posts he could fill over the following months; maybe he really could survive the Trump administration by focusing on judges. But how the evening unfolded demonstrated all of the problems with the Trump administration. The attorney general failed to show, Trump openly sneered at Rosenstein, and within thirty minutes of returning home, Trump was again defying McGahn's counsel and tweeting his complaints about the Mueller investigation.

"Why is that Hillary Clintons family and Dems dealings with Russia are not looked at, but my non-dealings are?" Trump tweeted.

The next morning, he tweeted again, about Rosenstein: "I am

being investigated for firing the FBI Director by the man who told me to fire the FBI Director! Witch Hunt."

McGahn's frustrations went beyond Trump, because he pinned a lot of the blame for the dysfunction on Priebus and Bannon. The chief of staff and the chief strategist were often unwilling to help McGahn when he tried to curb Trump's destructive impulses. Besides their inability to help McGahn stand up to Trump, they had acted, at times, in ways that McGahn thought were unbecoming of senior White House officials. One stark example of this had occurred in the first few months of the administration. Bannon had brought Tom Fitton, the head of the far-right-wing advocacy group Judicial Watch, to meet with Trump in the Oval Office to lobby the president to have the State Department speed up its production of documents and emails related to Hillary Clinton's use of a private email account. Sure, Judicial Watch had been one of Trump's greatest supporters, as it continuously pushed conspiracies about Clinton and other Trump enemies. But throwing open the door of the Oval Office for such an extreme partisan to discuss how the levers of government could be used against a rival showed bad judgment.

Working for Donald Trump and in this atmosphere was like parenting unruly toddlers, and for the second time in only five months on the job McGahn was ready to quit.

Instead of just impulsively walking away, he told Priebus and other White House officials that he was taking that Friday off. He needed a break, and it was his birthday. Then that Saturday was one of his young son's birthdays, and the family planned to take a trip an hour and a half south to the amusement park Kings Dominion in Virginia. McGahn loved riding roller coasters and thought it would all be a nice distraction. Sunday was Father's Day.

But the weekend got off to an odd start. That Friday evening, as McGahn flipped through the channels at home, he saw on Fox News a report that Trump had hired John Dowd—a retired Washington lawyer who had made his name in the late 1980s investigating the baseball star Pete Rose in a gambling probe—to be his personal lawyer. It was an unusual way for a White House counsel to learn whom the president had hired to be his personal lawyer in an investigation that directly involved the president's conduct in office. It was yet another example of Trump's lack of discipline. If the administration was going to survive the special counsel's investigation, the conventional wisdom said, everybody would need to be on the same page.

On Saturday morning, McGahn slept in. By the time he got up and looked at his phone, he saw that he had several messages from the White House switchboard.

Trump was looking for him.

Oh, great, McGahn thought.

At 2:23 p.m., Trump, who had just arrived at Camp David, finally reached McGahn. He'd had enough. It was time for Mueller to go. McGahn, Trump said, should call Rosenstein and have him remove Mueller because of his conflicts.

"You gotta do this," Trump told McGahn. "You gotta call Rod."

McGahn was furious that Trump had bothered him at home on his birthday weekend, and about an issue he had already made himself clear on. Trump was so impulsive that he obviously didn't care that firing the special counsel would imperil his presidency. Instead of erupting back at Trump, McGahn tried to stall the president. But this time, it wasn't working.

Several minutes later, Trump called back. He was manic.

"Call Rod, and tell Rod that Mueller has conflicts and can't be the special counsel," Trump said. "Mueller has to go," Trump said again, instructing McGahn to call him back immediately after he had made the call to Rosenstein.

McGahn had no intention of calling Rosenstein. He believed that if he even broached the subject with Rosenstein, the deputy attorney general might turn around and resign to ensure a safe landing for his reputation after the blowup over the Comey firing. It would also give Democrats and the media their Nixon moment, their Saturday Night Massacre, their Watergate echo of the moment when Nixon's attorney general and deputy attorney general had resigned after being ordered by the president to fire the special prosecutor investigating Nixon's campaign and administration. The moment that had transformed that scandal into a full-blown constitutional crisis. On the phone, McGahn didn't want to fight with

Trump; the easiest way to get off the call, he knew, was to give Trump the impression that he would call Rosenstein.

McGahn hung up the phone and decided he was going to resign. If Trump had had enough, well, so had he.

Since the first days of the administration, McGahn had instructed the lawyers in the counsel's office to have their resignation letters ready in case they needed to quickly leave. McGahn had carried his around with him, and now it was time.

President Donald J. Trump
The White House
Washington, DC 20501

Dear Mr. President:
By this letter, I hereby tender my resignation as Counsel to the President, effective immediately.

Sincerely,
Donald F. McGahn II

McGahn called Burck, telling him what Trump had told him to do and that he planned to resign.

Burck agreed with his client's decision.

"You cannot fire Mueller," Burck said. "You're walking yourself into a huge problem."

As McGahn's lawyer, Burck was most concerned about his client's criminal exposure, and playing a role in firing the special counsel would certainly have made McGahn a co-conspirator in Mueller's obstruction of justice investigation. On top of quitting, Burck told McGahn, he needed to take additional measures to protect himself. He instructed McGahn that he should avoid telling anyone—including his chief of staff, Annie Donaldson—why he was resigning. There were several reasons for this. One was that Burck was worried about McGahn's name being at all associated with Mueller's firing. If Trump did end up dismissing the special counsel, Burck did not want White House officials to have first heard of the idea from

McGahn. This decision would later have an impact on investigators' ability to substantiate McGahn's account of the incident.

After he got off the phone with Burck, McGahn called Donaldson. Without telling her why, he told her to meet him at the White House to help pack up his office. Because McGahn had done little by way of decorating his office, the packing went quickly. He had been unsure from the start how long he'd last in the job. He and Donaldson carried his belongings to his car, and McGahn then walked through the West Wing with his letter in hand looking for someone to give it to. It turned out that because it was the weekend, there were logistical obstacles to resigning. Trump was at Camp David, and there were few top White House officials—no Priebus or Bannon—in the West Wing.

Unable to resign, McGahn left the White House with the letter and drove home, believing he was departing the White House for the final time. Resigning would be a formality at this point.

It's unclear what happened next. But McGahn did not call the president and resign or email his resignation letter. Perhaps he got cold feet. That evening he did speak with Bannon and Priebus by phone. When McGahn said he was quitting, Bannon replied that he shouldn't do it and that he would get Trump to back off. Concentrate on the judges, Bannon said.

Trump and McGahn did not speak again that day, but from Camp David, Trump continued to foment his rebellion against Mueller to whoever would listen.

On Monday, McGahn dutifully returned to the office.

★★★

SUMMER 2017

AIRPORT PARKING LOT—I held my phone in my right hand just as the text came in.

"Landed."

"Great, I'll meet you at arrivals," I wrote back.

It was a little before 5:00 on a weekend morning in the summer of 2017. It was still dark. I pulled my mother's 2004 Volvo station wagon, which I had been given months earlier, up to arrivals and easily found him. He got in and we were off.

"How was your trip?"

Fine.

We made small talk. I said something about the weather. Then I gingerly moved the conversation toward Special Counsel Mueller.

I recounted some of the stories in the press that week and asked him what he thought was going on. He responded with a blunt assessment.

"Mueller's going for it on obstruction," he said.

I repeated those words back to myself in my head: *Mueller's going for it on obstruction.*

In a sense, I knew what that meant. Mueller's team wanted to build some sort of obstruction case against the president. But what did that exactly mean? Mueller's team could not indict the president under Justice Department policy.

I just wanted to keep him talking, so I repeated back to him what he said.

"So you think he's going for the president directly?"

The person said he did. He threw out some possibilities. Maybe, despite the department's policy that a sitting president could not be indicted, Mueller might try to move to charge the president. Trump had behaved so belligerently, he said, there was no way Mueller could look the other way.

Mueller had assembled a team of what we thought were some of the toughest, most skilled prosecutors in the country. Trump had, at the least, behaved unconventionally as president, and at worst his conduct had been criminal. It was hard to imagine, with all of Trump's attacks on the institutions of government, that there would not be some sort of immune response triggered, in this case from Mueller's prosecutors. Here, someone I trusted, who had visibility into what Mueller's office was thinking, was telling me that for Trump it was very serious indeed. He said Trump's lawyers had their heads in the sand and had little sense of how urgent the situation was. To make it all more consequential, Trump had shown no interest in curbing his behavior.

Most Washington reporters were more focused on the possibility that the Trump campaign had colluded with the Russians in their attacks on the election of 2016. I drove the source all the way to his house and dropped him off. I was going to have to focus on obstruction.

★ ★ ★

JULY 19, 2017

ONE YEAR, EIGHT MONTHS, AND THIRTY DAYS UNTIL THE RELEASE OF THE MUELLER REPORT

OVAL OFFICE—"The killers are here," Trump said cheerfully as I shook his hand.

I was joined by two White House correspondents from the *Times,* Maggie Haberman and Peter Baker, and we had just arrived in the Oval Office to speak with the president in an open-ended interview. It was my first time meeting him. From behind the Resolute desk, Trump began talking. Trying to decode the president's patterns of thought can at times be like trying to unzip fog, and that morning we were in for a master class in non sequitur. He sprinted from one unrelated topic to the next. Within the first few minutes, he discussed his own struggles with getting a health-care bill passed, and did we know that Hillary Clinton had failed to get one passed during her husband's presidency, and that Obama had taken more than a year with a healthy Senate majority, then straight to his recent one-night trip to France for the Bastille Day celebrations, and how much he enjoyed the military parade he watched there with the French president, Macron, and his desire to re-create it with the American military in Washington. Three nonconsecutive times he mentioned how much he loved holding hands with Macron. He then talked about Napoleon and the difficulty of fighting a war in Russia in the middle of winter.

Russia, of course, was on our minds, too. We wanted to get the president on the record about the Mueller investigation, the Comey firing, and the question of whether his campaign had colluded with the Russians. Baker took the first stab, asking Trump about a one-on-one conversation the president had had with Putin at the G20 summit a week and a half earlier.

The president happily set the scene for us. The G20 leaders, their spouses, and a few others were spread across a giant table in Hamburg, Germany. Trump had been seated between the wife of the Argentinian president, Mauricio Macri, and the wife of the Japanese prime minister, Shinzo Abe. The prime minister's wife spoke no English. Late into the meal—which Trump said he enjoyed very much—he had gotten up to go around the large table to say hello to his own wife, Melania, who happened to be seated next to Putin.

"While I was there, I said hello to Putin," Trump said. "Really, pleasantries more than anything else. It was not a long conversation, but it was, you know, could be fifteen minutes. Just talked about—things. Actually, it was very interesting, we talked about adoption."

Our ears perked up.

"You did?" Maggie said.

"We talked about Russian adoption," he continued. "Yeah. I always found that interesting. Because, you know, he ended that years ago. And I actually talked about Russian adoption with him."

Trump said it was notable that Putin had brought up adoption because Trump's son Don Jr. had just been in the news for his discussions with Russians about adoption.

More than two weeks earlier, my colleagues had reported that Don Jr., Jared Kushner, and the campaign chairman, Paul Manafort, had met at Trump Tower during the campaign with Russians offering dirt on Hillary Clinton. Don Jr. said that the meeting had largely focused on the issue of reinstating American adoptions of Russian orphans.

Unprompted, Trump defended his son's choice to take the meeting. "As I've said—most other people, you know, when they call up and say, 'By the way, we have information on your opponent,' I think most politicians—I was just with a lot of people, they said, 'Who wouldn't have taken a meeting like that?'"

It was a rhetorical question, begging for a proper answer, but was quickly followed by another swirl of free association—North Korea, Crimea, Syria, sarin gas.

Baker continually refocused Trump back to the email that the Russians had sent his son.

"All I know is this: When somebody calls up and they say, 'We have infor—'" Trump said.

Not finishing the thought, he swerved to the dossier and the allegation about the hookers and Obama's bed during Trump's trip to Moscow in 2013. The president said he had been in Moscow for only one day and that when Comey told him about the dossier in January at Trump Tower, he had known it was "really made-up junk" and "such a phony deal."

"In my opinion, he shared it so that I would think he had it out there."

"As leverage?" I asked.

"Yeah, I think so," he affirmed. "In retrospect. In retrospect."

Believing that a dossier of made-up junk might be used as leverage showed a highly sinister view of the world. But never mind, because in firing Comey, "I think I did a great thing for the American people."

"But look at the headache it's caused," I responded.

In an instant of quiet space a moment later, I asked one of the questions I'd come in with at the top of my notebook: What did Trump understand to be the scope of what Mueller could look at in his investigation?

Trump said he didn't know, because nobody from the investigation had contacted him about anything.

"Because I have done nothing wrong," he said.

Unbidden, he began to rage about Sessions's recusal and Rosenstein's appointment of Mueller.

"Sessions never should have recused himself, and if he was going to recuse himself, he should have told me before he took the job, and I would have picked somebody else."

This statement from the president would be big news within hours, because it was clear that he thought it was the attorney general's role to protect him from investigations, and in recusing himself from anything to do with the Russia matter, Sessions had, he felt, left him vulnerable. Personal loyalty to the president is not of course in the attorney general's job description. Sessions could not have known when Trump nominated him to run the Justice Department that a statement he made during his confirmation hearing to Senator Al Franken of Minnesota about his contacts with the Russians would force him to recuse himself from involvement with the Russia investigation, and lead to him becoming a singular object of the president's ire. But the velocity of this Trump monologue did not allow for nuance or the fact-checking of every single utterance, and it's harder to interrupt the president of the United States—especially one who speaks like a steamroller—than I thought it would be.

In the case of a president like this president, interviews are of only limited utility. Interviews will give you insight. Journalism will get you the truth. As Orwell said, journalism is about writing something that someone doesn't want you to write. Everything else is public relations.

"How do you take a job and then recuse yourself?" Trump continued. "If he would have recused himself before the job, I would have said, 'Thanks, Jeff, but I can't, you know, I'm not going to take you.' It's extremely unfair—and that's a mild word—to the president. So he recuses himself. I then end up with a second man, who's a deputy."

Baker again attempted to steer him back to the question of whether Mueller would be passing a red line if he looked at his finances. But Trump wanted to talk about Rosenstein's potential conflicts and said that he had a big hand in the Comey firing.

"Look, there are so many conflicts that everybody has," he said.

Before our time came to an end, I again wanted to know if he thought Mueller would be crossing some sort of red line if he were to investigate Trump's finances.

"Would it be a breach of what his actual charge is?" Maggie asked.

Trump said it "would be a violation," but of what it was not clear, and he wasn't able to say before immediately turning into a cul-de-sac about how he'd never done business in Russia and that his involvement with the Miss Universe pageant in Moscow had been minimal. It seemed as if he had logically connected a question about his finances with an answer about the extent to which he did or did not have business dealings in Russia.

"Would you fire Mueller if he went outside of certain parameters of what his charge is?" Maggie said, focusing her question.

"I can't answer that question," he said, "because I don't think it's going to happen."

McGahn only found out that Trump was giving an interview or what he might have said when we published our story about it. He knew then that Trump's fixation on punishing and humiliating Sessions had only intensified. At a greater level, the president was now in an open public war with his Justice Department, adding yet another ingredient to a smoldering pile of problems. Despite this and the heavily negative reaction to the interview, Trump was pleased with the coverage and the headlines it created. We got back word from the White House that the interview had been therapeutic for Trump, because he felt much better after publicly airing his grievances with Sessions.

With McGahn's persistent refusals to follow his order to fire the special counsel, Trump was undeterred and continued searching for someone who would do as he said. Although he had the power to fire Mueller, Sessions, and everyone else in the Justice Department, he appeared afraid to do it himself. Hours before we interviewed Trump in the Oval Office, the president, without telling McGahn, had met there with someone he thought might be the person for the job: his first campaign manager, Corey Lewandowski. In the middle of the campaign, Lewandowski himself had been fired by Trump, but like many others, Trump still took his calls and Lewandowski still said nice things about the president.

At the most basic level, government is supposed to be run by those inside the government. That precept ensures accountability. When the Article II branch—the executive—had been argued into existence by Madison and Hamilton in the Federalist Papers and then ratified in 1788, the idea was that presidents and those who worked directly for them would execute the executive functions under the Constitution, and legislative and judiciary branches would be able to "counteract" (Madison's word) the president's power should they need to.

But it's harder to counteract the power of a freelancer. Lewandowski had never joined the administration, but he had monetized his ties to the president through consulting contracts and book deals and was holding out hope that Trump would someday make him the White House chief of staff. During the campaign, Lewandowski had also served as a literal enforcer for the president, going so far as to get himself charged with misdemeanor battery in Florida in 2016 for grabbing a reporter who tried to approach Trump and ask him a question. Florida prosecutors ultimately decided not to pursue the charges.

In the Oval Office, Trump was getting an update from Lewandowski about a project they had discussed several weeks earlier. The previous month, Trump had asked Lewandowski to confront Sessions and persuade him to unrecuse himself from overseeing the Russia investigation. Specifically, the president wanted Lewandowski to tell Sessions to give a speech that lauded Trump and reestablished his control over the Mueller investigation. Trump had even dictated the exact language he wanted Sessions to use.

"I know that I recused myself from certain things having to do with specific areas," Lewandowski had scribbled down as the president dictated.

"But our POTUS . . . is being treated very unfairly. He shouldn't have a Special Prosecutor/Counsel b/c he hasn't done anything wrong. I was on the campaign w/ him for nine months, there were no Russians involved with him. I know it for a fact b/c I was there. He didn't do anything wrong except he ran the greatest campaign in American history.

"Now a group of people want to subvert the Constitution of the United States," Lewandowski wrote down. "I am going to meet with the special prosecutor to explain this is very unfair and let the special prosecutor move forward with investigating election meddling for future elections so that nothing can happen in future elections."

Since Trump first talked to Lewandowski, Sessions had still not given the speech, nor had he reasserted his control over the investigation. And the investigation had appeared only to intensify as the media reported that Mueller had staffed up with a team of experienced prosecutors—many of whom were Democrats—and the news had broken about the Trump Tower meeting during the campaign where the Russians had offered dirt on Clinton.

Now Trump wanted to know what Lewandowski had done with his demand.

What Lewandowski held back on telling Trump was that he had been concerned about discussing such a sensitive issue with Sessions. Lewandowski wanted to avoid talking to Sessions about it over the phone or in person at the Justice Department. He had scheduled a meeting with the attorney general at Lewandowski's personal office, but Sessions, after initially agreeing to see him there, had called it off.

Lewandowski told the president that he would follow through and would soon be communicating his message—and the speech—to the attorney general.

But by that night, after our interview was published in the *Times,* there would be no further need for Lewandowski to privately meet with Sessions. The president had loudly and clearly told the attorney general exactly what he thought of him.

★★★

JULY 22, 2017

ONE YEAR, EIGHT MONTHS, AND TWENTY-SEVEN DAYS UNTIL THE RELEASE OF THE MUELLER REPORT

ABOARD THE AIRCRAFT CARRIER *GERALD R. FORD* IN NORFOLK, VIRGINIA—McGahn watched as external factors continued to send Trump spiraling. On Friday night, *The Washington Post* reported that American intelligence intercepts showed that the Russian ambassador, Sergey Kislyak, had told his bosses in Russia that he had spoken with Sessions during the presidential race about campaign-related matters, more proof that Sessions hadn't told the truth in his confirmation hearing and another affirmation of his decision to recuse himself from the Russia investigation. The story once again tied Sessions to negative headlines about Russia and resurrected the recusal issue for Trump.

The following morning, Trump suggested that Clinton should be investigated, just like him.

"So many people are asking why isn't the A.G. or Special Council looking at the many Hillary Clinton or Comey crimes. 33,000 e-mails deleted?" Trump tweeted at 7:44 that morning.

The tweet was part of Trump's increasingly brazen effort to use the presidency to push an aura of criminality onto his former opponent. In an interview with the *Times* after his victory in November, Trump had said he was dropping his threats from the campaign to prosecute Clinton, saying that the best way to put a vicious campaign behind the country was to move on. But as he came under increased scrutiny in the White House, he began reversing course, saying that she, too, needed to be investigated.

As he flew on Marine One en route to Norfolk, Virginia, for the christening of a new aircraft carrier, the *Gerald R. Ford,* Trump decided it was time to oust Sessions, and he knew just the person to do it: Priebus. Trump told Priebus that Sessions needed to go. The president said it was Priebus's job to get Sessions to quit and that he was expecting a fresh resignation letter on his desk by that evening.

From the deck of the aircraft carrier, unsure of what to do, Priebus called McGahn, who only a month earlier had faced his own similar showdown with the president. Once the situation was explained, McGahn quickly recognized just how big a mess Trump was about to make for himself. First, the White House counsel and the chief of staff considered resigning themselves, right then and there—abandoning ship before Trump sank it completely. But then McGahn had another idea: Burck had been able to help maneuver him out of such requests from Trump; perhaps he could help Priebus as well. McGahn called his lawyer.

"I need you to talk to Priebus," McGahn told Burck.

Burck agreed, and McGahn called Priebus back to give him Burck's number, which Priebus scribbled down on a piece of White House stationery.

Still on the *Gerald R. Ford,* Priebus called Burck. Around the time of their call, Trump was giving a speech on the deck of the ship, admiring the "beautiful" $13 billion vessel and calling on the sailors in the audience to support his increased military spending proposals.

"Here's what's going on," Priebus told Burck. "He wants me to get Sessions's resignation."

Burck told his new client that he could not follow through on the president's demand. He said that if Trump continued to insist on it, both Priebus and McGahn needed to resign to protect themselves from being accused of obstructing justice.

Back in Washington that afternoon, Trump badgered Priebus to the point where Priebus assumed he was about to get fired over his refusal to oust Sessions.

"Did you get it?" Trump said. "Are you working on it?"

Priebus intended to follow Burck's instructions, but he was also afraid of the president. Digging himself in deeper, he told Trump that he would find a way to oust the attorney general. It was only later that day that Priebus hit on a short-term solution: He would tell the president that Sessions's ouster would lead other top Justice Department officials to resign en masse. That bought Priebus a few days.

Once again, Trump had been stymied behind the scenes. But he continued with the same rhetoric. On July 25, he again publicly attacked Sessions while simultaneously advocating for having the Justice Department prosecute Clinton.

"Attorney General Jeff Sessions has taken a VERY weak position on Hillary Clinton crimes (where are E-mails & DNC server) & Intel leakers!" Trump tweeted.

Message received. At the Justice Department, Sessions wrote a new resignation letter, and he would keep it in his pocket for the rest of his time as attorney general. Three days after the tweet, Trump fired Priebus.

For Burck, the incident involving Priebus showed him how dangerous and unusual a situation his clients found themselves in with the president and the challenge he had in helping to guide them. In the span of two months, Burck had gone from a complete outsider at the Trump White House to the voice on the other end of the phone for half a dozen senior White House officials scrambling to contain an unbound president and protect themselves at the same time. On long conference calls with other clients—like European companies in trouble with the Justice Department and Middle Eastern investors trying to do business in the United States—Burck's mind would often shift back to the intractable situation his clients had with the president. Burck had had a window into Trump's behavior for only a short period of time. He had never met Trump but could see through the profile emerging from his clients how the president was a mess, constantly creating legal problems for himself and for those around him while simultaneously testing the system in ways that had never before been contemplated. On top of it all, Burck believed there was a possibility the entire situation could spin out of control if Trump took a drastic measure—like firing Mueller or prosecuting a rival—and Trump was removed from office. Even though Burck thought Trump was awful and unfit to be president, the consequences of having him removed could potentially be worse. The entire fabric of the country, Burck thought, might unravel because 40 percent of Americans would see the removal as a coup, believe Trump had been overthrown, and resort to violence. The country might never recover from that, he thought. To head all of that off, his clients needed to be there to protect Trump from his worst impulses and protect the country from Trump.

"It's going to lead to much bigger problems for everyone," Burck later said. "He will get thrown out of office even before there's a report, and you will have the deplorables and everyone at war with each other."

The most important tenet of Burck's strategy was keeping his clients out of legal trouble. Even though Burck believed the country's future might hang in the balance, he knew that first and foremost it was his job to ensure that his clients did not break the law so that they might stand a chance of emerging from the administration with their reputations and livelihoods intact. The Mueller investigation came with a complicating factor that made it different from a typical Department of Justice investigation. There was widespread pressure on Mueller to release some sort of report. That meant that not only did his clients have legal exposure but their reputations were on the line. The investigators may stipulate that his clients did nothing wrong. But if Trump was accused of breaking the law and they were depicted as enabling him, it could ruin their names and destroy their careers. All of the Watergate co-conspirators carried the stain of their association with that administration for the rest of their lives. For Burck, to protect his clients' legal and reputational exposure, the answer was simple: He told his clients that if Trump tells you to do something and you believe it could be interpreted, even in the slightest, as illegal and potentially obstructing the investigation, don't do it. Either tell Trump to do it himself or tell Trump whatever he wants to hear to get out of the conversation, pretend as if you were going to do it, and then wait Trump out until he becomes preoccupied with something else. Burck reminded his clients that they had failed to do this with the Comey firing, and now that rash act had blossomed into an existential threat to the presidency.

"Start a pattern of hearing what he has to say and not doing it," Burck told his clients.

No doctrine is foolproof, and the Burck doctrine was no different. But there was a pattern to Trump's behavior that Burck had discerned that made him believe that stalling could contain the president: Despite Trump's unparalleled power as president, he seemed afraid to take actions himself.

"Ultimately, he doesn't want to do things himself," Burck reminded his clients.

That meant that Trump would often turn to one of his top aides, like McGahn or Priebus, to carry out his desired moves.

In nearly all other situations, a white-collar defense lawyer like Burck would tell his clients that they needed to quit in order to stop working for a boss who was telling them to do things that were potentially illegal. But Burck wanted his clients to remain in their positions. If Burck's clients quit or were fired, Trump would likely just replace them with more compliant, less principled people, who would be less squeamish about carrying out his every request, or even be initiators. After all, Trump had repeatedly told McGahn that he wanted a lawyer in the model of Roy Cohn—dirty fixer extraordinaire. It was challenging enough with Trump as president; the last thing the White House needed was a support staff of Roy Cohns.

"Don's view was it was his finger in the dike and 'if I go this entire thing collapses,'" Burck later said. "The problem with the collapse was not political; it was existential. There are going to be riots in the streets and this guy won't go quietly and there will be a total political meltdown."

Given Trump's unusual attraction to Russia and public taunting of Comey and others, a significant portion of the country believed Trump might be a Manchurian candidate who was using the powers of the presidency to protect himself. But Burck, through his clients, was hearing what Trump was saying behind closed doors to those closest to him and believed that Trump's problem was that he was simply stupid. Trump showed no sense of understanding how the government functioned and the norms that governed Washington.

"He's doing stupid shit," Burck said, "because he's a stupid person."

For Burck, though, it all came back to how removing Trump would create an everlasting fissure in the country, potentially inciting violence. Burck believed that based on everything he had seen until this point, the Justice Department was unlikely to find that Trump's moves—like firing Comey—broke the law. But Trump needed to be stopped from doing anything like that again, because that could be the end.

"The political moment can't deal with that type of meltdown, and if he does something like prosecuting Hillary Clinton and Jim Comey, it could create a real problem," Burck told me.

★★★

JULY 31, 2017

ONE YEAR, EIGHT MONTHS, AND EIGHTEEN DAYS UNTIL THE RELEASE OF THE MUELLER REPORT

McGAHN'S OFFICE ON THE SECOND FLOOR OF THE WEST WING—A bespectacled man with long gray hair and a large looping handlebar mustache walked into McGahn's office and announced that he had some good news.

The man, Ty Cobb, had joined the White House and in a matter of weeks leapfrogged McGahn as the most notable lawyer to Trump on the president's staff. Along with John Dowd, the lawyer who was assisting Trump from outside the government, Cobb was tasked with handling the White House's response to the special counsel investigation. It had been a long time since McGahn had heard anything that could be considered good news when it came to the investigation, so he was eager to hear what Cobb had to say.

Cobb told McGahn that he had just sat down with a representative of Mueller's team. Mueller, Cobb said, was conducting a mere box-checking exercise that would quickly resolve itself as long as the White House cooperated. All Mueller really wanted to do, Cobb said, was perform a few perfunctory interviews with White House officials about the Comey and Flynn firings.

Great, McGahn thought, *maybe this won't be so bad after all.*

But McGahn's momentary relief quickly subsided when Cobb started ticking off the names of the aides that Mueller's team said they wanted to speak with: Priebus, McGahn, and Spicer. *Holy shit,* McGahn thought, *we are the true inner circle, the people closest to Trump, who have seen his worst behavior.* Such an aggressive request, McGahn believed, signaled that, contrary to Cobb's rosy interpretation, Mueller's team was actually gunning for the president. To McGahn, this meant the White House should from then on approach dealing with Mueller with greater caution.

But making it all worse, in McGahn's eyes, Cobb said that Trump wanted the aides to talk to Mueller openly and offer whatever documents they had, without a fight. That strategy dumbfounded McGahn. Why would the president let someone come in from the outside and comb through whatever they wanted searching for evidence of crimes?

McGahn knew the president had done and said things regarding the Mueller investigation that Cobb likely did not know about. If prosecutors had direct access to McGahn and could learn everything he knew, there would, at the least, be serious questions about whether Trump had tried to obstruct justice. After all, McGahn and Priebus—two of the White House's top officials and two of the people Mueller had asked to talk to—had been so concerned that Trump was breaking the law that they hired a lawyer, Burck, to help guide them through the situation.

What Cobb did not tell McGahn is that he and Dowd had sold the president on a full cooperation strategy that Dowd believed would bring an end to the investigation by Labor Day. He had also told the president that he could even get Mueller to put out a statement saying Trump was not under investigation. Nearly all previous White Houses that faced investigations had conducted internal reviews of documents and interviewed aides to determine the facts and whether the president or any of his aides had criminal exposure. And presidents almost always fought to stop their White House counsels from cooperating with investigators, and lawyers, because of attorney-client privilege, were rarely allowed to speak with the authorities. In the normal run of things for a White House under investigation, competent counsel would do their best to hermetically seal the executive mansion.

But Dowd and Cobb had taken Trump at his word that he had done nothing wrong and were moving quickly to cooperate to bring it all to an end. And central to their plan was handing over McGahn.

For many years, Cobb and Dowd had been considered past their prime and no longer powerhouse Washington lawyers. It is unlikely that another president would have selected either of them to defend against such an existential threat as the Mueller investigation.

But with the urging of Kushner, Trump had hired Dowd, who touted his experience as a Marine as a way to relate with Mueller. Dowd, who was working out of his home office, then brought on Cobb to deal with the investigation from inside the White House.

"Trump's bringing on the pterodactyls to save us," McGahn told others at the time. "It's like *Night at the Museum*. Dowd's trying to rig it with his compatriot from the Hall of Fame of yesteryear."

After the meeting, McGahn was concerned that Cobb's decision could be bad for both himself and the White House. If Trump followed Cobb's advice, the question would change from whether Mueller would learn about Trump's obstructive behavior to whether he thought his obstructive behavior violated the law.

McGahn called Burck and tried to piece together what might be going on.

Besides incompetence, they failed to come up with a rationale for Trump's decision. McGahn and Burck both thought it was almost malpractice to allow Mueller to interview McGahn without some sort of initial fight. Mueller appeared to be knocking on the White House door. Why welcome him in?

"No, tell him no," Burck said to McGahn. "He can't talk to the lawyers."

Regardless of what McGahn thought, he was in no place to make that argument to the president because he had fallen out of favor with Trump over his refusal to dismiss Mueller. Still, he wanted to stop the interview from happening. He had witnessed several acts that prosecutors could easily see as obstruction. He had pressured Sessions to remain in control of the Russia investigation, and Trump had leaned on him relentlessly to fire Mueller. If McGahn detailed those episodes during an interview, an overzealous prosecutor might try to rope him into an obstruction of justice charge. Additionally, Burck, like most defense lawyers, wanted to head off an interview for his client because he believed that allowing McGahn to sit for one would only open him up to the possibility of being prosecuted for making false statements. To try to avoid the interview, Burck reached out to Cobb, believing he could reason with him about why the White House's approach was wrong.

"Why would you cooperate this way?" Burck asked Cobb. "You have multiple legal issues you could raise."

Burck said no other White House would hand the aides closest to the president—including the White House counsel—right over to prosecutors. He asked Cobb about why he had not conducted an internal review to learn what witnesses knew.

Cobb said the president had told him he had done nothing wrong. Anyway, if they fought Mueller, they would lose in court. Because of those factors, an internal investigation was unnecessary, Cobb said.

Burck said he thought he was making a grave mistake.

"You don't know what you don't know," Burck said to Cobb. "You guys don't know what your witnesses are going to say."

Burck knew that he knew more than Cobb. He had counseled McGahn through the Mueller firing attempt just weeks before advising Priebus through Trump's attempt to oust Sessions.

Burck and McGahn continued to confer about the White House's decision. Their inescapable conclusion was that Trump and his lawyers were setting up McGahn to take the fall. If Trump ever got accused of obstruction of justice, he would say that he was just listening to his lawyer.

"Nobody in their right mind would say, here's my lawyer, he's been involved in all of the serious and controversial matters, I'm going to send him in to talk to federal investigators, I don't want to know what he has to say, I don't care what he has to say, and he can answer any question he wants," Burck said to McGahn.

Then, in mid-September, one of my colleagues in the Washington bureau, the reporter Ken Vogel, went to lunch with a source at BLT Steak, the restaurant next to the *Times*' Washington bureau. Sitting at a table on the sidewalk in front of the restaurant, Vogel and the source ordered lunch. Shortly thereafter, the source spotted Cobb sitting at the table next to them.

"Isn't that the Trump lawyer?" the source asked.

Vogel turned his head slightly, noticing "the unmistakable visage" of Cobb, who was eating with Dowd, openly discussing some of the most sensitive issues related to the president's decision to cooperate with the Mueller investigation. Vogel took out his phone and began typing notes.

What occurred would play an integral role in how McGahn would approach his cooperation and demonstrated an incredible lapse of judgment by Cobb and Dowd. Within earshot of all those sitting around, Cobb described one White House lawyer he was working with as "a McGahn spy," adding that McGahn had "a couple documents locked in a safe" that Cobb wanted access to. Cobb said that one colleague had leaked to the media and tried to oust the president's son-in-law, Kushner, who had a tense relationship with McGahn.

When Vogel published a story based on what he had overheard, it erased any doubt in McGahn's mind that the president and his lawyers were setting him up to take the fall. McGahn settled on his own strategy of cooperation with Mueller's prosecutors. He had to make sure that Mueller's team learned about what was going on inside the White House from him, before they found it out from anyone else. McGahn had to show them that he had nothing to hide.

★★★

SEPTEMBER 11, 2017

ONE YEAR, SEVEN MONTHS, AND SEVEN DAYS UNTIL THE RELEASE OF THE MUELLER REPORT

COBB'S WINDOWLESS OFFICE ON THE GROUND FLOOR OF THE WHITE HOUSE—Dowd and Cobb continued to tell the president that the faster they cooperated, the quicker it would be over.

But by late summer more signs were beginning to emerge that that was not at all the case. And in the second week of September, Cobb circulated an Excel file to other lawyers in the counsel's office that laid out some of the first document requests from Mueller's prosecutors. The special counsel was casting a very wide net.

"Privileged and Confidential," the header of the document read, with "close hold do not distribute draft" on the line below.

The requests were broken into thirteen categories and had ranges of dates that the prosecutors wanted the White House to focus on for its search. Many of the categories were of little surprise. Mueller wanted essentially all the White House's documents—including emails, memos, handwritten notes, and phone logs—related to the firings of Flynn and Comey and Russia's election meddling. And Mueller's team asked for what the White House had on Manafort and his deputy, Rick Gates, who were publicly reported to be under investigation.

But the Excel sheet also contained requests that shed light on two new ominous paths Mueller's team was now heading down. Tucked at the bottom of the requests were the names of six men who had been part of Trump's foreign policy team during the campaign. Now Mueller wanted all the documents the White House had related to them.

The second request on the Excel sheet showed how investigators were also examining Trump's conduct. Mueller's team wanted all documents related to how the president and his aides had responded two months earlier to the *Times* story about Don Jr.'s meeting during the campaign with Russians offering dirt on Clinton. As part of that response, aboard Air Force One back to Washington from the G20 meeting in Hamburg, Germany, Trump himself had dictated a misleading statement to be given to the *Times*. The statement said the meeting had been mainly about adoption issues between the United States and Russia—a claim that would be directly contradicted by emails released by Don Jr. just two days after our story broke. The investigators now wanted to know whether there were drafts of the statement, who was with the president on the plane when he dictated it, and whom the president and his aides had been in contact with as they put it together. Compared with the other obstruction incidents that were being examined, Trump's role in crafting the statement created a new legal problem for the president, his lawyers calculated. There were constitutional arguments that the president had the right to fire his FBI director or end an investigation, no matter his intentions. But there was a far weaker argument that the president had a right to disseminate false information related directly to an investigation that could throw prosecutors off the scent and impede their work.

Beyond the legal arguments, the request signaled a far more significant development: The investigation had turned into a rolling, real-time creature that was sprouting new tentacles that were ensnaring the president. Along with looking at what had occurred before he was appointed, Mueller would now look at whether Trump had tried to obstruct Mueller's own work. The Flynn and Comey matters had occurred before Mueller had been appointed, and the requests about the foreign policy team related directly to the campaign. But the president's role in crafting a false statement had occurred a month and a half after Mueller first set up his office. Investigators had tipped their hand to the president and shown how they were closely watching what he was doing right under their noses. Based on his public actions—and what was being reported about what he did behind closed doors—the investigators were opening new lines of inquiry in real time. For any president, this would be a huge concern. But for a president who was now attacking the investigators and witnesses in public and trying to use his power to throw sand in the gears of their investigation, it was devastating. If Trump refused to curtail his behavior, he could create countless offshoots of the investigation in just a few tweets and calls to his advisers.

Despite now having written proof from Mueller that he was actively investigating the president, Dowd and Cobb refused to change course. They still wanted McGahn to go in, speak to Mueller, and tell investigators whatever they wanted to know.

★ ★ ★

FALL 2017

AIRPORT TERMINAL—This pickup was even earlier than normal. He was scheduled to arrive shortly before 4:00 a.m. That meant I had to get up at 3:00 a.m. I had gone to bed late, getting only three hours of rest. By the time I arrived at the airport, I had that weird and confused feeling of being jolted from sleep. I found him at the curb; he threw his bag in the back and hopped into the front.

"It's early," I said. "Where you headed?"

He gave me the address. I knew how to get there and took us in that direction. And without thinking much about it, as I tried to find the exit from the airport, I threw out something that I had been wondering about for weeks: Whatever happened to Pete Strzok?

Strzok was considered the top counterintelligence and counterespionage agent at the FBI. He had been the lead case agent on the Clinton email investigation. Comey had a soft spot for the counterintelligence agents because they thought more like him, and he found Strzok to be as competent an agent as there was in the bureau, and there was one thing about Strzok that Comey especially liked. When briefing Comey on the Clinton email investigation, Strzok did something that few agents ever did: He interrupted Comey and told him he was wrong. If Comey started saying something about the investigation and was off about a fact, even in the slightest, Strzok would say, "Sir, sir, you don't have that right," and he would explain it to him. Comey admired that and wished more people around him had the same nerve.

Strzok had a bit of a more polished background than other agents. He had graduated from Georgetown University and had been an Army intelligence officer. He knew he was smarter than most agents, and sometimes his arrogance showed. Four weeks after the Clinton email investigation ended, he became the lead case agent on the investigation into the Trump campaign's ties to Russia. He had flown to London to interview the Australian ambassador right after the bureau learned that the Trump campaign aide George Papadopoulos had talked about how the Russians had damaging information on Clinton in the form of her emails. After the appointment of Mueller, Strzok had joined Mueller's team. But then, abruptly in the middle of the summer, he had been moved off the Mueller investigation and assigned to human resources. To me, the move made no sense: Here was one of the most skilled agents in the bureau being removed from the most important counterintelligence investigation in FBI history. Beyond that, we knew nothing.

"I know about that," he said. "He had problems with his text messages. He was sending anti-Trump texts. Like, they showed bias."

I shut up and listened.

"There was a whole debate with Mueller about whether he should be removed. A lot of people didn't think he should have," the source said. "Frankly, I don't think they should have moved him."

I tried to assemble the pieces of what he was telling me. I repeated back to him what I thought he was saying: So the lead agent on the Trump-Russia investigation for Mueller sent text messages that showed he did not like Trump?

This would be a game changer. Trump would finally have what he had been grasping for publicly and privately for months: a real example of someone deep inside the investigation who might have expressed animosity toward him. Until that point, Trump's pushback in the first several months of the Mueller investigation had been anemic. Publicly Trump's lawyers signaled that they were fully cooperating with Mueller. This left the party faithful and the conservative media unsure of how hard to hit the special counsel's office. Mueller and his team had been roughed up shortly after his appointment when it was disclosed that he had hired six prosecutors who had made political donations to Clinton. That narrative struggled to gain traction because there was no evidence at all that politics was influencing the conduct of the investigation.

But text messages that included colorful language sent by the lead agent on the Trump-Russia investigation could easily be used by Trump and his allies as a cudgel against Mueller and a pretext to smear the whole investigation.

In December 2017, the *Times* would break the story about how Strzok had been removed from the Mueller investigation because of the texts. The disclosure came at a particularly ominous point in the investigation, because two days earlier Flynn had pleaded guilty and had agreed to cooperate with Mueller. Just as at many points where Trump appeared to be cornered, he had been thrown a lifeline. He would take full advantage of it.

★★★

NOVEMBER 30, 2017

ONE YEAR, FOUR MONTHS, AND NINETEEN DAYS UNTIL THE RELEASE OF THE MUELLER REPORT

A WINDOWLESS CONFERENCE ROOM IN THE SPECIAL COUNSEL'S OFFICE—The best prosecutions have reliable narrators. These witnesses have proximity to the wrongdoing and solid memories, and they are truthful. With the door to the West Wing thrown open by Dowd and Cobb, Mueller's team had a huge opportunity to run through the roster of senior White House officials in search of their own star witness. But while the first round of interviews turned up new leads and anecdotes that greatly enhanced Mueller's understanding of the soft, dark underbelly of the Trump White House, none of the witnesses checked all the boxes necessary to be a guide to Trump's obstruction.

One of the first to be interviewed was the CIA director, Mike Pompeo, who had been in a meeting with the president when he asked his intel chiefs to say publicly that there were no nefarious connections between him and Russia. Pompeo remembered so little that some investigators were suspicious he was not being completely forthcoming.

The by-then-former chief of staff, Reince Priebus, who had lasted just six months in the position before being fired by Trump, was the first senior White House official to be interviewed. He remembered far more than Pompeo and had been around the president during the Flynn and Comey firings and the efforts to oust Sessions. Priebus told them about how Trump had taken Sessions's resignation letter with him when he went on his first trip abroad, suggesting that Trump was hoping he could strong-arm the attorney general into reassuming control of the Russia investigation. But he too had memory problems, and despite being presented with many emails between transition officials to help him remember, he said he had no memory of whether he had been told in advance of Flynn's call with the Russian ambassador.

One of the first members of the White House counsel's office to be interviewed was McGahn's chief of staff, Annie Donaldson. She had a great sense of what had gone on between Trump and McGahn, but her knowledge was almost entirely secondhand, because McGahn would come back to his office after meeting with Trump and recount to her what he had said.

Mueller's team then had a shot at Vice President Pence. It had been Flynn's lie to Pence about his contacts with the Russian ambassador that set off the chain of events that ultimately led to Mueller's appointment. If there was a link between collusion and obstruction, Pence could provide it. He had overseen the transition when there were odd contacts between transition officials and foreign leaders. He had been in the room with Trump for discussions leading up to the firing of Flynn and Comey, had been alone with Trump and Sessions when Trump had held Sessions's job over his head. And he had been in the Oval Office to hear Trump rage about the Mueller investigation.

But Mueller treated Pence differently from all other witnesses.

Shortly after the special counsel's appointment, Pence's lawyer, Richard Cullen, met with Mueller to say that Pence wanted to cooperate and that if Mueller's team had any questions for him, his lawyer would be willing to answer them. With other witnesses, Mueller's team was asking for direct access. But in the fall, the prosecutors asked Cullen—a former prosecutor whose slight southern twang and aw-shucks congeniality put a friendly face on one of the country's most ruthless defense lawyers—to come in for a meeting.

No witness found himself in a more unusual position than Pence. Unlike all the other witnesses, he stood to benefit enormously if Mueller's team uncovered evidence that Trump had broken the law, because it could potentially clear a path for him to become president. But from the beginning of the investigation, Pence had given his aides and lawyers strict instructions: We need to do everything possible to help support the president and his defense. Pence wanted to be loyal. And to those around the president it was clear that Trump was flailing, obsessed with the Russia investigation and media coverage of it.

Trump's lawyers Dowd and Cobb had blithely taken Trump at his word that he did nothing wrong and told the president they could have the investigation wrapped up in a matter of weeks. But no top-tier lawyer involved in the investigation believed that any lawyer should take a client at his word and that such a high-profile investigation—involving the question of whether the president broke the law—could be so quickly wrapped up. So contrary to the approach of Trump's lawyers, Cullen in the late spring of 2017 conducted an internal investigation into what occurred around the Comey and Flynn firings. Following Pence's wishes, Cullen had met with Dowd to provide details on what he had found—many of which Dowd had no idea about because he had never done his own work. Cullen also provided Dowd with a legal opinion his lawyers had written about how an obstruction case would be highly difficult to build against Trump.

On October 11, six days after Donaldson went in for her first interview, Cullen went in to meet with Mueller and his investigators. He appeared to have two goals: get Pence out of having to sit for an interview and help Trump by showing the prosecutors why building an obstruction case around the firing of Comey was flawed. All the lawyers in the investigation wanted to keep their clients from sitting for questioning. Cullen feared Mueller might try to write a report and if Pence sat for an interview, his team could take a comment from Pence out of context or use the vice president against Trump.

Maybe if Cullen sat and told Mueller everything Pence knew, Mueller would decline to interview the vice president, for the sake of decorum and comity.

During the George H. W. Bush administration, Cullen had worked with Mueller when Mueller headed the criminal division at the Justice Department and Cullen served as the U.S. attorney for the Eastern District of Virginia, one of the more prominent offices in the country. The two liked each other; they picked up where they had left off years earlier and had a good rapport in the meeting.

Cullen started by laying out a fact he had uncovered during his internal investigation that he believed kicked the legs out from underneath the obstruction argument. He said how in the Oval Office the day before the Comey firing, McGahn's deputy, Uttam Dhillon, told Trump if he dismissed the FBI director, he would likely prolong the Russia investigation, trigger the appointment of a special counsel, and risk the release of damaging disclosures about himself. Trump told Dhillon and the others in the Oval Office—including Pence—he believed that Comey had to go and was prepared to bear whatever cost came with it.

Then Cullen took that piece of information and pivoted to laying out how no obstruction case could be built around the Comey firing. He asked, How could the firing be obstruction if Trump had been told that it would only make the investigation longer and lead to more damaging disclosures about him?

Mueller and the handful of investigators in the room said nothing in response to Cullen's argument. But Mueller, who appeared attentive, seemed to understand the contours of the investigation and asked several questions. He asked Cullen what Pence had told Trump about in regard to whether he should fire Flynn. Cullen said that Pence wanted to stay away from discussing the advice he gave the president. In the course of the meeting, Cullen mentioned how one of Pence's staffers had been involved in dealing with the Flynn firing. Mueller said that investigators would need to question that staffer.

The meeting ended with no discussion about Pence coming in to be interviewed. Cullen's play worked. Mueller's team never reached out to him to question Pence, nor did the investigators ever question the aide Mueller said they needed to talk to.

In late November, John Eisenberg—the brainy top national security lawyer for McGahn who was known as Mumbles for how he speaks—went in, but was not an impressive witness.

The day after Eisenberg's interview, McGahn went in for his interview. Within an hour, prosecutors realized what they had: McGahn was an extraordinary witness. He had a clear recollection of facts, seemed truthful, knew how to answer questions, had a good handle on how Trump's mind worked, and had created a paper trail to back up his work. He was likable and could even make a joke. He had an added layer of credibility with the investigators because he appeared reluctant to be speaking with them. In that session, he laid out the Flynn firing and Trump's elaborate efforts to use him to stop Sessions's recusal. The following day he was scheduled to return. But that morning, Flynn pleaded guilty to making false statements to FBI agents about his contacts with the Russian ambassador. In an early sign of how Trump loomed over the investigation, one of Mueller's prosecutors told Burck that given the massive attention to the Flynn plea and the potential for more cameras than usual to be staked out in front of their offices, they did not want to risk having McGahn photographed coming in—for his sake and theirs. It could enrage the president and make them and McGahn a target.

Two weeks later, McGahn returned, and over two days he spent hours discussing the lead-up to and the execution of the firing of Comey, as well as the White House's reaction and response to the appointment of Mueller. As the third day of interviews stretched on for several hours, Burck realized that the prosecutors had yet to ask about the attempt to fire Mueller. The prosecutors finished asking questions about all the incidents they knew about and then asked McGahn a standard question they always ask a witness at the end of an interview: Is there anything else related to what we discussed today that we should know about?

Burck jumped in. He knew that to stay in the good graces of the prosecutors, they needed to hear everything from McGahn first. Burck wanted to interrupt before McGahn had the chance to say no. If McGahn—knowing about the attempt to fire Mueller—said he had nothing to add, it could potentially raise questions about his credibility. So Burck led his client.

"There was an issue in June when Trump wanted Don to take action on Mueller," Burck said.

McGahn tensed. He knew that disclosing the incident could damage Trump. But he had to tell the truth. Reluctantly, he offered a few details.

Intrigued by a scene of potential obstruction that they had never heard of before, the investigators told Burck and McGahn that they were interested in hearing more about that and began talking to Burck about scheduling another interview after the first of the year.

McGahn had given Mueller's team a direct view of Trump's conduct from one of the people closest to him—someone the president had confided in and taken advice from as he tried to pull the levers of power to protect himself. It was hard to find such a narrator in most criminal investigations, and nearly impossible in one involving the president. Mueller's team had been investigating for only six months. But as the end of the year came to a close, they now had an incredibly important asset positioned right next to Trump. The team had an active investigation into whether the president was obstructing justice, and they were learning about new actions he had taken to thwart that investigation. For Mueller and McGahn, this information needed to be kept secret. If it got out, Trump might retaliate and fire what could be a potentially fruitful ongoing source for Mueller. But in the days after McGahn testified, word of what he said began to spread in Mueller's office, the FBI, and elsewhere in Washington.

★★★

DECEMBER 28, 2017

ONE YEAR, THREE MONTHS, AND TWENTY-ONE DAYS UNTIL THE RELEASE OF THE MUELLER REPORT

TRUMP INTERNATIONAL GOLF CLUB, WEST PALM BEACH, FLORIDA—Mueller's team had the building blocks for an obstruction investigation against Trump. And they could back it up by relying on one of the people closest to the president to demonstrate how determined Trump had been to interfere in the investigations into him and his associates.

But Trump apparently had no appreciation of this. His lawyers told him that there was nothing to the investigation, and he told aides he assumed that whoever went in would be loyal to him. This left Trump, by the end of 2017, with the impression that a box-checking exercise by Mueller would not be a problem for him.

"I think he's going to be fair," Trump said to me. "And if he's fair—because everybody knows the answer already, Michael."

Then Trump wanted to assure himself that I would treat him the same way.

"I want you to treat me fairly. Okay?" Trump said.

"Believe me. This is—" I said before Trump interrupted me.

"Everybody knows the answer already," Trump said about the investigation.

Trump and I were sitting in the middle of the grillroom of his golf club at a big round table with a white tablecloth on it. The president, wearing golf pants, a white polo shirt, and a white hat with the number 45 emblazoned on the side, had come off the course a few minutes earlier. I had managed to do an end around on the White House to land an interview with him. Now Trump and I were alone talking about the investigation.

A couple of weeks earlier, I had been sitting at my desk in the *Times*' Washington bureau when the bureau chief, Elisabeth Bumiller, approached me. Given the time of year, the look on her face, and who I was—single and Jewish—I had a good sense of what she was about to ask.

Can you spend Christmas vacation with Trump in Florida?

I had taken on this assignment two times over the previous three years, spending Christmases in Hawaii with President Obama. Although that might sound like an incredibly cushy assignment in the optimal locale, it was actually a lot of work, in part because Obama was highly active. On one day in 2015, I sat in the press van in Obama's motorcade for hours as he, in the wake of imposing new sanctions on North Korea, went to the beach with his daughters at an Air Force base, visited his grandfather's grave, spent time at his sister's house, hung out with the rock star Eddie Vedder, and then had dinner with friends just before we all got on Air Force One back to Washington.

But Florida, with Trump, sounded easier and I convinced myself that I was actually getting the better end of the deal than the *Times,* which would be paying for me to go on vacation. Trump would do nothing; I would feel no pressure to write anything.

So four days before Christmas, I went to Andrews Air Force Base to fly down to Florida with Trump on Air Force One. Over the course of the first week I spent in Palm Beach, my plan worked out pretty well. On my duty days, I joined the press pool early in the morning outside the hotel we were all staying in, got in a van, rode in Trump's motorcade to the golf club, didn't really see the president, and filed reports essentially full of nothing back to Washington done in plenty of time to enjoy the evenings.

One night, I had dinner at the Breakers hotel with one of the president's close friends and confidants, Chris Ruddy, the owner of the conservative media organization Newsmax. Ruddy—who brought two of Ralph Lauren's brothers to the dinner—was one of a cabal of individuals in Trump's orbit who often had his ear and who often took it upon themselves to freelance as the president's unofficial advisers, promoters, and press agents. In June, he had gone on television out of the blue to say that Trump was considering firing Mueller. And so, in the back of my head, I thought maybe a dinner with Ruddy could lead to an encounter with Trump.

I planted the seed with Ruddy, telling him that when he saw

Trump at Mar-a-Lago, where he said he was going the next day, to tell him I was around. It was just a flier, of course, but Ruddy said he would pass the message along. A few days later, I saw Ruddy again, and he said he had seen Trump but didn't mention to him that I was around. I told him it was fine. I didn't want to push it and was a bit relieved because I knew interviewing Trump would be a potential headache. Nearly a year into Trump's presidency, he had become so polarizing that every interview—and the transcripts from them—became fodder for the Right to call us "Fake News" and the Left to say we were not fact-checking the president in real time.

But the following night I saw Ruddy again out in Palm Beach at a restaurant called Buccan. And without telling anyone in the White House or Trump, Ruddy essentially appointed himself White House communications director for the evening and decided that Trump talking to me would be a good thing. He told me that the following day he was going to take me to lunch at Trump's golf club. Ruddy's idea was that we would go to the club at 12:30 p.m. and sit at the table directly next to Trump's, timing it to when he'd get off the golf course. When the president finished his round and came in to eat lunch, we'd see if he wanted to chat.

The following day I put on my black golf pants and red polo shirt and rode over to the course in my rental car, told the security guard at the gate I was there to have lunch with Chris Ruddy, drove up to the bellhop, got out of my car, got wanded by a Secret Service agent, and walked into the grillroom of the clubhouse at Trump's club. Nobody recognized me. I sat at the bar, ordered a Diet Coke, and tried to look as if I just walked off the course.

A few minutes later, Ruddy showed up, accompanied by two of his friends, Andrew Stein, the former Manhattan borough president, and Lee Lipton, a local restaurant owner. We sat down at the table adjacent to a larger one, where Trump usually sat, and we ordered lunch. I had the chicken salad and another Diet Coke.

Like clockwork, right after the food came, Trump walked into the dining room with his son, a few of his golfing buddies, and a pro golfer I had never heard of. Trump stopped at different tables to chat with members—but not with us—before eventually sitting down and taking off his white hat. Waiters and waitresses immediately scurried over to take care of him.

It took a few minutes, but Trump saw that Ruddy was right near him and told him to come over. Ruddy looked at me and the others, as if to signal that we should join him. As Ruddy walked over to the president, I came up behind him and he told Trump, "I've got Michael Schmidt of *The New York Times* with me."

Trump looked at me quizzically as if to say, "Why the hell is a reporter from *The New York Times* in the middle of my golf club?"

But Trump then turned affable.

"Michaaaaaaeeeeeel," he said slowly as I walked over to shake his hand.

I reminded him that I had interviewed him in July in the Oval Office. He remembered, and he repeated what I'd heard, saying that we had treated him fairly.

Then, without pausing or waiting a beat, the president immediately launched into something of a rant about the tax bill that Congress had passed just a few days earlier. Although Republicans controlled both houses of Congress, Trump had struggled all year for a major legislative accomplishment. Now he had one and wanted to talk about it.

I didn't know much about tax policy. But it was clear the president was energized, so I just shut my mouth and let him talk. I now thought I might have a chance of getting him to sit for an interview. But I was unsure how to broach the subject with him, so I walked up beside him, squatted next to him, like a catcher, which forced him to look down at me and kept him from being distracted by the throngs swirling nearby. One point about taxes turned into another and then another, and all these years after I'd retired as a Little League catcher, my legs quickly began to ache. Standing up at this point would signal that the conversation was over, so I interrupted him and told him that I thought what he was saying sounded new, and interesting, and that we should sit and do a quick interview so I could get it all down.

He said yes. He just wanted to finish his lunch (a salad that looked as if an entire head of lettuce had been cut up and doused in Thousand Island dressing), and then we could talk. I headed back to my table thinking it was a fifty-fifty shot that he'd actually call me back over.

But maybe five minutes later, I heard my name being called in an unmistakable voice.

"Michael, Michael . . . get over here," Trump said.

Interviewing the president—any president—is rare. But interviewing a president alone, without aides, in the grillroom of the clubhouse of his golf club, was even more unusual. Nothing like this would have happened, of course, with Obama or Bush or Clinton or any president maybe going back fifty years. But Trump was a president who just couldn't help himself when it came to the media, and because of his unusual routine, and the unusual sense of latitude that he gave to associates like Chris Ruddy, he was bizarrely accessible.

He started our interview by launching into his take on the situation, denying any collusion, calling the investigation a witch hunt, and insisting he won the election because he was "a better candidate by a lot" and had campaigned specifically to win the Electoral College. I didn't point out that running to win the Electoral College was not really a novel political approach.

Wasting no time, I made my first question about Mueller, asking him what his expectations were and when he thought he'd be wrapping up his investigation.

"I have no expectation," he said. "I can only tell you that there is absolutely no collusion."

He said it did not bother him that it was unclear when Mueller would be done because he is "going to be fair."

With rapid-fire repetitiveness, sixteen times in all, he insisted there'd be "no collusion" discovered by the inquiry, though he stopped short of demanding an end to it. He showed that he wanted a time limit on the investigation, saying that it "makes the country look very bad, and it puts the country in a very bad position. So the sooner it's worked out, the better it is for the country."

As he continued to say he'd done nothing wrong, he repeated accusations he'd been volleying at Democrats for months, on the dossier, on the Democratic National Committee, and on Hillary Clinton. I asked him if he thought the Justice Department should reopen the email investigation on his former opponent. Trump demonstrated his view of his powers as president and how the Justice Department was essentially a tool he could use as he wanted.

"I have absolute right to do what I want to do with the Justice Department," he said. "But for purposes of hopefully thinking I'm going to be treated fairly, I've stayed uninvolved with this particular matter."

The interview zigged and zagged wildly from there as he went on about China, the Alabama Senate candidate Roy Moore, and his former campaign chairman Paul Manafort. With Trump in front of me I had the opportunity to check some of my reporting. I had been told in the final weeks of the year that Trump, in complaining about Sessions and McGahn, had used the refrain about Holder protecting Obama, as Robert F. Kennedy had for his brother. As Trump went on and on about how disloyal Sessions had been, I asked him about Eric Holder.

"I don't want to get into loyalty, but I will tell you that, I will say this: Holder protected President Obama," Trump said. "Totally protected him. When you look at the IRS scandal, when you look at the guns for whatever, when you look at all of the tremendous, ah, real problems they had, not made-up problems like Russian collusion, these were real problems. When you look at the things that they did, and Holder protected the president. And I have great respect for that, I'll be honest, I have great respect for that."

The president seemed to be enjoying himself. At one point, the pro golfer he had played with that day, Jim Herman, came to say goodbye to the president. In front of Herman, Trump told me about how he had given him $50,000 years ago when he'd worked at Trump's golf club in New Jersey and was trying to make the PGA Tour.

Trump asked him how much he'd made on the pro circuit so far in his career.

Herman estimated $3 million.

"Which to him is like making a billion because he doesn't spend anything," Trump said. "Ain't that a great story?"

At another point, the president's body man came over with a cell phone to say that his top aide, Hope Hicks, was on the line. The president took the phone, and while I could hear only his side of the conversation, I could tell that someone in the grillroom had tipped her off to the fact that Trump had sat down for an interview with *The New York Times*. From what Trump said, she appeared to be trying to stop the interview. Trump told her that he knew who I was and thought I had treated him fairly before.

"Yeah, maybe he'll kill me in the piece," he said, but then added, lightly, that he often gets killed in the press, so what's the difference? He handed the phone back to his body man soon after that and continued, unbowed.

He finished off by saying that he was going to win a second term for a lot of reasons, including that "newspapers, television, all forms of media will tank if I'm not there, because without me, their ratings are going down the tubes."

"Without me, *The New York Times* will indeed be not the failing *New York Times* but the failed *New York Times,*" Trump said. "So they basically have to let me win. And eventually, probably six months before the election, they'll be loving me because they're saying, 'Please, please, don't lose, Donald Trump.'"

When Ruddy eventually came back over, the interview came to a close. But the president said that before I left, he wanted to show me something. We headed out of the grillroom, though we briefly stopped at a table where three people were sitting. The president introduced me to one of them, explaining that the guy in front of me was the richest man in Germany. Then he introduced me to another man at the table and told me that he was the second-richest man in Germany.

Then he looked at the supposed two richest guys in Germany, pointed to me, and said to them, "Mike hates Germans."

I had no idea what Trump was talking about. I was going to explain that my last name was Schmidt and that I had some German or Austrian roots, but I wasn't sure it was worth it. I had my interview, so I just smiled.

Then the president brought me over to what he wanted me to see—a plaque in the clubhouse that showed he had won the club championship several times and a framed copy of the scorecard from his low round at the course. I asked him how far he was hitting the ball these days, and in a rare moment of humility he acknowledged it was shorter and shorter the older he gets.

He said goodbye by asking me to be fair to him, repeating the phrase several times. I told him that I would treat him the same way we had in July. He invited me to play the course that afternoon. I told him it looked as if I had a story to file. We shook hands and he was off.

★ ★ ★

JANUARY 2, 2018

ONE YEAR, THREE MONTHS, AND SIXTEEN DAYS UNTIL THE RELEASE OF THE MUELLER REPORT

INSIDE THE WINDOWLESS CONFERENCE ROOM IN MUELLER'S OFFICE— When Don McGahn concluded his first series of interviews with Mueller's team, they told him and Bill Burck that if they remembered anything related to their questions, or if they felt the need to clarify what McGahn had said, they should reach out. Nothing unusual with that request; witnesses who are under pressure in an interview with prosecutors and FBI agents often remember facts and anecdotes days after their memories are first jogged. But Mueller's team added something else. James Quarles and Andrew Goldstein, the members of Mueller's team leading the obstruction investigation, said that going forward, if anything occurred along the lines of what they had questioned McGahn about, they should notify them. In other words, once McGahn returned to the West Wing, if the president did anything that walked up to the line of obstruction or could be relevant to their investigation, Burck should call to alert them.

For starters, it sounded a bit unusual for federal prosecutors to raise the prospect that the president of the United States—who was already under investigation—might break the law. Then again, an ongoing criminal investigation of the president was unusual. But the request also intimated something unmistakably audacious: that Mueller's team, at the very least, felt comfortable with the idea of some real-time information flow from McGahn to them as their investigation progressed. The idea of prosecutors using the president's lawyer as an active cooperator to learn about what occurred inside the walls of the White House felt so extraordinary that Burck struggled to take the possibility seriously. The CIA used that kind of tactic with moles around the world to penetrate adversarial governments to extract state secrets. At home, the Justice Department and FBI used informants in their most significant organized crime and terrorism investigations. Police departments in cities and towns used them to take down gangs who pushed guns and drugs on the streets.

But this investigation revolved around the sensitivities of the presidency. No way would Mueller's team try to "run"—investigative jargon for how the feds use informants—McGahn. With everyone from Rosenstein to Congress claiming to be paying close attention, the tactic would receive far too much scrutiny.

But who knew what could happen? Dowd and Cobb had made their bet on cooperation, throwing the door of the White House open to allow the investigators to rummage around in the West Wing's business and question the president's lawyers. At the center of the chaos sat the mercurial Trump. Burck and McGahn knew better than anyone else in Washington that given Trump's inability to control himself and the lack of guardrails around him, he would almost certainly do something that Mueller's team would want to know.

For the moment, though, they had only one option: hope. Maybe, they thought, the president would learn to restrain himself or become distracted by something else and avoid doing something to grab the investigators' attention. As legal strategies go, hope is particularly terrible. Especially when you are hoping for the impossible.

Back in their offices at Patriots Plaza, Quarles, Goldstein, and the rest of Mueller's investigators were building a timeline of what had occurred inside the White House. The team had obtained a wide array of evidence—witness interviews, White House documents, and some of the notes from McGahn's chief of staff that recounted conversations with Trump—and much of it involved Burck's clients. So as the prosecutors sorted through the facts,

Quarles, Goldstein, and an FBI agent working on the obstruction investigation repeatedly called Burck; it was one-stop shopping to clarify issues like what his clients remembered and what Donaldson meant in her notes and to schedule follow-up interviews. The normal back-and-forth between prosecutors and defense lawyers often involved these types of conversations. But at the end of these calls, after the prosecutors' initial inquiries had been answered, they began asking Burck general questions about what might be going on at the White House.

Is there anything else we should know about? Is there anything going on?

For Mueller's team to enter into this new and deeper relationship with the counsel for a client meant that they deeply trusted Burck. If they thought he would be a Trump lackey and relay these interactions back to the White House, they would never have asked such questions. The legal teams for defendants like Manafort had special pacts with Trump's lawyers—known as joint defense agreements—that allowed them to essentially be on the same team, share information about the investigation, and still keep it protected from prosecutors under attorney-client privilege. Lawyers for Trump and Kushner had made overtures to Burck about having a similar setup, hoping to glean information from the interviews with his clients and learn more about what Mueller's team was after. But Burck had avoided these pacts out of suspicion and out of a desire to show Mueller's team that his witnesses had no complicating allegiances.

"How do I know if my guys' interests line up with Trump's or Kushner's? I have no fucking idea," Burck told others at the time.

In McGahn's first round of interviews with investigators, Burck had shown his willingness to help the prosecutors. Instead of taking an adversarial approach, he kept a genial manner and reminded McGahn about facts that he believed would help the prosecutors. After all, it was Burck who had been the one to prompt McGahn at the end of his first round of interviews to disclose the attempted firing of Mueller.

Burck struggled to understand what had motivated Mueller's team to take such an approach. Maybe the prosecutors, who were now being roundly attacked by Trump on Twitter, operated under the belief that he might actually be a Russian agent and they needed to use every tool at their disposal to oust him. Why else would Trump lash out so much about Russia? Burck wondered.

In response to the general inquiries from Quarles and Goldstein, Burck said little. But he told McGahn that Mueller's team was asking questions about what was going on in the White House. McGahn told no one. He already knew his cooperation had been extensive, and he wanted to avoid bringing any additional attention to it. If Trump—who obsessed about loyalty and leaks—found out that Mueller's team was fishing with McGahn, he could erupt in anger and fire both McGahn and Mueller.

But in the early weeks of 2018, something happened that turned McGahn into an active cooperator, and the questions from Mueller's team about what Trump was saying behind closed doors in almost real time went from the general to the very specific.

★ ★ ★

WINTER 2018

ON AN AMTRAK TRAIN—I'd convinced myself that I'd worn out my welcome with one of my sources. For weeks, I'd struggled to get him to reengage with me on anything. My calls had gone unreturned, and when I texted him, he was nonresponsive. Sometimes a source gets cold feet weeks or months into a relationship when the story gets too hot. It was possible he thought he had shared too much or thought someone had figured out that we were talking. It was also possible that our exchanges had started to annoy him. Why should he be at my beck and call to help me write news stories?

But six months into the Mueller investigation, every juncture felt consequential, and every story more fateful. Mueller's prosecutors were taking in an extraordinary amount of evidence through witness interviews and document production from the White House, the campaign, and who knows where else. This source who had ghosted me knew what Mueller knew, and I needed to do everything I could to find him.

Finally, after weeks of silence, he messaged to say that he knew I had been looking for him and that he planned to take a train trip that afternoon and I should come along. For reporting, the train is the second-best option behind the car. For several hours, you have nowhere else to be. You're just two folks traveling. Wearing a baseball hat to disguise myself, I slid into a seat next to him. We began drinking cheap wine and chatting. There was no small talk or bullshit. We got right into talking about the investigation, and within the first hour I had hit on something.

"They're looking at his attempts to get rid of Mueller," he said to me.

I had to process that for a second. So Mueller is investigating Trump's attempts to fire him? Okay, that's big. Meta-obstruction of justice.

"He wanted to get rid of Mueller . . . ," I said, like a therapist repeating back what a patient says, just to establish that they've been heard.

He said he knew little more about the incident and what had gone on between Trump and McGahn. "Let me see what I can find out," he said.

Despite all of Trump's public bluster about Mueller, it had not yet been reported that he tried to fire him, or that Mueller was investigating it. Of course, it made sense. But like many features of the Trump presidency, it was unprecedented. Trump's public and private behavior had not been curbed by the investigation. Appeals from staff and lawyers to be more careful might as well have been in a foreign language. He had not been chastened. If anything, his behavior had grown only more erratic and angry. He had fired Comey the previous May. He had spent much of July trying to get Sessions to resign. Mueller was the next logical target. The way the president tried to do it also appeared to fit a pattern: Trump seemed afraid to take any action for himself and sought to use someone else—in this case McGahn—to do the deed.

It was also significant because it showed that Mueller's team had at the same time both tightened its focus and opened its aperture even wider, investigating actions the president had taken after Mueller had been appointed. An investigation that had started with a focus on the Comey firing had now become an ongoing inquiry into actions the president was taking to thwart the same investigation into him and his campaign. It also showed how Trump sought to use his power as the head of the executive branch to fire someone for reasons that his own lawyers believed were frivolous. Unlike other presidents, who fired heads of departments and agencies, Trump sought to reach down into the Justice Department and oust a particular prosecutor whose chief mission involved investigating him, his family, and his closest associates. Removing Mueller would send the unmistakable message to everyone else in the Justice Department: Investigate the president at your peril.

When we arrived at our destination, I got off the train and scribbled down everything I could remember from our conversation. And then I called my colleague Maggie Haberman.

"He tried to fire Mueller," I said.

I didn't have to say anything else.

* * *

JANUARY 25, 2018

ONE YEAR, TWO MONTHS, AND TWENTY-FOUR DAYS UNTIL THE RELEASE OF THE MUELLER REPORT

NEW YORK TIMES WASHINGTON BUREAU—At 8:14 p.m. on Thursday, January 25, six weeks after McGahn first told Mueller's investigators about the firing attempt, our story went up on the *Times* website under the headline "Trump Ordered Mueller Fired, but Backed Off When White House Counsel Threatened to Quit."

Trump was a man whose only measure of success or failure had always been his media coverage. By that measure, January 2018 had been a bruising and bountiful month. In the first week of the year, leaks from the first tell-all to be written about Trump's presidency began to seep into the news cycle—with cable news networks covering every scintillating excerpt from *Fire and Fury* by Michael Wolff as breaking news. It painted a damning picture of a chaotic White House run by an out-of-control president. Instead of ignoring it, Trump brought more attention to it by tweeting about it and threatening to sue one of the book's main sources—his now former chief strategist, Steve Bannon.

In the second week of January, *The Wall Street Journal* reported that Trump had paid off a porn actress to cover up an affair prior to the election—in probable violation of federal law. In discussions after the story appeared that involved McGahn and other senior aides, Trump lied to them, saying he knew nothing about the payments. Around that time, *The Washington Post* reported that Trump complained to aides privately that the United States accepted immigrants from "shithole countries."

Any one of those three crises—a tell-all, a campaign finance allegation tied to a porn star, or slurs by the president against other countries—would throw any White House off. But the news that the president had tried to fire Mueller was a next-level crisis, creating not only a media firestorm but also a legal threat from the special counsel's office, demonstrating that prosecutors had fresh evidence he had obstructed justice and were closely monitoring his conduct in office. He could see that Mueller's team was taking direct aim at him and was using one of the people closest to him to do it.

The White House's response to the story was a clinic in chaos—a near-perfect demonstration of how the Trump administration worked, or didn't work.

Without a plan, Trump, his lawyers, his aides, and Fox News started blindly counterpunching whatever and whomever they could. All of this meant that Burck and McGahn had to gird for the incoming, because Trump was on the loose. McGahn knew that he would be forced to fend off the president while also staying in Mueller's good graces.

Fox News went to work to undermine the story. Forty-five minutes after it posted, Sean Hannity's show started, and he immediately went on the attack.

"At this hour, *The New York Times* is trying to distract you," Hannity said. "They have a story that Trump wanted Mueller fired sometime last June, and our sources, I've checked in with many of them, they are not confirming that tonight. And the president's attorney dismissed the story and says, no, no comment, we are not going there. How many times has *The New York Times,* and others, gotten it wrong?"

But by the final segment of the show, Hannity changed his tune. "So we have sources tonight just confirming to Ed Henry that, yeah, maybe Donald Trump wanted to fire the special counsel for conflict. Does he not have the right to raise those questions? You know we'll deal with this tomorrow night."

Then he finished his show with "a shocking video of the day." He played footage of a police chase in Arizona that ended with a red SUV flying through an intersection and striking an oncoming car head-on.

The president was traveling home from the World Economic Forum in Davos, and Air Force One turned into a traveling rapid-response operation above the Atlantic Ocean, with Trump berating his lawyers over the phone and berating the aides with him. In response to Trump's rage, Dowd called Burck and told him that the president wanted McGahn to put out a statement refuting the story. Fat chance, Burck told Dowd.

Burck called McGahn. The two discussed Trump's demand, quickly agreeing they could not put out a statement contradicting what he had told Mueller. McGahn felt confident by that point in the investigation that he faced no legal exposure for his role advising the president. He wasn't about to jeopardize that by listening to the president now. Such a statement would be a lie, it would undermine McGahn's credibility with Mueller's team, and it would severely weaken an obstruction investigation against the president.

McGahn and Burck had few good options to satisfy Trump, and as with Comey almost exactly one year earlier, who had found himself dealing with an enraged president who was making requests that he could not accommodate, they sought to do something around the edges that could buy them some time and space. One of their few options was undermining the accuracy of the story. Maybe if Trump saw reports that called the story inaccurate, he would back off. McGahn and Burck believed the story gave the strong impression that McGahn had threatened to resign directly to Trump. Nowhere in the story had Maggie and I written that. Rather, we had written that after McGahn received the president's order to fire

Mueller, he had "refused to ask the Justice Department to dismiss the special counsel, saying he would quit instead." There might be an opening to confuse the story and mollify Trump.

McGahn called Robert Costa, a well-respected political reporter at the *Post*. McGahn had known Costa from his time representing Republican House and Senate members in the years before Trump ran for president. On background, speaking as "a person familiar with the episode," McGahn told Costa that he never told Trump directly that he planned to resign. The *Post* reported that, and McGahn crossed his fingers that the ploy would calm Trump down.

For a time, Trump's angst about the story dissipated. In the days that followed, as the story received less attention in the media, there is little evidence Trump did anything more than occasionally complain about it to aides. It would take more media coverage of the story to resurrect it as an issue for the president.

A week after the story broke, NBC's *Meet the Press* booked Reince Priebus to appear on that Sunday's show. Trump had fired Priebus in July, just six days after Priebus slow-walked an order by the president to get Sessions to resign. Unlike others, Priebus had been struggling to find his place in Washington in his post–White House life. He returned to his old firm as a private lawyer, marketing himself as a Trump insider who could help companies navigate Washington and the administration, Trump's humiliation of him notwithstanding. He remained loyal to Trump, hoped the president might give him another job, and worried about what the president thought and said about him.

In the lead-up to the appearance, Priebus had several conversations with Burck about what to say on the show regarding the investigation. Burck had by then established some general ground rules in an effort to keep his clients out of trouble. Priebus must refrain from having conversations with Trump about Mueller and stay away from any questions the press may ask about the investigation. But Priebus felt conflicted about what to do on *Meet the Press*. Trump, of course, would be watching, and Priebus would almost certainly be asked about the attempt to fire Mueller.

"I gotta say something, and I didn't know that was happening," Priebus told Burck, referring to Trump's attempt to fire Mueller.

Burck failed to understand why he had to say anything and wanted to protect Priebus from himself and stop him from going anywhere near discussing the investigation publicly.

Burck could tell from his interactions with Mueller's team that they were closely watching everything Trump tweeted and said publicly and everything that witnesses were saying in the media. Mueller's team already had questions about whether Priebus had been forthcoming about what he knew regarding Flynn's contacts with the Russian ambassador during the campaign. And now they would likely want to pin Priebus down on what he knew about specific events—like the Mueller firing—and any daylight between his public statements and what he told investigators could set off new problems. By that point in the investigation, Mueller's office had charged four Americans—Trump's former campaign chairman and deputy campaign chairman, a campaign foreign policy adviser, and the president's first national security adviser. Two of the four had pleaded guilty to only one charge: making false statements to investigators. Ringing up Priebus for lying would add another notch to the prosecutors' belts and help make the case that Trump's administration, like his campaign, was run through with corrupt liars.

"Why are you going to get in the middle of this thing?" Burck said. "You 'didn't know' doesn't change whether the story is true. All you can say is 'I don't know,' and the president isn't going to like that. Just say you can't talk about it."

Priebus knew "I can't talk about it" would not sit well with Trump. Unknown to Burck, Priebus had just received a call from Trump, who was at Mar-a-Lago. Priebus told the president that he planned to appear on *Meet the Press*. The president told him that the story about the attempt to fire Mueller was bullshit and that he never told McGahn to have Mueller dismissed.

In the time between that call and the interview, Priebus decided to completely defy his lawyer and ignore his advice. He would instead do his best to help the president.

"Of all the things that we went through in the West Wing, I never felt that the president was going to fire the special counsel," Priebus said on the air.

"I think it was very clear by the president's own words that he was concerned about the conflicts of interest that he felt that the special counsel had," Priebus added later in the interview. "And he made that very clear. Perhaps someone interpreted that to mean something else. But I know the difference between 'fire that person, why isn't that person gone,' to what I read in that *New York Times* piece. So when I read that, I'm just telling you I didn't feel that when I was there."

In a sense, Priebus might have been truthful, because McGahn never told him exactly why he planned to resign. But in other parts of the interview, Priebus was less truthful, saying that he never thought there was "some sort of collusion or some kind of obstruction situation going on in the West Wing."

That statement directly contradicted what he had told Mueller's investigators weeks earlier when he said that he himself had been prepared to resign the previous July when Trump asked him to force Sessions to resign so that he could install a more useful attorney general who could curtail the Russia investigation.

The Sunday of the *Meet the Press* appearance, Trump saw the show, called his former chief of staff to say he had done a great job, and repeated that he "never said any of those things about" firing Mueller.

Burck, who was in Minneapolis with his wife for that evening's Super Bowl between the Patriots and the Eagles, flew into a rage when he saw the transcript from *Meet the Press*. Just after Trump called Priebus, Burck called him, too. *What the fuck are you doing?* he screamed into the phone. Life with these White House clients was a nonstop crisis.

Mueller's team would of course have seen Priebus's performance on *Meet the Press*. And so to head off a potential problem, Burck called the special counsel's office on Monday to say that Priebus had made a mistake in what he said on television and stood by what he had told investigators. To Burck, the prosecutors did not seem too worked up by what Priebus had said, but in the weeks that followed, they would schedule another interview with Priebus to investigate whether Trump had tampered with their witness.

Burck had more immediate and bigger problems, though, because Trump was still on the loose.

The *Meet the Press* interview intensified public interest in stories about the firing attempt, putting it front of mind for Trump again. He renewed his complaints about it to aides, telling the White House staff secretary, Rob Porter, it was "bullshit" and saying that McGahn had leaked the story to the *Times* to make himself look good.

Trump thought something drastic had to be done to repair the damage the story had done to him. He told Porter he wanted McGahn to create a written record that said the president never told him to fire Mueller. The president wanted McGahn to document a lie. Porter, a lawyer, was conflicted. He found it hard to believe Trump had so explicitly told McGahn to fire Mueller the previous June, but at the same time realized the problems with the president leaning on a key witness. Porter told Trump he thought an issue like this should be dealt with by the West Wing's communications office. But Trump was insistent: McGahn needed to create an internal White House letter "for our records" to give the president something more concrete than a statement to the media to refute the story. The president then unleashed on McGahn, telling Porter that McGahn was a "lying bastard."

Then the president upped the ante even more.

"If he doesn't write a letter, then maybe I'll have to get rid of him," Trump said.

For Trump, this lie was becoming the condition for McGahn to keep his job.

In some ways, Trump's decision to lean on Porter made sense. He served as the staff secretary, spent much of the day with Trump, and had a relationship with McGahn. But the move appeared more sinister. Trump knew that McGahn knew that if he fired him, Porter would be a favorite to replace him. Porter had started dating Hope Hicks several months earlier. The two were spending time with Jared and Ivanka, who deeply distrusted McGahn for, among other things, raising questions about whether their business dealings violated federal ethics laws. Jared and Ivanka wanted Porter to become the White House counsel, and Dina Powell, a deputy national security adviser and ally of Jared and Ivanka's, had spoken with Porter about taking the position the previous month. But in targeting

Porter to pressure McGahn, Trump had once again found one of the most vulnerable people around him to do something that he was afraid of doing himself.

For reasons that had nothing to do with Mueller or McGahn, Porter was in the midst of his own scandal. Four days earlier, the *Daily Mail* reported that Hicks and he were dating and published photographs of them kissing in the back of a taxi. The tabloid attention led to reporters poking around his personal life, discovering that he had also been accused of physically abusing both of his ex-wives.

Porter, walking up to the line of helping Trump tamper with a witness, went to McGahn and told him what the president wanted him to do. McGahn shrugged off the request, saying the story was true. Porter then told McGahn that Trump said he might fire him if he refused to write the letter. "He's full of shit," McGahn said. For someone who had become famous on television for firing people, the president feared actually firing people, and he knew that the consequences for ousting McGahn could be catastrophic. But McGahn had again grown so frustrated working for Trump that a sort of fatalism had set in; if he was fired, his misery would be over.

"The fucking guy can't fire me, but maybe he will, fine," McGahn said. "So if he wants to fire me, fire me."

McGahn had been confiding in real time with Burck. He wanted a sounding board for how to navigate Trump, and he wanted someone to help him document what had occurred so that he could protect himself. Burck could see the pressure building on McGahn from Trump, and he decided he had to reach out to Quarles and Goldstein. Throughout the investigation, Burck always wanted to be the first in the door to tell the prosecutors about anything unexpected or potentially complicated that could come up with his clients. By being the first to tell the prosecutors, he could keep up the goodwill. But tactically, it also might soften the blow in case something went sideways and would likely keep the prosecutors from overreacting. And if the prosecutors first knew the version of events from Burck, it would be harder for accusations to come up later that McGahn had done something to help the president break the law. Burck believed this marked one of those occasions. In a telephone call, he told Mueller's team about how Trump had reacted to the story.

"I don't know what's going to happen, but there's a real possibility that he's not going to survive the next couple of weeks and I thought you should know," Burck told the prosecutors. "The president was very unhappy with Don for that article; he believes Don is the leaker, and Don may get fired sometime soon."

Burck also raised another possibility.

"He may also resign, because it's intolerable," he said.

Mueller's team thanked Burck and asked that he alert them as soon as he knew anything about McGahn's being fired or quitting.

Dowd found out that Trump wanted to meet with McGahn the following morning. Nothing good could come out of such a meeting. Dowd knew he had no control over his client or what he might do. So he went with the second option: calling Burck. If Dowd couldn't control Trump, maybe he could try to control how those around him reacted. Dowd told Burck that whatever happens in that meeting, McGahn could not resign. To Burck, it looked as if McGahn were one day away from finally being fired.

* * *

FEBRUARY 6, 2018

ONE YEAR, TWO MONTHS, AND TWELVE DAYS UNTIL THE RELEASE OF THE MUELLER REPORT

OVAL OFFICE—Don McGahn and John Kelly, who'd replaced Priebus as chief of staff in July, went into the Oval Office to meet with Trump that morning. Before the meeting, McGahn told Kelly he was not going to correct the story.

The relationship between McGahn and Trump had deteriorated to such a degree by that point that it was unusual for him to be in the Oval Office. The president started the conversation by going directly to the nut of his concern: The *Times* story looked bad for the president.

"I don't remember this," Trump told him.

"It is what happened," McGahn said.

"I never said to fire Mueller," Trump said. "I never said 'fire.' This story doesn't look good. You need to correct this. You're the White House counsel."

McGahn held his ground, telling Trump that the story was accurate, other than the impression it gave that he told him directly he wanted to resign.

"Did I say the word 'fire'?" Trump said.

"What you said is, 'Call Rod, tell Rod that Mueller has conflicts and can't be the special counsel,'" McGahn said.

"I never said that," Trump said.

The president said that all he wanted McGahn to do was call Rosenstein to tell him that Mueller had conflicts and that Rosenstein should figure out what to do with Mueller.

No, McGahn answered, that's not what happened. Indeed, he said, the president had told him to get rid of Mueller. "Call Rod," he recounted the president telling him. "There are conflicts. Mueller has to go."

"To me," McGahn said, "that means you want me to fire him or tell Rod to fire him; there's no other interpretation that makes sense to me."

Trump seemed unmoved and asked McGahn if he would "do a correction."

"No," McGahn said. "There is nothing to correct; it will just bring more attention to it."

McGahn tried to rationalize to Trump why it made no sense for him to leak the story or have it out there.

"Why would I stay if I leaked this?" McGahn said. "I'm not an idiot; I know you're going to lose your mind. Why am I going to leak this story while I'm in the White House counsel's office? How does that help me?"

Trump's reaction had proved McGahn's point.

McGahn had become convinced Cobb had leaked it, and he told that to the president.

Cobb, McGahn thought, knew about the incident and wanted McGahn out, so he leaked it so Trump would fire him and take his job.

"It's gotta be Ty," McGahn said.

McGahn reminded Trump that it had been Cobb who ran his mouth sitting outside BLT Steak just months earlier when he had lunch with Dowd and discussed intimate details about the investigation. "Remember he's the guy from BLT," McGahn said. "Of course it's Ty. But you'll fire me."

Trump continued to press McGahn about what he told Mueller's investigators, asking him why he had told them about Trump's attempt to have Mueller removed. This infuriated McGahn. Trump had been the one who decided he should cooperate with Mueller; now he blamed him for doing exactly what he said?

McGahn explained to the president that Trump—after being convinced by Dowd and Cobb—had decided to allow McGahn to cooperate fully with Mueller and that there was no attorney-client privilege on their conversations that could shield them from prosecutors.

"What are these notes?" Trump asked McGahn, referring to Donaldson's notes that had been given to Mueller. "Why do you take notes? Lawyers don't take notes. I never had a lawyer who took notes."

This infuriated McGahn, too. McGahn remembered how Trump often told him to write things down. Many times in response to such a request, McGahn would scribble on a legal pad, "President told us to write this down." It had been the president's lawyers, Dowd and Cobb, who decided to hand over the notes. Now Trump was blaming *him* for that? Anyway, McGahn thought, the notes helped Trump more than they hurt him because they showed how McGahn never went too far in going along with what Trump wanted.

McGahn said to Trump that he, like all real lawyers, kept notes in order to have a record of what occurred.

"I've had a lot of great lawyers, like Roy Cohn," Trump replied. "He did not take notes."

The meeting ended. McGahn still had his job. His statements to Mueller were intact. And Trump had increased his legal exposure by potentially tampering with Mueller's star witness.

Dowd then called Burck, saying that Trump was "fine" with McGahn.

...

Trump's behavior as president was so bizarre, and everyone around him had become so conditioned to it, that Burck and McGahn had adopted a new and demented sense of what they considered a positive outcome. To them, for a Trump meeting, it had gone better than they had thought it would. Trump had not fired McGahn. McGahn had not quit, nor had he done anything to undermine his own account to Mueller. And while the two men yelled at each other, it was far from the nastiest fight they had ever gotten into.

Burck called Mueller's team to update them on what occurred.

"Apparently, everything is fine," Burck said. "He went into the Oval and had a discussion, and everything seems to be fine now. He's not getting fired. He's not quitting."

Mueller's team thanked Burck for the update. In the days that followed, Mueller's office scheduled another interview with McGahn.

The back-and-forth between Trump and McGahn and the fact that Mueller's team received an almost-real-time readout of it marked a significant development for the special counsel's office. An investigation that had started by concentrating on the Comey firing had now become one that would look at witness tampering. Such an act added a powerful new layer to Mueller's case. Nearly all the episodes they had investigated directly involved powers that Trump had as the head of the executive branch—ending an investigation, firing the FBI director, and even pardoning witnesses. But the president had no right to influence a witness's testimony. Nixon and Clinton got themselves into trouble for just this type of behavior. When the House impeached President Clinton in December 1998, one of the two approved charges focused on the actions Clinton took to alter the accounts of key witnesses in an investigation into his conduct. In July 1974, the House Judiciary Committee approved an article of impeachment accusing President Richard Nixon of "approving, condoning, acquiescing in, and counselling witnesses with respect to the giving of false or misleading statements to lawfully authorized investigative officers and employees of the United States."

On top of that, Mueller's office was now receiving contemporaneous information about Trump's obstructive acts. Mueller's team wondered, If Trump was doing this with McGahn—someone whom he had encouraged to cooperate—what else was the president doing to interfere with the investigation?

Trump continued to complain to aides about McGahn and his refusal to correct the story on the attempt to fire Mueller. But the president largely left McGahn alone, and McGahn avoided Trump, which was a nice respite for McGahn.

Burck told McGahn that he needed to start putting the pieces in place to resign. McGahn, Burck argued, needed to be out of the White House by the time the report came out, because Trump was not going to like what he saw in it. But McGahn had mixed feelings about leaving. Yes, he was sick of Trump and all the chaos—and while he had a high threshold for pain, he could only take so much.

But he had concerns about what Trump would do without him there. Who knew who would follow him as White House counsel? Was it really outside the realm of possibility that Trump could hire someone akin to Michael Cohen to succeed him? No, it was not. Who would be there to say no, to protect Trump from himself and the country from Trump? McGahn trusted Kelly and thought he would serve as a firewall, but he did not want to leave him to do it alone.

On a deeper level, though, McGahn knew that his chief mission in the White House—stacking the courts—had not been completed. And as someone who closely watched the Supreme Court, McGahn knew there could be a huge reason to stay: another open Supreme Court seat. Justice Anthony M. Kennedy had served on the court for thirty years. McGahn had built a close relationship with him during his time in the White House, with Kennedy often weighing in on possible nominations for judgeships in lower courts. Kennedy had said nothing to McGahn about leaving, but McGahn's sense was that his time was near.

So the possibility of Kennedy's open seat gave him a reason to stay. But in the meantime, another intractable problem involving the president and his children was headed directly for his desk.

VII

★★★★★

NORMS OF PRESIDENTIAL CONDUCT 101

FEBRUARY 16, 2018

ONE YEAR, TWO MONTHS, AND TWO DAYS UNTIL THE RELEASE OF THE MUELLER REPORT

McGAHN'S OFFICE ON THE SECOND FLOOR OF THE WEST WING—Dating back to the transition, the intelligence community, the FBI, and senior members of the Obama administration knew of evidence that foreign countries wanted to gain access and leverage over the incoming administration by exploiting Trump's adult children.

Trump had made a show of ceding control of his real estate business—which had properties all over the world—to his sons after the election to demonstrate that he would try to keep the operation of his businesses separate from governing the country. Before he was inaugurated, though, intercepted communications by the intelligence community revealed evidence of foreign officials from more than one country discussing how they wanted to do business deals with the kids in order to gain closer access to the administration. A wiretap picked up the United Arab Emirates' ambassador to the United States, Yousef Otaiba, discussing how he wanted to help Jared and Ivanka find a home in Washington, where they planned to move from New York before the president took office. Perhaps it was just a friendly gesture. Or perhaps it was a way to burrow in closer to the Trump children. It was difficult to say, because in the modern era there had not been a president who remained vested in any business interests while in the White House.

Counterintelligence officials had concerns about the attempts by foreign countries to buy influence with Trump's children, but they only went so far. Sure, these countries could seek to exploit the children to gain access to Trump. That was bad. But foreign countries routinely had their officials and spies cozy up to the family members of elected leaders. Next on the ladder of concerns for American counterintelligence officials is ensuring that potentially vulnerable or compromised people are restricted from having access to classified information. The good news was that none of the children were going to be able to know the country's most sensitive secrets. The president's sons Don Jr. and Eric were going to remain out of government to run the family business. And while Trump's son-in-law, Jared Kushner, and daughter Ivanka planned to join the administration, they had said that reports during the transition that they would seek security clearances when they joined the White House staff were false.

But as the inauguration drew near, Kushner and Ivanka quietly began completing the background forms and extensive paperwork needed to get a top-secret-level clearance. Improbably, given his paucity of experience in the area of foreign policy or international relations, Kushner planned to take the lead on negotiating Middle East peace; of course, having a security clearance would be essential to that role. From the start, there were problems. In a section of his application in which he was required to disclose all of his foreign contacts, Kushner failed to list multiple meetings with Russians during the campaign and transition. The omission suggested that he may have broken the federal law that says those filling out the forms must be forthcoming and truthful.

"I have never seen that level of mistakes," said Charles Phalen, the top Trump administration official dealing with background checks for security clearances.

To fix the paperwork issue, which was becoming a public relations problem that Kushner had his press aides spend an inordinate amount of time spinning, Kushner hired a high-profile former Justice Department official. After at least four revisions to Kushner's background check document—in which more than a hundred names were added to his list of contacts with foreigners—the issue largely receded from the headlines, and Kushner was issued a temporary clearance, pending his background check, which entailed a proper vetting by the FBI.

A year into Trump's presidency, Kushner still hadn't received a clearance, and this remained a source of real concern among senior White House staff. Then, in mid-February 2018, after Rob Porter was fired following spousal abuse accusations about him in the media, it was revealed that he, like Kushner, had been working since the beginning of the administration with only an interim security clearance. Porter had been the staff secretary, a position not widely known outside the White House but one of the more consequential jobs in the West Wing. As staff secretary, Porter was in charge of all the paper that is supposed to go in front of the president, including the most sensitive national security documents that were routinely sent for the president's review and approval by the intelligence community and the Pentagon.

Some officials operate with an interim clearance at the beginning of an administration while the FBI conducts a background check, and the White House's personnel office can then make a determination about whether they should be granted a clearance. But when an official continues to work under an interim clearance for a year, it means that something has been uncovered in the background check that has raised questions about whether the official should have access to classified information. In Porter's case, former top national security experts from Democratic and Republican administrations were appalled, saying that no person should be able to hold such a high position without a permanent clearance. By delaying a decision about Porter's clearance, the experts contended, the White House had effectively allowed Porter to skirt the process that had been set up to ensure that compromised people were never given access to sensitive materials.

The White House came under intense scrutiny for not adhering to the norms of previous administrations in dispensing security clearances. In response to the outcry, John Kelly and Don McGahn worked together to put into effect a new policy: White House officials who had had interim security clearances for more than six months would have their clearances downgraded or revoked. The new policy directed attention squarely on Kushner and his security clearance. As was the case with Porter, there were problems in Kushner's background. Along with the omissions and revisions, intelligence officials had concerns about Kushner's business dealings and personal relations with foreign leaders. At the time, Kushner's family owed more than $1 billion for their mortgage on 666 Fifth Avenue—a boxy commercial skyscraper in midtown Manhattan—and the Kushners were seeking funding from countries like China and Qatar. Among the concerns was that foreign leaders would seek to do personal business with Kushner to gain access to the White House.

Trump's indifference to norms—like protecting state secrets—had created a problem that hit very close to home and was now very public. But in a balkanized West Wing, concern over adhering to some vestige of White House norms had long since split the staff down the middle.

On one side were Kelly and McGahn, who believed that, given Trump's carelessness with several of the most important elements of the presidency, they had to act in the best interests of both the government and the country and serve as presidential guardrails. Kelly and McGahn felt as though they tolerated more petulant and self-destructive behavior from the president than anyone to have ever held the positions of White House chief of staff and White House counsel. Between policing Trump's ignorance of presidential traditions and norms of conduct and his obsession with settling scores and fighting with the media, both men felt as if they had time for little else. They were forces for good, they believed, and they resented having to serve as the "bad cops" for the whims and ethical lapses of "the family." Both men thought that "the kids" were caricatures of entitlement, but they knew the president had no appetite for putting any limits on their power.

On the other side were Kushner, Ivanka, and their allies, who resented any checks on their power, believing Kelly and McGahn were using this issue as a way to limit their power because they saw them as rivals. Trump liked the conflict between his children, on the one hand, and Kelly and McGahn, on the other, because it meant that they were distracted by undercutting each other and less focused on containing him. And with the president disengaged from the issue, the battle over security clearances would be a fight for survival pitting the chief of staff and the counsel against the president's family, with Kelly and McGahn fighting for the traditional process that ensured the security of sensitive material and Kushner fighting to maintain his dominance over the senior appointees in the West Wing.

Among the reasons that red flags had been raised in the intelligence community about Kushner's security clearance were his business connections in Israel, Russia, and the United Arab Emirates. But Kelly and McGahn's crackdown was met with an escalation from Jared's camp. On February 16, within hours of the new policy being put in place, Kushner released a statement through his lawyer, Abbe Lowell, acknowledging the holdups with his clearance but misleadingly stating that the issues were merely routine. Lowell said that he had been in touch with officials dealing with the security clearance at the White House and that they "again have confirmed that there are a dozen or more people at Mr. Kushner's level whose process is delayed" and "that it is not uncommon for this process to take this long in a new administration."

Lowell added that "the current backlogs are being addressed, and no concerns were raised about Mr. Kushner's application," and he said that Kelly's announcement that day of the new clearance policy would have no impact on "the very important work he has been assigned by the President."

That evening, as I sat at my desk at the *Times,* I got a message from a source who said he had new information on Kushner's security clearance. The source said that Kushner had a "high-level law enforcement problem."

I had never heard that term before. In the media, we had obsessed about who in the administration was and was not under investigation. The more I thought about it, the more I realized it was sort of a cute way of saying that Kushner was under investigation.

"It's something significant," the source said. "Jared has a significant problem."

The source said that the Justice Department, through Rosenstein, had warned Kelly that week that the authorities had some sort of "derogatory information" on Kushner. Rosenstein told Kelly that while he had to refrain from discussing an ongoing investigation, the issue was unlikely to be resolved anytime soon.

The source said Kelly had relayed this anecdote to the president's personal lawyer John Dowd, who often had trouble keeping his mouth shut. Dowd had told others, and word had gotten around town. "Dowd said Jared has a high-level law enforcement problem; nobody will tell Kelly what it is," the source said.

"Kelly tried to figure it out," the source added.

But the source said he did not know any more about how much progress Kelly had made other than learning that Kushner had a "high-level law enforcement problem."

The source told me that this development had further complicated Kushner's already-troubled security clearance. And Kelly's investigation would make coming up with a determination about what to do with Kushner's clearance even more fraught.

All I could find on my desk to write on was a paper plate left over from another dinner eaten at my desk, so I scribbled on it as the source talked.

This new information provided the clearest proof yet that reassurances from Kushner's side that "Jared was fine" and had nothing to worry about regarding the Mueller investigation or any other Justice Department inquiry might be false. Dowd was known to be indiscreet, but he was also known to be accurate. All the same, this seemed dangerous. I kept the plate with my scribbled notes as a reminder and picked at it with sources over the next several months.

I would later confirm while working on this book that the information I had was true: Kelly had in fact been briefed on the Justice Department investigation into Kushner. Under the new procedures created by Kelly and McGahn, those aides who had their background checks languish unresolved would have their clearances downgraded within a week. Of course, Kushner's clearance created a distinctive problem because he was the president's son-in-law, his clearance had already attracted a lot of unwelcome attention, and any decisions made about his access to classified documents would be highly scrutinized by the media and Congress. A year into the presidency, McGahn had learned many measures he could take to protect himself when faced with a difficult situation: Either Annie

Donaldson would take contemporaneous notes, or he would write memos to the file himself. For the Kushner problem, McGahn needed to create a record, just in case. The issue was already receiving tons of media scrutiny. Kelly had been briefed on highly sensitive national security information about Kushner. And Kushner's lawyer had put out a misleading statement to the media about how the clearance was being dealt with. Someday, McGahn knew, he might have to explain this.

So on February 23, McGahn sent a two-page memo to Kelly that laid out why he believed Kushner's clearance should be downgraded. The memo was marked "Sensitive, unclassified, privileged and confidential." McGahn began by memorializing the new policies that had been put in place in the aftermath of the Porter debacle. He said that among those whose clearances remained unresolved were some of the highest-ranking officials in the West Wing, including an assistant to the president and two special assistants to the president.

McGahn then tackled the biggest issue at hand.

"There remains the question of one assistant to the president, however, whose daily functions will be considerably impacted by the implementation of today's roll off," McGahn wrote, referring to Kushner. "As you're aware, there have been multiple reports in the media regarding this particular assistant to the president that have raised questions about the individual's fitness to receive the most sensitive national security information."

The White House counsel then laid out a sanitized version of what I had been told the previous Friday night by a source: Kelly had recently received a classified briefing about Kushner and had briefed McGahn about what he had learned.

"The information you were briefed on one week ago and subsequently relayed to me, raises serious additional concerns about whether this individual ought to retain a top security clearance until such issues can be investigated and resolved," McGahn said.

McGahn said he had been unable to receive the briefing or "access this highly compartmented information directly" about Kushner.

Given all these factors—the unresolved background check and

the derogatory information Kelly had been briefed on—McGahn made his recommendation, saying his clearance should be downgraded.

"According, in my judgement, the roll off of this individual for interim access to TS and TSSCI information, including the PDB (presidential daily briefing), is only appropriate at this time," McGahn said.

"Interim secret is the highest clearance that I can concur until further information is received," McGahn concluded, referring to the level of classified information Kushner would be able to access.

By reducing Kushner's clearance from top secret to secret, McGahn and Kelly had restricted Kushner's access to the PDB, the closely held rundown provided by the intelligence community six days a week for the president and his top aides, and other highly sensitive intelligence that exposed sources and methods.

McGahn did note that there was a possibility that when the background check was complete, it could be resolved in Kushner's favor, or there could be a recommendation that he not receive a clearance.

And then McGahn conceded that Trump could if he chose simply disregard any security concerns and circumvent any standard procedures and grant Kushner the security clearance himself.

"As you know," he wrote to Kelly, "the executive power vested in the president by the Constitution allows him to determine ultimately which individuals may have access to national security information. The president may unilaterally grant security clearance to an individual regardless of a BI [background investigation] or any staff's recommendation. Should the president of the United States wish to bypass the established process of which to evaluate whether a member of his staff should have access to national security information by being evaluated for and grant a security clearance, he personally is the one who needs to make the determination if desired."

It was in 1883 that Congress had first implemented a standard process for examining a government employee's "fitness" for a job, and since then a system of culling government officials' backgrounds had been created and refined. What it had evolved to was far from perfect. But it had a track record of ensuring that state secrets remained secret and that foreign countries had to overcome great obstacles to infiltrate the president's inner circle and influence American domestic and foreign policy. Now that system faced a test—a test probably greater than any that has ever been publicly known. And that test came from the two people closest to the president. Kelly and McGahn believed that when pushed whether to side with the children or the country, Trump would pick the children. But they were not going to let Trump do that without a fight.

★ ★ ★

MARCH 8, 2018

ONE YEAR, ONE MONTH, AND TEN DAYS UNTIL THE RELEASE OF THE MUELLER REPORT

SPECIAL COUNSEL'S OFFICE—McGahn and Burck returned to the windowless conference room in Mueller's office exactly a month after Trump pressured McGahn to change his account of his attempt to fire Mueller. For hours, McGahn recounted how Trump had argued with him over what he had told Mueller about the firing attempt and asked him to create a White House document to refute what he had told investigators. Burck helped fill in gaps in the story, describing his conversations with Dowd and providing the prosecutors with text messages Dowd had sent him about how McGahn could not resign no matter how hard Trump pressured him.

Quarles and Goldstein were operating in a remarkable investigative space. They essentially had a member of Trump's legal team helping the government build a case against Trump. With investigations into previous presidents—most recently Bill Clinton—White House counsels had stymied every effort to gain information, access, and insight of any kind. But with Cobb paying little attention, Quarles and Goldstein seized the moment and exploited the opportunity, turning McGahn into their main channel of information. This access to McGahn allowed the special counsel's office to operate at lightning speed. In a little more than a month, Trump had taken an action that raised questions about whether he had obstructed justice; the prosecutors learned about it almost as soon as it happened and had secured statements from McGahn to document the incident. Quarles and Goldstein essentially had a real-time cooperating witness against the president inside the White House who could be there to collect evidence on how Trump continued to obstruct the investigation.

Now Quarles and Goldstein wanted more.

The prosecutors could see a new and disturbing trend in Trump's behavior; he not only wanted to obstruct the Mueller investigation and make it more difficult for investigators to uncover damning facts but also wanted to use his power to destroy and prosecute his rivals, like Comey and the deputy FBI director, Andrew McCabe. In addition to the publicly available evidence—the president's Twitter feed was a living, breathing evidentiary record—to make a stronger case, prosecutors would need to secure statements from those around the president to show that behind his bluster was a real effort to use the power of the Justice Department to target his enemies.

With McGahn's lavish cooperation, what Trump was saying behind closed doors was potentially just a phone call away, and the prosecutors wanted to try to use that lever to collect more evidence on the president. One of the first issues Quarles and Goldstein pushed on related to McCabe. Eight days after Mueller's team interviewed McGahn in March about Trump's attempts at witness tampering, Sessions, working with Rosenstein, fired McCabe. The stated reason was that McCabe had misled internal watchdogs at the bureau about his role in providing an investigative journalist with details for a story.

The firing came with an extra punitive twist. After twenty-one years in the FBI, McCabe was fired just one day away from retiring and collecting his full government pension. The move by Rosenstein and Sessions made it appear as if they were doing Trump's bidding, because the president had publicly broadcast his views on the issue several times.

"FBI Deputy Director Andrew McCabe is racing the clock to retire with full benefits. 90 days to go?!!!" Trump had tweeted in December.

The prosecutors knew that Trump had pressured Sessions to reassert his control over the Russia investigation to essentially stop it from ensnaring him. And Trump had leaned on Sessions by holding his job over his head. They now wanted to know whether that pressure had manifested itself in the firing of McCabe. In the days after the firing, Quarles and Goldstein reached out to Burck to ask whether Trump had played a role in the firing.

Burck knew that he had to answer their questions. If he refused to answer, it would raise questions about whether he was covering something up. So he checked with McGahn, who had continued to fall out of favor with Trump and was spending little time with the president. McGahn told Burck he didn't know anything about what Trump might have done to force the McCabe firing but said he might have discussed the prospect of firing McCabe with Sessions and Rosenstein.

Burck relayed that information—sketchy as it was—to Mueller's office.

The ask by Mueller's team angered McGahn, because it served as a stark example of the consequences of the decision by Trump, Cobb, and Dowd to allow Mueller unfettered access to McGahn. He could now see the investigators trying to use him to dish on Trump in real time.

How can I do my job? They might as well send an FBI agent around with me to take notes, McGahn thought.

★★★

APRIL 9, 2018

ONE YEAR AND NINE DAYS UNTIL THE RELEASE OF THE MUELLER REPORT

OVAL OFFICE—Hours after FBI agents in New York raided the offices of Trump's personal lawyer Michael Cohen, Rosenstein—who had signed off on the search warrant—walked into the Oval Office to meet with Trump and McGahn. Rosenstein was there for a meeting to assuage the president's concerns about the Justice Department's delay in releasing documents from the Clinton email investigation. Trump wanted the FBI producing more and more documents to show Clinton in a negative light and demonstrate how Comey had made the wrong call in refusing to recommend her prosecution. To put Trump at ease, Rosenstein had brought someone the president had come to like and trust: Dana Boente, the FBI's general counsel, who had overseen the Russia investigation at the Justice Department the previous year. But as often happened with the president, events in the news had distracted him.

Trump, furious, wanted to talk about the Cohen raid.

When pressed by Trump for details on the raid, Rosenstein told the president the investigation involved Cohen's business dealings unrelated to Trump. While it was true that the agents in New York were investigating Cohen's taxi medallion business, they were also examining his role in arranging payments to silence a porn star about her relationship with Trump in the month before the 2016 election. Rosenstein had been briefed extensively on that part of the investigation, but he portrayed it to Trump as if it had nothing to do with him.

As the investigation intensified in the coming months, Trump would repeatedly tell his personal lawyers that Rosenstein had assured him that the investigation of Cohen had nothing to do with him.

Less than a week after the Cohen raid, excerpts of Comey's book, *A Higher Loyalty,* began appearing in the media. The book chronicled Comey's career and included several chapters on his relationship with Trump. Comey described Trump as an unethical and untruthful leader, comparing him to the mob bosses he used to investigate as a federal prosecutor in New York. Comey poked fun at Trump's tanning regimen and the size of his hands.

ABC News aired an hour-long interview with Comey, conducted by the network's top political anchor, George Stephanopoulos, reigniting negative coverage about Trump's decision to fire Comey, whether the president had obstructed justice, and the dossier. Comey had never been briefed about the dossier's central source casting doubt on the entire document, and in the interview lent credence to the dossier, telling Stephanopoulos that at its core it "was consistent with the other information we'd gathered during the intelligence investigation." Comey described Steele as "a credible source, someone with a track record, someone who was a credible and respected member of an allied intelligence service during his career." He continued: "And so it was important that we try to understand it, and see what could we verify, what could we rule in or out? . . . There's no doubt that he had a network of sources and sub-sources in a position to report on these kinds of things."

Comey described how he informed Trump of the raw intelligence in the dossier about the supposed incident from 2013 in which Russian intelligence filmed him in the presidential suite of the Ritz-Carlton hotel in Moscow in the company of prostitutes.

"He interrupted very defensively," Comey said, "and started talking about it: 'You know, do I look like a guy who needs hookers?'"

Stephanopoulos asked Comey how graphic he got with Trump.

"I think as graphic as I needed to be. I did not go into the business about—people peeing on each other. I just thought it was a weird enough experience for me to be talking to the incoming president of the United States about prostitutes in a hotel in Moscow."

Comey then left open the possibility that the allegation was true.

"I honestly never thought these words would come out of my mouth, but I don't know whether the current president of the United States was with prostitutes peeing on each other in Moscow in 2013," Comey said. "It's possible, but I don't know."

The coverage sent Trump into a rage. In his four decades as a businessman in New York, Trump had followed a familiar routine when he felt he had been wronged by rivals: He would claim they broke the law and threaten to sue them. Occasionally, he actually filed a complaint against them in court. Now, as president, even though he controlled the executive branch of the U.S. government, his preferred medium to settle scores was Twitter.

"James Comey is a proven LEAKER & LIAR," Trump tweeted on April 13. "Virtually everyone in Washington thought he should be fired for the terrible job he did-until he was, in fact, fired. He leaked CLASSIFIED information, for which he should be prosecuted. He lied to Congress under OATH. He is a weak and . . . untruthful slime ball who was, as time has proven, a terrible Director of the FBI. His handling of the Crooked Hillary Clinton case, and the events surrounding it, will go down as one of the worst 'botch jobs' of history. It was my great honor to fire James Comey!"

Trump had leveled so many similar accusations as president that the tweet quickly dissipated in the ether. Despite his accusing Comey of felonies for leaking classified information and lying to Congress, the media generally treated Trump tweets like empty threats, or entertainment, and the coverage of this particular tirade focused on the president's calling Comey an "untruthful slime ball." What was unknown at the time—what we all missed—was that Trump had broadcast publicly exactly how he had sought to use his power behind closed doors. Now, confronted with a new irritant from Comey, Trump realized he needed more than just tweets and arm-twisting. *Goddamn it,* Trump said to his aides, he was president of the United States. He needed to take the law into his own hands. He would prosecute them himself if he had to.

So, in the middle of April, Trump turned to one of the few people in the White House who, in spite of their differences, he believed could actually get something done: Don McGahn. In an Oval Office meeting, the president complained to McGahn about Sessions for his refusal to prosecute Clinton and Comey. Trump told McGahn that he wanted to order Sessions to prosecute them. If Sessions did not want to do it, Trump said he wanted to use his power as president to prosecute Clinton and Comey on his own. It was a startling disclosure for even Trump. Immediately, McGahn realized that the president's determination to use the justice system to selectively direct prosecutions against his enemies was an enormous problem. Trump was already under investigation for obstructing justice for his firing of Comey. Now, his push for revenge, a blatant abuse of presidential power, could put Trump in the position of trying to prosecute a potential chief witness against him.

Trump's request also showed McGahn that the president had little idea how prosecutions actually functioned, because the president had no power to order someone to be charged with a crime.

"First of all," McGahn told the president, "you can't prosecute anybody. Second of all, that's the Department of Justice's job, and if you do that, they're all going to quit."

Trump said he did not understand. He was the president and ran the executive branch. Why couldn't he tell the Justice Department whom to prosecute?

At this point in the presidency, McGahn thought he knew how to tame Trump.

"How about I do this? I'm going to write you a memo explaining to you what the law is and how it works, and I'll give that memo to you and you can decide what you want to do," McGahn said.

McGahn knew what the memo would say: Trump had no power to prosecute anyone. That decision is made by apolitical Justice Department prosecutors who present evidence to grand juries, which are controlled by the judicial branch and indict individuals. The president could ask the attorney general to investigate someone. But the perception of that move—especially because it flouted the norms that had been established in the aftermath of Watergate to shield justice from politics—could further imperil Trump's presidency.

The move to write the memo showed McGahn's cunning ability to deal with Trump. If McGahn had simply told Trump he could not do as he wished, it could easily cause the president to lash out and make an irrational move, like firing him or Mueller. But by offering to write the memo, McGahn was both memorializing their exchange—a written record that showed he opposed this effort—and buying himself time for Trump to become distracted by something else. And McGahn knew that whatever the memo said, there was no chance Trump would sit down and read it. By that time, it was well known around the White House that Trump was not much of a reader, especially when it came to detailed and lengthy documents, like the memos. He preferred that their contents be summarized for him in a short conversation. The president had not read one book during his time in office.

McGahn briefly considered asking the Justice Department's Office of Legal Counsel—the arm of the department that helps interpret laws—to provide advice on what the president could do. But it was such an elementary question and McGahn feared it could leak.

Instead, he asked the lawyers who worked for him in the White House counsel's office to write a memo laying out the problems with the president trying to prosecute his rivals.

The lawyers in McGahn's office—conservatives who had been raised in the Federalist Society legal culture—had joined the administration to be on the front lines of the most serious legal clashes over executive branch power, such as how the president could use his authority to carry out his agenda on issues like trade and immigration. They believed in that work and had no interest or any expectation that in their jobs in the White House counsel's office they would be pressed into service to answer a fairly basic, but politically toxic, question about how the president could and could not use his power. But at McGahn's request, several attorneys in his office put their legal acumen to the extraordinary task of trying to protect the president from his most self-destructive impulses.

McGahn's lawyers researched the question with the same vigor they put into more fulfilling policy briefs. From their offices in the Eisenhower Executive Office Building, they pored over Supreme Court decisions, the Constitution, presidential history, and law review writings from a range of lawyers and judges spanning the political spectrum. That work resulted in several drafts—addressed from the White House counsel to the president—that in the annals of the American presidency may well be without equal. The drafts totaled nearly ten thousand words and ran dozens of pages. They carried subject lines like "DIRECTING CRIMINAL ENFORCEMENT" and "Privileged, confidential and deliberative."

The memos were written in a way that didn't leave any doubt about how the White House lawyers felt about the question. Unlike many legal opinions on gray-area issues and other White House memos, McGahn did not offer any counterargument to his assessment that Trump could not initiate a prosecution against anyone, much less a figure whom he had run against for the presidency. The lawyers labored over the language, to ensure that no sentence could be taken out of context and construed as permission for such action. In dry but clear legal writing, the paragraphs build a powerful and comprehensive rebuke of the president's desire to use his position atop the executive branch to carry out his vendettas. As a reading experience, one cannot escape noticing that the writers seemed to be acutely aware of the strangeness of this brief—to, essentially, teach an introduction-to-the-Constitution class to a president in training.

From the top, the briefs address the question that had increasingly showed up in Trump's private conversations, tweets, and remarks to the media. "You've asked what steps you may lawfully take if you disagree with the Attorney General's decision not to pursue criminal prosecution or not to conduct further criminal investigation," McGahn said in the opening paragraph of one memo. The line seemed charitable to Trump, who had rarely asked his lawyers whether something he wanted to do was legal. In fact, he once asked McGahn why he had to follow international law; McGahn explained it was in the Constitution. It's not as if Trump had gone to McGahn and specifically asked what was "legal"; he just wanted to know how he could throw Clinton and Comey in prison.

From there, McGahn made three overarching points: *Don't do it.* If you do try this, you will likely get into huge trouble and could even be impeached. And, if you're really upset about all of this, your only recourse is to fire the attorney general.

"There is a strong constitutional norm against political involvement in decisions about prosecution or criminal investigations," McGahn told Trump.

The American people and Justice Department officials "share strong aversion to even the appearance that law enforcement decisions reflect political calculations rather than the sound exercise of legal judgement."

"Particularly over the last several decades, consensus has emerged that a key component of ensuring fair criminal proceedings is avoiding even the appearance of political motivation for prosecution or criminal investigation," McGahn wrote.

The memos educated Trump on the powers a president actually had under Article II of the Constitution. Despite being the head of the executive branch and the person who appoints the attorney general, he had no authority to actually prosecute someone himself. Only the attorney general had that power.

"You do not have authority however to initiate an investigation or prosecution yourself or circumvent the Attorney General by directing a different official to pursue a prosecution or investigation," McGahn wrote.

To give the president proper context, McGahn detailed the evolution of American justice from the country's founding, to show how politics had been slowly extracted from prosecutions over the 242 years of American history. Presidents Washington, Adams, and Jefferson, McGahn said, all instructed district attorneys on when to start and end prosecutions. The country had just been formed, and the federal government and its law enforcement powers were in their infancy. For our first presidents, leading a prosecution "was not something controversial" that they sought to keep from the public.

"Presidents were rather open about their direction, discussing their control in published speeches and proclamations," McGahn wrote to Trump. Directing prosecutions became so openly accepted that the Senate once asked President Adams to have a district attorney prosecute a newspaper publisher for slandering the Senate. "President Adams complied, sending a letter to the district attorney for Pennsylvania instructing him to prosecute the man," McGahn wrote. "Again, modern practice differs markedly."

Skipping ahead 150 years in American legal history to the 1940s, McGahn demonstrated just how far the country had moved from its founding toward a clear separation between politics and the pursuit of justice. President Franklin D. Roosevelt's attorney general, Robert H. Jackson, argued in 1940 directly against what Trump wanted to do eighty years later, the memo said.

"The most dangerous power of the prosecutor," Jackson wrote, was that "he will pick people that he thinks he should get rather than pick cases that need to be prosecuted."

But not until Watergate—and its shocking revelations of corruption and criminality that reached all the way to the Oval Office—did the public truly begin to pay close attention to the need for an independent Justice Department. McGahn used remarks made just three years after Nixon resigned by President Carter's first attorney general, Griffin Bell, to show the scars the scandal had left.

"In our form of government there are things that are nonpartisan and one is the law," Bell said. "But the partisan activities of some attorneys general in this century combined with the unfortunate legacy of Watergate have given rise to an understandable public concern that some decisions at Justice may be the products of favor, or pressure, or politics."

Bell added, "White House influences on the Justice Department, real and suspected, had contributed greatly to the public opinion."

McGahn used other remarks by Bell to drive home the importance of a president keeping his distance from the Justice Department.

"The president's best served when the attorney general and the lawyers who assist him are free to exercise their professional judgment," Bell said. "Just as important, they must be perceived by the American people as being free to do so."

Despite the post-Watergate reforms to police the relationship between the White House and the Justice Department, McGahn wrote, scandals have still arisen.

"These policies have not fully averted controversy," according to McGahn.

McGahn laid out how in 2006 President George W. Bush had abruptly fired seven U.S. attorneys. Those dismissals gave rise to allegations that the prosecutors were dismissed for going after Bush's allies and refusing to target his rivals. The consequences were painful.

"Following a 2-year investigation, the Department of Justice inspector general concluded that the removals were handled improperly and recommended that the attorney general appoint a special counsel to investigate whether political influence over the pending prosecutions motivated at least one of the removals, though a special counsel was never appointed," according to McGahn. "Thus, not only is there a strong constitutional norm against political influence over law enforcement, but there is also specific tradition that this norm imposes strict limits on the appropriations on the White House involvement in individual criminal matters."

McGahn even cited a 2001 *Harvard Law Review* article by Elena Kagan, one of the Supreme Court justices appointed by President

Obama, to show, as she said, that "the crassest forms of politics (involving, at the extreme, personal favors and vendettas) pose the greatest danger of displacing professionalism and thereby undermining confidence in legal decisionmaking."

The memos then cited a justice from the other end of the political spectrum. "Congress . . . can impeach the executive who willfully fails to enforce the laws . . . and the courts can dismiss malicious prosecutions," Justice Antonin Scalia wrote in *Morrison v. Olson*.

But leaving aside the chance he may face political consequences, the memo was intended to explain to Trump that the norms against prosecutions were designed to protect individual citizens from being unreasonably targeted and that the president should not have a law enforcement role when it comes to individual citizens.

"The gulf between the overwhelming power of the federal government and the vulnerability of the individual citizen may be nowhere starker than in the criminal prosecution or an investigation," McGahn said. "That is why, among other protections for the accused," the Constitution demands that "no person should be deprived of life, liberty or property without due process of law."

The president faced dire consequences if he even appeared to meddle in the Justice Department's decisions about prosecutions, McGahn said.

"There are several political and pragmatic reasons why the president should exercise caution before deciding to get involved in any criminal matter," McGahn warned.

The first obstacle Trump would likely face is Congress, which McGahn said stood best positioned to take on the president. Describing Congress as "perhaps the most likely and formidable foe in a potential conflict of presidential involvement in a specific criminal matter," McGahn explained that it has "many tools if it perceives (even wrongly) that the president had crossed a line."

Either the House or the Senate could conduct "intrusive and protracted oversight to investigate the motivations and details of the president's involvement." That oversight could come with restrictions on funding that could hurt the executive branch's ability to "continue an investigation or prosecution."

Of greatest significance, "Congress could seek to ***'impeach and remove'*** the president if it concluded that he abused the power of intervening in a criminal matter," McGahn wrote, using bold and italics to emphasize Congress's powers.

The next obstacle Trump could face is the courts. McGahn acknowledged that the courts would likely not be as proactive as Congress at taking on the president, but the courts had several levers that judges could pull to thwart the president. If someone who had been targeted by the president was charged with a crime, a judge could dismiss the indictment, saying it was "selective or vindictive." If the president played a direct role in someone's prosecution, that individual could sue the federal government under the Federal Tort Claims Act for a "malicious prosecution" and claim the president's "involvement improperly" influenced the case.

The president could also face problems within his own administration. His own Justice Department officials—like Sessions—could refuse to carry out his orders. And, McGahn wrote, even if Trump were to fire the attorney general, law enforcement officials within the Justice Department would still retain the sole authority to prosecute individuals for federal crimes. McGahn suggested that the department's remaining officials might want to disrupt any prosecutorial decisions that they saw as corrupt—causing further political issues and delaying the political prosecutions.

"Defiant executive officials could substantially disrupt any effort to direct a criminal proceeding and the process would further fan the flames of political opposition," McGahn wrote.

Outside government, the American people could ultimately hold the president accountable were he to seek reelection. "The norm against political influence in law enforcement is enforceable by the American people at the ballot box," McGahn wrote.

Trump could fire the attorney general, McGahn wrote, and seek to replace him with someone more willing to do his bidding. Such a dismissal may be the president's only constitutional avenue to direct the Justice Department's prosecutorial decisions. But, McGahn added, taking such a move could spawn new and perhaps greater problems for the president.

First, and most obviously, there would likely be significant political blowback to the dismissal, because it would appear as if the president were undermining the independence of the Justice Department that had been considered nearly absolute in the decades since Watergate.

The McGahn memos are also remarkable for the balance they strike between being respectful and restrained, peremptory and proscriptive. While McGahn cautioned Trump against executive actions that could hurt himself, it's hard to ignore that by this point in his presidency Trump had already done much of what he was being warned against. McGahn knew that the president had asked Comey to end the Flynn investigation, he had fired Comey, he had called for the prosecution of Comey and Clinton, he had declared that he would not have made Sessions his attorney general if he knew he was going to recuse himself from any matters related to the Russia investigation, and he had tried to fire Mueller.

McGahn's office completed the memos by the end of April, and McGahn had them delivered to the president. There is no evidence that Trump ever read them.

In spite of McGahn's wariness about providing the special counsel's office with information about what Trump had said about ousting McCabe, Mueller's prosecutors pressed on, undeterred. By the end of April, the prosecutors had contacted Burck with another request. They wanted to know whether Trump had followed through on what he was saying publicly about Comey. Mueller's team told Burck, We see the tweets about how Comey should be in jail, and they asked, Is he saying anything about that privately? Is he explaining that to Don?

Burck knew the answer. McGahn had told him about Trump's desire to prosecute Clinton and Comey. Now Mueller's team had hit on an unfolding incident that he knew something about. The White House had told McGahn to cooperate with the special counsel's investigation. Being interviewed is one thing, but this type of ongoing back-and-forth was different from Cobb's original green light on cooperation. Although Burck and McGahn had found Cobb's decision to be strange, they now understood that McGahn was required to answer any questions Mueller put to him about past events. However, when it came to delivering documents in real time and divulging ongoing discussions, neither of them felt that Cobb's directive applied. Neither the president nor his lawyers could know whether something of questionable legality would be discussed in the future, including on the obstruction question, so it is unlikely that Cobb's directive had been meant to commit McGahn to open-ended future cooperation with prosecutors.

But Burck could not lie to the prosecutors. Both he and McGahn could get into trouble for that. So he answered the question.

"He's talked to Don about wanting to prosecute Hillary and Comey, and Don wrote him a memo about it," Burck told the prosecutors.

All of this obviously interested Quarles and Goldstein, who were determined to show that the president had obstructed justice. Having the White House counsel's office documenting the president's conduct—in writing—could be extraordinarily damning evidence of just how reckless Trump's behavior had gotten. But Quarles and Goldstein also clearly knew they were on treacherous ground asking the president's lawyer to hand over a document that clearly belonged to the White House.

If we ask for it, will you consider providing it to us? they asked.

"Let me think about it," Burck said.

Clearly, Burck, McGahn, Quarles, and Goldstein were heading into a new type of cooperation, with one side asking real-time questions and the other secretly providing responses.

Burck and McGahn's understanding of the White House's decision to allow them to cooperate was that they could go in and talk about events that had happened in the past. There was a question about whether McGahn's meeting with prosecutors after Trump's witness-tampering attempt violated that. For McGahn, there was a potential ethical problem, too: On the one hand he was a lawyer providing advice to a client, and on the other he would be contemporaneously providing information to prosecutors about what his client was saying to him as he sought that legal advice.

Of course, it was Trump's own behavior that had created this dilemma. But still, how could McGahn secretly cooperate against Trump while being his lawyer?

"This is getting a little uncomfortable, with no one representing the White House's interests," Burck told McGahn in a phone call.

McGahn was in a vise. Did he have an ethical obligation to tell the administration that there was no lawyer protecting Trump or the office of the presidency? Somehow, Burck and McGahn needed to ensure that the interests of the presidency were being protected without alienating Mueller or tipping off Trump that Mueller's office was working so hard to get him that they were trying to turn McGahn into a cooperating witness.

Burck and McGahn had several options.

The first option was to deny the request from Mueller's team and let them know that they would be unable to provide any real-time documentation or cooperation. Taking that path could immediately backfire. Turning down any request could easily lead Quarles and Goldstein to believe that McGahn was holding back other important information. Faced with an uncooperative McGahn, the prosecutors could subpoena him and spark a legal firestorm that could plague the remainder of McGahn's time in the White House. And regardless of the response from Mueller's side, Burck and McGahn did not like any option that would appear adversarial to the investigation, because they understood that there would be a very public report produced at the conclusion of the process. If Mueller's team included one or two negative facts about McGahn and how he helped Trump obstruct justice, it could significantly damage McGahn's reputation or even put him in legal jeopardy.

The second option would be to simply notify the White House of the request and hope that Cobb would put a stop to the line of inquiry. But that option also came with complications. If Mueller's team found out that Burck and McGahn were going back to the White House and discussing their responses with the lawyers defending the president, it could appear to prosecutors that the White House lawyers were all just getting their stories straight and that McGahn's cooperation was not entirely genuine. Alerting the White House could also introduce legal questions of witness tampering because McGahn might end up communicating his understanding of events to Trump—a potential witness—allowing Trump to tailor what he would end up saying if questioned by investigators.

A third option was to simply comply with the request and hand over the memos McGahn had written for Trump to Mueller's team. The White House was supposed to determine what did—and did not—get handed over to Mueller. Burck and McGahn could make that decision on their own, but if they were caught, Cobb would likely tell Trump, who might fire McGahn.

Mueller's team had circumvented the White House like this before. Dowd had claimed in a January 2018 letter to Mueller that investigators did not need to question the president, because the White House had handed over McGahn's "extensive internal file memo." But that was not the whole story. The White House had only given the special counsel's office some of his chief of staff's notes.

Knowing they lacked the full trove, Quarles had turned to Burck for help.

"Is there any chance we can get the whole thing?" Quarles asked Burck.

Quarles declined to say why they wanted all of Annie Donaldson's notes.

Burck checked with Donaldson and McGahn to see if they would object to handing them over. They said that they would not object. For Burck, Cobb and Dowd had given him the green light to cooperate. Burck even had emails from Cobb to back that up.

The legal pads were brought over to the special counsel's office, where they were copied and then returned to Burck.

The fourth option was to pack up and leave the White House, which McGahn was actively considering.

Burck still believed resignation might be the best option. A lawyer always wants his client as far away as possible from someone who might break the law. Burck thought Mueller could be done with his report within weeks or months. McGahn had to be gone by then. So why not just go now? But McGahn knew that he was getting closer to the beginning of July, when Justice Anthony Kennedy would decide whether to retire and open up a seat on the Supreme Court.

The reports coming into spring 2018 reflected that Kennedy

seemed invigorated, savoring the moment. He appeared more outspoken than was typical, like someone trying to cement his legacy of conservatism. He voted more with the conservative majority than at any point in the past nine years.

He's writing for history, McGahn thought.

Surely this was his last term. McGahn decided that he could withstand the bizarreness of the White House until July 4. That meant he would be there through the end of the Court's term in late June, when justices typically retire. McGahn sensed that Kennedy was concerned about who might succeed him on the Court. If McGahn remained, it would show Kennedy that he could indeed retire and allow McGahn to shepherd an appropriate replacement through the thicket of confirmation.

Burck and McGahn realized that if Mueller's team continued to lean on them for cooperation, McGahn would likely have to quit. But McGahn wanted to remain in the White House to see what Kennedy would do. So Burck and McGahn concluded that their best option was to try to oust Cobb and replace him with someone with deep experience who would take a more adversarial approach to defending the president in an investigation. The legal team was already in turmoil; Dowd had quit in March in part because he had realized Trump "was a fucking liar," as he told others. Burck and McGahn had one person in mind: a lawyer named Emmet Flood, whom Burck had worked closely with during the George W. Bush administration. A year earlier, Flood had flirted with taking the job but turned it down amid concerns that Trump's personal lawyers—not he—would lead the legal team. Now, not only would McGahn have to persuade Trump to hire Flood, but Burck would have to persuade him to take the job. McGahn began circulating Flood's name in the West Wing. Burck called Flood, telling him that Trump needed a lawyer inside the White House. Trump's legal team was being rebuilt, Burck said, allowing Flood to be in charge and call the shots.

"Ty looks like he's on his way out, the president looks like he is ready to get rid of him, and Dowd is gone," Burck told Flood.

Burck didn't care if Trump's legal defense was strong or not. He had no allegiance to the president.

"I'm a lawyer for a witness; I've got to protect his interest only," Burck said. "I can't be looking out—nor should I be looking out—for the interests of the White House."

Regarding the president, Burck added, "I don't give a shit about Trump."

What Burck did care about was the prosecutors' continued requests for information from McGahn—a fact that Burck held back from Flood. But Burck had worked so closely with Flood, and trusted him so much, that he was confident that if Flood took over Cobb's role, it would put an end to the free-flowing cooperation and the real-time requests for information.

Trump was initially skeptical of Flood because he had been part of the legal team that defended Bill Clinton during his impeachment proceedings in the late 1990s. But aides made the case to Trump that Flood was the right lawyer for the new and more adversarial relationship to the special counsel's office. Trump had grown exasperated with the pace of the investigation, particularly after being sold on the notion, by Dowd and Cobb, that if he cooperated, it could be wrapped up in a matter of weeks. Now, nearly a year later, it appeared to be mushrooming instead, especially after the FBI had raided the offices of Trump's personal lawyer Michael Cohen.

Trump's new posture had been based on a careful calculation by his side. The Justice Department had informed the White House that Mueller would be bound by the department's guidelines, which said a sitting president could not be indicted. Essentially, Trump and his aides thought the president had no criminal exposure and only faced a threat from impeachment. And to them, impeachment, which would be determined by the House of Representatives, was a political problem, not a legal one. To defend himself, Trump needed to do everything he could to undermine Mueller's credibility with the public and ensure that Mueller received as little information as possible that he could use in the report to taint Trump. To execute that strategy, Trump believed he needed both an outside public relations attack dog and a behind-the-scenes litigator to jam up Mueller. The attack dog would go on cable television, speak to newspaper reporters, and more vigorously defend him regardless of the truth. This would satisfy Trump, who had long told aides that he thought he was the only person out there defending himself and he wanted someone else to go on the offensive with him.

To play the public attack dog role, Trump hired the former New York City mayor Rudy Giuliani. To do the real legal work, he met and spoke with a range of lawyers, including William Barr, who served as attorney general under George H. W. Bush and went on to become the general counsel of Verizon. Barr, who had made millions of dollars in the private sector, came close to accepting the job but decided against it, telling others he did not believe it was the right time. Ultimately, Trump settled on Flood to work inside the White House.

While the hiring of Giuliani got the most headlines—especially because the former mayor made a string of outlandish claims about the investigators—Mueller's team saw the addition of Flood as the real game changer. Flood came from Williams & Connolly, the Washington law firm that had a reputation for being one of the most aggressive litigators in town, with a long history of creating massive headaches for the Justice Department. But Flood was potentially more than an aggressive defense attorney. He came with particularly strong views of how special counsel investigations were unfair endeavors that needlessly wrecked presidencies. Through his experiences representing Clinton and working in the George W. Bush White House, he had become convinced that these types of investigations—with their unlimited money and time—were set up to ultimately come to only one conclusion: that the person under investigation broke the law. With these views came a hardened perspective: Trump, like other presidents, had to take a more confrontational approach to the investigators and do everything possible to avoid an interview. Putting aside Trump's problematic relationship with the truth, in Flood's eyes an interview came with massive risk for any president under investigation and turned the prosecutors into the judge, jury, and executioner of the presidency. By sitting with prosecutors, a president would be giving them a whole new set of evidence that they could pick over, identify any misstatement or omission, and then make the case the president committed perjury. But Flood faced a challenge on this issue. He was walking into a White House where the president wanted to sit for an interview because, as Trump told his aides repeatedly, he believed he could explain to Mueller that he did nothing wrong and his aides and previous lawyers had indulged that thought.

On the day the White House announced that it had hired Flood, it also said Cobb was leaving. In a sign of how differently Flood viewed the world than Cobb, that day Cobb was interviewed on a podcast to discuss his time at the White House. During the podcast, he suggested that Trump's remaining lawyers would likely allow Trump to be interviewed.

"I can't really say how likely it was at any given time, but it's certainly not off the table and people are working hard to make decisions and work toward an interview," Cobb said. "And assuming that can be concluded favorably, there'll be an interview."

Later that same night, Giuliani discussed the same topic on *Hannity.* He said that Trump himself was pushing to sit down with Mueller.

"If they're objective, we can work something out," Giuliani told Hannity.

For Flood the entire approach had to change. Instead of negotiating with Mueller's team about what the interview would look like, the discussion had to be about whether Mueller could go to court and legally compel Trump to answer questions.

But Flood had a more immediate issue: stopping the free flow of information to Mueller. Flood wanted to establish new boundaries between the White House and Mueller's team and tell them in no uncertain terms that he was slamming closed the open door to the West Wing. About two weeks after he started at the White House, an unmarked government car brought Flood over to Mueller's office, and he entered through a back entrance. In a windowless conference room, Flood laid out, in blunt but civil terms, how he viewed the investigation. A new sheriff had arrived in town, and the days of unfettered cooperation under Cobb were coming to an end. Flood told Mueller's team his beliefs about their investigation: It was designed to take down Trump, and it had started based on an illegal leak of information by Comey.

"I'm going to conduct myself according to those perspectives," Flood told the investigators.

He said that going forward, prosecutors would need to prove to him why they wanted certain documents and interviews from the White House.

Mueller, who attended the meeting, and the other prosecutors said little in response. In the weeks that followed, members of Mueller's team complained to friends about Flood's new approach. One of the prosecutors asked a friend whether Flood's old law firm, Williams & Connolly, had thrown a party when Flood left because he was such a pain in the ass.

★ ★ ★

MAY 21, 2018

332 DAYS UNTIL THE RELEASE OF THE MUELLER REPORT

MCGAHN'S OFFICE ON THE SECOND FLOOR OF THE WEST WING—By May, Kushner's background check had been completed, and McGahn and Kelly had to make a determination about whether to grant him a security clearance and at what level.

As he had done in February, McGahn wanted to create a record of how he handled the matter, and so he wrote another memo to Kelly.

The subject line read, "Re: Security clearances for Jared Kushner and Ivanka Trump."

"Background investigations, BIs, for both Mr. Kushner and Ms. Trump are both complete," McGahn wrote. "Individuals in the personnel security office were divided on opinion on whether to recommend granting a TS clearance at this time based on the unclassified information in the BI.

"The Central Intelligence Agency does not recommend granting the SCI clearance at this time," McGahn wrote, using the acronym for the most sensitive compartmented information.

"Given this situation as well as additional classified and sensitive information available to the White House counsel that it is not within the BIs [background investigations] review of the personal security officers or Central Intelligence Agency, the White House counsel does not recommend granting any adjudicated clearance at this time," McGahn wrote.

"Additional time and information may resolve some of these issues," he wrote. And in the final paragraph of the letter, in language that echoed his February memo, McGahn acknowledged that the president ultimately determines who should have access to the nation's secrets and could well ignore his recommendation.

"The president may ultimately grant a security clearance to an individual regardless of a BI or his staff's recommendation," McGahn wrote. "Should the President of the United States wish to bypass the established process by which the adjudicate clearances or override the recommendation of the staff and direct the granting of a clearance to Mr. Kushner or Ms. Trump, he may either by executing an order in his own hand or by issuing an order to the Chief of Staff to do so."

* * *

MAY 22, 2018

331 DAYS UNTIL THE RELEASE OF THE MUELLER REPORT

CHIEF OF STAFF'S OFFICE, THE WEST WING—McGahn's recommendation meant nothing to Trump. The following day he told Kelly that despite the concerns of the agencies and over McGahn's objections, he would grant Kushner and Ivanka "Top Secret" security clearances.

Like McGahn, Kelly felt the need to take measures to protect himself.

"Memorandum for the file," read the memo at the top.

The subject line read, "Re: Security Clearances for Jared Kushner and Ivanka Trump." The memo was only one paragraph.

"The President of the United States has ordered that Jared Kushner and Ivanka Trump be allowed to access national security information up to the Top Secret Level," Kelly said. "Accordingly, Jared Kushner and Ivanka Trump shall be granted Top Secret security clearances. Mr. Kushner and Ms. Trump shall be notified of their grant of Top Secret level security clearance."

Kushner wasted no time. The following day, his lawyer, Abbe Lowell, put out the word that Kushner's security clearance had been restored to "Top Secret."

The spin from Kushner's side effectively shifted the narrative in his favor. He had been vindicated by the process, went the spin. Whatever cloud from the Russia investigation that might have been hanging over him had cleared. At the *Times,* we fell for the spin, and under the headline "Jared Kushner Gets Security Clearance, Ending Swirl of Questions Over Delay," we wrote a front-page story that said the decision to give Kushner the security clearance ended "a period of uncertainty that had fueled questions about whether Mr. Kushner was in peril in the special counsel investigation." We also reported incorrectly that the president was not involved in the process and that the decision had been made by career officials.

Lowell either lied to the public about what occurred or was lied to by the White House about what had actually happened, because his public statements were entirely inaccurate.

"With respect to the news about his clearances, as we stated before, his application was properly submitted, reviewed by numerous career officials and underwent the normal process," Lowell said. "Having completed all of these processes, he's looking forward to continuing to do the work the president has asked him to do."

That afternoon on CNN, Lowell compounded the lie, saying, "There was nobody in the political process that had anything to do with it, there was nobody who pressured it, it was just done the normal, regular way."

★★★

MAY 30, 2018

323 DAYS UNTIL THE RELEASE OF THE MUELLER REPORT

OVAL OFFICE—By May, McGahn had turned into the Mueller team's personal Forrest Gump: the guy with the front-row seat to all the awful history of the Trump administration he had never wanted to witness.

More disturbing to McGahn was that he'd been put in the position of being asked by prosecutors for real-time reporting about Trump's conduct. It made for a harrowing existence, and to make matters worse, Trump steamrolled McGahn and Kelly for trying to heed the intelligence community's warnings about keeping Kushner and Ivanka away from the country's most guarded secrets.

McGahn cared less about the turf battle with the president than about the nagging feeling that intelligence and law enforcement officials, who had probably seen everything in their careers, were so concerned about the president's daughter and son-in-law that they did not believe they should have top security clearances.

McGahn kept some sort of equilibrium by focusing on the transformational impact he was having on the courts. Between the kinds of judges he was putting forward for appointment, the long careers they would have, and the possibility that Justice Kennedy would soon retire and leave Trump with another Supreme Court vacancy, McGahn felt if he could survive Trump's West Wing without getting ensnared in any legal trouble or career-ending scandal, the opportunity to shape the Court for a generation would have been worth it.

But Trump found new ways to test McGahn's patience again and again.

With a month to go before the end of the Supreme Court term and Kennedy's retirement decision, a rumor began to circulate around the West Wing that Trump would not be the only reality star and social media sensation in the White House on Wednesday,

May 30. None other than Kim Kardashian was scheduled to meet in the Oval Office that day with Trump about one of the president's most sacred and absolute powers: pardons.

What could go wrong? McGahn wondered.

And sure enough, shortly after 4:30 p.m., Kardashian walked into the Oval Office to meet with Trump, Kushner, Ivanka, and other aides. McGahn attended with a mix of dread and despair.

Kardashian had supported Clinton during the campaign. But she had insinuated her way into the West Wing by reaching out directly to Ivanka, who thought that a meeting with Kushner to discuss criminal justice reform was in order. Kardashian had gone back and forth with the White House for months about the meeting but then settled on May 30, because it was the birthday of an incarcerated woman whom she wanted the White House to pardon. Before coming to the White House that day, Kardashian tweeted about the woman, Alice Marie Johnson, a grandmother who had already served twenty-two years of a life sentence for nonviolent cocaine-trafficking charges and had had her clemency request turned down by the Obama administration.

"Happy Birthday Alice Marie Johnson. Today is for you," Kardashian tweeted.

Most issues advocates would have a hard time getting a few minutes with a member of their state legislature. But Kardashian was beginning her lobbying career in the Oval Office. One of the things that had irritated Trump the most in his presidency was his lack of support among celebrities, and in particular the notable absence of famous entertainers at his inauguration. He was, after all, one of them. Now a celebrity supernova was sitting across from him in the sanctum sanctorum of the American government, and McGahn watched the bizarre tableau in utter disbelief. Kardashian expertly appealed to Trump's ego, posing for pictures with him as she lobbied for Johnson's pardon.

There are careful processes in place for everything that a president can do. Or there were, anyway, before the presidency of Donald Trump. And McGahn could see right in front of his eyes one of the greatest failures of his time as White House counsel. Despite his best attempts, he had failed to prevent the pardon process from becoming potentially corrupted by Trump's indifference to the rule of law and norms and by the whims of his children.

Since the first several months of the administration, McGahn had tried to instill some structure in the West Wing to ensure the integrity of the pardon process. Pardons were supposed to provide the executive branch with a powerful tool to right the wrongs of the legal system and show mercy on convicts who had paid too high a price. But early on, Trump demonstrated that he viewed pardons as similar to White House memorabilia: gifts to be handed out to allies, supporters, and celebrities.

The power to pardon is among the most unambiguous powers a president has. Unlike making laws, which requires Congress, or stripping away regulations, which requires consulting with federal agencies, when it comes to granting pardons and clemencies, whatever a president says goes. No one can stop him. McGahn understood that the power was so great, and the potential blowback so substantial, and Trump's impulsivity so uncontrollable, that such power in Trump's hands was another problem waiting to happen. President Clinton's pardon of Marc Rich in the final hours of his administration had led to a criminal investigation into whether the pardon was sought unlawfully. When President George W. Bush commuted the thirty-month sentence of Dick Cheney's former chief of staff, Scooter Libby, in 2007, Democrats accused the president of doing a political favor for a former aide. If Trump was going to use this power, McGahn had wanted there to be a process to at least give it the veneer of being done in a thorough and thoughtful manner.

But in the first few months of the administration, in the spring of 2017, Trump had started talking about his desire to use his pardon power to help the Arizona sheriff Joe Arpaio. Instead of being wronged by the system, Arpaio, the evidence clearly showed, had sought to use the system to wrong others; he was preparing to go on trial for his refusal to stop detaining people simply based on the suspicion that they were illegal immigrants. McGahn, Sessions, Porter, and others shot down the idea, saying that it would be inappropriate for the president to intercede in an investigation and that he should allow the case to go to trial.

The staff advice initially appeared to deter Trump.

On April 21 of that year, McGahn had sent a memo to all White House staffers about how pardons should be handled. The memo had a blunt message: No White House officials, other than those lawyers in the counsel's office specifically designated to deal with pardons, should be involved in the process.

That meant no one—including Trump's children—should be out in the world talking to anyone about pardons without first involving McGahn.

McGahn's directive reminded White House officials that there was a long-standing, systematic process in place between the White House counsel's office and the pardon attorneys at the Justice Department for handling these requests.

"This process involves extensive fact gathering and research before any application is presented for the president's consideration," it read.

By this time in Trump's presidency, it was clear that a handful of Fox News hosts and a circle of Trump allies outside the government had an outsized influence on Trump's decision making. McGahn was trying to avoid a situation in which every trip to Mar-a-Lago, Christmas party, fundraiser, or Fox News segment turned into an opportunity to lobby the president and his advisers on pardons.

"At times it may be unclear if a request is simply asking for a meeting to discuss an ongoing issue, past sentence or a more formal request for clemency," the memo continued. "You should err on the side of caution and consult the White House Counsel before taking any action."

Four months after McGahn sent his memo to all White House staff, Trump made clear what he thought of McGahn's warnings. At 9:00 p.m. on a Friday in August, with a category 4 hurricane steaming into the Gulf of Mexico, Trump pardoned Arpaio.

Rod Rosenstein was particularly agitated by the way the Arpaio pardon had gone through. He reached out to McGahn to tell him that the White House needed to get a handle on the pardon process. The deputy attorney general complained to McGahn that all sorts of people from the White House were calling over to the Justice Department to ask about pardons. Rosenstein feared that Trump could use his power corruptly and urged McGahn to nudge Trump toward a more normal process. In response, McGahn had said that from then on only he and his top deputy, Uttam Dhillon, would be in communication with the Justice Department about pardons.

Despite the misgivings of the deputy attorney general and McGahn's memo urging a more official and defensible process, the power to pardon would become one of the president's favorite toys. In the nine months between the Arpaio pardon and the Kardashian meeting in the Oval Office, Trump granted clemency to four people—all of whom were fast-tracked by lobbying efforts from celebrities or Trump allies. Sholom Rubashkin—the former CEO of a kosher meat producer who was serving a twenty-seven-year sentence for financial fraud—received a commutation of his sentence in December 2017 after the celebrity lawyer Alan Dershowitz—who was also providing legal advice to Trump at the time about how he could direct his attorney general to investigate his rivals—made the case directly to the president. Three months later, Trump pardoned a former sailor in the Navy who pleaded guilty to mishandling classified information and had been sentenced to a year in prison. Days earlier the sailor had appeared on *Fox & Friends,* one of Trump's favorite shows, to argue that his punishment was unreasonably harsh when compared with Hillary Clinton, who he said had committed a similar crime.

The following month, Trump pardoned Scooter Libby—a step further than Bush was willing to go for his own man. Libby's case had been advocated at the White House by Victoria Toensing, a conservative lawyer and regular Fox News guest who briefly represented the president. Then, less than a week before Trump met with Kardashian, he issued a posthumous pardon for Jack Johnson, a Black boxer who had been convicted in 1913 for transporting a white woman across state lines. Johnson's pardon was pushed by another celebrity, Sylvester Stallone, who posed for a photo with Trump as he granted the pardon.

Now, in front of McGahn, Trump, Kushner, and Ivanka were doing an end around on his process, degrading pardons even further by allowing a reality television star to lobby Trump, who had little knowledge of the law and even less interest in it. There had been no formal review process by McGahn or the Justice Department, nor an informal one, for that matter. There had been no discussion with McGahn beforehand about how the president should have such a conversation with someone lobbying him for a pardon. But now Kardashian, using her celebrity, had gained access to Trump to make her case, and she played him expertly.

Shortly after the meeting, Kardashian tweeted about Trump. "I would like to thank President Trump for his time this afternoon. It is our hope that the President will grant clemency to Ms. Alice Marie Johnson who is serving a life sentence for a first-time, non-violent drug offense," she said.

Seven days later, Trump commuted the woman's sentence.

McGahn would later tell others that it was after this favor for Kim Kardashian that he knew he had to leave the White House. It wasn't that the commutation itself was indefensible. It was legal; Trump had the power to do what he did. It wasn't that McGahn was offended by Trump's refusal to be "politically correct." In fact, he'd been attracted to Trump's willingness to go against the political establishment. It was, rather, the cumulative effect of Trump's heedless efforts to remove Sessions and Mueller, combined now with Ivanka and Jared stomping all over the process he had tried to put in place to preserve the sanctity of presidential pardons. He could no longer ignore the possibility that there was more behind the president's repeated overreach into the Justice Department and his flagrant disregard for concerns among the intelligence community over Jared and Ivanka's clearances. But there was only a month left until he would know whether Kennedy would step down. He had suffered enough to get to this point. There was no reason to quit just yet.

And then, at the end of June, a longtime clerk for Kennedy called McGahn to tell him that the justice planned to retire. McGahn arranged for Kennedy to quietly come to the White House to tell Trump the news in person. Kennedy, Trump, and McGahn met in the Oval Office. In the week and a half that followed, Trump went back and forth on whom he might want to nominate as he seriously considered three conservative appeals court judges: Brett Kavanaugh of the D.C. Circuit Court of Appeals; Amy Coney Barrett of the Seventh Circuit Court of Appeals; and Raymond Kethledge of the

Sixth Circuit Court of Appeals. Trump expressed skepticism about Kavanaugh's ties to the George W. Bush administration, where he served as the staff secretary. But McGahn convinced Trump of his bona fides by playing up the fact that he went to Yale both as an undergraduate and for law school. That did it, and on July 9, Trump nominated Kavanaugh.

★ ★ ★

JULY 31, 2018

261 DAYS UNTIL THE RELEASE OF THE MUELLER REPORT

FLOOD'S WINDOWLESS OFFICE IN THE BASEMENT OF THE WEST WING— By the middle of the summer, Quarles and Goldstein had asked Flood to interview Chief of Staff John Kelly and Press Secretary Sarah Sanders. The topics the investigators wanted to talk to Sanders about seemed minor, but Flood, in a departure from Cobb's all-access approach, imposed a time limit on how long they could talk to her. Allowing Kelly to speak was far more problematic. Flood considered Kelly perhaps the second most important official in the West Wing—someone who spent a lot of time with Trump. Flood had some inkling that McGahn had spent countless hours with Mueller's team, and he wanted to do everything possible to ensure the same thing didn't happen with Kelly. By now, Trump's relationship with Kelly had begun to sour. Who knew what Kelly had stopped Trump from doing? Making it all the more troubling for Flood, Kelly insisted that he didn't need a lawyer. He wanted to just go in and tell the truth. Flood calculated that he couldn't stop Kelly and that the White House needed to make an effort to allow the interview to hopefully bring the investigation to an end. So Flood reached a deal with Mueller's team that he would come in with Kelly and they could interview him about a narrow set of topics. An open-ended McGahn-style questioning was completely off the table.

"You can have him for two hours," Flood told Mueller's team.

On August 2, Kelly and Flood met with investigators. The interview focused on Trump's efforts earlier in the year to pressure McGahn to release a statement saying that the president had not asked to fire Mueller. Kelly's testimony bolstered McGahn's account.

Throughout the investigation, Mueller had never conducted any of the interviews. But during many in the first year of the investigation, he would come in, shake the hand of the person being questioned, thank him or her for coming in, sit for a portion of the interview, and then leave. If there ever was an interview for him to do that for, it would have been Kelly's. Just like Mueller, Kelly was a Marine—a four-star general—and as chief of staff he was perhaps the most powerful official to sit for an interview. But Kelly talked to the prosecutors for two hours and left without Mueller making an appearance.

Meanwhile, now that Flood had reframed the White House's perspective on cooperation, he shifted his focus to quashing any chances of Mueller's interviewing the president.

★ ★ ★

AUGUST 1, 2018

260 DAYS UNTIL THE RELEASE OF THE MUELLER REPORT

ON THE SIDEWALK IN FRONT OF THE WHITE HOUSE—After spending nearly an hour talking to McGahn in front of the White House, I walked back to my office soaked but invigorated. I'd spent a year trying to deepen my understanding of how Mueller's team was investigating Trump and what they had learned about how the president used his powers to protect himself and interfere in the investigation. Over that time, I had become convinced that Mueller was using one of the people closest to the president to build the case that he had obstructed justice. I had written stories about how Trump had pressured McGahn to stop Sessions from recusing himself, how McGahn sought to stop Trump from sending a ranting letter to Comey when he fired him, and how Trump had complained endlessly to McGahn about how he needed a lawyer like Roy Cohn to defend him and run the Justice Department. I had also gained access to the questions that Mueller's team wanted to ask Trump in an interview and what investigators had asked other witnesses. All of this showed me one thing: McGahn was essential to the government's case against Trump. Yet, despite everything I wrote, I had struggled to convey that idea in my writing. In meetings in our bureau, I would tell my colleagues and editors, "I think McGahn did a lot of damage to Trump. I think he really hurt him." But there was a difference between being convinced of something and being able to prove it. The extent to which McGahn had hurt the president was to that point entirely unknown, a secret kept between investigators and McGahn and his counsel, Bill Burck.

And then I had my not-so-chance encounter with McGahn in front of the White House gate.

I headed straight back to the bureau, where in a dark office with no one around I took down everything I could remember from our conversation. I tried to figure out a way to write what I was now more convinced of than ever: McGahn was one of Mueller's key witnesses. I'd learned to pay close attention to what a source didn't say. Usually, when I was talking with someone, if I said something that was untrue, the person would without hesitation knock it down. McGahn had done that in our conversation when I told him that I had heard he got a haircut when John Kelly had taken over as chief of staff, to show respect to the four-star Marine general. Not true, he said. But when I had accused him of flipping on the president, he had demurred. Of course, Trump had no idea of the degree to which McGahn was cooperating, or McGahn wouldn't still be working at the White House. Trump had fired people for much less than providing hours upon hours of cooperation to a special counsel whom Trump was so enraged by that he often spent mornings tweeting insults at Mueller and his team.

I had McGahn's non-denial, which didn't count as confirmation, but it meant that I was onto something. I started doing the math, thinking that if I could quantify McGahn's cooperation, it would give us the hook we needed. So I worked backward. I learned that the FBI had information that McGahn had at least three meetings with Mueller's team and that each meeting had lasted several hours, if not the entire day. I did the math on what that amounted to in hours and then ran that figure by some of the people who knew the answer. They said my figures were right, if not low. We now had a figure—thirty hours—to hang a story on. The top lawyer in the executive branch, who had a country to run, had instead spent at least thirty hours with Mueller's team, and the president knew little about it.

About a week after my encounter with McGahn, I went to meet a lawyer who had worked for McGahn at the White House. The lawyer, not wanting to be seen with me, agreed to talk but wanted to do it walking around the residential neighborhood on Capitol Hill instead of sitting at a restaurant or coffee shop, where we'd be more conspicuous and easier to spot.

At the end of our walk, we ended up outside Union Station, just north of the Capitol, and I told him about our story.

"We're going to write that McGahn cooperated extensively with Mueller, thirty hours, told him everything," I said.

The lawyer, whose insight I had grown to appreciate and respect, gave a frank response.

"You can't write that," he said.

McGahn, the lawyer said, was one of the few good people around the president; he ballasted the ship. He could stop the president from taking actions that were illegal or would hurt the country.

If Trump knew about this cooperation, the lawyer said, he would almost certainly use it as an excuse to finally get rid of McGahn. "Who knows what will come in his place?" he said. "You can't trust it will be someone who will say no."

Most times when we are asked not to publish something, the call comes from the top official at the FBI, CIA, or Pentagon with a plea to withhold details because revealing them could get Americans, allies, or intelligence sources killed or jeopardize a sensitive operation. Sometimes the request would come in a meeting in the Oval Office between the president and the publisher and executive editor of the *Times,* like during the George W. Bush administration when the president asked the paper to not publish stories about secret surveillance programs created after the attacks of September 11,

2001. But this request was not coming from the president, obviously. It was coming from a staffer who had come to view the president as a dangerous figure whose malign impulses needed to be thwarted at every turn, as much as possible. This person and people like him were a marvel to me, and I thought the situation they faced was likely unique in American history. But it underscored the strangest dynamic of all of these events: As the president they feared shredded norms with abandon, and used the extraordinary powers of his office to protect himself, *they* were bound to abide by those same beleaguered norms. If the president was left to his own devices, these people believed, there would be a level of chaos even worse than anything anyone had seen to date.

I got where he was coming from and the dangers of the information we had. If we reported something about McGahn that got him fired and Trump went out and did something drastic—including firing Mueller—then we would be blamed for having set in motion a series of events that might damage the country significantly. At the same time, though, we were talking about the president of the United States; we have an obligation to report aggressively and write what we find. What were we in the media supposed to do if we have to live with the implicit threat that when we report something that bothers the president, we're responsible for whatever bad thing he does in response?

The exchange felt paradigmatic of the entire experience of reporting on the Trump administration. I told the lawyer that we would talk about his concerns but that it was unlikely we were going to delay publishing or withhold information from the public because we feared what the president might do. He said he understood, and we parted ways.

I headed back to the office and told my editor, Amy Fiscus, what the source had said.

"He said we'll be responsible if he fires McGahn," I said.

Amy and I both knew what the answer was: We could not take that into consideration.

Three days later, on a Saturday afternoon, we published our story:

> The White House counsel, Donald F. McGahn II, has cooperated extensively in the special counsel investigation, sharing detailed accounts about the episodes at the heart of the inquiry into whether President Trump obstructed justice, including some that investigators would not have learned of otherwise, according to a dozen current and former White House officials and others briefed on the matter.
>
> In at least three voluntary interviews with investigators that totaled 30 hours over the past nine months, Mr. McGahn described the president's fury toward the Russia investigation and the ways in which he urged Mr. McGahn to respond to it. He provided the investigators examining whether Mr. Trump obstructed justice a clear view of the president's most intimate moments with his lawyer.
>
> It is not clear that Mr. Trump appreciates the extent to which Mr. McGahn has cooperated with the special counsel. The president wrongly believed that Mr. McGahn would act as a personal lawyer would for clients and solely defend his interests to investigators, according to a person with knowledge of his thinking.

That night, I went out for a jog and ran into another one of McGahn's lawyers on the street.

"I read your story. It's wrong," he said.

"What?" I said.

"He just had to go in and answer a few questions," he said.

I looked at him. He worked for McGahn but still did not appreciate what had gone on. I started trying to explain to him how much McGahn had helped Mueller and how it was becoming clear that Mueller was building some sort of obstruction case around McGahn's statements about Trump.

He continued to argue with me. I realized nothing I said would change his mind. Someday we would read the Mueller report and we could see who was right. So I smiled, said I had to go, and jogged off.

The lawyer on the street was not the only person agitated and refusing to accept what we had written. Trump went into one-man rapid-response mode, issuing a barrage of angry tweets, and even calling Maggie and me "fake reporters."

> I allowed White House Counsel Don McGahn, and all other requested members of the White House Staff, to fully cooperate with the Special Counsel. In addition we readily gave over one million pages of documents. Most transparent in history. No Collusion, No Obstruction. Witch Hunt!

> The failing @nytimes wrote a Fake piece today implying that because White House Councel Don McGahn was giving hours of testimony to the Special Councel, he must be a John Dean type "RAT." But I allowed him and all others to testify—I didn't have to. I have nothing to hide.. . . . . and have demanded transparency so that this Rigged and Disgusting Witch Hunt can come to a close. So many lives have been ruined over nothing—McCarthyism at its WORST! Yet Mueller & his gang of Dems refuse to look at the real crimes on the other side—Media is even worse!

> Some members of the media are very Angry at the Fake Story in the New York Times. They actually called to complain and apologize—a big step forward. From the day I announced, the Times has been Fake News, and with their disgusting new Board Member, it will only get worse!

> The Failing New York Times wrote a story that made it seem like the White House Councel had TURNED on the President, when in fact it is just the opposite—& the two Fake reporters knew this. This is why the Fake News Media has become the Enemy of the People. So bad for America!

In the aftermath of the story, Burck had tried to keep Trump calm and possibly stop him from firing McGahn by leaking to the press that he had given Trump's lawyers a high-level overview of what his client told investigators. Burck's leak was technically correct: He had given Dowd a few broad details about McGahn's discussions with Mueller. But he did not get into many specifics and did not tell him about several other meetings that McGahn had with Mueller and the several other requests for information Mueller's office had made to Burck in the months after.

As Trump attacked us, we wrote a follow-up and reported that the White House was blindsided by the disclosure of McGahn's cooperation and that even some of Trump's lawyers had known little about what he had told the authorities. We wrote that at the time McGahn decided to cooperate, he believed that Trump and his lawyers were setting him up to take the fall for any wrongdoing. Motivated by that fear, McGahn decided to cooperate as fully as possible, in part to demonstrate he had nothing to hide:

> President Trump's lawyers do not know just how much the White House counsel, Donald F. McGahn II, told the special counsel's investigators during months of interviews, a lapse that has contributed to a growing recognition that an early strategy of full cooperation with the inquiry was a potentially damaging mistake.

The Monday after our story about McGahn's cooperation, Goldstein called Burck, and McGahn's importance to Mueller's case became even clearer.

Prosecutors are always wary that witnesses may waver from their testimony. In this case especially, it was vital that they be assured that what McGahn had testified to was solid and reliable. On the phone, Goldstein's tone was serious. He had three questions for Burck.

The first question related directly to the case the special counsel was trying to build against Trump, a case with which Burck was by now intimately familiar. Goldstein had seen Trump's tweets and how the president seemed to have little appreciation for what McGahn had said to prosecutors.

"Does he stand by his testimony?" Goldstein said.

Burck assured Goldstein that McGahn did.

Then Goldstein asked a more penetrating question that went directly at McGahn's motives for what he had told prosecutors.

"Was he really concerned about being screwed?" Goldstein asked Burck.

Burck explained to Goldstein how McGahn struggled mightily to understand how the White House had conceived of a strategy that would have allowed him to speak with Mueller. Why had

Trump's lawyers done no internal investigation to figure out what Trump had done? Why had they made no effort to stop McGahn from telling prosecutors all that he knew, knowing well that his testimony would almost certainly be made public someday?

Burck told Goldstein that he and McGahn believed the White House was "insane" for allowing McGahn to talk.

McGahn deduced that one of the only explanations for allowing him to cooperate to that extent was that they were setting him up to take the fall, Burck said.

Finally, Goldstein pushed Burck even further. Goldstein trusted Burck. But now he wanted a little more information about what Trump's lawyers knew about the contours of McGahn's cooperation.

"You don't have to tell us, we're just asking, but did you debrief the lawyers?" Goldstein said, probing to find out what Burck might have told Cobb and Dowd after McGahn met with investigators.

"I'm happy to tell you: I didn't go into a lot of the details," Burck said.

Burck explained to Goldstein the skepticism he had for helping Trump's lawyers and the others who represented witnesses close to the president. Unlike a majority of the lawyers involved in the investigation, Burck said he had refused to be a part of the joint defense agreements. Burck saw those agreements as essentially putting the witnesses and defendants on one side against the government prosecutors. If Burck was convinced that his clients did nothing wrong, why would he want to ally himself with the potential targets of the investigation? "I have no joint defense agreements, because I don't know whether any of my clients' interests really align," Burck said. "Am I going to be in a joint defense agreement with Donald Trump and Jared Kushner?"

Burck told Goldstein about how early in Dowd's tenure as Trump's lead lawyer, Dowd had tried to organize a weekly call among the lawyers, where they could share details they had learned about the investigation. For Burck, these calls were potentially dangerous for his clients, and he refused to participate because of what prosecutors might think about their allegiances to each other.

When Burck relayed the call to McGahn, both of them realized that there was no way Goldstein would have called if Mueller's team did not believe that McGahn would be central to their case and a key part of their report.

In the aftermath of the story, Burck realized that McGahn could easily be fired by Trump at any point, even though McGahn was in the middle of overseeing the Kavanaugh nomination.

The weekend after the story ran, McGahn went with his wife and two young children to his parents' home still in Brigantine, New Jersey, right outside Atlantic City, to see his ailing father.

In late August, McGahn learned from Annie Donaldson that Kushner was now moving to take over the pardons process. Kushner, adding to his varied and expanding portfolio, had, sans expertise, taken on criminal justice reform. He announced in a meeting that he planned to use the pardon power as a central policy tool in what he described as an Obama-like approach to freeing felons who had received lengthy sentences for nonviolent crimes. That might have been a valid idea and a good tool for criminal justice reform. But Kushner had never once discussed it with McGahn, and it was the view of the White House counsel's office that Kushner was the wrong person to oversee pardons. In fact, allowing him to do so was rife with potential conflict. Kushner would have a direct hand in fundraising for the 2020 campaign—meaning the top person asking for money would also be in charge of giving out pardons.

Around that time, McGahn heard again that Kushner was calling over to the Justice Department to get language for pardons. That same week, Burck received a series of calls from reporters, telling him they were hearing that McGahn was trying to block the president from pardoning Paul Manafort, who had been convicted on fraud charges by Mueller's team. The news made no sense for several reasons. McGahn's relationship with the president had deteriorated so badly that, outside discussing judges, the two men had not had a substantive one-on-one conversation in months. And since Manafort had been convicted, McGahn had not been asked by anyone in the White House what he thought of pardoning him. Burck told the reporters that the rumor was not true, but the calls kept coming in all the same. The relentlessness of the calls led McGahn and Burck to believe that Kushner and Ivanka were driving a campaign of misinformation, planting such a volume of stories that Trump would take notice and become convinced that McGahn was an impediment to him, or worse, and needed to be removed.

It was the last week in August, but between Trump, Mueller, Kavanaugh, Kushner, and Ivanka, McGahn could not relax. One of his friends who lived in the area called, hoping to distract him for a few hours. The friend, William J. Hughes Jr., was the son of a former Democratic congressman and had recently become close to McGahn. A defense lawyer and former federal prosecutor, Hughes knew that the stress of McGahn's job had weighed on him, and he had come up with an idea.

"Why don't you bring the kids and Shannon and come down to the beach with us?" Hughes said. So the McGahns loaded up the kids and hauled their gear down the shore. Their kids and Hughes's four boys played in the small gullies that formed on the shore when the tide went out. At first, McGahn seemed like his old self. But as he sat on the beach, Hughes noticed that something was off about his friend. McGahn, who loved to talk, just stared out into the ocean, saying nothing.

The accumulated stress of the previous nineteen months, combined with our public disclosure about his cooperation with Mueller's prosecutors, weighed heavily on him. He was certain that Jared and Ivanka were plotting against him, and tilting against such flagrant and powerful nepotism weighed on him as well. McGahn knew they had never gotten over his role in subjecting them to such scrutiny over their security clearances, nor his determination to enforce some kind of separation between their businesses and their work for the administration.

All of his worries conspired to make sure that McGahn couldn't take pleasure in a day at the beach, or in much of anything. He just stared out at the waves, one after another.

"Things kind of crazy?" Hughes asked him.

"You have no idea," McGahn said. "It's unbelievable."

"I can't imagine," Hughes said.

"Look, my time is short," McGahn said. "I'm getting out soon. I can't handle it."

The following Monday morning, McGahn was in his office at

around 9:30 when John Kelly came bursting in. Kelly looked as nervous as McGahn had ever seen him.

"I can't believe you didn't tell me you had decided to go," Kelly said.

McGahn had no idea what Kelly was talking about.

"The president just tweeted that you're leaving once Kavanaugh is done," Kelly told him.

McGahn thought Kelly was joking.

"Lay off, Chief, I got shit I gotta deal with today," McGahn told Kelly.

McGahn then realized that Kelly was not kidding.

That's when it dawned on both of them: From the residence, the president had just pushed out the White House counsel without telling his chief of staff. McGahn had told Trump that he wanted to leave but Trump now made it appear like he had the final say.

* * *

SEPTEMBER 27, 2018

203 DAYS UNTIL THE RELEASE OF THE MUELLER REPORT

ANTEROOM OF ROOM 216, HART SENATE OFFICE BUILDING, WASHINGTON, D.C.—The morning had been devastating for Brett Kavanaugh. Testifying before the Senate Judiciary Committee in a hearing possessed of a rare tension, Christine Blasey Ford had utterly captivated the nation. She had taken the country back to the summer of 1982, high school days, and with a breathtaking combination of composure and pain had recalled in detail how a young and drunk Kavanaugh had climbed on top of her and tried to remove her clothes while she attempted to escape.

Back in the White House, governing had slowed while Trump and many of his senior aides followed the testimony closely. With a four-to-four ideological split on the nation's highest court, a lifetime elevation for Kavanaugh, fifty-three, from judge to justice would skew the Court conservative for years, if not decades, after Trump left office. After Ford's testimony ended midday, news began to leak out of the West Wing that Trump believed Ford had dealt a devastating blow to Kavanaugh during her time in front of the committee. The president wanted to pull the nomination and try anew with someone else. Kavanaugh himself was scheduled to testify in the afternoon, but after Ford's wrenching testimony all seemed lost.

McGahn had watched the testimony from the office of Thom Tillis, the Republican senator from North Carolina, and believed Ford's testimony had cast enormous doubt on Kavanaugh's chances of getting confirmed. He saw the reports about Trump's desire to pull Kavanaugh. If that happened, everything else that McGahn had achieved in reshaping the federal judiciary would be overshadowed by this blowup. His time in government was coming to an end, and despite needing no Democratic votes to fill the vacancy left by Kennedy's retirement, he was nonetheless going to come away with the blame for Kavanaugh's failure.

McGahn assumed then, as he just about always assumed, that the damaging leaks about Kavanaugh were coming from Jared and Ivanka, who McGahn believed wanted a more liberal justice. McGahn actually understood why Trump might want to pull Kavanaugh and could not fault him for it.

McGahn went in to meet with Kavanaugh to prepare him for the biggest moment of his career. He believed Kavanaugh needed to give up the conciliatory approach he had attempted earlier that week during an interview with Fox News. In fact, when McGahn huddled with Kavanaugh, the nominee's wife, and several aides inside an anteroom in the Hart building, McGahn grew angry when he heard a former clerk suggest to Kavanaugh that he ought to be measured, just as he had been on Fox.

"Did I tell you that you could say that?" McGahn snapped. He cleared the room before anyone else could offer any more advice.

McGahn had a strategy in mind, one that he had discussed with Senators Orrin Hatch and Lindsey Graham beforehand. Kavanaugh was angry because he felt as if he were being treated unfairly. Moments before the hearing was to resume, McGahn told him that he had to use that anger to push back at the Democrats as hard as possible and defend himself and his character as if it were the last battle he would ever fight. It had to come from the heart. The angrier, the better.

During one of the breaks in Kavanaugh's testimony, Donaldson relayed to McGahn, with Kavanaugh within earshot, that Trump was trying to reach him. McGahn knew that Kavanaugh had seen the reports that Trump wanted to pull the nomination. But McGahn wanted Kavanaugh to know that it was them versus the world, and that he was going to do everything to stick with Kavanaugh and get him through the process.

"Tell him I don't talk to quitters," McGahn said to Donaldson loud enough that Kavanaugh could hear it.

A couple of minutes later, as Kavanaugh prepared to testify, McGahn stepped aside and called Trump. The president seemed calm and said that he was sticking with his nominee.

Just over a week later, on October 6, 2018, after an explosive nomination process that racked the nation and left the painful allegations raised by Dr. Ford forever unresolved, Kavanaugh took his seat on the U.S. Supreme Court. Good to the president's tweet on the subject, McGahn left the White House a week and a half later. In a farewell meeting with Trump in the Oval Office, the president, like a boss moving along a summer intern, said he was happy to provide McGahn a recommendation for his next job. Trump said that McGahn got high marks for most of his work, but low ones for his inability to stop Sessions's recusal and Mueller.

★★★

FEBRUARY 28, 2019

FORTY-NINE DAYS UNTIL THE RELEASE OF THE MUELLER REPORT

SPECIAL COUNSEL'S OFFICE, WASHINGTON, D.C.—For the prosecutors and agents working on the Mueller investigation, the jobs came with an added layer of stress that went beyond the long hours. Their lives were under more scrutiny than at any other point in their careers. Trump publicly ridiculed them, his allies dug through their backgrounds looking for evidence of bias, and judges picked over their legal filings for mistakes. The American public demanded the investigation be done correctly, and Democrats wanted it completed yesterday. If the investigators failed to turn over every rock, they could close up the inquiry, present their findings to the attorney general, and then learn months later that they missed a key piece of evidence, and their entire investigation could be called into question.

Despite all of that, investigators live to be a part of the hardest, most high-profile investigations, and being on "Mueller's team" marked a lifetime opportunity, because they might never otherwise get a chance to work on such an important and stimulating investigation. There was also the allure of being in the know and on the inside for the most closely watched inquiry in American history. The investigators knew what they were finding, whom they were building cases against, and what the answers were to central questions such as whether the presidential election of 2016 had not only been marred by the Russian active measures but also been further compromised by collusion between the Trump campaign and Moscow. Sometimes that could be frightening. Other times it could be amusing, such as when they watched reporters, pundits, witnesses, and lawyers make flagrantly mistaken pronouncements about the investigation. The investigators' friends and families wanted to know what they knew and what they were working on, but Mueller's team was extraordinarily disciplined and resisted the impulse to talk about their work.

One issue the investigators were baffled about were the wildly inaccurate predictions about when the investigation would be over. The first round of incorrect claims began in the months after Mueller's appointment in May 2017, when Trump's first team of lawyers, Dowd and Cobb, said they could get the investigation wrapped up within six to eight weeks. When they missed that date, Cobb publicly made another baseless claim, saying it would be over, at the latest, by Thanksgiving 2017. That proved untrue, too, when the investigation appeared to be gaining momentum by Thanksgiving. A week after the holiday, Flynn went into federal court in Washington, pleaded guilty to lying to the FBI, and agreed to cooperate with Mueller's investigation.

The joke among Trump's second team of lawyers, which replaced Dowd and Cobb in the spring of 2018, was that Dowd and Cobb had actually been right about Thanksgiving but had just had the year wrong. In October 2018, Bloomberg reported that Mueller would issue his findings soon after November's midterm congressional elections. But by Thanksgiving 2018, the investigation was still moving forward, and a week after *that* holiday Trump's personal lawyer Michael Cohen pleaded guilty to lying to Congress about the timing of negotiations over plans to build a Trump Tower in Moscow. By December, NBC News reported that Mueller was expected to submit his report to the attorney general as early as mid-February. Then, in mid-February, CNN and NBC News reported that the Department of Justice was preparing to announce the end of the investigation by the end of the month. On Thursday, February 21, CBS News said the report could be sent the following day.

In reality, by the end of February, the obstruction investigation on Trump was still active and ongoing. In fact, at least one witness was still being asked for documents and to sit for yet another interview: McGahn. Mueller's team—led by Goldstein and Quarles—was still trying to shore up McGahn's account about Trump's attempt to oust Mueller in the late spring of 2017. The problem stemmed from how Burck helped McGahn navigate the episode at the time. The pressure Trump put on McGahn to have Mueller fired so unnerved McGahn that he had been in constant contact with Burck throughout that entire weekend. In the course of those conversations, Burck advised McGahn to refrain from talking to anyone in the White House about what Trump wanted him to do. That included McGahn's chief of staff, Annie Donaldson, whom McGahn had habitually confided in so that he would have a witness to back up his accounts of what Trump had ordered him to do and how McGahn had responded. That meant the only person who knew what occurred was McGahn's wife, Shannon. After all, she had heard and seen a lot of what was going on because McGahn had grown upset that Trump was calling him at home on a Saturday to tell him to fire Mueller and then, in a fit of rage, drove to the White House with his resignation letter and packed up his office.

Mueller's obstruction team trusted McGahn. They'd already spent more than thirty hours with him. But to claim, at the end of a two-year investigation, the president had obstructed justice, they needed some additional piece of evidence to bolster his credibility, and the only two people who knew about how the president had behaved—Burck and McGahn's wife—were highly problematic witnesses. The Justice Department shies away from using lawyers or spouses as witnesses for a slew of reasons, particularly because their credibility is so easily attacked and juries are less likely to believe them because the perception is that they will say whatever is necessary to back up the witness.

This left McGahn standing alone. The investigators knew that McGahn had spoken on the phone with Trump that weekend. Maybe, they thought, if they could get McGahn's phone records, they could show that Trump had indeed been calling him. Such evidence would not show what they actually discussed, but at least it would substantiate that the calls were made.

But even producing evidence of the calls proved tricky. In a normal investigation, a prosecutor could simply get a grand jury subpoena and send it to the telephone company for the records. But Mueller's team had decided early to avoid using the grand jury in the obstruction investigation. If they used the grand jury, Trump could more easily try to fight the prosecutors' efforts by citing executive privilege. And if they obtained testimony or documents through the use of a grand jury, it would ultimately be harder to hand those materials over to Congress for an impeachment proceeding because there are even more restrictions on such evidence.

Without those tools, the investigators brainstormed other ways of getting the phone records. Goldstein went back to Burck in late 2018 with a homework assignment: Please tell McGahn to go get the phone records himself.

McGahn had been a hockey dad since leaving the White House in October 2018, as he planned his move to the private sector. He called his phone carrier and requested the phone records that the investigators were seeking. Because the dates that he needed were more than ninety days old, the company had to go back and get them manually and mail them to McGahn. This process took several weeks. But finally, McGahn received them in the mail and sent them to Burck, who, in turn, gave them to Goldstein.

Armed with the records, the investigators built a spreadsheet that charted every call that McGahn and Trump had made in the days around the attempted firing incident. Still, the investigators knew that they needed more to understand the sequence of calls and wanted to talk to McGahn again.

But interacting again with McGahn could be potentially dicey for everyone involved; if Trump found out they were still meeting with McGahn, he'd rain down on both sides with renewed vitriol. Since Emmet Flood had taken over from Ty Cobb in May 2018, Mueller's team had stopped trying to speak to McGahn. But in late February, Goldstein went around the White House again and called Burck. He asked him to arrange a conference call with McGahn to go over the records.

At 2:00 p.m. on February 28, McGahn went to Burck's ninth-floor offices just four blocks from the White House. For about forty minutes, Goldstein, Quarles, and an FBI agent working on the obstruction case talked to McGahn and Burck to go over the sequence of calls between Trump and McGahn on the dates of the president's order to have Mueller removed. Burck had been convinced since he first brought McGahn in to be interviewed by Mueller's team in November 2017 that McGahn could be their star witness. While the final interview seemed like a logical step for the investigators, it heightened Burck's concern that if the report became an impetus for the president's impeachment by a new Democratic House majority, McGahn was in for a long road ahead as the central narrator of the president's illegal conduct.

McGahn had held on to hope throughout the entire process that maybe something would transpire that would spare him from having to be the person to testify against the president. He had hid his cooperation with Mueller from everyone ranging from the president to the president's lawyers to his fellow senior White House officials. But the incident drove home to McGahn that as much as he might hate his fate, there was only one reason Mueller's team was coming back to him this late in the game: The investigation into the president was a serious threat to the Trump presidency, and he would be a witness against the president he'd served.

⋆ ⋆ ⋆

MARCH 5, 2019

FORTY-FOUR DAYS UNTIL THE RELEASE OF THE MUELLER REPORT

ATTORNEY GENERAL'S CONFERENCE ROOM—Five days after McGahn's last interview with Mueller's team, Mueller, William Barr, and their aides met at the Justice Department to discuss how Mueller would be concluding his twenty-two-month-long investigation.

Twenty-six years had passed since Mueller served as the head of the criminal division under Bill Barr when he was the attorney general during the administration of George H. W. Bush. At the time, both were young stars of the Justice Department. In the years that had passed, they had remained friendly. Their wives had been in a Bible study group together, and Mueller had attended the weddings of two of Barr's daughters. Barr became a multimillionaire as the top lawyer for Verizon and Mueller the FBI's most important director since J. Edgar Hoover.

Throughout their careers, Barr had been considered in conservative circles an intellectual heavyweight and a willing partisan political operator. Despite holding such a prominent position, Mueller had recoiled at all of Washington's partisan debates during his twelve-year tenure at the FBI, eschewing politics and establishing complete independence from the presidents he served.

Now, as they sat across from each other again, they would each be driven by very different objectives and worldviews. Barr entered the room with a long-standing belief that special counsels were too powerful and designed to undermine the presidency. Once Trump fired Jeff Sessions in November 2018, ending his tortured run as attorney general, Barr was in line for his reappointment to run the Justice Department, having vaulted to that position, in part, by writing a nineteen-page memo—addressed to Deputy Attorney General Rod Rosenstein in June of that year—that outlined how he thought an obstruction case against Trump was preposterous. In a sign of Flood's influence on the trajectory of the investigation, he had made the case to Trump that he should pick Barr. The new attorney general thought Trump and his campaign had been unfairly tainted by the Russia investigation, and he knew that, more than anything, Trump wanted to have the cloud of the investigation lifted and to be exonerated. Those goals became Barr's reason for being once in office.

And now, sitting across from his old colleague, he had an even more urgent concern: to protect the president from impeachment. He would do so unabashedly, with none of the reserve in that mission that his predecessor had evinced. I learned in reporting for this book that senior Justice Department officials were deeply concerned at the time that Mueller's report would essentially turn into an impeachment referral that could drive Trump from office. With Trump's presidency potentially on the line, Barr faced the ultimate test of his legal and political skills. Mueller had come to the meeting with a Marine's sensibility—focused on doing right by the honorable work of his team of prosecutors and investigators who, under near-constant and withering public attacks from the president and his allies, had indicted thirty-four individuals and secured six guilty pleas and one other conviction. For Mueller's report to have credibility and to stand up in the hyperpartisan climate of the Trump presidency, Mueller needed to muster his decades-long reputation for fairness and rectitude.

But it would not be a fair fight. Barr was as vibrant, smart, funny, and cunning as he had ever been. But Mueller seemed to be a shell of his former self. As he spoke in the meeting, his voice trembled, his hands shook, and he seemed at times confused. To Barr, it was sad to see what had happened to Mueller. But this was not the time for sentimentality for his old colleague and friend. Barr controlled how the report would be released, giving him some ability to sculpt the narrative's findings, influence how its conclusions would be interpreted and understood, and shape the ultimate outcome for Trump.

Mueller and his team laid out how his office had found no criminal evidence that Trump's campaign had conspired with the Russians. But on the question of whether Trump had obstructed justice, it was a much more complicated and nuanced result. They tried to explain what his team had concluded, saying they had declined to make a decision on whether Trump had broken the law. The disclosure from Mueller angered the department officials on the other side of the table. At the most basic level, prosecutors had a duty: to make a decision about whether someone has broken the law. The entire investigation had created massive questions about Trump's conduct and whether he had committed crimes. Mueller was supposed to bring clarity to that. But here, Mueller was saying that in the most high-profile criminal investigation in a generation his team had declined to make a determination about whether the president had committed a crime.

In some ways, this was good for Trump. With Mueller not making a determination, Barr knew that he could easily impose his will and clear Trump of wrongdoing. But at the same time, Mueller's conclusion might leave the question unanswered in the public's mind. Barr pushed back on Mueller and his team, trying to force them to explain their logic, saying that he did not understand their rationale. In an example of how differently the men would come to view Mueller's decision to not make a decision, Barr asked Mueller why he continued to investigate if he knew that he was never going to charge the president.

Mueller tried to explain his reasoning but struggled to articulate it. It was hard to fault Mueller for his inability to clearly lay out the decisions his prosecutors had made about whether Trump broke the law. The decision was based principally on the Justice Department's policy that a sitting president cannot be indicted. In a demonstration of both the paradox of criminally investigating a president and the probity of Mueller's approach, his team reasoned that if a sitting president cannot be indicted, then it would be unfair to accuse Trump of a crime while he is in office. Without a criminal indictment, due process would be impossible, the thinking went, and so it would be impossible for Trump to clear his name until he was out of office. So instead, Mueller's prosecutors decided to simply accumulate facts about whether Trump broke the law. Then later, after Trump left office, prosecutors could decide whether to charge him.

Mueller's team returned to their offices to put the finishing touches on their report. At the Justice Department, officials debated what to do. They could have asked Mueller to make a decision about whether the president had any criminal liability. But if that happened, Mueller could come back with an answer that they did not want to hear. Department officials could have brought in another team of prosecutors to look at the evidence and make a decision. But that would only prolong the investigation, and that ran counter to Barr's mission to bring the investigation to a close.

Two weeks later, at noon on Friday, March 22, an agent from Mueller's office delivered several hard copies of the report to the Justice Department for Barr, Rosenstein, and other top officials to read. They quickly went through the report looking for new pieces of information that they had not been briefed on that might drastically change their understanding of the investigation. But as they read the report, they could see no new facts would alter the overarching conclusions: There was no provable criminal conspiracy between Trump's campaign and Russia, and Mueller had declined to make a decision on obstruction. At 4:00 p.m. that Friday, as hail began to fall from the sky outside the Justice Department, Barr sent a letter to Congress saying that he had received the report, was reviewing it, and might be able to publicly announce Mueller's baseline conclusions as soon as that weekend.

Both Barr and Rosenstein stayed in the office late Friday night to read over the report and decide what kind of determination had to be made. Each worked in his respective office and turned page after page for hours. To dig through the nearly 448-page document, Rosenstein attempted to get comfortable, taking off his shoes and relaxing in the club chair in his office.

That Sunday, Barr, not Mueller, would frame Mueller's nearly two-year-long investigation to the world. By being the first to describe Mueller's findings, Barr would have immense sway over what the first and most lasting impressions of Mueller's work would be. As it would turn out, Barr's spin of the report—and Mueller's determination to let the report speak for itself—would establish a popular narrative of the report's contents that was highly favorable to Trump.

Barr wrote in a letter to Congress, "As the report states: '[T]he investigation did not establish that members of the Trump Campaign conspired or coordinated with the Russian government in its election interference activities.'"

That was a far more generous description than what Mueller actually said in the report, because Barr parsed the language and failed to quote the entire sentence from the report, which read, "Although the investigation established that the Russian government perceived it would benefit from a Trump presidency and worked to secure that outcome, and that the Campaign expected it would benefit electorally from information stolen and released through Russian efforts, the investigation did not establish that members of the Trump Campaign conspired or coordinated with the Russian government in its election interference activities."

Barr would devote far more ink in the letter to shaping the special counsel's conclusions on obstruction. He said that because Mueller had declined to make a decision, he had to make the decision himself. Barr said that he and Rosenstein had concluded that there was insufficient evidence to charge the president with an obstruction offense. As a dose of insurance or an attempt to assuage the Mueller team, Barr included this from the obstruction section: "While this report does not conclude that the president committed a crime, it also does not exonerate him."

Barr downplayed the obstruction findings by depicting them as a summation of facts that the public already knew much about. In describing the potential incidents of obstruction that Mueller investigated, Barr wrote that "most" of them had been the subject of public reporting and that "many" of the incidents occurred in public.

Around 3:00 p.m. on Sunday, one of Barr's aides called Trump's White House lawyer, Emmet Flood, who had decamped to Mar-a-Lago with Trump. Over the phone, the aide read Flood the text of the letter that Barr planned to send to Congress. Flood and the new White House counsel, Pat Cipollone, then went into the residence at Mar-a-Lago and briefed Trump on the findings.

Trump's lawyers were entirely satisfied with Barr's letter. Despite Mueller's refusal to exonerate the president on obstruction, Trump took it as the exact opposite.

"It was a complete and total exoneration," Trump said on the tarmac of the Palm Beach International Airport shortly before boarding Air Force One at 5:00 p.m.

Instead of savoring his apparent victory, Trump said that it was time to turn the tables and go after those who had investigated him.

"It's a shame that our country had to go through this," he said. "To be honest, it's a shame that your president has had to go through this for—before I even got elected, it began. And it began illegally. And hopefully somebody is going to look at the other side. This was an illegal takedown that failed. And hopefully somebody is going to be looking at the other side."

As Air Force One approached Andrews Air Force Base in Maryland, the president stood in the cockpit for the landing. The following morning, the Israeli prime minister, Benjamin Netanyahu, visited the White House. Around noon, the media was brought into the Oval Office for a photo op with Netanyahu. The only subject of interest that day was the Mueller report.

Trump publicly gave Barr the go-ahead to release the entire report to Congress.

"Up to the attorney general, but it wouldn't bother me at all," Trump said.

The lawyers were jubilant. Later that afternoon, Rudy Giuliani and another of Trump's personal lawyers, Jay Sekulow, attended a ceremony in the Oval Office to honor the Washington Capitals, who had won the 2018 Stanley Cup. Giuliani texted me a screenshot of a fake *New York Times* front page with the headline "WE'RE SORRY MR. PRESIDENT" and below that "We were wrong. We are Fake News. You win."

"Cute," I responded.

But as Trump claimed exoneration, a standoff was brewing between Mueller's team and Barr over his characterization of the report. Barr's letter to Congress made many members of Mueller's team irate, and they cried out to each other that Barr had spun the report. They could not identify outright falsehoods in the letter but contended it failed to capture many of its key aspects, especially in the obstruction section.

At the center of the issue was that Barr had failed to include thirteen pages of executive summaries that Mueller's team had written, intending them to be released to the public on announcement of the report. When they turned in the report, Mueller's team believed that Barr would quickly release the summaries to Congress as they were submitted and then later put out the entire redacted report. But Barr decided against it. Despite Mueller's team reminding the Justice Department of the summaries just hours before Barr sent his letter, the attorney general ultimately decided to write his own synopsis of Mueller's conclusions. Shortly before it was sent off to Congress, the Justice Department offered to let Mueller's team review the letter, but Mueller's team declined.

A day after Barr sent the letter to Congress, Mueller's office conveyed its concerns about how Barr portrayed the report and wrote a letter to the attorney general that contained the report's introduction and summaries of the Russia and obstruction volumes that had been redacted for grand jury information so they could be released to the public.

Two days later, Mueller sent a far more harshly worded letter to Barr. The attorney general did not receive it until the following day. In a lawyerly way, it called out Barr for spinning the report and asked him to immediately release the introduction and summaries.

The letter Barr sent to Congress, Mueller said, "did not fully capture the context, nature, and substance of this Office's work and conclusions."

"There is now public confusion about critical aspects of the results of our investigation," Mueller said. "This threatens to undermine a central purpose for which the Department appointed the Special Counsel: to assure full public confidence in the outcome of the investigations."

"Release at this time would alleviate the misunderstandings that have arisen and would answer congressional and public questions about the nature and outcome of our investigation," the letter said.

Barr claimed to aides that he did not understand Mueller's concerns. He insisted he had accurately summarized the core findings of the report without getting into the nitty-gritty details that would later be released. Senior Justice Department officials said they had given Mueller a chance to review Barr's letter prior to its sending, but Mueller had declined to do so. Now Mueller looked as if he wanted to rewrite history.

Barr and senior Justice Department officials did not believe that

Mueller actually wrote the letter. They thought that Mueller, in a diminished state, had been manipulated by the angry members of his team, who thought they could get away with making an impeachment referral without actually calling it one. They theorized that someone like Michael R. Dreeben—one of Mueller's prosecutors—had written it and that the upset team members had pressured Mueller into sending the letter. Barr thought the letter was "snitty," and was frustrated that Mueller would not just pick up the phone and call him if he had a concern.

To stop a more lengthy paper trail from being created between Mueller and Barr, the two got on the phone for a fifteen-minute conversation with staff members listening in. Mueller told Barr he was not trying to accuse him of misleading the public, but instead he felt people did not have enough information to understand the basis of the report's reasoning.

"What we're principally concerned about is the fact there is not enough background on obstruction analysis," Mueller said over the phone. "What you said in the letter was not inaccurate, but we would prefer more context and background on the obstruction analysis."

Mueller pushed again for the summaries his team had written to be made public, as they were originally intended to be. But Barr did not like the idea at all. He thought he was clear in saying the four-page letter was just the top-line conclusions and that the reasoning and process of the investigation would be released in full when they were ready. His intention was never to provide an all-inclusive summary, he said; he just wanted to let Congress know if the president was going to be charged with a crime or not.

Barr told Mueller that releasing the summaries would add to the confusion and cause people to draw incorrect conclusions before the full details were released. He did not want a drip, drip, drip of information and believed it should all be released at once.

"Let's get it out as quickly as we can," Barr said. "If we don't put out the whole thing, we'll be back in the same boat we're in."

At the end of the discussion, Mueller agreed that his team would work on the redactions with the attorney general's office, and Barr let him know that he was unhappy with how Mueller had communicated with him. "Bob, we've known each other for a long time, just pick up the phone and give me a ring," Barr said. "By the way, here is my cell if you want to call me over the weekend."

Barr later told Congress that he had declined to release Mueller's summaries because he believed it was akin to releasing a small piece of the report—that could be analyzed, dramatized, and used as political weaponry—without releasing the rest of the report as context.

"I think—I think—I suspect that they probably wanted more put out," Barr later told Congress. "But in my view, I was not interested in putting out summaries or trying to summarize, because I think any summary, regardless of who prepares it, not only runs the risk of, you know, being underinclusive or overinclusive, but also, you know, would trigger a lot of discussion and analysis that really should await everything coming out at once."

Barr told lawmakers that it did not matter what Mueller wanted; Mueller worked for Barr, and it was up to the attorney general to decide what was released.

"It was my baby," Barr told lawmakers.

My baby. Mueller, the embodiment of by-the-book, rule-of-law independent justice in America for a generation, had been rolled by the attorney general. In the spring of 2017, the president had angrily complained that in Sessions and Rosenstein he had two disloyal men running his own Justice Department.

Finally, he would tell others, he had found someone who was loyal—he had found his Roy Cohn.

* * *

APRIL 16, 2019

TWO DAYS UNTIL THE RELEASE OF THE MUELLER REPORT

DEPUTY ATTORNEY GENERAL'S CONFERENCE ROOM, JUSTICE DEPARTMENT— Emmet Flood and Trump's personal lawyers trekked to the Justice Department to read the full Mueller report. For the entire day, they examined all 448 pages that Attorney General Barr planned to release to the public on Thursday of that week. Because executive privilege had been preserved, the president's lawyers needed to sign off on the information going public.

The lawyers were comforted, a bit, that there were no major surprises. They believed the new incidents were similar to the ones that had already become public. The calculus was both cynical and valid. Throughout the investigation, the president had flagrantly attacked it and there were countless disclosures about how he sought to interfere with it. Because so much of it had been out there, however, it would be hard to shock the public with Mueller's findings—a numbness that would work to the White House's advantage.

But the report painted a damaging portrait of a president determined to use his power to protect himself from an investigation into his own conduct and the conduct of those closest to him. The report detailed ten episodes of obstruction. Some of Trump's lawyers could see how the Democrats were going to be able to easily weaponize the report against the president and build an argument that he should be impeached for obstructing justice.

Flood, in particular, thought the report was an abomination. It had clearly been written as an impeachment referral—something that the rules the special counsel operated under had not called for. Among his litany of complaints with the report, it contained no exculpatory evidence that Flood knew Mueller had obtained in his two years of investigating the president. Flood knew from Burck that McGahn told Mueller's team that despite everything Trump told him to do, McGahn never believed that Trump actually broke the law.

Legally, Mueller's team would argue, it made no difference how McGahn felt about whether Trump had broken the law; that was not a determination for him to make. But Flood thought that in what essentially amounted to an obstruction referral, it was deeply unfair to not include McGahn's opinion. For Flood, it was yet more evidence that Mueller's team was out to get the president.

After reading the report, Trump's lawyers conferred and discussed whether McGahn might be willing to put out a statement reiterating what he had told the investigators. Flood said he would call Burck.

"There's nothing really new," Flood said to Burck about the report. "But Don is the centerpiece of the report."

Duh, Burck thought.

"It would be helpful if he put out a statement," Flood said, adding that if McGahn put a statement out after the report was released, it could potentially calm Trump as the media broadcast the obstruction incidents.

To Burck, Flood's request made sense. Burck knew that McGahn—and all of his other clients who worked for Trump—wanted to do everything to avoid drawing the president's ire. An adversarial Trump would only complicate McGahn's life and haunt his future.

Burck called McGahn, laying out what Flood wanted. McGahn knew how to manage Trump as well as anyone, and a statement that gave even the slightest hint that McGahn was still in Trump's camp just might keep "Kong" off the Empire State Building.

★★★

APRIL 18, 2019

THE DAY THE MUELLER REPORT WAS RELEASED

PRESS ROOM, JUSTICE DEPARTMENT, WASHINGTON, D.C.—It would take the Justice Department officials and Mueller's team four weeks to go through the report and redact it. In that time, a narrative that Trump had essentially been cleared took hold. With the report still cloaked in secrecy, Democrats were powerless to push back on the hardening story line that Trump had done nothing wrong. But Barr was still determined to guide the end of the investigation and enshrine that result. The day the report was released, Barr offered a pre-rebuttal for Trump, holding a press conference at the Justice Department. Some Justice Department officials had warned Barr against using language—like "no collusion"—that could be perceived as defending Trump by echoing his own refrain.

But as Barr addressed the country from the lectern, it took just a few minutes for him to repeat the exact phrase that Trump wanted to hear.

"The Special Counsel found no evidence that any Americans—

including anyone associated with the Trump campaign—conspired or coordinated with the Russian government or the IRA [Internet Research Agency] in carrying out this illegal scheme," Barr said. "Put another way, the special counsel found no collusion by any Americans in the IRA's illegal activity."

Barr—who was flanked by Rosenstein and the top department official who oversaw Mueller on a day-to-day basis, Ed O'Callaghan—mentioned some form of "no collusion" five times in his twenty-two-minute-long remarks.

Shortly after 11:00 a.m. on Thursday, April 18, the Justice Department released the report. Mueller's report—hundreds of pages of detailed investigative findings about Trump and his associates—was, on its face, one of the most damning documents ever written about a sitting president.

Particularly in the second volume—the 182-page section laying out more than a dozen incidents in which Trump appeared to be close to or at the point of obstructing justice.

Barr had said that most of what was included in the obstruction section of the report was already publicly reported or something Trump had done in public. But the report contained stark new examples. Despite failing to learn from McGahn about how Trump wanted to prosecute Clinton and Comey, the report contained a similar incident. Trump, according to the report, held Sessions's job over his head at the same time he pressured him to investigate Clinton and Comey: "According to Sessions, the President asked him to reverse his recusal so that Sessions could direct the Department of Justice to investigate and prosecute Hillary Clinton, and the 'gist' of the conversation was that the President wanted Sessions to unrecuse from 'all of it,' including the Special Counsel's Russia investigation. Sessions listened but did not respond, and he did not reverse his recusal or order an investigation of Clinton."

The report also detailed the time that Trump had instructed his former campaign manager Corey Lewandowski to meet with Sessions and get him to publicly announce his unrecusal. If Sessions refused, the report stated, Trump wanted Lewandowski to tell Sessions that he was fired. Sessions never gave in to that request, which rankled Trump endlessly. Trump had fired Sessions the morning after the midterm elections in 2018.

In tortured fashion, the report declined to say whether any of these incidents actually amounted to a violation of the law, leaving it to legal experts to play prosecutor. Out of the incidents, the experts said, at least four were clear-cut examples of Trump breaking the law. They were all tied to Trump's efforts to contain the Mueller investigation. They included the new incident involving Lewandowski. But, of greatest significance to our reporting, they also included the attempt to fire Mueller and the attempt to force McGahn to go back on what he had told Mueller about the firing attempt after we broke our story.

There were so many instances of obstruction documented in the report that they crowded each other out, preventing one salient example from rising to the country's consciousness. It is a great irony that, as with so much else with the way that Trump operates, a cascading chaos dulls the senses, sows confusion, and has the effect of protecting him. One or two instances of a president obstructing justice is relatively easy to understand. Ten instances of a president obstructing justice is overwhelming and disorienting. In the weeks that followed, obstruction failed to catch on.

It would take me a year to put together the pieces of what I believe is one of the most important parts of the report: what it did not contain. Back in May 2017, the FBI had opened a two-pronged investigation into whether Trump obstructed justice and whether he was a Russian agent. When Mueller took over the investigation, the acting FBI director, McCabe, had briefed him on this. Over nearly two hundred pages, Mueller's team took on the question of whether Trump had obstructed justice. But nowhere in the unredacted version of the report was there a thorough examination of Trump's ties to Russia. The report did examine whether members of the campaign broke the law for conspiring with the Russians and found no evidence of a criminal offense. But the report said nothing about whether Trump posed a threat to national security or whether his long-standing ties to Russia were problematic.

In reporting for this book, I spoke to several people involved in the Mueller investigation. They told me that investigators never undertook a significant examination of Trump's personal and business ties to Russia. For instance, they said, investigators knew of financial documents that might show Trump's ties to Russia, but they never pursued them. Further, in intense negotiations with Trump's lawyers in seeking an interview with the president, Mueller's team showed little interest in questioning Trump beyond issues related to the election. And when Mueller's team ultimately sent Trump questions for him to respond to in writing, they never asked anything other than questions about what occurred during the campaign.

Mueller would later tell Congress that his investigators had not closely examined Trump's finances, but his disclosures received little attention. In his testimony before the House Intelligence Committee, Mueller engaged in an exchange with Congressman Raja Krishnamoorthi of Illinois that captures what can only be described as a profound failure to present the full picture of Trump's ties to Russia.

"You described your report as 'detailing a criminal investigation,' correct?" asked Krishnamoorthi.

"Yes," Mueller answered.

"Director, since it was outside the purview of your investigation, your report did not reach counterintelligence conclusions regarding the subject matter of your report?" Krishnamoorthi asked.

"That's true," Mueller said.

"For instance, since it was outside your purview, your report did not reach counterintelligence conclusions regarding any Trump administration officials who might potentially be vulnerable to compromise of blackmail by Russia, correct?" Krishnamoorthi asked.

"Those decisions probably were made in the FBI," Mueller said.

"But not in your report, correct?" asked Krishnamoorthi.

"Not in our report. We avert to the counterintelligence goals of our investigation which were secondary to any criminal wrongdoing that we could find," Mueller said.

"Let's talk about one administration official in particular, namely President Donald Trump. Other than Trump Tower Moscow, your report does not address or detail the president's financial ties or dealings with Russia, correct?" Krishnamoorthi said.

"Correct," Mueller said.

"Similarly, since it was outside your purview your report does not address the question of whether Russian oligarchs engaged in money laundering through any of the president's businesses, correct?" Krishnamoorthi asked.

"Correct," Mueller said.

"And, of course, your office did not obtain the president's tax returns, which could otherwise show foreign financial sources, correct?" asked Krishnamoorthi.

"I'm not going to speak to that," Mueller said.

"In July 2017, the president said his personal finances were off limits, or outside the purview of your investigation and he drew a 'red line,' around his personal finances," Krishnamoorthi asked, referring to our 2017 interview with Trump in the Oval Office. "Were the president's personal finances outside the purview of your investigation?"

"I'm not going to get into that," Mueller said.

While Mueller had addressed the question of what his team had or had not investigated, he didn't explain himself. If the American public or official Washington had expected the Mueller investigation to answer questions of the president's loyalties that only a counterintelligence investigation could answer, it would not. In reporting for this book, I discovered why. During the struggle between McCabe and Rosenstein in May 2017, it appeared as if McCabe had come out on top, as Rosenstein had appointed Mueller to pick up where McCabe and the FBI had left off on their obstruction and counterintelligence investigations of Trump. But in handing off the investigation from McCabe to Mueller, Rosenstein had suspended the counterintelligence investigation into Trump. He believed that the decision by McCabe and the top counterintelligence investigators at the FBI to open the inquiry into whether Trump was a Russian agent in the first place had been precipitous and premature. Without informing McCabe, Rosenstein told Mueller that his investigation should concentrate on whether crimes were committed, and it should not be a fishing expedition into whether Trump was a Russian agent. If Mueller's prosecutors wanted to expand their investigation, they could come back to Rosenstein and ask for the authority to do so. But in the meantime, they were to concentrate on whether the Russians had broken the law in their election meddling, and whether any Americans had broken the law in connection with those activities.

Deputy Attorney General Rod Rosenstein had foreclosed any deeper inquiry before the investigation even began.

A month before the report was released, Burck had begun representing the New England Patriots owner, Robert Kraft, after he was accused of soliciting sex at a massage parlor in Florida. Burck was now working around the clock to persuade a judge in Florida to keep video of the alleged incident secret. But as soon as Mueller's report was released, Burck, who was working from his study at home, dropped everything and began reading. While it was true that McGahn was the centerpiece, there were many others—ranging from characters like Lewandowski to Sessions—who implicated the president in obstructive behavior, showing that Trump had done far more than try to use McGahn to control the investigation. Along with all the damaging details about Trump, there was a small surprise: an anecdote that showed Trump bad-mouthing McGahn. The report said that as Trump sought to pressure McGahn to recant that he had told him to fire Mueller, Trump told Porter that McGahn was a leaker and a "lying bastard."

Two years of desperately trying to keep the presidency within the bounds of the law, and that's the thanks he gets. When McGahn heard what Trump had said, he no longer wanted to put out a statement. And Burck agreed that putting out such a statement on the occasion of a report awash in obstruction would look weird. And after being called a liar? No way.

That afternoon, Flood called Burck to find out when they would be putting out the statement. Burck said it was not the right time and explained their rationale.

"What would the purpose be?" Burck said.

Flood grew very agitated—more agitated than Burck had heard him in the dozen years they had known each other and worked closely together. The president, Flood said, was raging. And then

Burck heard a refrain he had so many times in the previous two years.

"The president's going to fire me," Flood said.

Burck thought it sounded like an empty threat from Trump. And so what if he fired Flood? Flood would just return to private practice, where he worked for a great firm and made a nice living. He would not be putting out that statement.

In the days that followed, Flood did not call Burck back.

That Friday night, I checked in with Rudy Giuliani, who had been in constant contact with Trump and was preparing to go on Fox News. Giuliani told me he would call back when he finished his interview. After the interview, he called and I asked him about McGahn. Giuliani said that McGahn had made inaccurate statements to the special counsel.

"It can't be taken at face value," Giuliani told me. "It could be the product of an inaccurate recollection or could be the product of something else," he said, intimating that McGahn had lied.

Giuliani denied that Trump ever asked McGahn to have Mueller fired. The former mayor said that he wanted the chance to cross-examine McGahn on the witness stand.

I sent Giuliani's remarks to Burck and asked him for a response. Minutes later, Burck fired back at Giuliani.

"It's a mystery why Rudy Giuliani feels the need to re-litigate incidents the Attorney General and Deputy Attorney have concluded were not obstruction," Burck said. "But they are accurately described in the report."

Then Burck, with McGahn's approval, took a dig at Trump, drawing attention to how McGahn had played such a key role in the nomination of judges—arguably Trump's greatest political accomplishment.

"Don, nonetheless, appreciates that the president gave him the opportunity to serve as White House Counsel and assist him with his signature accomplishments."

On Saturday afternoon, Flood called Burck back. He said he had a message to pass on from the president. Two days had passed since the report was released, and it had sunk into Trump just how much damage Burck's clients had done to him in the report. Trump knew who Burck was. In a conversation two weeks earlier with Kraft, the president had told him that Burck was a great lawyer and that Kraft was in good hands. Trump now had a different perspective.

"The president wants you to know you're a dirtbag and all the people hurting him are the dirtbags who hired you," Flood said in his dry tone. "Consider this your speaking to."

Two weeks later, Trump again told Priebus that Burck was a great lawyer.

* * *

MAY 25, 2019

ONE YEAR, FIVE MONTHS, AND NINE DAYS UNTIL THE 2020 PRESIDENTIAL ELECTION

FRONT STEPS OF QUARLES'S HOUSE—I spent so much time with the obstruction section of the Mueller report that I would find pages of it covered in notes and highlights tucked between my sheets and comforter. I wrote many stories about its conclusions and talked obsessively to my colleagues about where Mueller had ended up. It was clear there were many unanswered questions, and it seemed as though there was a thread that ran through all of them.

It still made no sense why Mueller had not pursued an interview with Trump. The investigation turned on why the president took so many potentially obstructive actions that made it harder for the government to investigate Russian interference. Yet there was nothing in the report about whether Trump was a Russian agent or was potentially compromised by the Russians. On obstruction, the decision to not make a decision was viewed by many as a dodge. And Mueller had closed up his investigation before Flynn had been sentenced and his prosecutors had had a chance to try Roger Stone, who was Trump's longtime confidant and the point person between WikiLeaks and the Trump campaign. All of these points lead to this question: Why did Mueller, whom we had made out as such a tough and thorough prosecutor, take such a weak approach as the investigation concluded?

We had studied similar investigations—like the ones conducted by Ken Starr of Bill Clinton and Lawrence Walsh of Iran-contra—and it seemed as if the personalities of those leading the inquiries had as much bearing on the final results as the facts themselves.

In trying to answer these lingering questions, I started to stitch together bits and pieces of my own reporting on Mueller over the previous year that I had never been able to fully run down or understand.

A sense that something might be amiss with Mueller had crept in during the summer of 2018. Time and again, as we reported on meetings between Mueller's team and Trump's lawyers about the president sitting for an interview, we were told that Mueller had been nowhere to be found. In the first year of the investigation, Mueller almost always showed up for the meetings with Trump's legal team when the stakes were far lower. But it was odd that he had sort of ducked out just as the negotiations were hitting a fever pitch.

Mueller's team had given Trump's lawyers no indication of where Mueller had gone. I wondered what was going on. Maybe the prosecutors were holding Mueller back from the negotiations for strategic reasons, planning to deploy him at a crucial point. Or maybe we were overthinking it. Maybe Mueller was busy; after all, it was a sprawling investigation. And on top of that, his team was writing a report; maybe he was playing editor.

These are of course difficult and delicate questions to ask. But the question of where Mueller was only intensified as the investigation entered its final months. The inescapable sense was that more and more, at crucial times, he simply wasn't there. When John Kelly went in for his interview in August, Mueller did not show. Then, by November, with the negotiations over the Trump interview at a standstill, Trump's lawyers demanded a meeting with Mueller's team and staffers for Rosenstein who were supervising Mueller. The meeting was convened in Rosenstein's conference room at the Justice Department. Giuliani and Trump's whole gang of lawyers showed. If there was a time for the prosecutors to use Mueller, this would have been the meeting. But, again, Mueller failed to show.

Not once during the investigation—including when his team indicted the Russians behind the hacking and disinformation—had

Mueller held a press conference. Then, as the investigation concluded, there was no sign of Mueller. He had remained silent as his team sent the report to the Justice Department. He had allowed Barr to spin the conclusions without saying anything publicly. And when the report was finally released, he declined to stand with Barr at the press conference, opening the door even wider for the attorney general to sculpt the conclusions. We knew that Mueller's team was upset with how the report had been portrayed. But Mueller still said nothing publicly. In Mueller's career, he had testified before Congress more times than almost any other living American. Yet he was afraid to talk as the most consequential investigation he had overseen was being distorted by the president, the attorney general, and the Republicans in Congress?

By the end of May, about a month after the report had been released, the calls for Mueller to testify were becoming louder and louder. Senior Justice Department officials lobbied members of Congress to hold off on subpoenaing Mueller. They claimed Mueller was not going to say anything more than what he had written in the report, so there was no need for a hearing. Their insistence that Mueller not testify seemed curious to me. Why not let it all play out? Were they afraid he would say something that would tip the narrative against the president? Or were they trying to shield Mueller from something?

As the Justice Department sought to fend off Congress about a hearing, I heard more and more about Mueller and the questions percolating inside the Justice Department, the White House, and Mueller's office about Mueller's acuity. I learned the details about how in the March meeting with Barr, Mueller's hands shook, and he struggled to articulate his team's conclusions. But that information left us at a loss about what to do. Without having medical files or seeing Mueller speak and interact in the flesh, how could we write a story, and what would we say? A lot of those who were pushing the questions about Mueller's command were on the Barr-Trump side of the equation. But it was unclear whether their talking about it was simply gossip about someone they had a strategic interest in diminishing or if it was an effort to deter Mueller from testifying.

I was at a loss. Mueller's position was of such consequence that the state of his cognitive abilities was equally important. The only idea I had for examining this question was to just directly approach members of Mueller's team and inquire. They knew there were questions about whether he would testify. If we told them how this was being pushed by the Barr-Trump side, maybe they would engage in the hopes of setting the record straight. I knew if we tried to reach out to anyone on Mueller's team at the office, we would be rebuffed. But maybe we could try one of the most aggressive and rarely used moves in reporting: approaching someone at their home.

So one evening, I persuaded my colleague Adam Goldman, who had a great history of success with door knocks and was always willing to try to get anyone to talk, to take a drive to the home of Jim Quarles in Bethesda, Maryland. I was sort of scared to make the approach, as I had far less success in this area. Would he erupt at us for showing up at his house? I banked on the fact that along with everything I had reported on in the previous two years, I had learned that of all the folks on Mueller's team Quarles was the most genial and thoughtful. In the worst-case scenario, maybe he would just tell us to leave. We knocked on the door of his tidy, fairly large house in a cul-de-sac. About a minute later, he came to the door, wearing sweatpants and what looked like a large football jersey.

"Hey, Mike Schmidt and Adam Goldman from the *Times,*" Goldman said.

He smiled.

"Not talking," he said.

I tried to make small talk. He did not respond to anything. Goldman went on about how we were just trying to get the story right, and Quarles muttered something along the lines of: We just don't talk. In other words, as the Mueller team, we don't talk.

Our only hope was to keep him talking about anything, even the weather or the grass in the front yard. I made a joke about how ridiculous it was that we had come out there.

"Are we among many who have come out here to bother you?" I asked.

He said we were the first. I thought worse of my colleagues in the media who had not made a similar try.

I had to make a last-ditch effort. I thought that if our reporting was true, Mueller and his team were headed for a problem. If he testified and was diminished, it would undermine the report. And if he did not testify, it would only stoke questions about his tenure leading the investigation. So I threw it all out there: You know, I said, they're saying all this stuff about how Mueller has lost it and there's something wrong with him.

Quarles did not bite, gave a slight nod, and closed the door.

His reaction left me with no clues. But I did not want to give up. I thought we had to take another shot at someone on Mueller's team. Goldman and I then found the nearby home address of Quarles's investigative colleague Andrew Goldstein. We drove just a few minutes to his home. It didn't look as if anyone was there. Then we saw who appeared to be his wife and children walk into the home. We waited a few more minutes and then walked up to his front door. The doorbell was broken, so we knocked. We could hear voices inside, but no one came to the door. At this point, I thought better of the entire ploy. Given that his children were there and that it would be potentially uncomfortable for them to see two reporters confront their father, I turned to Goldman and said this had gone too far, and we headed back to the car without knocking again.

At this point, I thought we had no choice but to put all of our cards on the table. That Saturday morning, I went to a coffee shop in my neighborhood and wrote a letter to Mueller's chief of staff, Aaron Zebley. I thought that our only choice was to level with them, tell them what we knew, and hope they would engage, given that if there was some sort of problem with Mueller, they would eventually have to disclose it. I wrote three or four drafts of the letter and then called a cutout I knew who could get the letter to Zebley without having to go through the press office. That afternoon, I sent the letter on its way to Zebley.

> Aaron:
>
> I apologize for reaching out to you. We've hit on some fairly serious information that has put us in an unusual position. We're trying to do everything to deal with it as delicately and fairly as possible. I don't believe we can do that without trying to com-

municate directly with you and I need your help making sure we get it right.

Off the bat, I want you to know that I only know you by reputation but if you tell me there is nothing to the gist of this I will take what you say at face value. If there is indeed something to this, I urge you to deal with us, as it seems that this is building towards coming out and we are prepared to deal with it with great care.

Reporting on someone's fitness is something we often try to avoid given the invasive and deeply personal nature of this issue. But under the current circumstances, there are few people aside from the president whose status is more important than Mr. Mueller's given his outsized role in what has gone on over the past two years. In the past few days the narrative in the media has been that Mr. Mueller will decline to testify publicly to avoid the spectacle. While this may be true it is not the full picture of the decision to shield Mr. Mueller from the public. Through our reporting, we've learned that there are deep concerns among those close to Mr. Mueller that he lacks the mental acuity to do this. Mr. Mueller, we're told, has good days and bad days and there's a risk that a public hearing could undermine the public's view of his fitness.

What we've learned builds on other reporting we have developed over the past year. We're told that in the March 5 meeting with Barr and his aides that Mr. Mueller's hands significantly shook and that he struggled to articulate his views. Starting last summer, Mr. Mueller was less and less involved in the interactions the special counsel's office had with the Justice Department, the president's lawyers and lawyers for witnesses. After initially participating in some of the negotiations about a potential Trump interview, Mr. Mueller faded from the discussions with the president's lawyers. On the Justice Department side, you increasingly took the lead dealing directly with the DAG's office. Those who did interact with Mr. Mueller said that it was as if "his fastball consistently landed three feet short of the plate." We're told that in the initial months of the investigation, it was clear that Mr. Mueller was "not the Mueller of his early FBI days."

We're not interested in chronicling every episode that may raise questions about Mr. Mueller's status. Instead we are focused on the larger issue of why he may not want to testify publicly. We have indications at this point that Main Justice, the White House, the president's lawyers and others are aware of this issue. And we have reason to believe other media outlets may know about it as well. We believe we are best positioned to deal with this in the most responsible and fair way. I'm available to talk anytime this weekend and would meet you wherever whenever if you'd like.

Thank you,
Mike Schmidt

That evening, I received a message back that what I had written was flat wrong. Mueller was fine. Then, a day later, Mueller's spokesman reached out to me to say that what I had heard was wrong and that it was almost offensive that I asked the question. We had hit a dead end, because it was going to be pretty hard to write a story in the face of such a denial. If Mueller ever testified, we would learn the truth.

★ ★ ★

MAY 29, 2019

ONE YEAR, FIVE MONTHS, AND FIVE DAYS UNTIL THE 2020 PRESIDENTIAL ELECTION

PRESS BRIEFING ROOM, JUSTICE DEPARTMENT, WASHINGTON, D.C.—In the weeks following the Mueller report's release, congressional Democrats sought to highlight its findings and amplify the portions most damaging to Trump. They clamored for the Justice Department to make two concessions: First, they wanted the entire report given to them unredacted, and second, they wanted Mueller to testify.

Adam Schiff, the California representative and chairman of the House Intelligence Committee, went on television and said that

Mueller had to testify if the American people wanted to hear the unfiltered version of what he found.

"He is going to testify," Schiff said. "The American people have a right to hear what the man who did the investigation has to say and we now know we certainly can't rely on the attorney general who misrepresented his conclusions."

By the end of May, the Justice Department believed it had found a compromise that might dampen the Democrats' demands. Mueller had continued to remain a department employee in the months after his investigation had concluded, but now he was going to officially close his office. Perhaps, Justice Department officials thought, if Mueller gives one final press conference, he could satisfy the desires for additional public comments.

So, in the late morning of May 29, Mueller stood behind a Department of Justice lectern and announced the closing of his special counsel office. It marked the first time he had spoken publicly since the investigation began two years earlier. For less than ten minutes, he read his prepared remarks off the podium and only occasionally looked up. When discussing his decisions on obstruction of justice, Mueller suggested the president might have committed a crime.

"And as set forth in the report after that investigation, if we had had confidence that the president clearly did not commit a crime, we would have said so," Mueller said.

Mueller gingerly pointed out that while his team had declined to make a decision, there may be another way to hold the president accountable.

Citing the Justice Department guideline that a president cannot be indicted, Mueller said that "the Constitution requires a process other than the criminal justice system to formally accuse a sitting president of wrongdoing."

And while he did not speak the word, it hung in the air all the same. "Impeachment."

Mueller also tried to slow the calls for his testimony by saying that if called, he would offer nothing more than what had already been written in his report.

"I hope and expect this to be the only time that I will speak to you in this manner," Mueller said. "There has been discussion about an appearance before Congress. Any testimony from this office would not go beyond our report. It contains our findings and analysis and the reasons for the decisions we made."

Mueller's report had been completed. The public had consumed it. It seemed like a natural time for Mueller to end his investigation. But by walking away at this point, Mueller was doing something that similar investigators—like Lawrence Walsh during the Reagan and Bush years—had shied away from. Walsh had remained as the independent counsel for more than six years, seeing his cases through their sentencing. By doing this, he ensured the independence of his investigation to the end. And while Mueller's work seemed as if it were done, it really was not. That fall, Trump's longtime political adviser Roger Stone was scheduled to go on trial for lying to Congress about his contacts with WikiLeaks about its stolen emails during the campaign. And Flynn had still not been sentenced for lying to FBI agents about his contacts with the Russian ambassador. Justice Department officials said that these cases would be handled by Mueller's prosecutors who remained at the department to ensure continuity and that they came to a proper conclusion. But they would do so now without the structure or imprimatur of the special counsel's office, giving the attorney general—who thought little of the special counsel's work—more control over the directions of those cases.

⋆ ⋆ ⋆

JULY 24, 2019

ONE YEAR, THREE MONTHS, AND TEN DAYS UNTIL THE 2020 PRESIDENTIAL ELECTION

HEARING ROOM 2141, RAYBURN HOUSE OFFICE BUILDING, CAPITOL HILL—Mueller's press conference failed to satisfy Democrats, and they continued to publicly pressure him to come up to the Hill and offer his testimony—hoping that he could lay out in detail all of the most damaging scenes for the president. Despite being asked, however,

Mueller had resisted. It wasn't until June 25, when both the House Intelligence and the House Judiciary Committees subpoenaed him, that Mueller finally agreed to testify.

Scheduled to appear the following month, Mueller had the opportunity to reassert control over the messaging around his investigation, which had been subverted by the attorney general. He could add more legal analysis on the events within the report, offering the public a fresh understanding of the president's actions. He could change the public narrative, and direct Congress or the American people to take the next step.

In preparation, Zebley, the deputy special counsel, Goldstein, and Quarles sat down with Mueller to prepare him for the questions he was bound to face. Their sessions went badly. Mueller struggled to remember basic facts or articulate the central findings and conclusions of his report. Congressional staffers, who had heard rumors similar to the ones I had about Mueller's deteriorating condition, asked Goldstein if Mueller was doing all right. Goldstein told them that Mueller was fine.

In the days before his appearance, there were signs that Mueller was looking for some help with his testimony. Mueller's representatives asked House Democrats if Zebley could sit next to Mueller when he testified so he could assist and answer questions if needed. The committees pushed back but ultimately allowed Zebley to attend in a largely advisory role.

On July 24, Mueller sat down next to Zebley and took questions first from Judiciary and then from the Intelligence Committee members. Within seconds of his beginning to speak, it was clear that something about him was off.

Throughout the day he struggled to answer questions, including about the president who had appointed him as U.S. attorney in Massachusetts. More than a dozen times he asked lawmakers to repeat their questions. There were small difficulties, like when Mueller had a hard time coming up with the word "conspiracy." But there were larger ones, like when he gave the wrong answer to one of the central questions of his investigation.

"I'd like to ask you the reason, again, that you did not indict

Donald Trump is because of OLC [Office of Legal Counsel] opinion stating that you cannot indict a sitting president, correct?" Representative Ted Lieu, Democrat from California, asked Mueller.

"That is correct," Mueller answered.

Mueller failed to realize that he gave a contradictory answer to what was in the report during his testimony and only cleaned up his remarks after a break in the hearing.

At one point in the proceedings, the Republican congressman Jim Jordan, the Judiciary Committee's ranking member, not known for his empathy, turned to a member of his staff sitting nearby and said, "I feel bad for the guy."

EPILOGUE

★ ★ ★ ★ ★

PRESIDENT TRUMP FINDS HIS ROY COHN

JULY 25, 2019

ONE YEAR, THREE MONTHS, AND NINE DAYS UNTIL THE 2020 PRESIDENTIAL ELECTION

WHITE HOUSE RESIDENCE—Mueller's testimony left Trump feeling and acting triumphal, vicious, and emboldened. The Mueller report had two volumes: volume 1 on Russian election interference and whether the Trump campaign had colluded with the Russians; and volume 2 on whether Trump obstructed justice and used his power as president inappropriately. A mere eighteen hours after Mueller finished answering lawmakers' questions, Trump combined the worst accusations of volumes 1 and 2 into a single act.

On July 25, 2019, on a call shortly after 9:00 a.m., Trump, from the White House residence, asked the newly elected leader of Ukraine, Volodymyr Zelensky, to interfere in the 2020 American election on his behalf by having his country use its law enforcement powers to conduct investigations that Trump wanted. Trump said the Ukrainians should look into the business dealings of the son of the former vice president Joseph R. Biden Jr., his most likely challenger in the election, and into whether the Ukrainians had interfered in the 2016 election to help the Democrats. Trump said he wanted the Ukrainian president to help his personal lawyer Rudy Giuliani, who was investigating the matters for Trump, and his own attorney general, Bill Barr, whom Trump wanted to prosecute the Bidens and the Democrats.

"I will tell Rudy and Attorney General Barr to call. Thank you," Trump told the Ukrainian president, according to a White House document created at the time to memorialize the call.

On the call, Trump appeared to combine his request for investigations with the conditional offer of a White House meeting with the new Ukrainian president. Zelensky very much wanted the meeting, to demonstrate the strong bond between Ukraine and the United States, especially as his country was fending off Russian-backed separatists.

"Whenever you would like to come to the White House feel free to call," Trump said. "Give us a date and we'll work that out. I look forward to seeing you."

As they typically do for calls with top foreign leaders, many administration and National Security Council officials listened in, including Secretary of State Mike Pompeo. In reaction to what Trump said, Pompeo did nothing, actually believing the call had gone well compared with Trump's other ones with leaders—particularly Europeans—which often turned into Trump screaming at them. But the call alarmed several officials on the National Security Council for two reasons. First, Trump was using his power as the head of the country's foreign policy to solicit assistance from another country for his domestic political campaign. Second, Trump had for weeks been curiously withholding $391 million in military aid—which Congress had already appropriated—from the Ukrainians that they desperately needed. Now Trump appeared to be using that aid as leverage as he asked the Ukrainians for a major favor. Later that day, two Army lieutenant colonels on the National Security Council—the twins Alexander and Yevgeny Vindman, who immigrated to the United States from the Soviet Union as children—went to John Eisenberg, the top lawyer on the NSC. Eisenberg, who in the early days of the administration oversaw the White House's response to the concerns raised about Michael Flynn's contacts with the Russian ambassador, had seen several actions that concerned him over the two and a half years of Trump's presidency. He had become skilled at taming the fallout, having survived longer than McGahn. He told the Vindman twins he would look into the matter, and in the aftermath of the meeting he restricted access to the White House document memorializing the call.

The NSC typically "back briefs" analysts and officials at agencies like the CIA after the president has calls with foreign leaders. In the course of back briefing, NSC officials spoke with a CIA analyst in his early thirties who covered Ukraine. The officials were alarmed by what the president had done.

The analyst was already on alert for the obvious intertwining of American foreign policy with Trump's personal political desires. As an expert on Ukraine, he studied the country—its news, its leaders, its scandals, and its trajectory. If an action or event was poised to shift the dynamic between the United States and Ukraine, it was the analyst's job to track it and understand how the Ukrainians would likely react and how it could impact American interests.

Throughout the spring, the analyst had watched as Giuliani had set out on a campaign to upend American-Ukrainian relations as the president's personal lawyer pursued his own foreign policy to Ukraine. The analyst saw how Giuliani used media appearances to publicly push all sorts of conspiracy theories about Ukraine, its role in the 2016 election, and Biden's son. Giuliani spoke dramatically about how Trump had been wronged by the Mueller investigation and needed to strike back against his potential opponent. In repeated television appearances and interviews with print journalists, Giuliani attacked Biden, a clear indication that Trump saw Biden as the Democratic candidate who could beat him in the election. The analyst noted how Giuliani used his position as Trump's personal lawyer to open doors with Ukrainian officials to lobby them directly to conduct the investigations he wanted. Giuliani had discussed plans to travel to Ukraine in May but canceled the trip amid a public outcry that he was seeking to get the Ukrainians to meddle in the election. By May 2019, the analyst learned there were deep concerns throughout the American government that Giuliani was working outside normal diplomatic channels to pursue Trump's personal political errands in Ukraine.

Giuliani's foray into Ukrainian relations had been largely overshadowed by the Mueller investigation and report. But in Ukraine, the story had left an indelible mark and created some suspense as to whether satisfying Giuliani would unlock better relations with the United States and the military aid needed to defend the country against Russia. The analyst had heard about Trump's call and could only think that it constituted the next step in a pressure campaign.

The request floored the analyst who thought to himself, *What the fuck?* Trump's behavior on the call had been highly problematic and potentially illegal, he believed. The analyst had been dealing in foreign affairs his entire career. How was it that Trump could withhold the aid from Ukraine at the same time he was pressuring the country's president to investigate his political rival? Wasn't that illegal?

But what could he do? He was a mid-career analyst at the CIA—just one of roughly twenty thousand agency employees and tens of thousands in the entire intelligence community. The president was the head of the executive branch—the most powerful person in the world. Trump had survived more embarrassing disclosures than any other American president, and he'd survived the Mueller investigation. Nothing could stop him. The analyst believed it was his duty—both as someone seeking to keep American-Ukrainian relations intact and as a public servant who swore an oath to the Constitution—to do something. Like Comey and McGahn before him, he wondered, Whom do you call when the president of the United States is the one undermining American interests?

Through the analyst's training, he knew that he should report any potential wrongdoing to the CIA general counsel's office. In the days after the call, he met with a CIA lawyer. The analyst explained how he had been informed about the details of Trump's conversation with Zelensky by multiple White House officials who had either been listening to the call or read a summary of the call in the days following.

The lawyer agreed with the analyst that what he was reporting was troubling and said that the CIA's general counsel, Courtney Simmons Elwood, would work with the White House to figure out what to do. Soon after, Elwood called Eisenberg and told him what she had learned. Within days, however, the CIA's counsel's office told the analyst that it seemed as if the White House was not going to be taking this seriously.

The idea that the White House was looking the other way bothered the analyst even more. He was convinced something troubling had occurred, and he felt as though he'd taken the proper and necessary steps. But now the White House was smothering it. A sense of dread began to set in. He was one of only a handful of people who knew both about the president's call and how it fit into the larger story of Giuliani's pressure campaign and the risk that withholding the money created for Ukraine and its ability to hold back the Russian-backed separatists. But there was no one else up the chain of command who could overrule the White House. The analyst figured his only option was Congress.

The analyst contacted a friend and former NSC colleague who now worked as a staffer for the Democratic chairman of the House Intelligence Committee, Adam Schiff, who had been determined to expose Trump since the early days of the presidency. The analyst gave his friend a rough idea of what had occurred. The friend told him that what he had uncovered was extremely serious. But in order for the committee to investigate it, the analyst would need to do something through official channels, like filing a whistleblower complaint. To do that, the analyst would need a lawyer to guide him through the process.

But finding a lawyer was complicated. He needed someone who understood whistleblower complaints. Few lawyers practiced that type of law and had experience dealing with the complexities that came with it. The analyst searched through his network of contacts, including the dozens of officials from the intelligence community and the Obama administration who had left government and were now lawyers in private practice. Through searching, he saw that one former official who had worked on the Obama National Security Council might have some expertise in this area, and the analyst reached out to him.

They met at a coffee shop just blocks from Capitol Hill.

To the lawyer, the analyst did not seem nervous or frantic. Instead, he appeared solemn, as if he were carrying a great burden and trying to do the right thing and navigate a part of Washington that he knew little about.

"I want to be very cautious. I don't want you to tell me anything classified or privileged," the lawyer said.

"If I'm understanding what I believe happened, I think people need to look at it," the analyst said.

The analyst laid out a skeleton of what he knew, very elliptically. He said he had not witnessed the incident but had been told about it. He intimated that it involved a senior administration official. He said he believed the law might have been broken. And he said that he thought becoming a whistleblower was likely his only pathway forward, but he wanted to know what that entailed.

The lawyer believed that he was referring to something that President Trump had done. But the lawyer was not completely sure, and the lawyer declined to press on that issue. Instead, the lawyer gave him his counsel.

"I think I've heard enough to give you some guidance," the lawyer said.

While the lawyer said he had experience dealing with whistleblowers, this type of case was different and required a high level of expertise. It almost certainly involved classified information, issues of executive privilege, the president's conduct, and navigating the intelligence community and the political winds of Capitol Hill.

"I think I have the person for you," the lawyer said.

After they had parted, the lawyer deleted the calendar event he had created in his phone for the meeting. He was unsure where the entire matter was headed but believed that to ensure the analyst's identity remained secret—and that none of the people who worked for him learned who the analyst was—it was safest to delete the event. Within a day, he introduced the analyst to a lawyer named Andrew Bakaj.

Eight days after Trump made the call to the Ukrainian president, the analyst called Bakaj, who had just returned home from vacation with his wife's family and was in the parking lot of a golf course in northern Virginia preparing to play nine holes. Bakaj had worked as a lawyer in the office of the inspector general at the CIA earlier in his career and had become a whistleblower himself after he reported wrongdoing in his office. He was retaliated against and then left the government to work as a lawyer representing whistleblowers and intelligence community personnel who had problems with their security clearances. Bakaj knew that whistleblowers came in all forms. Some were paranoid and conspiratorial. Others were extreme rule followers who saw the world in black and white and wanted to call attention to the smallest of infractions. The remaining few were people who truly had stumbled across some wrongdoing and were simply trying to do the right thing. After he spoke with the analyst, Bakaj's initial reaction was that the analyst fell into the third category.

Over a long conversation, the analyst laid out what he found so alarming about Trump's call, how access to the transcript had been limited, and concerns he had about the broader campaign by Trump and Giuliani to mix Trump's political desires with foreign policy.

Bakaj told the analyst he essentially had two options: file a whistleblower complaint through the inspector general for the intelligence community or do nothing. The analyst said he had no interest in doing nothing. Bakaj backed up that notion, saying that government employees had a duty to report wrongdoing when they saw it. He explained to the analyst how President George H. W. Bush had issued an executive order in 1989 establishing the "principles of ethical conduct" for federal workers, which required all government employees to "disclose waste, fraud, abuse, and corruption to appropriate authorities."

Over the next week and a half, Bakaj and the analyst went back and forth about putting together a complaint. Bakaj told the whistleblower that he had to write the complaint on his own because it involved classified information. On classified computers at the CIA, the analyst put together a nine-page complaint that began with Giuliani's earliest efforts to lobby the Ukrainians and walked through the events up to Trump's saying he was planning on inviting Zelensky to the White House.

"Multiple White House officials with direct knowledge of the call informed me that, after an initial exchange of pleasantries, the President used the remainder of the call to advance his personal interests," the complaint read. "Namely, he sought to pressure the

Ukrainian leader to take actions to help the President's 2020 reelection bid."

On August 3, Bakaj and the whistleblower met at Bakaj's office on Connecticut Avenue, a few blocks from the White House. The analyst had finished the complaint and was prepared to transmit it. The two discussed how, once the analyst filed it, the entire matter would be outside their control.

The possibilities of how it could go wrong were endless. Whistleblowers' identities are supposed to be protected. But given how the Trump administration functioned and the potential damage the complaint could do, the analyst's name could be revealed, subjecting him to harassment ranging from nasty social media posts to professional retaliation to death threats.

While both the analyst and Bakaj felt a sense of dread of what could come, Bakaj told the analyst it was unlikely the complaint would lead to much. After all, Bakaj thought, Mueller's report had done nothing to move Democrats. And then Trump had promptly done something similar with yet another country. Why would more of the same move the needle?

That afternoon, the whistleblower emailed the complaint on the classified networks to the inspector general of the intelligence community, known as the ICIG, which was led by a career Justice Department official named Michael Atkinson.

The following day the inspector general's office reached out to the whistleblower to tell him the complaint had been received, and the office began an investigation to determine whether it was credible and urgent—the standards required to transmit it to Congress. As part of that investigation, the inspector general's office secretly interviewed the whistleblower and several NSC staffers without telling the White House. Within two weeks the inspector general's office determined that it was indeed credible and urgent, and Atkinson prepared to report it to Congress.

But then, on September 5, the whistleblower's quest looked doomed. The inspector general's office told the whistleblower that the acting director of national intelligence, Joseph Maguire, had decided against sending his complaint on to Congress. It was made clear to the whistleblower that Atkinson was not happy about Maguire's decision. What the whistleblower did not know was that Trump had been told about the complaint in August and that the White House and Justice Department had instructed Maguire not to send it to Congress.

Bakaj had never before heard of a complaint that an inspector general deemed urgent and credible being stopped from transmitting to Congress—he didn't even think that Maguire had the power to stop it from being sent to Congress. To Bakaj, it reeked of the way officials tried to cover up wrongdoing during Watergate—the exact event that caused the formation of the inspectors general offices in the first place. Concerned now both for his client and for the sanctity of the entire whistleblower system that formed the backbone of government transparency and accountability, Bakaj decided to take matters into his own hands. Over the weekend he drafted a letter to the chairs of the House and Senate Intelligence Committees, saying that his client's complaint had been deemed urgent and credible by the inspector general but, in an apparent violation of the law, had been blocked from being sent to Congress.

On the afternoon of September 9, Bakaj decided to hand deliver the letter to the Senate and House Intelligence Committees. He first went to the Senate, where the staff of the Republican chairman, Richard Burr, showed no interest in speaking with him. But when he arrived at the office of Schiff, his staffers were intrigued.

Bakaj sat down with three of the committee's top attorneys in the office's library. The group talked for about thirty minutes, building an overview of the complaint Bakaj was bringing to the lawyers' attention. Bakaj made sure not to say too much in an effort to avoid any future allegations of leaking, but he also wanted to say enough to pique the lawyers' interest in the hopes they would put pressure on Maguire for the complaint.

The lawyers seemed to have some understanding of what the whistleblower knew and began ticking off the topics. They mentioned Ukraine, and Bakaj cut them off.

"It may have something to do with that," Bakaj said.

The lawyers started peppering Bakaj with questions.

Was it about a presidential communication?

It was, Bakaj said.

Did it involve the president of Ukraine?

Bakaj said he couldn't tell them either way on that, but he essentially gave it away with a hint.

"You're warm on that one," Bakaj said.

Just as the lawyers were asking their last questions and wrapping up the meeting, someone knocked on the library's door. One of the lawyers answered the knock and briefly left the room while Bakaj and the other two attorneys continued chatting.

When the staff lawyer returned, he looked ashen.

"Andrew, we just received a letter from the ICIG," the staff lawyer said. "It matches up exactly with what you came in here with today."

It was one thing to have the lawyer of a whistleblower come into the House committee to say that his client had filed a complaint that they might be interested in. That did not happen every day, but it was not an infrequent occurrence. But the letter from the inspector general was a game changer. In Atkinson's two-year tenure, he had never deemed a complaint both "credible" and "urgent." On top of that, Atkinson was saying that he was being stopped from sending it to Congress. In the letter, he was alleging that Maguire had violated the law by failing to pass along the complaint.

Maguire's decision to withhold the complaint from Congress "does not appear to be consistent with past practice," the letter said.

The lawyers wouldn't show Bakaj the letter, but he knew exactly what it was about. He was more shocked than anything. Just a week earlier he was not expecting there to be too much news or drama coming out of the complaint. And he definitely was not expecting the complaint to be blocked from reaching the Hill. But now, at basically the same exact time, both he and the inspector general were running to the House Intelligence Committee to highlight what they saw as a massive cover-up.

As he drove home that afternoon, it dawned on him that the complaint might have a far greater impact than he originally believed. He was one of the few people in the world who knew what was in it. And when it came out, it could transform Washington. But Congress still did not have the complaint, and it was unclear how that would happen.

Four days later, Congressman Schiff sent a subpoena to Maguire asking for the complaint. Given the investigation fatigue in the wake of the Mueller report and the fact that it was unclear whom the complaint was related to, it received little attention in the media. But that changed days later when the media reported that the complaint had been filed against the president.

The story created another massive scandal for Trump. As the allegations made in the complaint came into focus, and the gravity of the charges became clear, Congress and the country were tempest tossed yet again. During the Russia investigation and after the Mueller report, as several members of her caucus agitated to impeach the president, Speaker of the House Nancy Pelosi stood firmly against the idea. Let the election sort it out. Any impeachment that could be seen as political would not be good for the country, she thought. But then the whistleblower complaint exploded into the news, and like a dam bursting, the Ukraine scandal inundated Washington. And soon the Speaker, who had been so resolved against putting the country through an impeachment, realized that the House of Representatives would likely have no choice, whatever the political consequences may be. Regardless of the politics. Either the Constitution meant something and was worth defending, or it wasn't, Pelosi contended. The Senate would almost certainly not convict, but that wasn't the point. This was for the record and for history.

The whistleblower had accomplished what everyone before him had failed to do: He had stopped President Trump in his tracks and had him on the path to being impeached.

Two months later, on a Saturday afternoon in mid-November, as Democrats moved toward their impeachment vote, Trump made an unexpected visit to Walter Reed National Military Medical Center. The White House played off the trip as part of the president's annual physical but provided no other details about the examination, raising questions about the president's health. In reporting for this book, I learned that in the hours leading up to Trump's trip to the hospital, word went out in the West Wing for the vice president to be on standby to take over the powers of the presidency temporarily if Trump had to undergo a procedure that would have required him to be anesthetized. Pence never assumed the powers of the presidency, and the reason for Trump's trip to the doctor remains a mystery.

* * *

JANUARY 23, 2020

285 DAYS UNTIL THE 2020 PRESIDENTIAL ELECTION

NEW YORK TIMES WASHINGTON BUREAU—Three months later there was no question that the whistleblower's account was correct. Democrats in the House had already voted to impeach Trump. The remaining question was whether there would be enough pressure applied to Senate Republicans—who held a fifty-three to forty-seven majority—to persuade twenty of them to convict the president and have him removed.

Even before the Senate received the impeachment referral from the House, Republicans were signaling their intention to vote on the articles and close the case as soon as possible; that meant no new witnesses. Now, with the clock ticking down, we in the media saw it as our role to get as many facts out as possible before the final vote was taken.

One of the few gold mines of information left largely untouched was Trump's former national security adviser John Bolton. He had served in the Trump White House for seventeen months and left as most others had—disaffected and changed by the experience, transformed from Trump champion into Trump critic—a Trump enabler who could now be an impediment. Bolton left in early September 2019, just as the Ukraine scandal was building. During the House investigation, he had not testified. Unlike many of the witnesses whom the Democrats had called, Bolton had a particularly high standing with Republicans because he had been a leading national security hawk for decades, spending countless hours on Fox News.

In a normal situation, it would be difficult to know what Bolton would testify to. He had left the White House on the day before Trump released the aid to the Ukrainians and was said to have become disillusioned with the president. We could talk to his friends, colleagues, and aides to get a sense of what he knew and how he viewed Trump, but that reporting could take us only so far. And Bolton had created a highly unusual situation. He had signaled he had something damaging to say about Trump, but refused to testify before House impeachment investigators. That made it look like he was hoarding his damaging information about Trump for a book he planned to publish. Democrats and some Republicans said they wanted to hear what he had to say. At the *Times*, we felt that, given the high stakes, we had to find out what was in the book. It would put us in a ridiculous race against time, scouring for leads and even receiving a tip from a private eye.

In December, I attended a meeting with top editors in New York about our impeachment coverage. I mentioned what I thought was our best chance to move the impeachment story forward.

"If we could figure out what's in Bolton's book, it would allow us to write what he would testify about," I said.

A masthead editor in the room laughed at the notion, saying there was no chance we could get that. In journalism, like sports, you sometimes need motivation and sometimes have to find it in weird places. I was upset that the editor had scoffed at the notion. Why not help me brainstorm ideas on how to go after it? But I tried to channel those feelings toward motivation. A top editor thought we couldn't do it?

The best I could come up with was talking to Bolton's lawyer, Chuck Cooper. Throughout the Trump administration, I had met a range of lawyers who represented clients caught up in the investigations of Trump's presidency. Out of all of them, Cooper was probably the most compelling character. When Jeff Sessions got into trouble for misleading Congress about his contacts with the Russian ambassador, Cooper swooped in to represent his old friend, helping guide him through the congressional investigations and serving as an outside adviser as Sessions sought to maintain his job. It ate Cooper alive to watch his friend get taken apart and humiliated by Trump, someone Cooper believed was uncouth, unprincipled, and a threat to the country. It was in his representation of Sessions that I met Cooper. He was a younger, better-looking version of Sessions and had his strong Alabama accent. But different from Sessions, Cooper understood the law and the complexities of the Trump administration better than anyone involved in the story.

Cooper had started representing another close friend who had attracted Trump's ire, Bolton, in connection with the impeachment investigation. I knew that Cooper had decamped to his house in Florida for December. I considered flying down and inviting him to dinner in the hopes of figuring out Bolton's potential testimony. I thought I might be able to glean a few small pieces of information that would enable us to read the Bolton tea leaves. Instead, we just talked over the phone. In our conversations, I tried to lightly bring up the issue. But every time, Cooper refused to talk to me about it. Despite the media's clamoring for information throughout the Trump story, Cooper had shown himself to be loyal to his clients and their interests. He knew Bolton did not want him to say anything, so he was unhelpful.

"Not talking about it," Cooper would tell me every time I asked about Bolton.

I listened for what I was not hearing, and the silence seemed to signal something ominous. But I knew nothing more than that. At that point, I sort of gave up. I had no other ideas.

In January, as the Senate held the impeachment trial for Trump, Elisabeth Bumiller called me late on a Thursday afternoon as I worked on this book in the Manhattan offices of a friend. "What do you know about Bolton and what he would testify about?" she asked.

Republicans were still signaling that they wanted no new witnesses to testify at trial, and Democrats were saying that there was no way they could vote on whether to convict without hearing from him.

I said I did not know much, other than that it would probably be bad for Trump and that he was writing a book.

"We should really be talking to Maggie because she knows all about this," I said.

Eight days earlier, Maggie had written a short article about Bolton buried at the bottom of a live briefing online about impeachment. It said that Bolton was close to finishing his book. Maggie reported that Bolton planned on detailing his view of the Ukraine matter, including Trump's efforts to pressure the Ukrainians to announce an investigation into Joe Biden's son. Given the question about Bolton's testimony, it should have received great attention. Maggie had broken nearly every major story in the Trump era. But for some reason, it slipped through the cracks and no one seemed to notice.

I called Maggie. "I talked to Bumiller," I said. "We gotta figure out what's in the Bolton book."

Maggie reminded me that she had already written about this.

Like children talking about their parents, I said to Maggie: "They never know what they're talking about, just ignore them. Let's take a shot at this."

She repeated what she had written, saying that "Bolton's book is going to be bad for Trump on Ukraine."

"We gotta figure out how to write that," I said.

"I already wrote that," she said.

"We gotta find a way to write it again," I said.

That Friday, I put out calls to my sources and spent hours in a car riding with someone I wanted to talk to for this book. By that evening, I learned that the White House had obtained a copy of Bolton's book and was reviewing it as part of the prepublication process to ensure it did not contain classified information. In Washington, that's as incremental a development as there could be. But in Bolton's case it was highly important. If the White House had the book, and the book dealt with Ukraine, then the White House knew what Bolton would testify to. Now it made more sense why the White House had recently begun pressuring congressional Republicans not to call Bolton as a witness.

That development gave us something to go back to our sources with. By that Sunday, we learned Bolton wrote in his book that Trump wanted to hold off on releasing the aid to Ukraine until they committed to pursuing the investigations he was seeking. It moved the story forward because no one who had testified had been in the room with Trump when he tied the aid and the investigations together.

The story jolted Republican senators on Capitol Hill who were trying to put an end to the impeachment trial as soon as possible and without witnesses. The new revelations changed the minds of some Republicans, who, at least momentarily, appeared newly open to the idea of calling witnesses.

"I think it's increasingly likely that other Republicans will join those of us who think we should hear from John Bolton," Mitt Romney said soon after the story was published.

A day later we published a second story that said Bolton and Barr had confided in each other about their concerns over Trump's dealings with the authoritarian leaders of China and Turkey. Bolton had written about how Barr was worried that Trump had suggested to the foreign leaders that he had the authority to alter independent Justice Department investigations. The story showed that Barr, the administration official most seen as willing to do Trump's bidding, actually had concerns about how Trump had meddled in the work of the Justice Department.

The story had no impact on the Republicans. There was likely more in the book that was newsworthy, but by this point it felt as if we had tapped as much information as we could.

That evening, though, I learned of another possible way we could find out what was in the book. I received a call from a man I had never heard of. He said that several years earlier he had sat next to my father on a train and he had followed my work. The man said that he worked as a private investigator of sorts in the Washington area and had been trying to figure out what Bolton had written in his book. A friend had told him at a Rotary Club meeting that Bolton was taking sections of his book and sending them out to friends to review and comment on. The friends were then mailing them back to him, and he was throwing them in his trash. Bolton had apparently done this because he did not want to create an electronic record of his correspondences. The man said that he had been scouting Bolton's wife's office and their house on the nights he put his trash out. After Bolton moved the trash onto the street, he went through it. On a recent night he had found a large envelope that he said looked big enough to hold a manuscript. But there was nothing in the envelope. The envelope showed that it had been sent by a woman who worked for a top American ambassador who was abroad at the time and whom Bolton had been close with. It seemed as if the ambassador might have sent the package to her home, where the employee redirected it to Bolton.

I was willing to entertain wild ideas at this point to find out what else might be in the book. In that vein, I thought the name of the employee gave us a lead. The chances were low, but the stakes were high. Why not send one of our reporters to take a cold shot at her? Maybe the woman was less schooled with the media than the ambassador. And if we sent one of our reporters who specialized in getting people to talk to her house, maybe she would talk. I asked Bumiller for authority to arrange this, and she gave me the go-ahead. But in a subsequent conversation with the private eye, he said that that Thursday morning was trash pickup day in Bolton's neighborhood. I made sure not to tell him whether he should go through the trash again. I knew that what he wanted to do was likely legal, but the idea of the *Times* aligning ourselves with a private eye was potentially troublesome. So I shelved the idea.

That Wednesday, I received a message through a cutout from someone in Bolton's world: Bolton was convinced we did not have the book because despite our two stories we had missed the best parts.

I called Maggie and told her what I heard.

"What?" she said, sounding exasperated.

"I don't know, we missed stuff," I said.

"What, that doesn't make any sense," she said.

We had one job—to inform the public record. There was information that was apparently important to the public that we did not have, and we had to race to get it.

We had to move quickly. The Senate was scheduled to vote on whether to remove Trump from office at 5:00 that afternoon. At noon we reported that Bolton had first been told to assist Trump with his Ukraine pressure campaign in early May, during an Oval Office meeting with other top White House officials. According to Bolton, Trump asked him to call the president of Ukraine and get him to meet with Giuliani, who was planning on traveling to Ukraine to push for the investigations Trump was after. It was yet another example of Trump's mixing his official duties with his personal political desires.

But again, Republicans remained unmoved. On Wednesday, the Senate voted to acquit Trump on both articles of impeachment. Mitt Romney, seven years after starting the ball rolling on the Benghazi attacks, would be the only Republican to vote to convict Trump—on the first article, for abuse of power.

The Senate acquittal came at the end of a lengthy cycle of public investigations and damaging revelations. But the president had won again. The impeachment of Donald John Trump had been the last stand for the institutions. Inevitable once all the facts were known, equally inevitable that it would end in failure.

Trump had defeated everyone who had tried to contain him. All of the role players, big and small, who had found themselves facing the realization that . . . feeling strongly that . . . having a gnawing sense that . . . something was not right in the Trump presidency. All who sought to stop him or slow him failed. The FBI director. The acting FBI director. The White House counsel. The deputy attorney general. The Speaker of the House. The intelligence community. All positions of tremendous power and consequence failed.

Now, to come out on top against the next obvious challenge that stood in front of him, the 2020 election, Trump was going to have to convince voters that his transgressions were nowhere near as bad as Democrats made them out to be.

Or maybe yet, given the president's penchant for calling things "fake," perhaps he'd even be so brash as to assert that his transgressions weren't transgressions at all. *I did nothing wrong.* He was no transgressor; the other side, they were the transgressors. And look what they had put him through. *Hoax!* They would have to pay. "No president should ever be put through that again" became a more or less constant refrain.

It was as if all the people who had crossed him had been cogs on a giant gear, turning inside a giant machine, and in the months after impeachment was done, the giant gear stopped and then slowly lurched into motion again, only this time in the opposite direction. To undo everything.

Luckily for the president, his attorney general, William Barr, had already begun planting the seeds to delegitimize the Russia investigation, and all the investigations undertaken to assert the primacy of the law, reaffirm Madison's separation of powers, and contain the power of a heedless president. And now, the institutional prerogatives having run their course, Barr set out to use the power of the Justice Department to counterattack. The giant machine, now in reverse.

Here's how it would go.

Prior to taking over as Trump's attorney general, and in the opening months of the job, Barr began to drop hints about his view of the Russia investigation.

In the fall of 2017, he told the *Times* that he saw more reason for the Justice Department to investigate Hillary Clinton for her alleged involvement in a uranium deal that was approved during her tenure in the State Department—a conspiracy pushed by the author Peter Schweizer of *Clinton Cash* fame—than there was reason to investigate alleged collusion between Trump and Russia.

As attorney general, after he cleared Trump of the wrongdoing found in the Mueller report, Barr told a Senate Appropriations subcommittee in April 2019 that he believed the FBI had engaged in "spying" on the Trump campaign in 2016—providing institutional credibility to Trump's attacks on the intelligence community, FBI, and Obama administration.

"I think spying on a political campaign is a big deal," Barr said. "I am going to be reviewing both the genesis and the conduct of intelligence activities directed at the Trump campaign during 2016."

The next month, we reported that Barr had called on John H. Durham, the U.S. attorney for Connecticut who Sessions had asked back in 2017 to investigate Comey for leaking, to investigate the early days of the Russia probe and determine whether the FBI and intelligence community had overstepped their authority during the Russia investigation.

Two months later, the president thought so much of Barr's willingness to help him that he asked the Ukrainian president to coordinate the investigations Trump wanted with Barr.

By October, Barr himself was traveling the globe and looking into the origins of the Russia investigation. He traveled to Italy twice to talk to officials about a meeting that happened there between George Papadopoulos, the Trump campaign aide, and a Maltese professor who Trump's allies believe is an intelligence asset.

In January, the *Times* reported that Comey was under investigation for a years-old leak of classified information.

Then, in February, Barr took his most audacious act as attorney general up to that point. Prosecutors who had won a conviction against Roger Stone for lying to Congress and witness tampering were preparing to sentence him. The prosecutors—including one left over from Mueller's office—recommended Stone receive a seven- to nine-year sentence. Around 2:00 on the morning after the sentencing, Trump tweeted that the original recommendation was "very unfair" and a "miscarriage of justice." Hours later, Barr overruled the prosecutors and, with the special counsel's office gone, went to court to have the sentencing recommendation significantly lowered. The prosecutors who had worked on the case quit in protest.

Stone was ultimately sentenced to just over three years in prison, leaving only one major Mueller case pending: Flynn. Flynn had pleaded guilty in December 2017. But he had still not been sentenced. He had switched lawyers and then told the court he wanted to renege on his guilty plea. Members of Mueller's team who watched this unfold thought that Flynn was trying to make a case for Trump to pardon him.

In April, Trump fired Michael Atkinson—the inspector general who had kicked off impeachment by sending the whistleblower complaint to Congress.

But then in May, Barr did Flynn something even better than a pardon. He decided the Justice Department would ask the judge to drop the Flynn prosecution altogether. In response to the move—but before it was publicly announced—the lead prosecutor against Flynn, who had been a member of the Mueller team, withdrew from the case in protest.

"People sometimes plead to things that turn out not to be crimes," Barr said after the Justice Department asked for the case to be dropped, arguing his move was a step to "restore confidence in the system."

By asking the judge to drop the Flynn case, Barr was finally accomplishing what Trump had asked Comey to do on the twenty-sixth day of his presidency. "I hope you can see your way clear to letting this go, to letting Flynn go," Trump had said back in February 2017. Now Barr had.

Several years ago, when I wrote the story of Trump's appeal to his FBI director, a sense of emergency had come over the capital, and a special counsel had been summoned. Three years later, Trump's new attorney general had granted his request.

The president had bent Washington to his will.

AFTERWORD

★ ★ ★ ★ ★

JULY 28, 2017

189 DAYS INTO THE PRESIDENCY

ABOARD COAST GUARD ONE ABOVE THE UNITED STATES—AS John Kelly navigated the fledgling Trump administration in its first six months as the secretary for the Department of Homeland Security, he had two moods.

The dominant mood was Marine general steady. In that state, Kelly, with the seriousness and grit that came with being a four-star Marine general in the post-9/11 era, was unflappable and projected an aura of "I've seen worse" that stabilized those around him during the turbulent early months of the Trump presidency. Affable and talkative, Kelly embraced his role as one of the most high-profile members of the new administration and the leader of the department that dealt with the most complex and controversial issues—like immigration—but came with far less prestige than running the Pentagon or State Department. He gave attaboys, joked with subordinates, asked about their family members whose names he would often remember, told stories about growing up in Boston and about combat in Iraq, and proved far more approachable, and relatable, than his standing suggested.

On some occasions, though, Kelly would become pensive and preoccupied. He would stare blankly as he worked on a problem, and the stare would give way to a pained expression, as if he were suffering a migraine. When Kelly became like this, he was almost always grappling with some awful mishap from the increasingly dysfunctional Trump administration that he had decided to work for even though many mainstream Republicans and veteran national security hands had pointedly declined to serve. Instead of lashing out and yelling, or unloading his burdens on his team of senior staff, he tended, perhaps strategically, to essentially shut down to the outside world and attempt to solve his problems internally without letting his emotions get in the way. Often he would walk off by himself so he could clear his mind, leaving aides wondering where he had gone. Sometimes he would even go to Arlington National Cemetery to visit the grave of his son, Robert, a Marine who had been killed in Afghanistan. On the last Friday in July 2017, almost exactly six months after Donald Trump was sworn in as president, Kelly boarded Coast Guard One—the sixteen-seat jet that the Department of Homeland Security uses to ferry its secretary around the world—in San Diego after visiting with his only surviving son at Marine Corps Base Camp Pendleton as he prepared to deploy to Iraq.

To the small group of aides traveling with Kelly, it was abundantly clear that he was in a dark mood. But because he was on a small jet, there was nowhere to be alone, no way to escape.

Kelly sat in a large bucket chair facing the front of the plane, joined by a couple of his top aides. He said little and pulled out his iPad, which he used to catch up on the news created by the Trump administration. For anyone who was not a Kelly mood reader, taking out the tablet was his universal sign of saying: I want to be left alone.

About thirty minutes into the trip, as flight attendants came around to serve food and beverages, Kelly's chief of staff, Kirstjen Nielsen—who was sitting across the aisle—broke the silence, turning to him with a question. She was one of the few people who could consistently understand what Kelly was thinking, and she realized that something significant was bothering him.

"Did you talk to the president again?" Nielsen asked.

Confirming Nielsen's hunch, Kelly said he had just spoken to Trump, who was pressing him again to become chief of staff to replace Reince Priebus.

Recalling to Nielsen the conversation with the president, Kelly explained how he reinforced to Trump that indeed he needed better staff but that he was not the man for the job.

"I still do think you need to surround yourself with better people," Kelly had told Trump. "Our job as staff wherever we are is to make sure the president makes informed decisions."

But Trump had refused to take no for an answer.

To move Trump off the idea of his becoming chief of staff, Kelly said that if he took the position, it would be too disruptive to the Department of Homeland Security, the arm of the government that was taking the lead on immigration, the issue that Trump had run on and meant the most to his base.

"I'm not sure I'm the best guy to be your chief of staff. I believe in the mission of DHS; I can make a big difference at DHS," Kelly told Trump.

But Trump continued to press Kelly, who tried to buy himself more time, telling the president that he would come to speak with him in person when he returned to Washington.

Trump said Kelly should come in on Saturday or Sunday to discuss it.

Kelly, who lived over an hour's drive from the White House, said it would be best to connect after the weekend.

"Can we talk on Monday? I'm just flying back now," Kelly said.

"Yeah, yeah, okay, we'll talk about it, come in on Monday," Trump said.

Kelly believed he had pacified the president for the moment, but as he flew back to Washington, he remained deeply conflicted: He didn't want the job; few in their right mind would welcome the chaos engulfing Trump. Besides, he had an important job with a clear mission; that's where he belonged. But Kelly was a military man, and when the president asks you to do something, that is not a request you can take lightly. Moreover, it was by now very clear that the White House operation was a mess, with weak leadership and no professional organization.

"No decisions have been made, but I am worried about where things are," Kelly told his aides.

What Kelly held back from laying out in detail was that his concerns were rooted in how the lack of stability in the West Wing could have catastrophic consequences for the country. As the secretary for the Department of Homeland Security, Kelly was serving in a political role for the first time in his life. He was a military commander by training. He had spent a career reading and studying military history, and he had a special interest in understanding the events that set off military conflicts. To Kelly, it was simple: A vacuum of leadership was clearly emerging around Trump where he did not have sober and well-informed people who could provide him with the best information so he could make the right decisions. And when such a dynamic exists at the top of the American government, it has the potential to destabilize the world order and lead to destruction and death. Kelly feared if a natural disaster or some sort of terrorist or cyberattack occurred that required a quick response from Trump, the president might easily take the wrong action. Trump had shown himself to be undisciplined, and from studying wars, Kelly knew that simple miscommunication between countries—the misreading of public statements or military movements—could set off a chain reaction and put the United States at war with a country like North Korea that had nuclear weapons. There was just no wiggle room for any missed signal. Kelly and Nielsen had already confronted this when Trump would proclaim something outlandish—such as Mexico is going to pay for the wall—and they would immediately try to head off a tit-for-tat response, calling top Mexican leaders to tell them that Trump had no idea what he was talking about.

In March, less than two months into the administration, Kelly had become so concerned about the staffing problems that he raised it directly with Trump in a phone call, saying that his staff was failing him. In response to Kelly's criticisms, Trump said, why don't you take the position?

In the weeks that followed that exchange, Trump began asking aides and friends what they thought about Kelly taking over—a telltale Trump move that often foreshadowed what he was planning to do, regardless of what people told him. And while it was known among administration officials that Kelly did not want the job, the idea of his heading to the White House had circulated among other cabinet secretaries, like Secretary of State Rex Tillerson and Secretary of Defense James Mattis, who saw Kelly as an ally and believed he could be a beacon of stability amid Trump's inexperienced staff.

Throughout the spring, Trump had continued to try to give Kelly bigger jobs in the administration. In the days after he fired James Comey as the FBI director in May, Trump had reached out to Kelly more than once, asking him to become FBI director while also continuing to serve as secretary of homeland security. Kelly rebuffed Trump's request again, telling him it would be unfair to the mission at DHS. But the president refused to relent, and Kelly ended up having to go to the Justice Department over Mother's Day weekend to meet with Attorney General Jeff Sessions to discuss the possibility.

In a subsequent call with Trump, Kelly continued to try to explain to him that it was almost humanly impossible to do both jobs, and even if it was possible, it would be a disservice to the country to do either role part-time.

On one of the calls between Kelly and Trump about becoming FBI director, Kelly would witness an early and important example of Trump's appetite for shattering norms and politicizing the justice system. Trump told Kelly he needed an FBI director who would be loyal to the president—and only to the president.

The request made Kelly deeply uncomfortable, because it all but said that the FBI director would have to look the other way on Trump's behavior in order to keep the position. Such an arrangement would shred any notion that the United States was a country where no one—including the president—was above the law, a fundamental tenet of American democracy that Kelly, like many top national security officials, took as seriously as anything.

Kelly, sensing the immense problems with that idea, immediately shot it down.

"I'll be loyal to the Constitution," he had told Trump.

Trump dropped the idea.

But the unsettling episode had left Kelly with the false sense that he, through explaining, teaching, and patience, could help keep Trump on the straight and narrow and potentially talk him out of bad ideas.

As his plane approached Washington, Kelly weighed the reasons why he should and should not take the position. He didn't realize it at the time, but he was making the most serious miscalculation of his life. Kelly had seen what seemed like endless blunders in the first six months of the administration, whether it was the botched Muslim travel ban, the firing of the FBI director, the White House's inability to execute simple policy rollouts, or calls with outlandish demands at 11:00 p.m. from Stephen Miller, Trump's top immigration aide, with orders from the president. He thought the White House's problems stemmed from the incompetent and inexperienced staff. It was the people *around* the president who simply needed to be taught how to run the government.

For Trump, and by extension the country, to be successful, Kelly concluded, the president needed a strong leader of his West Wing to impose discipline and create a process to ensure that he made the most informed decisions in the best interest of the country. Whether it was on the battlefield or serving as the top uniformed adviser to the secretary of defense, Kelly had learned that having a clearly articulated and enforced process was the only way to run any large organization. Leaders would make mistakes, but these mistakes would be ones of good faith, if they followed a process that ensured they had made their decisions based on hearing the best information from the best people who were subject matter experts. As erratic as Trump seemed, Kelly assumed that the president wanted to do the right thing for the country. So to help put Trump's presidency back together, someone had to create a process.

The excruciating aspect of Trump's entreaty was that Kelly knew he was one of the few people who could create that process to stabilize the West Wing. His willingness to serve had very little to do with the person who had won the election: He would have served in Hillary Clinton's administration if she had prevailed and asked him. Service was Kelly's hard wiring. In fact, few Americans had lived a life more clearly associated with duty than Kelly, who had risen to become a Marine general after enlisting as a grunt during the Vietnam War. His two boys had become Marines and had served in the Iraq and Afghanistan wars. In 2010, his younger son, Robert Michael Kelly, had been killed by a land mine while leading a Marine patrol in the Helmand province of Afghanistan, making Kelly the highest ranking American military officer to lose a child in the wars fought in the aftermath of the September 11, 2001, attacks. Less than a year after his death, Kelly had visited the base where Robert had been stationed in Afghanistan. His daughter had married a Marine who had had part of one of his legs amputated after suffering a battlefield wound, also in Afghanistan and had gone on to work for the FBI. They had met at Walter Reed National Military Medical Center as he recovered.

There were other reasons why Kelly was seriously considering the job. If he declined the position, some of the other potential candidates terrified him. Kelly had watched as Trump tried to put Kris Kobach, a Kansas Republican who had helped Trump push the lie that millions of people had voted illegally in the 2016 election, in as the deputy secretary at the Department of Homeland Security—a move Kelly had killed. Kelly had a sense that Trump had surrounded himself with yes-men and hacks. Reince Priebus seemed like a good guy to Kelly but had no handle on the West Wing. If Trump moved to replace him with someone like Kobach or any other political crony, the situation could easily become even worse—and the chances of a crisis spinning out of control would be greater.

On the other hand, becoming chief of staff would be truly crossing a line that Kelly saw as almost sacred. Among the most important ethos Kelly had come to embody was that there should be a significant divide between the military and partisan politics. Even though he had joined an administration in one of its most political positions, and had retired from the military a year and a half earlier, he still viewed the world through the eyes of a four-star Marine general. If he were to leave the cabinet to go to work in the White House, the move would put him at the center of partisan politics. And the fact that Trump was such a polarizing figure, and found himself embroiled in an investigation into his ties to Russia, made taking the post all the less appetizing.

Whatever was going through Kelly's mind as Coast Guard One landed at Reagan National Airport in Washington late on Friday afternoon, he was convinced that he had the weekend to weigh the decision in the hopes Trump would become distracted by something else, and he and his staff were looking forward to finally having a quiet weekend—a respite from the blistering first six months of the administration.

On the tarmac, Kelly's security detail met him, and he got into an unmarked government car and began his ride home. Nielsen got into her car as well, taking a call with her staff, as she typically did at the end of each day. As she talked to her team, she received an alert on her phone that Trump had just posted a tweet. She quickly glanced down at it.

"I am pleased to inform you that I have just named General/ Secretary John F. Kelly as White House Chief of Staff," Trump had tweeted, saying that Kelly "has been a true star of my Administration."

"I would like to thank Reince Priebus for his service and dedication to his country," Trump wrote. "We accomplished a lot together and I am proud of him!"

"Oh, shit," Nielsen said to her staff on the call. "I have to go, the president just announced Kelly as chief of staff—I've got to go call him."

She hung up and immediately called Kelly.

"Sir, he just tweeted it," Nielsen told Kelly. "The president just tweeted you're chief of staff."

"No, we're talking about it on Monday," Kelly said.

"No, the tweet is out," Nielsen said.

"Are you sure the tweet went out, are you sure it's not a draft?" Kelly asked, referring to how the White House occasionally shared with the department media releases it was planning to send out.

"I'm looking right at it," Nielsen said.

"Holy shit—oh, I gotta call Karen," Kelly said, referring to his wife.

Kelly was trying to stop his wife from learning about it from anyone but him. He had told her that Trump wanted him to become chief of staff and she felt strongly that her husband should not take the position.

As Kelly called his wife, Nielsen and her staff scrambled to figure out how to respond to an almost certainly unprecedented scenario in American history where a cabinet secretary, who had just told the president that he did not want a position, was learning on social media minutes later he had been named to arguably the most important staff position in the White House.

Some of Kelly's aides discussed the possibility of putting out a statement saying Kelly had never committed to the job. But Kelly knew that the tweet had sealed his fate. His concerns about how unstable the White House was meant he had only one choice: He would take the position. Who knew what could happen if a cabinet secretary put out a statement denying a presidential announcement that he was going to become chief of staff? Trump would probably fire Kelly, wreaking even more havoc and instability at the White House and the Department of Homeland Security.

Kelly told his press aide to confirm to reporters that indeed he would be taking the position.

With that, Kelly had become Trump's second White House chief of staff.

On the phone with Nielsen, Kelly was almost speechless. "I just talked to the president this morning and we agreed on this plan—how does this happen?" he asked.

Three days later, on Monday morning, Kelly met with his aides in a large conference room at a Department of Homeland Security office building a few blocks from the White House. Kelly was solemn. "This is a great job," he said, referring to the cabinet position he was leaving. "That's not a great job. But the president has asked me to do it."

Kelly said little more. Moments later, he went to the men's room, where he ran into one of his longtime aides.

"Sir, we're going to miss you—go get 'em," the aide told him.

In response, Kelly muttered the words "fuck" and "goddamn."

To the aide it was clear what Kelly was saying: *I know I'm fucked.*

He would later acknowledge to confidants the miscalculation he had made about Trump and the true root of the administration's problems: "I didn't know they made people like that."

As the conventional wisdom in Washington went at the time, if anyone could impose order on the forty-fifth president's chaotic management style, it would be the retired four-star Marine general. There had been a sense in Washington that whereas Priebus had spent a lot of time working the phones in an effort to control any unflattering coverage of himself, Kelly would start from scratch, reforming the West Wing from a cliquish and dysfunctional cult of personality into a functioning White House. Trump often touted the generals he had appointed to high positions, like Kelly and Secretary of Defense James Mattis, talking endlessly about "my generals" as if he thought they would be obligated to follow his every command. But Kelly and Trump did appear to share strong views about the border and were roughly the same age, baby boomers who grew up in the aftermath of World War II and the chaos of the 1960s and 1970s.

But the two men could not have been wired more differently. And in their views of country and honor and service, they might as well have been from different species.

Trump's view of the military was that anyone who served was a sucker, anyone who was injured in the line of duty was a loser, and prisoners of war were less noble than soldiers who didn't get captured by enemy armies—all things Trump would later tell Kelly, even though Trump knew that Kelly's son had been killed in battle and his son-in-law had lost part of a limb. As a young man, Trump had gone to great lengths to avoid military service. He had faked a condition that was among the disqualifiers: bone spurs.

Kelly lied about his bone spurs too, but the difference was that he actually had them and asked a recruiter to look the other way so he could join the Marines. Kelly grew up in a gritty, Irish-Catholic neighborhood in Boston, surrounded by veterans of World War I, World War II, and the Korean War, and becoming a Marine was all he had ever wanted to do. One of his neighbors was a veteran of World War I who had sustained serious injuries from a gas attack on the battlefield. Kelly's father—a career postal carrier who left the house to deliver the mail at 5:30 every morning for forty-five years before later in the day heading downtown to work on the railroad—was a World War II army veteran himself, having served in the Pacific. From as early as Kelly could remember, he wanted to serve; it's what everyone else around him had done, and he wanted to follow in their footsteps.

Although Kelly had been born five years after World War II ended in 1945, the triumph of the United States over the evil of Hitler's Germany and the horrors of the Holocaust indelibly shaped his childhood. Kelly's father taught him the names of the major battles and turning points in the war. When Kelly was ten and the movie *Exodus*—which tells the story of how Jews founded Israel in the aftermath of the Holocaust—was released, his father sat him down to explain the movie's opening scenes. *Exodus* begins at a Nazi concentration camp, and Kelly's father—who barely had a high school education and fought in the Pacific—explained what Hitler had done and how the United States played a role in stopping him. And, his father said, even though Jews practiced a different religion from the Kellys, who were Catholic, everyone should be treated the same.

Kelly had a zest to see the world and as a teenager hitchhiked from Boston to Seattle and then rode freight trains back home. Soon after, he became a Merchant Marine, serving on a boat that delivered tons of beer, frozen food, tanks, and ammunition to American troops in Vietnam and South Korea.

Kelly could have used his time as a Merchant Marine to secure a two-year deferment from Vietnam, as many his age were seeking to do given the backlash to the ongoing war. But instead, when he returned home, he went down to his local recruiting center and tried to enlist at the age of twenty.

The military was desperate for service members, and the recruiter told Kelly that he could take his physical immediately. If the doctor said that Kelly was healthy enough for service, it would almost guarantee that he would be sent off to boot camp.

On the day of Kelly's physical, he stood around in his underwear with dozens of other young men as they went through a gauntlet of tests and screenings. Kelly noticed that many of the young men around him had bundles of papers in their hands.

After the physicals, when the potential enlistees were meeting with the doctor to find out their determination, Kelly saw many of them hand the papers to the doctor. The papers, Kelly realized, were letters from doctors or psychiatrists laying out reasons—or likely excuses—for why they could not serve.

Kelly had no papers, nor did he want any.

When Kelly met with the doctor, the doctor told him what the doctor claimed was good news.

"You are medically disqualified," the doctor said.

To Kelly this was terrible news.

"You have to qualify me," Kelly said.

"If your eyesight didn't disqualify you, your bone spurs would," the doctor said.

"What are bone spurs?" Kelly asked.

Kelly could literally feel his heart sink as his lifelong dream of being in the Marines appeared to be crashing down before him. He protested with the doctor, who, apparently seeing Kelly's interest and knowing that the military needed as many service members as possible for Vietnam, decided to ignore Kelly's health issues.

"Army or Marines?" the doctor asked.

"Marines," Kelly replied.

He left for boot camp within a week.

★★★

JULY 31, 2017

192 DAYS INTO THE PRESIDENCY

WEST WING—Kelly arrived at the White House shortly before 9:30 a.m. the Monday after Trump's tweet that announced Kelly's appointment, meeting him in the Oval Office. One of the first things that Trump told Kelly was that he had to go down the hallway and fire the White House communications director, Anthony Scaramucci, whose call with a reporter days before had been published, showing him criticizing Reince Priebus and Steve Bannon and saying that he wanted to "fucking kill all the leakers." Kelly was a bit taken aback by the fact that Trump wanted to get rid of him, because Scaramucci had been in the job for only eleven days, and Kelly told Trump that he could find a way to work with anyone. It was also sort of odd that Trump was asking Kelly to fire someone as his chief of staff's first act. But Trump said he had to go, and Kelly said he would do it. First Kelly needed to officially become chief of staff, so moments later he was sworn in in an Oval Office filled with staff he was now charged with leading. Then, as aides mingled in the office, Kelly ducked out to fire Scaramucci.

To Kelly, there was no more important time for work than Monday morning, but to his surprise the aides were still mingling in the Oval Office when he returned. The fact that no one had anywhere to go or anything to do, including the president, and that the Oval Office served essentially as a sort of lounge for the idle West Wing staff was an early sign of just how little structure there was to Trump's day.

The rest of the day was even more bizarre.

In the first several hours of his tenure, Kelly learned of a rumor circulating the West Wing: The beleaguered and soon to be former chief strategist to Trump, Steve Bannon, had installed some sort of listening device in the chief of staff's office. It was unclear where Bannon was, or what he was up to, and there was a sense that Trump was preparing to fire him. Nevertheless, the possibility that he could be listening in on Kelly's first day was real. So throughout the day, as Kelly was familiarizing himself with the basics of the West Wing and figuring out where the nearest men's room was, he whispered as he spoke with aides like Nielsen (whom Kelly had persuaded to come with him to work in the West Wing) when they were in his office. When he wanted to speak in normal tones, he would step out onto the small patio just off his office. It was like something out of a bad spy movie.

Throughout the day West Wing aides paraded into Kelly's office, where they wanted to gossip with him and Nielsen, telling them their version of events about how Priebus had been fired. One top aide, the deputy national security adviser, Dina Powell, told Kelly and Nielsen that she thought she was going to become chief of staff and had been surprised that Kelly had been brought in to replace Priebus. Kelly was unsure how to respond.

"Okay, I don't know what to say about that," Kelly told Nielsen after Powell left the room.

"Who *are* these people?" Nielsen asked Kelly.

As Kelly and Nielsen began to assess what seemed increasingly like another planet, they realized that there were four groups of aides in the West Wing they would have to contend with. There were those, like Bannon and Sebastian Gorka, who had little to no experience in government, were creatures of the fringes of the Republican Party, and were never going to like Kelly, because they saw him as an entrenched representative of the Deep State. The second group was young, equally inexperienced aides who had risen high in Trump's orbit largely because more established government hands had no interest in working for Trump. These aides were often more concerned with the superficial trappings of the job, like office size, and were looking for some sort of adult figure to come in and give the West Wing order and direction. In the first days of Kelly's tenure some of them complained with tears in their eyes about how promises made to them by Jared Kushner, like for a prestigious West Wing office, a title of assistant to the president, or the use of the government plane for a trip, had gone unfulfilled. The third group was those who actually had expertise and experience working in government or running things. But because they often had deeply held beliefs, and were so put off by the incompetence and lack of process around them, they refused to collaborate or tell others what they were working on. The fourth group was Trump's family members, specifically his son-in-law, Kushner, and daughter Ivanka, who appeared to operate as their own power center, although it was unclear what they actually did.

Kelly sensed that the problems at the White House needed an initial two-pronged solution. In addition to managing Trump, he realized that someone had to dedicate their time to managing the fractured and rudderless staff. Kelly decided that he would take Trump and that Nielsen, who had worked as a homeland security official in George W. Bush's administration, would oversee the staff. This made sense for several reasons. First, Kelly had more experience dealing directly with Trump and had the gravitas Trump was likely to respect. Kelly was also a man, and although Kelly and Nielsen had not worked extensively with Trump, they assessed that given his almost obsession with his generals Kelly was going to be more successful at managing the president than Nielsen might be.

Managing the impulsive, undisciplined president was a job unlike any White House chief of staff had ever faced, and figuring out the best strategy for it would take some time. But whatever shape it would take, Kelly wanted to start a routine that he believed would help create stability and allow him to best serve the president. So on his second day, he began a regimented schedule. He would wake up around 3:30 a.m., shower, and shave. Then he would put on broadcasts of CNN or Fox while he scrolled through *The New York Times, The Washington Post, The Wall Street Journal, Politico,* and Breitbart. Between 4:30 a.m. and 5:30 a.m., a car would pick him up and drive him to the White House, where a CIA officer would take ninety minutes to present him with that day's intelligence briefing. Kelly would then turn to the flow of information that seemed most important to the president: cable news. Between 6:00 and 8:00 a.m., Kelly often followed along with Fox News' programming because he knew that Trump was most likely watching upstairs in the residence and he wanted to be prepared if the president brought up one of the topics the hosts discussed. Along with Fox, Kelly would come to watch MSNBC's *Morning Joe.* Although Trump had repeatedly claimed that he did not watch the show, it would become evident to Kelly from complaints Trump would make that he was closely watching what Joe Scarborough—who would often address Trump directly through the television and tell him just how poorly he was doing as president—was saying about him. At the same time, Kelly and his staff had to maximize this time to take care of the regular day-to-day work of the government, because after Trump came down from the residence, the rest of the day would be lost. Trump would typically return to the residence around 5:00 p.m. In that first week on the job, Kelly was highly attuned to everything occurring around him. He had to pick up as much information as possible about how the place functioned, how Trump took in information, and which aides had the best expertise and ability to communicate with the president. The faster he did this, the faster he could create a process and put the White House on track to function like previous administrations. But as Kelly keyed in on those issues, he found oddity after oddity that showed him how the problems with the process were far graver than he could have imagined.

In the mornings, Trump was generally nowhere to be found. He would saunter down from the residence sometime around 11:00 a.m. Kelly did not expect everyone to possess his military discipline, wake up before the crack of dawn, and digest every piece of American intelligence. But here was the president of the United States, who was supposed to be solving the country's problems and taking in the best information so he could make the best decisions, coming to work an hour before most people began eating lunch and expressing no interest whatsoever in the greatest threats to the country.

Half a dozen years earlier Kelly had served as the top military adviser for the defense secretaries Leon Panetta and Robert Gates, whose schedules were mapped out down to the minute weeks and months in advance. Their jobs were so important that no time could be wasted. From working for them, Kelly also had an appreciation of how the West Wing functioned because he often arranged for them to attend meetings with the president they served under, Barack Obama, who kept a similarly regimented schedule. But nothing like that existed for Trump. There was literally no schedule.

"It's not rocket science shit," one West Wing official told me, describing the chaos. The official said that there were no "weekly scheduling meetings, no knowing where principals were going to be, no submitting schedules, no making decisions about where to go, no calendars—shit you do in a freshman congressman's office."

Aides Kelly spoke to said that the flow of the day was dictated by when Trump came to work and whatever was on his mind. That was the schedule. The Oval Office operated like a lounge that was an open free-for-all where Trump held court and anyone—from Mar-a-Lago hangers-on, to low-level aides, to television personalities, to the national security adviser—could wander in and tell Trump something. It was not uncommon for aides to have one discussion with Trump about an issue, leave, and then return several hours later to discover that Trump was still talking about it but had changed his mind about what he wanted to do.

From Kelly's time working for the defense secretaries, he learned that anything that came to their desk had to be vetted to ensure that it was the legal, ethical, or smart thing to do. Nothing that had not passed through that gauntlet of oversight could be thrown in front of the president. But whether it was an idea for a tweet, a piece of legislation, or how to deal with a foreign adversary like North Korea, Trump might act on it, without consulting with anyone who might be in a position to know better and guide him.

As Kelly in his early days as chief of staff peeled back the layers to assess the size of the problem, he discovered issues that were plainly frivolous but that had become major affairs of state and were taking up far too much time and attention of West Wing aides. Omarosa Manigault Newman, the former *Apprentice* star who became the director of a little-known White House office, was having parties at the White House pool, which is supposed to be reserved for the First Family. Might the new chief of staff do something about that? Yes.

Another major issue was the ongoing competition between Ivanka and Melania Trump. Kelly had been told that earlier in the presidency Ivanka had wanted to take over the title of First Lady and assume many of the ceremonial roles that came with that title, following a similar model to the presidency of the unmarried James Buchanan, who, in the mid-nineteenth century, turned to his niece to fulfill the duties of First Lady. Melania and Trump's youngest son, Barron, had moved down to Washington in June 2017, short-circuiting that plan. But Kelly had further learned that Ivanka was still trying to take on some of the First Lady's responsibilities, like choosing who would attend White House events and who would sit at what table. Kelly had been told that the Office of the First Lady wanted him to referee this family squabble and rein in Ivanka.

Trump himself also wanted Kelly to intervene in family matters. In the first week, he told Kelly that he needed for him to fire Jared and Ivanka. "I need you to get rid of them—send them back to New York," Trump told Kelly in one of their one-on-one meetings after the Oval Office had cleared out. "I don't want them here. They're a distraction." To Kelly it was unclear what Jared and Ivanka actually did in their roles at the White House, but it was clear to both the chief of staff and the president that they were not qualified to hold top positions in the government, because they had so little relative experience and expertise. In some of their early interactions with Kelly they had struggled to articulate what they actually were assigned to do. Kelly, who had no previous relationship with anyone in Trump's family, thought that it was inappropriate for him to intervene in a family matter and that Trump needed to deal with his own family. "No," Kelly told Trump in response to his request. "That's family, I'm not doing that, you deal with your family. If you want to fire them, fire them." Trump was too afraid to dismiss them on his own, and so they remained in the West Wing, building their fiefdoms.

Kelly's unwillingness to fire Jared and Ivanka would haunt his tenure as chief of staff, because the two would exploit opportunities to undermine his authority. Early in his time in the White House, Kelly had Nielsen by his side to help him manage the staff and protect his blind side. But in December 2017, Trump had Nielsen installed as secretary of DHS, taking her out of Kelly's day-to-day orbit in the West Wing. Two months after Nielsen left, Kelly suffered his most significant setback as chief of staff when he was widely criticized in the media for initially defending Rob Porter, the White House staff secretary, who had been accused of domestic abuse by both of his ex-wives. Kelly later told others he had wrongly taken Porter—who Kelly saw as one of the most qualified aides in the West Wing—at his word when he initially told him he had done nothing wrong. The incident was a public humiliation for Kelly, and his enemies pounced. In his first several months in the West Wing, Kelly had regularly reminded Jared and Ivanka that they worked for him and had to go through him in order to deal directly with the president on official matters. The president's daughter and son-in-law paid Kelly lip service but went around him anyway. In the wake of the Porter debacle, they would tell the president that Kelly had embarrassed him and they began the drumbeat that Kelly had to go.

It's a wonder the White House was functioning at all. Kelly had initially believed the problem was the staff—now he traced the chaos to its source: Trump himself. As a nonpartisan figure, Kelly had long heard the stories about Trump being a damaged and potentially dangerous person. He had seen for himself the showman's impulse to get attention by saying outrageous and offensive things. But he had dismissed what he had seen Trump do during the campaign as mere politics: There was no way someone could believe the stuff that Trump was saying. But Kelly now realized that he had been wrong. While Trump held court in the Oval Office, Kelly sat in one of the wooden chairs that surrounded the Resolute desk, closely listening to Trump's every word. If Kelly was going to serve the president, he needed to know as much as he could about how the man's mind worked, how he took in information, how he saw the world, and how he made decisions. As Kelly sat there listening, he could see how Trump was far more limited, petty, immoral, incurious, and, frankly, stupid than he ever could have imagined. He seemed to care only about how anything reflected on him and personal loyalty, and he was impervious to facts.

In front of Kelly, no matter the subject, Trump would go on as if he were an expert, particularly on matters like foreign policy and immigration, where Kelly knew Trump had no expertise. When Trump discussed these matters, he would base his assertions on incorrect information or exaggerated talking points, like when he claimed to Kelly that countries had gamed the U.S. visa lottery system. Trump told Kelly that the lottery was how foreign countries were able to send their burglars, rapists, and other criminals to the United States, where they would overstay their visas and live illegally.

"That's not the way it works," Kelly told Trump about how the visa lottery system functioned.

Kelly explained that a significant portion of the undocumented immigrants were actually just visitors who arrived legally and overstayed their visas.

"Most illegal immigrants are from all over the world and don't go home; it's not just people from Central America, and most people who come from there come and stay and obey the laws. Yes, some are criminals but not all of them," Kelly told Trump.

But Kelly was coming to understand that Trump simply could not tolerate disagreement and could not be told he was wrong—

about anything. And he had no ability to deal with nuance, particularly about issues that were red meat to his base. After all, his political ascent was built on a racist lie about President Obama turbocharged by a xenophobic promise to keep Mexicans out of America by building a wall along the southern border, topped by the laughable claim that the wall wouldn't cost American taxpayers a dime; the Mexican people would pay for it, went the oft-repeated lie.

In the early days of Kelly's tenure as chief of staff, Trump also showed he had no grasp on the basics of American foreign policy.

"Why did we go to war in North Korea?"

Kelly then explained the basics of the Korean War to the president. "Why the fuck are we in NATO?" he would ask Kelly.

Kelly sensed that Trump's question had to do not with the philosophical arguments about whether the United States should be in a multi-country alliance but with the simple basics.

Kelly explained the basis of the alliance to the president.

"Sir, it came as a result of the Second World War," he tried to explain.

Trump seemed to have no interest in and be confused by Kelly's explanation that nations created a deterrence against Russia by committing to a collective defense.

"What the fuck?" Trump said.

Kelly tried again to explain.

"This is how it came about," he told Trump. "The Soviets were taking over Europe, so NATO's defense strategy deterred incursions by the Soviets."

Trump seemed to have no appreciation that the alliance had fostered peace and stability for seventy years.

In meetings with Kelly and other top aides, Trump happily dismissed criticism or expert information if it clashed with his gut feelings and instincts. Even when briefing material was provided, he never seemed interested in reading or listening to more information before making a decision.

Kelly would tell aides, "He has this thing that he knows more than the generals, the economists, the geologists. He is incapable of saying, 'I don't know anything; I need some advice.'"

In the first few weeks of Kelly's tenure, Trump expressed to him a growing frustration with his generals' unwillingness to go along with what he wanted. Whatever Trump wanted to do on an issue like immigration, they always seemed to say it was a bad idea, impractical, or illegal. During the transition and in the early part of the administration, Trump had publicly praised the generals, put them in his cabinet, and believed they would be there to faithfully do whatever he wanted, in the same way his underlings at the Trump Organization had followed his every command during his four decades masquerading as a business tycoon in Manhattan. But by the time Kelly became chief of staff, Trump had grown wary of the generals.

"Why aren't you loyal?" Trump asked Kelly. He meant Kelly, James Mattis, and H. R. McMaster, whom Trump had installed in his cabinet and other top administration posts.

Trump was hitting on an area that Kelly believed was one of the most important tenets of the U.S. government: the divide between civilians who controlled the military and the generals who executed the orders. Now Kelly finally thought he had a moment to privately explain to the president why he was so misguided.

"We're loyal to the Constitution," Kelly explained.

He told Trump that the generals, and everyone else who served in his cabinet, actually had taken an oath to the Constitution and were not there to serve a politician or political party. The generals believed in following the law, following the facts, and doing what was prudent for the country. They were not servants or lackeys.

Trump still didn't understand.

"Why can't the generals be like the German generals?" Trump asked.

Kelly, who was steeped in the histories of World Wars I and II, was shocked to hear Trump bring up the Germans and hoped that the president was not referring to Hitler's generals.

"Are you talking about the German generals during the Prussian times?" Kelly asked, using the proper term for Germany during World War I.

"Or, when they tried to kill Hitler three times?" Kelly asked, referring to how generals under Hitler had plotted to topple him during the war.

Trump indicated that he was talking about how he thought the German generals had been loyal to Hitler during World War II but said little more. Kelly was shocked that anyone—particularly the president—would admire anything about Hitler's Germany. It was even more troubling that Trump's view was based on an incorrect understanding of what had actually gone on.

Trump's comments had insinuated a loyalty-based relationship between generals and the commander in chief that made the military look like an arm of the government there to simply serve at the whims of the president. But as Kelly was now explaining to Trump in the Oval Office, all officials in the government took an oath "to protect the Constitution against all enemies, foreign and domestic"—not a pledge to a particular leader.

Trump still said he did not understand. *Did the generals really believe that?*

Yes, Kelly said.

Trump seemed mystified by the concept.

"Do you really believe you're not loyal to me?" he would ask Kelly.

"I'm certainly part of the administration, but my ultimate loyalty is to the rule of law," Kelly replied.

Kelly might as well have been speaking another language. The principle, familiar to anyone who paid attention to American history, would infuriate and baffle Trump throughout his presidency.

In his four decades in the Marines, Kelly had been taught how to kill a foreign enemy on the battlefield. He had learned how to invade a country and had actually led his own Marines in doing just that in Iraq in two different wars. He had sat through local tribal council meetings in Iraq as an insurgency engulfed the country, trying to build relationships with ruthless sheikhs in the hopes of creating a lasting peace in that country. He had served as the top aide to two defense secretaries, sitting beside them as they negotiated the country's most serious national security issues with their counterparts from Russia and China. And he had sat in the same Oval Office with other top uniformed generals and President Obama, telling that commander in chief his blunt assessments about threats to the United States. But in none of his training or experiences had he ever contemplated the situation he was now facing: What do you do, whom do you call, what textbook or user manual do you turn to when you realize the president of the United States is potentially a threat to the country he is leading?

Obviously, there was no real answer.

For Kelly, quitting was not an option. He would never have quit if he was losing on the battlefield, so there was no way he would do that now. And if imposing order on the West Wing had been an important enough reason to drop his cabinet post and go to the White House, then realizing the gaping holes in Trump's intelligence and character was surely enough reason to stay.

"I had a sense of *holy shit,*" Kelly later told confidants. "If I thought it was important before to put order to this place, now it was even more important."

Kelly boiled it down to a simple equation: Trump would be far more prone than his predecessors to make mistakes that could cost lives because he was too ignorant, uninterested, and egotistical to stick with the facts and listen to those who knew more than he did. So Kelly was going to construct a process whereby the president would be surrounded by facts and experts, increasing the chances that he made a decision that was not based on his whims that could hurt the country and the world.

"This is probably not going to work out," Kelly told aides at the time. "But I'm going to continue to operate how I operate and push back against him."

Kelly would try to convince himself in the months that followed that maybe, just maybe, somewhere deep in Trump's mind or soul there was someone who was willing to listen and do the right thing. He would never find that side of Trump. "There were a lot of people trying hard," Kelly later told confidants about West Wing aides. "But there was another, darker influence that was preventing any real organization to the staff," Kelly said, referring to Trump. "You had the president, who just called a lot of people who had no idea how to be in government and listened to their 'good ideas.'"

At one point in the early days, Kelly said something that Trump did not like, and the president snapped at him.

Kelly pushed back.

"Mr. President, that's the last time you ever say that to me—the next time I'm gone—I don't give a fuck, I'm gone," Kelly told him.

Trump backed down.

One of the most significant challenges for Kelly was conveying to Trump how he would take instructions from the president. Trump seemed to think that communicating with his chief of staff via his Twitter was a good idea.

"Did you see that tweet I sent last night?" the president would ask.

"Yes, sir, I did," Kelly said.

"What did you think?" Trump asked.

"Well, I know it's going to dominate the rest of my day; it already has been," Kelly responded. "I thought it was inappropriate and not based on the facts."

Kelly then sought to lay down some markers with Trump, particularly about his tweeting.

"I will never take what you send out as a tweet as guidance," Kelly said. "If you sent out a tweet, 'Ready. Aim. Shoot,' I'll never take that as guidance. If you want me to motivate this administration to do something, look me in the eye and tell me, but I'll never take your tweets as guidance."

No problem combined the White House's process deficiencies and Trump's character issues more than North Korea. As Kelly was becoming chief of staff, Trump and Kim were exchanging language publicly about using force that Kelly had never seen an American leader and an adversary use. Trump seemed to be treating Kim like he was just another Republican candidate whom Trump belittled and attacked during the run for the party's nomination in 2016. The heated language meant that the margin for error was incredibly small and just one missed signal or spark could set off a conflict that could easily kill tens of thousands of people within the span of a few hours.

The examples of the problem had played out right in front of Kelly's face. On August 8, 2017, eight days after Kelly arrived at the White House, in response to North Korean threats of "physical action," Trump had said at an event at his golf club in Bedminster, New Jersey, that "they will be met with fire and fury and frankly power, the likes of which this world has never seen before."

The language would have been problematic if some rogue undersecretary had said it, but coming from the president of the United States, the declaration was a five-alarm fire. Kelly was a student of how major military conflicts were set off, and he knew that many times one side launched a preemptive attack because they feared that they were in imminent danger. Kelly could envision the worst-case scenario where Trump would fire off an incendiary tweet insulting Kim or North Korea. Kim, fearing looking weak, would respond by launching a missile at South Korea or an intercontinental ballistic missile at the United States. The Americans would shoot down the missile, but it would be too late; a war would begin and tens of thousands of people would die on the Korean peninsula. In another scenario Kelly told others he feared, a North Korean general might fire off a missile toward South Korea believing it was what Kim wanted in the face of Trump's rhetoric, leading American troops there to respond with force.

In one-on-one conversations in the days that followed, Kelly tried to gently nudge Trump away from his incendiary language toward North Korea, telling him that he could unintentionally set off a conflict if his language was misread.

"You're pushing him to prove he's a man," Kelly said to Trump. "If you push him into a corner, he may strike out. You don't want to box him in."

Kelly tried to explain to the president that Kim would be forced to use all available means to counter American military force because he would need to appear like a strong leader to his country's elites, who could overthrow him if he looked weak.

"He is trying to appeal to his elites to survive," Kelly told Trump.

But Trump showed no interest in toning down his Twitter posts. To Kelly, Trump wanted to treat Kim like another real estate developer in New York or rival on the campaign trail, and had no appreciation that dealing with a foreign enemy like this could incite mass violence. This was incredibly scary to Kelly: The president of the United States had no appreciation for the fact that he could bring the country not just to the brink of a war at any moment—but a nuclear war that could easily escalate into the most dangerous one in world history.

Three days after his "fire and fury" comments, Trump tweeted, "Military solutions are now fully in place, locked and loaded, should North Korea act unwisely. Hopefully Kim Jong Un will find another path!"

Over the next few weeks, the North Korean military fired several missiles into the sea, including some directly over Japan—essentially taunting the U.S. military.

In this cycle of escalation, the tensions only got worse. Trump goaded the dictator in Pyongyang further in September with a speech to the UN in which he threatened to "totally destroy North Korea" if Kim, whom he referred to as "Rocket Man," continued his military threats. Kim responded by calling Trump a "mentally deranged U.S. dotard."

Later that month, Trump, unhappy with a speech given by the North Korean representative at the United Nations, posted a tweet without consulting with Kelly that could easily be read as threatening American military action.

"Just heard Foreign Minister of North Korea speak at U.N. If he echoes thoughts of Little Rocket Man, they won't be around much longer!" Trump wrote.

What scared Kelly even more than the tweets was the fact that behind closed doors in the Oval Office, Trump continued to talk as if he wanted to go to war. He cavalierly discussed the idea of using a nuclear weapon against North Korea, saying that if he took such an action, the administration could blame someone else for it to absolve itself of responsibility. The problems with that idea were obvious to Kelly, who tried to use reason to explain to Trump why it was a terrible idea. "It'd be tough to not have the finger pointed at us," Kelly told the president. With war now a distinct possibility, Kelly tried to rely on process. To make sure Trump understood the possibilities of what he could set off, Kelly brought the military's top officers to the White House to brief the president on how easily war could break out and how, given the number of weapons the North and South Koreans had pointed at each other, the ensuing back-and-forth would be devastating. Along with painting a stark picture of the potential casualties of war, military officials ran through the various options for Trump. The possibilities ranged from doing nothing, to sanctions, to launching an offensive military strike.

Kelly thought that by demonstrating to Trump just how many people could be killed, he would appeal to his moral and human instincts. From Kelly's life in the military, and particularly with the death of his son, he had a deep appreciation for the horrors of war. He did not expect everyone to have such a defined view. But he was astonished by how little understanding or care Trump had for how just horrific war could be. The potential loss of life argument had no impact on Trump. Kelly seemed to be able to grab Trump's attention only when he told the president that war would almost certainly hurt America's economy and, in turn, reflect poorly on him. But the argument of economic damage could hold Trump's attention for only so long as he would turn back to the possibility of war, including at one point raising to Kelly the possibility of launching a preemptive military attack against North Korea.

Kelly did not believe that Trump actually had the guts to launch a military strike—the rhetoric was just an extension of Trump's insecurities and use of tough language to cover them. But what Kelly feared was that Kim would take some sort of action that would leave Trump slighted—whether it was a public statement, military test, or actual military action—and Trump, believing that he looked weak, would be forced to quickly respond and would do so by launching a nuclear weapon or some sort of devastating attack that would send the countries spiraling into a conflict that would kill tens of thousands of people in a matter of hours.

When Trump would bring up the idea of using a nuclear weapon or launching a preemptive attack, Kelly would tell Trump that if he wanted to make such a drastic move he would need to receive congressional approval, because he did not have the authority to take such an action when there was no imminent threat to the country. Such obstacles baffled and annoyed Trump.

The private rhetoric was nearly as troubling to Kelly as the public threats because of how sloppy Trump could be discussing the matter. It was well known among senior American officials over the past several decades that the North Koreans had sought to spy on senior American decision makers as tensions between the two countries grew. So, it was alarming to White House aides that Trump would repeatedly talk on unclassified phones, with friends and confidants outside the government, about how he wanted to use military force against North Korea.

There was no indication that the North Koreans had a source inside the White House, but the possibility that they were listening in on Trump's phone calls or those of the people he spoke to was well within the realm of American intelligence assessments. And if that was the case, the North Koreans would know that Trump was truly considering the same kinds of military strikes he was threatening publicly, possibly leading Kim, in an effort to gain the upper hand, into a preemptive attack on an American ally in Asia or the U.S. territory of Guam.

Kelly would have to remind Trump that he could not share classified information with his friends.

Trump dismissed Kelly's concerns, saying that his chief of staff was "paranoid" and exaggerating the problem.

Unsure of what else to do, Kelly would express his frustration to other top White House officials. The White House chief of staff was coming to the realization that his boss, the president of the United States, might be just as volatile, irrational, and unpredictable as the North Korean dictator who ran his country like a prison camp. "There are two people here with tremendous egos, and both have to come out of this winning," Kelly said, referring to Trump and Kim. "If one of them feels like they lost, we have a problem. It's a save-face situation."

Since Trump appeared unmoved by the moral and strategic arguments that Kelly was trying to make and continued to carelessly approach an issue that could set off a world war, Kelly searched for another approach. He decided that he would appeal to Trump's ego, and the strategy that Kelly finally settled on to stave off conflict with Pyongyang was as desperate as it was clever. Knowing that Trump would likely respond well to a narrative that cast him as a hero, Kelly decided that the quickest way to de-escalate with Kim would be a direct appeal to Trump's narcissism. When Kelly and Trump would talk about North Korea, Kelly began to slip in another option: building a friendly diplomatic relationship with Kim and negotiating with the North Koreans face-to-face. Kelly sweetened the pitch by telling Trump that engaging with Kim could prove once and for all that he was the "greatest salesman in the world."

"Maybe there's a better way to do this," Kelly told Trump.

Trump had obsessively compared himself to past presidents. Playing on that insecurity, Kelly told Trump that he could do something that no other president had accomplished.

"No president since North Korea became a communist dictatorship has ever tried to reach out," Kelly told Trump. Kelly told Trump that he could engage directly with Kim and negotiate the greatest deal in American foreign policy history. "No president has tried to reason with this guy—you're the big dealmaker, why don't you do that," he said.

Kelly knew that such an interaction was highly unlikely to result in the United States and North Korea reaching a deal on anything, much less one that would lead North Korea to give up its nuclear weapons program, or result in Western sanctions being lifted and the birth of a new era of relations between the countries that have been bitter enemies for more than half a century. But Kelly's calculation was that the most important problem was to simply get both Trump and Kim to back off their rhetoric of nuclear holocaust. Kelly held back on telling Trump his entire calculation. But he continued to push on Trump's narcissism, pointing out that the presidents he was obsessed with outperforming—like the Bushes and Obama—had failed in their efforts to deal with North Korea.

To Kelly's surprise and relief, Trump liked the idea and took the bait. He loved the prospect of outmaneuvering Kim and achieving a better outcome in North Korea than any president before him. Just as Kim and the North Koreans were pausing their missile tests by December 2017, Trump was beginning to consider a more diplomatic relationship. A review of his public statements in the following two months shows a more restrained approach. Although he occasionally insulted the North Korean leader on Twitter, he soon moved from the militaristic taunting to the more traditional talking points of sanctions and denuclearization.

What else occurred in private is unclear, but some secret communications between the two countries were sent, signaling that Trump, indeed, wanted to come to the table and negotiate directly with Kim. By February 2018, as the Winter Olympics in Pyeongchang, South Korea, brought some temporary calm to the Korean peninsula, the White House publicly signaled a willingness to hold diplomatic meetings with the North Koreans, even planning a secret meeting between them and Vice President Pence. In March 2018, an envoy from South Korea came to the White House carrying a message from the North Koreans saying Kim wanted to meet with Trump. The president immediately agreed.

Kim and Trump met in Singapore in June 2018 and agreed to an exchange that many American military leaders were unhappy with: North Korea would commit to full denuclearization and the United States would suspend its military exercises in South Korea. Then an extended and bizarre exchange of letters between Kim and Trump ensued, which Trump called "love letters." In the letters, Kim addressed Trump as "Your Excellency" and compared their relationship to a "fantasy film." The two leaders met again in Hanoi in early 2019, and one final time in June 2019 in the demilitarized zone between North and South Korea.

"He truly believed that he could get Kim to do what he wanted him to do," Kelly later told associates.

Trump would leave office with North Korea no closer to denuclearization, its weapons program unaffected by the professed intimacy between the two leaders. But Kelly's ruse had worked: A massive military conflict had not broken out.

In the end, it might be said of Kelly's tour as Donald Trump's chief of staff that chaos resists order and that some egos are beyond discipline. Ultimately, Kelly was unable to reform Trump's White House, but he had worked diligently to curb the president's worst impulses, from his penchant for lying to his obsession with judging people by their physical appearance, and he would come away from the experience with as clear an understanding of Trump's character as anyone else in the country.

By the close of 2017, as the Mueller investigation was intensifying, the head of Trump's legal team, John Dowd, called Kelly. Dowd, a Marine who had sold Trump on hiring him because he could deal with his fellow Marine Robert Mueller, revered Kelly and often took his advice. Trump had been insisting in public and private that he wanted to sit with Mueller's team for an interview, and Dowd was in negotiations with the special counsel's office about having the sit-down at Camp David.

"What do you think about him talking to Mueller?" Dowd asked Kelly.

Kelly immediately recognized the catastrophe this could be for Trump, saying allowing him to talk to Mueller was a bad idea. It was not Kelly's fear that Mueller would get the truth out of Trump and the president would incriminate himself; Kelly's worry was that the president would lie and get himself into more trouble.

"He's not the most truthful guy," Kelly said. "He's just not very truthful."

Kelly had become conditioned to Trump's indifference to the truth firsthand. In January 2018, Maggie Haberman and I had broken the story in *The New York Times* on how Mueller's team had learned from the White House counsel, Don McGahn, that Trump wanted him to fire Mueller. The story enraged Trump, who in the days that followed launched a campaign to force McGahn to refute what we had reported, which culminated the following month in an Oval Office meeting with Kelly and McGahn during which Trump told McGahn to create a fake document that went back on what he had told Mueller's investigators. McGahn refused, but the moment would make both Kelly and McGahn witnesses to one of Trump's most brazen acts of obstruction of justice during his time in office.

In the spring of 2018, as Trump considered firing Secretary of State Rex Tillerson, he queried Kelly about whom he should pick to replace him.

"Who should be secretary of state?" Trump asked Kelly.

"I think Mike Pompeo," Kelly responded.

"What about Haley?" Trump asked, referring to Nikki Haley, the former governor of South Carolina whom Trump had appointed to be ambassador to the United Nations.

"I don't know," Kelly said, adding that he thought that Pompeo's experience running the CIA had been more substantial than Haley's experience at the UN.

"She doesn't look good for me—she has that skin thing, she doesn't look good for me," Trump said, as he repeated a complaint he previously made to Kelly about how Haley had a blotchy complexion.

It was demented logic. The president of the United States was arguing that an appointee's apparent skin problem would hurt how the public saw him.

(Trump had also derided the looks of his lawyer, Dowd. By March 2018, the president had soured on him, in part because he didn't believe Dowd looked good representing him in public. Trump told Kelly that Dowd was too fat and not a good enough public speaker to be his lawyer in such a high profile investigation.)

There might have been better reasons not to promote Haley to lead the State Department, but for Trump, in that moment, it was all about her appearance. But there was no more powerful calculus to Trump than popularity, and as Haley's star continued to rise, he would come to consider her for an even more important job.

In October 2018, around the time that Haley stepped down as the ambassador to the United Nations, Trump asked Kelly what he thought about replacing Pence on the 2020 Republican ticket with Haley.

"Do you think she would make a good president?" Trump asked Kelly.

"As good as anyone," Kelly said.

"How about vice president?" Trump asked.

Trump then turned the discussion into a rant about Pence.

"I saved Pence, he was going to get defeated," Trump said, referring to how Pence was likely to lose reelection as governor of Indiana in 2016, when Trump picked him to be vice president. "He owes me, I saved him.

"I saved him," Trump said. "I saved him. He owes me."

Throughout the summer of 2018, Kelly hit different breaking points, where he thought he had no choice but to quit.

On August 25, with the death of John McCain, Washington fell into a bipartisan grief. A Republican in a city now deeply divided along partisan lines, McCain was unusually well liked on both sides of the aisle. Senator Mitch McConnell, the Republican leader of the chamber McCain served in for more than thirty years until his death, quickly arranged for McCain to be officially mourned in the Capitol. Chuck Schumer, the top Democrat in the Senate, suggested an office building on Capitol Hill be named for McCain. But Trump, who had long resented McCain for his occasional criticism of the president, was having none of it. He swatted away insistence by top aides to issue a respectful statement about the death and to lower the flag atop the White House to half-staff. Two days after the death, Kelly called Trump at 7:00 a.m. and asked the president to allow his staff to issue comments on McCain.

"We have to support him," Kelly said.

McCain's family requested a full military funeral, which Trump would have to approve, but the president refused. Kelly believed it would be unconscionable to decline the request. He told Trump that he would resign if he did not go along with what McCain's family wanted.

Later that day, Trump relented, approving the military funeral, and released a statement that read, "Despite our differences on policy and politics, I respect Senator John McCain's service to our country"—but not before privately raging about McCain to Kelly.

"He was last in his class and he got shot down," Trump said regarding McCain's time at the U.S. Naval Academy and his military service in Vietnam, during which he was held for more than five years as a prisoner of war. For Trump, the attacks weren't just malicious statements to hurt a political opponent; the president would often complain that soldiers who were injured or wounded in war were getting too much praise.

"Why the fuck do you think they're heroes?" Trump asked. "They're losers."

After their fight over the McCain funeral, it was clear to both Trump and Kelly that their relationship was beyond repair. Kelly's frustration grew to the point where one afternoon he grabbed his briefcase and stormed out of the White House, yelling, "I'm tired of this fucking place," only to return the next morning.

By this time, Kelly's views about Jared and Ivanka had also hardened. Despite Kelly's attempts to rein them in, they largely maintained their power and direct line to the president. Kelly thought Ivanka was too focused on staying in the limelight and "didn't come to work all that much," he told confidants. He thought that Kushner was clearly intelligent but focused far too much of his energy on altering American foreign policy to benefit Israel. Kelly believed having a strong Israel was a critical feature of American foreign policy and it was one thing for any administration to pursue strong pro-Israel policies. But Kushner's approach puzzled him, because it seemed as if he worked day and night to do whatever the Israeli prime minister, Benjamin Netanyahu, wanted, as if he were an Israeli acting in the best interest of that country, not the United States. Kelly was also struck by how there was a range of Muslim countries in the region that were critical to brokering peace—like Egypt and Jordan—but Kushner seemed to concentrate only on the wealthy ones like the United Arab Emirates and Saudi Arabia. By the end of the administration, to friends Kelly would refer to Ivanka and Jared as "the royal couple."

Despite all of this, Kelly had remained, believing that if he left, whoever came after him would be far less willing to curb Trump's worst impulses than he had been and the consequences would be terrible for the country. At times Kelly would privately try to make his case to members of the media about why he had stayed.

"He's the president of the United States; if he gets it wrong, we could be in a war," he would say. "If he gets in a war, he could create a depression—Americans could be adversely affected. He's the fucking president. I know he attacks you people, but right now he's our president. I'm not saying you should be nice to him, but if I don't make this place function, you'll have no idea what can happen."

★★★

NOVEMBER 10, 2018

ONE YEAR, NINE MONTHS, AND TWENTY-ONE DAYS INTO THE PRESIDENCY

THE U.S. AMBASSADOR'S RESIDENCE IN PARIS—By November 2018, Kelly had endured working for Trump for fifteen months. By then, he was openly expressing his hatred of the president to aides and confidants, even telling one administration official outside the Situation Room that he couldn't wait "to get the fuck out of here." Occasionally, there were events that Kelly cherished being a part of, like when he had the chance to spend time with service members and Gold Star families. And early that November, Kelly was looking forward to the hundredth anniversary of the end of World War I. To honor that occasion, Trump and his top aides—including Kelly—were planning to fly to Paris and meet with other world leaders, hold a commemorative ceremony at the Arc de Triomphe, and visit the Aisne-Marne cemetery outside Paris, where thousands of American veterans of World War I are buried.

On the flight to France on Air Force One, Trump showed his lack of basic knowledge about world history.

"Who were the good guys in World War I?" the president asked Kelly.

"By definition anyone we were with were the good guys," Kelly said. "So anytime you ever have a question about who the good guys are, if we're in the war, we're with the good guys."

Kelly tried to explain Germany's role by connecting World Wars I and II, which he knew most people understood because of the world-historic darkness of Hitler's Holocaust against the Jews of Europe.

"Well," Trump responded, "Hitler did a lot of good things."

Trump attempted to convince Kelly of his reading of history. Germany, he told Kelly, was only able to gain economic dominance in Europe because of Hitler. Kelly, stunned that an American president would make such an argument, told Trump that he was profoundly wrong. And in any case, Hitler's economic philosophy was utterly irrelevant given the obvious fact that he was one of the most notorious genocidal maniacs in history.

"You cannot *ever* say anything supportive of Adolf Hitler," Kelly said. "You just can't."

After landing, Trump would continue to show Kelly he had little understanding of the world or of history. After a dinner commemorating the end of World War I, where the French president, Emmanuel Macron, and the German chancellor, Angela Merkel, had been seated near the head of the table, Trump raged to Kelly. It was as if he were cast aside, he told Kelly, and he thought that Macron had ignored him the whole time.

Kelly tried to calm Trump and assure him that the seating arrangement should be taken not as a slight but simply as a reflection of the world war they were there to commemorate.

"Sir, in World War I the heavy lifting on the Allies' side was done by the British and French, and the Americans had a relatively small role," Kelly said. "The vast majority of our casualties in that war were from the Spanish flu, so this is the seating arrangement."

"I should be number one," Trump said.

"They kind of got an order of the Allies; we came to the war late," Kelly said.

On the first afternoon in France, Trump was scheduled to travel about fifty miles east of Paris with Melania to visit the Aisne-Marne cemetery. It was raining and Trump told Kelly he didn't want to go. He didn't want his hair to be ruined, and he didn't understand why he would visit a memorial site for troops who had been killed.

"They lost," Trump told Kelly as they stood in a room at the ambassador's residence. "They're losers. Suckers in the war," Trump said. "These guys are losers. I like people who win."

Kelly had lost a son in battle and was angered by Trump's suggestion that sacrificing one's life in war somehow made a service member anything less than heroic. He told the president that he had to go to the cemetery. Macron and Merkel would be attending a similar ceremony outside Paris, and skipping the event would make Trump look as if he didn't support the troops, Kelly said.

"They're going to kill you if you don't go," Kelly said. "If you don't go and we can't tell the press you had a coronary, you're going to get killed."

"Why two cemeteries?" Trump asked. "What the fuck?"

Exasperated, Kelly then said, "I'll cancel it—you're not going."

Kelly traveled to the cemetery with Joseph Dunford, the chairman of the Joint Chiefs of Staff, and each of their wives. Walking through the cemetery, Kelly cried, deeply moved by the moment and the example of sacrifice laid out before him. In another way he was happy that Trump had not come, because someone who had so little understanding of war and sacrifice had no business being present at such an important moment. That was it for John Kelly; he had reached his breaking point and could no longer work for Donald Trump, no matter the consequences. He had decided to stay as long as he could take the pain. Now he knew he had to leave.

In the days after the trip, Kelly told Trump that his time was coming to an end, and also told the president that it was going to be difficult to find his replacement. He already knew, because he had reached out to potential candidates to see whether they might be interested in the position.

"You shitting me—taking your job? You're out of your fucking mind," one of those people told Kelly.

Kelly told Trump, "No one wants the job, no one decent. No one credible wants it."

A few weeks later, as Kelly's days in the West Wing were winding down, the former president George H. W. Bush died. As if affirming Kelly's decision to leave, Trump behaved badly in response to the news. He had always been disdainful of the Bushes and had not attended Barbara Bush's funeral earlier in the year, and now hated the idea that the elder Bush would be considered a war hero for his service in the Navy during World War II.

"You think he's a hero?" Trump asked. "He was shot down."

"One of the biggest problems with his narcissism," Kelly would tell confidants, "was that he was absolutely convinced he was better than Reagan, better than the Bush family, better than Obama. He was driven always to make the case that he was the greatest president ever."

In early December, Kelly went to the Oval Office prepared to finally resign. By then, Trump had been intentionally going around him and cutting him out of important discussions, knowing that Kelly was apt to tell him he couldn't or shouldn't do whatever it was that he was planning to do.

"You don't take my recommendations," Kelly told Trump. "And you're going around me in the process."

"You want to go?" the president answered. "It's fine."

In leaving, Kelly presumed to give Trump one last piece of advice.

"Mr. President, don't pick a bootlicker, don't pick a yes-man," he said. "If you do, you will be impeached."

"Nah, nah, nah," Trump answered.

"You will be impeached," Kelly repeated. "You need someone to help you stay on the tracks."

In December, Trump announced that he had picked Mick Mulvaney, director of the Office of Management and Budget, to be the White House's interim chief of staff. Mulvaney told the West Wing staff in a meeting at the time that his approach would be far different from Kelly's.

"We're going to do this differently," Mulvaney said. "We're going to let the president be the president—that's how to be successful, let the president be the president."

Almost exactly a year after Mulvaney took over, the House of Representatives impeached Donald Trump for the first time.

ACKNOWLEDGMENTS

TO COMPLETE THIS PROJECT, I had to stand on the shoulders of many colleagues, friends, and family. Without them, I'm unsure I would have finished the book.

First, I want to single out my researcher and co-pilot for the past two years, Matt Cullen. Every step of the way, Matt kept this project on track. Matt learned the subject matter we covered in this book as well as anyone else. He developed a nearly encyclopedic knowledge of what documents contained, what our reporting showed, and what we had written in drafts. He looked at every angle of the story with incredible thoughtfulness and perspective. Matt is a promising young journalist, and I can't wait to see what he does in the years to come.

I want to thank my dear friend Wyatt Lipman for the countless hours he put in with me, talking through what this era meant, what it said about politics and human nature, and how to turn that into a story. His incredible depth of knowledge and sense of story helped me figure out how to tell this tale in a way that gave it a larger meaning. Working this through with him made for some of the most enjoyable moments of writing the book. Wyatt is a great, loyal friend, and I'll forever be indebted to him for his help.

I'm incredibly grateful to my cousin Aaron Cohen, who helped me try to think like a book author and turn my reporting into something larger. He told me to keep writing and everything else would fall into place. It sounds like simple advice, but it was essential and helped get me home.

One of the great cheerleaders of this project was my friend and *Times* colleague Jason Stallman. Even when my drafts made little sense, he read them, gave me great feedback, and told me that what I had was great. He's an incredible editor, and I hope I get to work for him in the years to come.

I'm especially appreciative to my agent, Gail Ross, who reached out to me, told me that I needed to write a book, gave me guidance on how to do it, and made sure that it got done. Gail was a calming presence who made sure the project stayed on track, pushed me when needed, and listened when I was lost. Working with her was a highlight of this experience. I also want to thank her partner, Howard Yoon, who played a big role in helping me come up with what this book could look like. His early guidance put this on the right path.

I am incredibly grateful for the relationship I've developed with my publisher, Random House. Andy Ward, Tom Perry, and Mark Warren are three of the great pros and mensches of the world. Mark's editing of the book elevated and streamlined it in ways I never could have imagined. He made me a better reporter and storyteller, and forced me out of my comfort zone to find new ways to see this story. I'll forever be indebted to him for that and his time and patience. And speaking of professionalism and patience, I am also very grateful to our copy editor, Ingrid Sterner, for improving this book when it mattered most. I am deeply grateful for Random House legal counsel Matthew Martin for the care and insights that he brought to this book. An enormous thank-you as well to Carlos Beltrán for designing the powerful and arresting cover. Our publicist, Greg Kubie, and our marketer, Ayelet Gruenspecht, were all-in on this book, and complete this amazing team.

Working as a reporter at *The New York Times* has been the highlight of a lifetime. The Sulzberger family, led by A.G., is one of the great treasures of the United States. Unlike nearly every other paper in the country, the *Times* is more robust today than it's ever been—

and that is directly a result of the family's decision to protect the newsroom. Dean Baquet, our executive editor, is one of the great lions of journalism. He's the most inspiring journalist I've ever worked with. His deputy, Matt Purdy, is one of the most thoughtful and gracious editors around, and above all he's a great person. He's guided me through my career, always keeping me focused and in line.

My home base for the past eight years has been the *Times* Washington bureau. The bureau exists because of an extraordinary group of people. Our bureau chief, Elisabeth Bumiller, has led us fearlessly in the Trump era, as we've expanded as a bureau to produce more stories a day than anyone ever could have imagined. Elisabeth has kept us on mission and done it with charm. Her husband and longtime *Times* reporter, Steve Weisman, is a great friend. My editor in the bureau, Amy Fiscus, has been the steady hand that has guided us through covering the Mueller investigation and all the other craziness that came after it. She made us better reporters and writers, and is a great friend and someone you want in the foxhole with you. My editors early in my tenure in the bureau—David Leonhardt, Carolyn Ryan, Bill Hamilton, and Rebecca Corbett—should be rewarded for the patience they had with me. They were great tutors and allies to have. The backbone of the bureau is formed by Tahirah Burley, our senior operations manager, and our technology specialists, Cliff Meadows and Jeff Burgess. The laptop Cliff arranged for me to have to write the book is one of the greatest electronics I've ever had. Without it, I never would have finished on time. I'm also thankful to work for and alongside: Dick Stevenson, Thom Shanker, Carl Hulse, Julie Davis, Helene Cooper, Matt Apuzzo, Katie Benner, Matt Rosenberg, Nick Fandos, Peter Baker, Sharon LaFraniere, Eileen Sullivan, Julian Barnes, Charlie Savage, Michael Shear, Ken Vogel, Michael Crowley, Noah Weiland, Zolan Kanno-Youngs, Annie Karni, Scott Shane, Mark Landler, Eric Lipton, Eric Schmitt, and many others.

There are four people I'm closest to at the *Times* who are some of the greatest friends I've ever had. Mark Mazzetti selflessly became the editor of our Russia coverage after the election. It was as daunting an assignment as anyone could take on. He did it with grace.

He's as good a journalist as he is a person. I still want to be like Mark when I grow up. Maggie Haberman is far and away the greatest reporter of her generation. She covered the Trump campaign better than anyone else. And after Trump won, she selflessly threw herself at the story, taking on the most important political story of our time with a singular goal of just covering it. No one did it better—and no one has given more to the paper than her. No one can do the improbable in journalism better than Adam Goldman. He has more raw reporting power than anyone else I've worked with. If Adam wants the story, he will get it. It's quite something to watch. Adam is as loyal a friend as there is. Emily Steel and I spent countless days in a small conference room at the *Times* in 2016 and 2017 reporting out the story of Bill O'Reilly's sexual harassment settlements. It was an incredibly difficult assignment. But there is no one else I would have rather worked with it on and I'm incredibly grateful for the friendship we have.

Mom, Dad, Molly, J.J., Tim, Nicolle, and Liam, you are what sustains me. Words cannot express what you all mean to me.

NOTES

★ ★ ★ ★ ★

For this book, I examined over a thousand pages of documents from across the federal government that had never been previously made public. I spent hundreds of hours with current and former senior government officials, and others outside the government intimately involved in the story, often speaking to them on the condition of anonymity because they did not want to be identified discussing sensitive, privileged, or classified information.

ACT ONE

I. Rule of Law, Rule of Trump

7 **By the end of the second year:** Barry J. McMillion, "Judicial Nomination Statistics and Analysis: U.S. District and Circuit Court, 1977–2018," Congressional Research Service, March 21, 2019.

10 **Indeed, in 2008:** Jason Szep and Caren Bohan, "McCain and Obama Call Political Cease-Fire for 9/11," Reuters, September 11, 2008.

10 **But on September 11:** "American Killed in US Consulate Attack in Benghazi: Official," Agence France-Presse, September 11, 2012.

11 **In Cairo, reports indicated:** Tamim Elyan, "Egyptians Angry at Film Scale U.S. Embassy Walls," Reuters, September 11, 2012.

11 **The embassy in Cairo:** "U.S. Embassy Condemns Religious Incitement," U.S. embassy in Cairo, September 11, 2012, web.archive.org/web/20120912144752/http://egypt.usembassy.gov/pr091112.html.

11 **At the far end of the party:** Michael Cooper, "Palin, on Offensive, Attacks Obama's Ties to '60s Radical," *New York Times,* October 4, 2008.

11 **Trump falsely suggesting:** "Blitzer and Trump Go at It over Trump's 'Birther' Claims," CNN, May 29, 2012, politicalticker.blogs.cnn.com/2012/05/29/firing-off-trump-stands-by-birther-comments/.

12 **"From the point of view":** Gabriel Schoenfeld, *A Bad Day on the Romney Campaign: An Insider's Account* (New York: Penguin Group, 2013).

12 **Stevens, Romney's chief strategist, and policy adviser Lanhee Chen:** "What They Said, Before and After the Attack in Libya," *New York Times,* September 12, 2012.

13 **Even some Republicans:** Daniel Larison, "The Attacks in Benghazi and Cairo," *American Conservative,* September 12, 2012.

13 **at 7:22 a.m.:** "What They Said, Before and After the Attack in Libya."

13 **"Guys, we screwed up":** Mark Halperin and John Heilemann, *Double Down: Game Change 2012* (New York: Penguin Press, 2013).

17 **a total of fewer than eighty thousand:** Philip Bump, "Donald Trump Will Be President Thanks to 80,000 People in Three States," *Washington Post,* December 1, 2016.

19 **"Highly conflicted Bob Mueller":** Donald J. Trump (@realDonaldTrump), Twitter, September 15, 2018, 6:08 p.m., twitter.com/realDonaldTrump/status/1041086383505465345.

ACT TWO

II. The Institutionalist

31 **In February 2015:** Michael S. Schmidt, "F.B.I. Director Speaks Out on Race and Police Bias," *New York Times,* February 12, 2015.

31 **"a nation of cowards":** Helene Cooper, "Attorney General Chided for Language on Race," *New York Times,* March 7, 2009.

31 **"I believe the job":** "Statement by FBI Director James Comey Regarding Dylann Roof Gun Purchase," FBI, July 10, 2015, www.fbi.gov/news/pressrel/press-releases/statement-by-fbi-director-james-comey-regarding-dylann-roof-gun-purchase.

31 **Roof had said he committed:** "The Dylann Roof Trial: The Evidence," *New York Times,* December 9, 2016.

32 **the president broke into song:** Michiko Kakutani, "Obama's Eulogy, Which Found Its Place in History," *New York Times,* July 3, 2015.

32 **roughly twenty thousand arrests a year:** "Federal Table 3," Federal Bureau of Investigation, 2016–2017, ucr.fbi.gov/crime-in-the-u.s/2015/crime-in-the-u.s.-2015/home.

32 **In the early 1990s:** Clyde Haberman, "An Idaho Family, and Federal Tactics, Under Siege," *New York Times,* October 26, 2014.

32 **government investigators placed:** "A Review of the FBI's Handling of Intelligence Information Related to the September 11 Attacks," U.S.

Department of Justice Office of the Inspector General, November 2004, oig.justice.gov/special/0506/final.pdf.

33 **In June 2004:** "Remarks of Deputy Attorney General James Comey Regarding Jose Padilla," U.S. Department of Justice, June 1, 2004, www.justice.gov/archive/dag/speeches/2004/dag6104.htm.

33 **the *Times* ran the story:** Michael S. Schmidt, "Background Check Flaw Let Dylann Roof Buy Gun, F.B.I. Says," *New York Times,* July 10, 2015.

34 **agents and their supervisors initiated:** "Hillary R. Clinton Part 05 of 41," FBI Records: The Vault, vault.fbi.gov/hillary-r.-clinton/Hillary%20R.%20Clinton%20Part%2005%20of%2041/view.

35 **"You know you are":** James Comey, *A Higher Loyalty: Truth, Lies, and Leadership* (New York: Flatiron Books, 2018).

36 **"We should skype sometime":** Alana Goodman, "Anthony Weiner Carried On a Months-Long Online Sexual Relationship with a Troubled 15-Year-Old Girl Telling Her She Made Him 'Hard,' Asking Her to Dress Up in 'School-Girl' Outfits and Pressing Her to Engage in 'Rape Fantasies,'" *Daily Mail,* September 21, 2016.

41 **In 2015, the FBI had found:** Michael S. Schmidt and Matt Apuzzo, "David Petraeus Is Sentenced to Probation in Leak Investigation," *New York Times,* April 23, 2015.

44 ***Oh, my God:*** Andrew G. McCabe, *The Threat: How the FBI Protects America in the Age of Terror and Trump* (New York: St. Martin's Press, 2019).

45 **"We sat together on a couch":** Áine Cain, "FBI Director James Comey Reflects on His Time at the College," *Flat Hat,* November 17, 2014, flathatnews.com/2014/11/17/fbi-director-james-comey-reflects-on-his-time-at-the-college/.

III. The Point of No Return

In this chapter, when discussing Lawrence E. Walsh's actions surrounding the 1992 presidential election, I referenced Walsh's 1997 book, *Firewall*, and Bob Woodward's 1999 book, *Shadow*. For the section on links between Trump and Russia, I referenced the Wikipedia page entitled "Timeline of Russian interference in the 2016 United States elections," which I found to be a useful compendium of events, details, dates, and articles.

53 **"There is evidence to support":** "Statement by FBI Director James B. Comey on the Investigation of Secretary Hillary Clinton's Use of a Personal E-mail System," FBI, July 5, 2016, www.fbi.gov/news/pressrel/press-releases/statement-by-fbi-director-james-b-comey-on-the-investigation-of-secretary-hillary-clinton2019s-use-of-a-personal-e-mail-system.

53 **"This is a great man":** "Transcript of Pelosi Press Conference Today," Office of Nancy Pelosi, July 8, 2016, www.speaker.gov/newsroom/24531.

54 **"highest standards of integrity":** Tim Kaine, interview on *Fox News Sunday,* October 16, 2016, archive.org/details/FOXNEWSW_20161017_020000_Fox_News_Sunday_With_Chris_Wallace/start/960/end/1020.

54 **"Generations of prosecutors and agents":** Matthew Miller, "James Comey's Abuse of Power," *Washington Post,* July 6, 2016.

55 **"I'm here because we're mystified":** "FBI Director James Comey to Testify Before House Committee on Clinton E-mail Probe. Aired 10–10:30a ET," CNN, July 7, 2016, transcripts.cnn.com/TRANSCRIPTS/1607/07/cnr.03.html.

55 **"We did not find evidence sufficient":** "Continuing Coverage of FBI Director Testimony Before Congress. Aired Noon–12:30p ET," CNN, July 7, 2016, transcripts.cnn.com/TRANSCRIPTS/1607/07/lvab.01.html.

57 **"Russia, if you're listening":** Ashley Parker and David E. Sanger, "Donald Trump Calls On Russia to Find Hillary Clinton's Missing Emails," *New York Times,* July 27, 2016.

58 **Less than five hours:** Special Counsel Robert S. Mueller III, "Report on the Investigation into Russian Interference in the 2016 Presidential Election," U.S. Department of Justice, March 2019.

62 **From a plain-looking building:** Adrian Chen, "The Agency," *The New York Times Magazine,* June 2, 2015.

64 **He first traveled to the Soviet Union:** Megan Twohey and Steve Eder, "For Trump, Three Decades of Chasing Deals in Russia," *New York Times,* January 16, 2017.

64 **his children toured the Kremlin:** Matt Apuzzo and Maggie Haberman, "Trump Associate Boasted That Moscow Business Deal 'Will Get Donald Elected,'" *New York Times,* August 28, 2017.

64 **"Whether you like him or don't":** Noah Bierman and Chris Megerian, "As Candidate, Trump Sought Friendlier Ties with Russia While Eyeing Big Money in Moscow," *Los Angeles Times,* November 30, 2018.

64 **At a business conference in Moscow:** Twohey and Eder, "For Trump, Three Decades of Chasing Deals in Russia."

64 **Trump profited enormously:** Robert Frank, "Only in Palm Beach: The $95 Million Tear-Down," *New York Times,* August 27, 2016.

65 **"In terms of high-end product":** Brennan Weiss, "Trump's Oldest Son Said a Decade Ago That a Lot of the Family's Assets Came from Russia," *Business Insider,* February 21, 2018.

65 **Russia's state-run bank provided:** Rob Barry, Christopher S. Stewart, and Brett Forrest, "Russian State-Run Bank Financed Deal Involving Trump Hotel Partner," *Wall Street Journal,* May 17, 2017.

66 **"This story is completely fabricated":** Eric Trump (@EricTrump), Twitter, May 8, 2017, 6:32 a.m., twitter.com/EricTrump/status/861529156701564929.

66 **When Letterman cracked a joke:** *Late Show with David Letterman,* CBS, October 17, 2013, www.youtube.com/watch?v=PR_SoJpWzOA.

66 **"Do you think Putin will be going":** Donald J. Trump (@realDonald Trump), Twitter, June 18, 2013, 11:17 p.m., twitter.com/realDonald Trump/status/347191326112112640.

67 **The Russians paid Trump $20 million:** Katie Rogers, "How Trump's 'Miss Universe' in Russia Became Ensnared in a Political Inquiry," *New York Times,* July 11, 2017.

67 **an oligarch close to Putin:** Stephanie Baker, "Billionaire Ally of Putin Socialized with Kushner, Ivanka Trump," Bloomberg, February 4, 2014.

67 **"I was in Moscow recently":** Philip Bump, "How Well Does Trump Know Putin? A Chronology," *Washington Post,* July 7, 2017.

67 **"They're terrific people":** Hugh Hewitt, "Donald Trump Returns," *The Hugh Hewitt Show,* September 21, 2015, www.hughhewitt.com /donald-trump-returns/.

67 **Trump signed a letter of intent:** Mueller, "Report on the Investigation into Russian Interference in the 2016 Presidential Election."

67 **"We were stablemates":** Christopher Massie, "Trump and Putin Appeared on '60 Minutes' Together . . . from Different Continents," *BuzzFeed News,* November 10, 2015.

68 **Flynn had scheduled a trip:** Nicholas Schmidle, "Michael Flynn, General Chaos," *New Yorker,* February 18, 2017.

68 **After he was pushed out:** Adam Goldman and Michael Schwirtz, "Michael Flynn Was Paid by Russian-Linked Firms, Letter Shows," *New York Times,* March 16, 2017.

68 **Cohen sent an email to a spokesman:** Mueller, "Report on the Investigation into Russian Interference in the 2016 Presidential Election."

70 **Manafort received a contract:** Jeff Horwitz and Chad Day, "AP Findings on Trump Associate's Work for Russian Oligarch," Associated Press, March 22, 2017.

70 **the two met in New York:** Mueller, "Report on the Investigation into Russian Interference in the 2016 Presidential Election."

71 **Two days earlier:** "Review of Four FISA Applications and Other Aspects of the FBI's Crossfire Hurricane Investigation," U.S. Department of Justice Office of the Inspector General, December 2019, www.justice .gov/storage/120919-examination.pdf.

81 **"I am certain his behavior continues":** Sydney Leathers, "Two Thumbs Down on Weiner Doc," Washington Babylon, August 11, 2016.

82 **the *Daily Mail* paid her $30,000:** Benjamin Weiser, "Anthony Weiner's Lawyers Question Motivation of Sexting Victim," *New York Times,* September 14, 2017.

82 **more than 300,000 emails:** "A Review of Various Actions by the Federal Bureau of Investigation and Department of Justice in Advance of the

2016 Election," U.S. Department of Justice Office of the Inspector General, June 2018, www.justice.gov/file/1071991/download.

84 **the Dutch could see precisely:** Huib Modderkolk, "Dutch Agencies Provide Crucial Intel About Russia's Interference in US-Elections," *De Volkskrant,* January 25, 2018.

89 **Walsh and his team contended:** Lawrence E. Walsh, *Firewall: The Iran-Contra Conspiracy and Cover-Up* (New York: W. W. Norton, 1997).

90 **Bush talked to Attorney General William P. Barr:** Bob Woodward, *Shadow: Five Presidents and the Legacy of Watergate* (New York: Simon & Schuster, 1999).

92 **On October 31:** David Corn, "A Veteran Spy Has Given the FBI Information Alleging a Russian Operation to Cultivate Donald Trump," *Mother Jones,* October 31, 2016.

IV. "Oh, God"

95 **82 percent chance of winning:** Josh Katz, "2016 Elections Forecast: Who Will Be President," *New York Times,* November 8, 2016.

99 **"It was only a matter of minutes":** "U.S. Senate Judiciary Committee Holds a Hearing on the U.S. Attorney Firings," U.S. Senate, May 15, 2007, gulcfac.typepad.com/georgetown_university_law/files/comey.transcript.pdf.

100 **"standing up for what he believed":** President Barack Obama, "Remarks by the President at Nomination of James Comey as Director of the FBI," White House Press Office, obamawhitehouse.archives.gov/the-press-office/2013/06/21/remarks-president-nomination-james-comey-director-fbi.

101 **"a phony, a fraud":** "Transcript of Mitt Romney's Speech on Donald Trump," *New York Times,* March 3, 2016.

102 **"What Jim Comey did":** Jerrold Nadler, interview on *New Day,* CNN, November 14, 2016, archive.org/details/CNNW_20161114_110000_New_Day/start/2040/end/2100.

103 **"Can you imagine":** Donald J. Trump (@realDonaldTrump), Twitter, December 12, 2016, 8:17 a.m., twitter.com/realDonaldTrump/status/808299841147248640.

104 **"If Russia, or some other entity":** Donald J. Trump (@realDonald Trump), Twitter, December 15, 2016, 9:24 a.m., twitter.com/realDonaldTrump/status/809403760099422208.

104 **For only four of the previous sixty years:** Chris Canipe, "Republicans Take Control," *Wall Street Journal,* January 20, 2017.

105 **The Russians had meddled:** "Assessing Russian Activities and Intentions in Recent US Elections," Office of the Director of National Intelligence, January 6, 2017, www.dni.gov/files/documents/ICA_2017_01.pdf.

106 **six human sources:** Bob Woodward, *Fear: Trump in the White House* (New York: Simon & Schuster, 2018).

107 **uniquely important in identifying:** Julian E. Barnes, Adam Goldman, and David E. Sanger, "C.I.A. Informant Extracted from Russia Had Sent Secrets to U.S. for Decades," *New York Times,* September 17, 2019.

108 **"some guy in his home":** "Donald Trump on Russia, Advice from Barack Obama, and How He Will Lead," *Time,* December 7, 2016.

109 **He asked one of his aides:** Josh Campbell, "'No Turning Back Now': The Inside Story of James Comey's Trip to Trump Tower," CNN, September 16, 2019.

110 **"I don't believe in human sources":** Woodward, *Fear.*

110 **Trump fixated on the prostitutes:** James Comey, memorandum, January 7, 2017.

112 **"very smart":** Donald J. Trump (@realDonaldTrump), Twitter, December 30, 2016, 2:41 p.m., twitter.com/realDonaldTrump/status/814919370711461890.

112 **In the column:** David Ignatius, "Why Did Obama Dawdle on Russia's Hacking?," *Washington Post,* January 12, 2017.

ACT THREE

V. The Road to Mueller

In this chapter, when examining the history of Atlantic City and the life of Paddy McGahn, I referenced Nelson Johnson's 2002 book, *Boardwalk Empire,* and Timothy L. O'Brien's 1998 book, *Bad Bet.*

118 **every U.S. president since John Adams:** Betty C. Monkman, "John and Abigail Adams: A Tradition Begins," White House Historical Association, www.whitehousehistory.org/john-and-abigail-adams-a-tradition-begins.

118 **Obama's crimson drapes:** Katie Kindelan, "Donald Trump Brings Gold Curtains, Winston Churchill Bust to the Oval Office," ABC News, January 21, 2017.

126 **His mother suggested:** Nelson Johnson, *Boardwalk Empire: The Birth, High Times, and Corruption of Atlantic City* (New York: Fall River Press, 2002).

131 **He was even so appreciative:** Michael Daly, "The Decorated Marine Who Called Trump a 'Draft-Dodging Bastard' to His Face," *Daily Beast,* November 29, 2016.

131 **"Jack, I'm 13 and 0":** John R. O'Donnell, *Trumped! The Inside Story of the Real Donald Trump—His Cunning Rise and Spectacular Fall,* with James Rutherford (Hertford, N.C.: Crossroad Press, 2017).

132 **Paddy had charged Trump:** "Trump Sues Former Lawyer Patrick 'Paddy' McGahn," *Press of Atlantic City,* October 6, 1995.

132 **"expert at interpreting things":** Kendall Taggart and Chris Geidner, "Trump's Lawyer: We Met with Him in Pairs to Avoid Lies," *BuzzFeed News,* October 6, 2016.

133 **"There's three sides to every story":** Donald F. McGahn II, "A Conversation with Don McGahn," Stockton University, January 23, 2020.

135 **McCabe told Flynn:** Andrew McCabe, *The Threat: How the FBI Protects America in the Age of Terror and Trump* (New York: St. Martin's Press, 2019).

136 **they could see Trump telling movers:** James B. Stewart, *Deep State: Trump, the FBI, and the Rule of Law* (New York: Penguin Press, 2019).

136 **The agents said that:** FD-302 for Michael Flynn, Federal Bureau of Investigation, February 15, 2017, assets.documentcloud.org/documents/5633260/12-17-18-Redacted-Flynn-Interview-302.pdf.

137 **"What a beautiful black sky":** McCabe, *Threat.*

144 **Flynn's son had been fired:** Matthew Rosenberg, Maggie Haberman, and Eric Schmitt, "Trump Fires Adviser's Son from Transition for Spreading Fake News," *New York Times,* December 6, 2016.

144 **"Not again, this guy":** Special Counsel Robert S. Mueller III, "Report on the Investigation into Russian Interference in the 2016 Presidential Election," U.S. Department of Justice, March 2019.

145 **"Why does it matter":** "Full Transcript: Sally Yates and James Clapper Testify on Russian Election Interference," *Washington Post,* May 8, 2017.

146 **"The head of the FBI":** James Comey, *Higher Loyalty: Truth, Lies, and Leadership* (New York: Flatiron Books, 2018).

146 **At 6:20 p.m.:** James Comey, memorandum, January 28, 2017.

146 **Morticians embalmed:** Conrade C. Hinds, *The Great Columbus Experiment of 1908* (Charleston, S.C.: History Press, 2012).

146 **Eleanor Roosevelt greeted the pilot:** Maurine H. Beasley, *Eleanor Roosevelt and the Media: A Public Quest for Self-Fulfillment* (Champaign: University of Illinois Press, 1987).

150 **"so-called judge":** Donald J. Trump (@realDonaldTrump), Twitter, February 4, 2017, 8:12 a.m., twitter.com/realDonaldTrump/status/827867311054974976.

150 **Blumenthal said that Gorsuch:** Julie Hirschfeld Davis, "Supreme Court Nominee Calls Trump's Attacks on Judiciary 'Demoralizing,'" *New York Times,* February 8, 2017.

150 **Trump then publicly called:** Donald J. Trump (@realDonaldTrump), Twitter, February 9, 2017, 6:57 a.m., twitter.com/realDonaldTrump/status/829660612452036608.

150 **When Comey entered the White House:** James Comey, memorandum, February 8, 2017.

156 **Flynn had in fact spoken:** Greg Miller, Adam Entous, and Ellen Nakashima, "National Security Adviser Flynn Discussed Sanctions with Russian Ambassador, Despite Denials, Officials Say," *Washington Post,* February 9, 2017.

156 **On Saturday night in Florida:** David A. Fahrenthold and Karen DeYoung, "Trump Turns Mar-a-Lago Club Terrace into Open-Air Situation Room," *Washington Post,* February 13, 2017.

156 **"I don't know about that":** Matthew Rosenberg and Glenn Thrush, "Trump Will 'Look Into' Reports That Flynn Discussed Sanctions with Russia," *New York Times,* February 10, 2017.

157 **"General Flynn does enjoy":** Madeline Conway and Tara Palmeri, "Spicer and Conway Send Split Signals on Flynn's Future," *Politico,* February 13, 2017.

157 **"We'll give you a good recommendation":** Mueller, "Report on the Investigation into Russian Interference in the 2016 Presidential Election."

158 **"That sounds better":** Mark Mazzetti et al., "Intimidation, Pressure, and Humiliation: Inside Trump's Two-Year War on the Investigations Encircling Him," *New York Times,* February 19, 2019.

158 **"Good afternoon":** "Press Briefing by Press Secretary Sean Spicer," White House, February 14, 2017, www.whitehouse.gov/briefings-statements/press-briefing-press-secretary-sean-spicer-021417/.

160 **At 4:15 p.m.:** James Comey, memorandum, February 14, 2017.

163 **at least two meetings:** Adam Entous, Ellen Nakashima, and Greg Miller, "Sessions Met with Russian Envoy Twice Last Year, Encounters He Later Did Not Disclose," *Washington Post,* March 1, 2017.

164 **"became President of the United States":** Jason Kurtz, "Van Jones on Trump: 'He Became President of the United States in That Moment, Period,'" CNN, March 1, 2017.

165 **"This is bullshit":** Julie Hirschfeld Davis and Michael D. Shear, *Border Wars* (New York: Simon & Schuster, 2019).

166 **"You're telling me":** Mueller, "Report on the Investigation into Russian Interference in the 2016 Presidential Election."

166 **The showdown in the Oval Office:** "Video Shows Heated Oval Office Meeting," CNN, March 5, 2017, www.cnn.com/videos/politics/2017/03/05/heated-oval-office-meeting-bannon-trump-nobles-newday.cnn.

167 **Trump put out a series:** Donald J. Trump (@realDonaldTrump), Twitter, March 4, 2017, 6:25 a.m., twitter.com/realDonaldTrump/status/837989835818287106.

168 **When McGahn wasn't looking:** Mueller, "Report on the Investigation into Russian Interference in the 2016 Presidential Election."

168 **WikiLeaks had repeatedly teased:** WikiLeaks (@wikileaks), Twitter, February 4, 2017, 5:38 a.m., twitter.com/wikileaks/status/827828627488268290.

172 **He secretly told McGahn:** Mueller, "Report on the Investigation into Russian Interference in the 2016 Presidential Election."

172 **From the Oval Office:** Ibid.

174 **"I can't go into the particulars":** Kailani Koenig, "Schiff: 'More Than Circumstantial Evidence' Trump Associates Colluded with Russia," NBC News, March 22, 2017.

175 **Trump started the call:** James Comey, memorandum, March 30, 2017.

178 **Comey missed the call:** James Comey, memorandum, April 11, 2017.

179 **Trump proudly told McGahn:** Mueller, "Report on the Investigation into Russian Interference in the 2016 Presidential Election."

180 **Feinstein accused Comey:** Adam Goldman, "James Comey 'Mildly Nauseous' Over Idea He Swayed the Election," *New York Times,* May 3, 2017.

181 **In the exchange with lawmakers:** "Read the Full Testimony of FBI Director James Comey in Which He Discusses Clinton Email Investigation," *Washington Post,* May 3, 2017.

181 **"This is terrible, Jeff":** Mueller, "Report on the Investigation into Russian Interference in the 2016 Presidential Election."

182 **"He told me three times":** Ibid.

190 **"Dear Director Comey":** Ibid.

190 **"Few events have represented":** Adam Goldman, "Andrew McCabe, Ex-F.B.I. Official, Will Not Be Charged in Lying Case," *New York Times,* February 14, 2020.

193 **McGahn and Dhillon also tried to appeal:** Mueller, "Report on the Investigation into Russian Interference in the 2016 Presidential Election."

193 **Comey began his day in Jacksonville:** "Hours Before His Firing, FBI Director James Comey Was at Law-Enforcement Conference in Jacksonville," Action News Jax, May 9, 2017, www.actionnewsjax.com/news/local/hours-before-his-firing-fbi-director-james-comey-was-at-law-enforcement-conference-in-jacksonville/521019494/.

196 **Comey landed at Reagan National Airport:** Flight data for JENA625, May 9, 2017, flightaware.com/live/flight/JENA625/history/20170510/0103Z/KLAX/KDCA.

199 **"Only seven days after Donald J. Trump":** Michael S. Schmidt, "In a Private Dinner, Trump Demanded Loyalty. Comey Demurred," *New York Times,* May 11, 2017.

200 **"James Comey better hope":** Donald J. Trump (@realDonaldTrump), Twitter, May 12, 2017, 8:26 a.m., twitter.com/realDonaldTrump/status/863007411132649473.

203 **Trump had disclosed highly sensitive intelligence:** Greg Miller and Greg Jaffe, "Trump Revealed Highly Classified Information to Russian Foreign Minister and Ambassador," *Washington Post,* May 15, 2017.

213 **"I could record the President":** Stewart, *Deep State.*

222 **"It's your fucking fault":** Philip Rucker and Carol Leonnig, *A Very Stable Genius: Donald J. Trump's Testing of America* (New York: Penguin Press, 2020).

222 **"You're *weak*":** Ibid.

223 **"Oh my God":** Mueller, "Report on the Investigation into Russian Interference in the 2016 Presidential Election."

223 **"We've got a problem":** Chris Whipple, "'Who Needs a Controversy over the Inauguration?': Reince Priebus Opens Up About His Six Months of Magical Thinking," *Vanity Fair,* February 14, 2018.

223 **"Jeff, what's going on":** Ibid.

223 **But the following morning:** Mueller, "Report on the Investigation into Russian Interference in the 2016 Presidential Election."

ACT FOUR

VI. "He's Saying Some Crazy Shit"

In this chapter, when detailing Trump's efforts to pressure Sessions through Lewandowski and Priebus, I regularly referenced the Mueller report.

230 **at least eighty-three different gifts:** Ken Klippenstein, "The Insane Gifts Saudi Arabia Gave President Trump," *Daily Beast,* September 4, 2017.

231 **Trump had taken Sessions's resignation:** Special Counsel Robert S. Mueller III, "Report on the Investigation into Russian Interference in the 2016 Presidential Election," U.S. Department of Justice, March 2019.

233 **In an effort to shield Nixon:** "Dean Disbarred in Virginia for 'Unethical' Acts," Associated Press, February 7, 1974, www.nytimes.com/1974/02/07/archives/dean-disbarred-in-virginia-for-unethical-acts.html.

237 **Late on June 14:** Devlin Barrett et al., "Special Counsel Is Investigating Trump for Possible Obstruction of Justice, Officials Say," *Washington Post,* June 14, 2017.

238 **"Why is that Hillary":** Donald J. Trump (@realDonaldTrump), Twitter, June 15, 2017, 3:43 p.m., twitter.com/realDonaldTrump/status/875438639823675392.

238 **"I am being investigated":** Donald J. Trump (@realDonaldTrump), Twitter, June 16, 2017, 9:07 a.m., twitter.com/realDonaldTrump/status/875701471999864833.

240 **At 2:23 p.m.:** Mueller, "Report on the Investigation into Russian Interference in the 2016 Presidential Election."

240 **"Call Rod, and tell Rod":** Ibid.

242 **Concentrate on the judges:** Ibid.

245 **"While I was there, I said hello":** Peter Baker, Michael S. Schmidt,

and Maggie Haberman, "Citing Recusal, Trump Says He Wouldn't Have Hired Sessions," *New York Times,* July 19, 2017.

245 **More than two weeks earlier:** Jo Becker, Matt Apuzzo, and Adam Goldman, "Trump's Son Met with Russian Lawyer After Being Promised Damaging Information on Clinton," *New York Times,* July 9, 2017.

248 **Hours before we interviewed Trump:** Mueller, "Report on the Investigation into Russian Interference in the 2016 Presidential Election."

249 **Lewandowski had also served:** Maggie Haberman and Michael M. Grynbaum, "Corey Lewandowski, Donald Trump's Campaign Manager, Is Charged with Battery," *New York Times,* March 29, 2016.

249 **"I know that I recused":** Mueller, "Report on the Investigation into Russian Interference in the 2016 Presidential Election."

250 **On Friday night:** Adam Entous, Ellen Nakashima, and Greg Miller, "Sessions Discussed Trump Campaign-Related Matters with Russian Ambassador, U.S. Intelligence Intercepts Show," *Washington Post,* July 21, 2017.

251 **"So many people":** Donald J. Trump (@realDonaldTrump), Twitter, July 22, 2017, 7:44 a.m., twitter.com/realDonaldTrump/status/888726438265966592.

251 **In an interview with the *Times:*** Julie Hirschfeld Davis and Michael D. Shear, "Donald Trump Drops Threat of New Hillary Clinton Investigation," *New York Times,* November 22, 2016.

251 **The president said it was Priebus's job:** Mueller, "Report on the Investigation into Russian Interference in the 2016 Presidential Election."

252 **"Did you get it":** Mueller, "Report on the Investigation into Russian Interference in the 2016 Presidential Election."

252 **"Attorney General Jeff Sessions":** Donald J. Trump (@realDonald Trump), Twitter, July 25, 2017, 6:12 a.m., twitter.com/realDonaldTrump/status/889790429398528000.

259 **Then, in mid-September:** Kenneth P. Vogel, "'Isn't That the Trump Lawyer?' A Reporter's Accidental Scoop," *New York Times,* September 19, 2017.

261 **Trump himself had dictated:** Ashley Parker et al., "Trump Dictated Son's Misleading Statement on Meeting with Russian Lawyer," *Washington Post,* July 31, 2017.

270 **"I think he's going to be fair":** "Excerpts from Trump's Interview with the Times," *New York Times,* December 28, 2017.

271 **Trump was considering firing Mueller:** Michael D. Shear and Maggie Haberman, "Friend Says Trump Is Considering Firing Mueller as Special Counsel," *New York Times,* June 12, 2017.

283 **In the second week of January:** Michael Rothfeld and Joe Palazzolo, "Trump Lawyer Arranged $130,000 Payment for Adult-Film Star's Silence," *Wall Street Journal,* January 12, 2018.

283 **"shithole countries":** Josh Dawsey, "Trump Derides Protections for Immigrants from 'Shithole' Countries," *Washington Post,* January 12, 2018.

283 **"At this hour":** Erik Wemple, "Fox News's Sean Hannity Is Suddenly an Expert on Trump and Mueller," *Washington Post,* March 19, 2018.

284 **"So we have sources tonight":** Callum Borchers, "Fox News Hits Peak Trump Sycophancy, as Opinion Hosts Disregard the Network's Own Reporting," *Washington Post,* January 26, 2018.

286 **"Of all the things":** Kailani Koenig, "Reince Priebus Disputes Report That Trump Tried to Fire Robert Mueller," NBC News, February 4, 2018.

287 **called his former chief of staff:** Mueller, "Report on the Investigation into Russian Interference in the 2016 Presidential Election."

288 **telling the White House staff secretary:** Ibid.

288 **"If he doesn't write a letter":** Ibid.

289 **Four days earlier:** Martin Gould, "White House Romance! Trump's Comms Director Hope Hicks Is Seen Canoodling with President's High Level Staff Secretary Rob Porter," *Daily Mail,* February 1, 2018.

291 **"I never said to fire Mueller":** Mueller, "Report on the Investigation into Russian Interference in the 2016 Presidential Election."

292 **"What are these notes":** Ibid.

293 **In July 1974, the House:** Chuck Todd, Mark Murray, and Carrie Dann, "Impeachment Seems Much More Likely After Thursday's Bombshell Report," NBC News, January 18, 2019.

VII. Norms of Presidential Conduct 101

296 **they had said that reports:** Mark Landler, "Trump Will Have Wide Latitude to Let Family into Government's Secret Circles," *New York Times,* November 16, 2018.

296 **In a section of his application:** Maggie Haberman et al., "Trump Ordered Officials to Give Jared Kushner a Security Clearance," *New York Times,* February 28, 2019.

296 **"I have never seen that level":** Kara Scannell, "Background Check Chief Has 'Never Seen' Mistakes and Omissions at Level of Jared Kushner Forms," CNN, February 13, 2018.

298 **Kushner's family owed more than $1 billion:** Charles V. Bagli and Kate Kelly, "Deal Gives Kushners Cash Infusion on 666 Fifth Avenue," *New York Times,* August 3, 2018.

299 **"again have confirmed":** Shane Harris et al., "New White House Security Clearance Policy Could Put 'Bull's Eye' on Kushner," *Washington Post,* February 16, 2018.

302 **It was in 1883:** "An Act to Regulate and Improve the Civil Service of the United States (Pendleton Act)," National Archives, January 16, 1883.

304 **The stated reason:** Matt Apuzzo and Adam Goldman, "Andrew McCabe, a Target of Trump's F.B.I. Scorn, Is Fired Over Candor Questions," *New York Times,* March 16, 2018.

304 **"FBI Deputy Director Andrew McCabe":** Donald J. Trump (@realDonaldTrump), Twitter, December 23, 2017, 3:30 p.m., twitter.com/realDonaldTrump/status/944666448185692166.

306 **Comey described Trump:** James Comey, *A Higher Loyalty: Truth, Lies, and Leadership* (New York: Flatiron Books, 2018).

306 **ABC News aired an hour-long interview:** "Transcript: James Comey's Interview with ABC News Chief Anchor George Stephanopoulos," ABC News, April 15, 2018.

307 **"James Comey is a proven LEAKER & LIAR":** Donald J. Trump (@realDonaldTrump), Twitter, April 13, 2018, 8:01 a.m., twitter.com/realDonaldTrump/status/984763579210633216.

320 **"was a fucking liar":** Bob Woodward, *Fear: Trump in the White House* (New York: Simon & Schuster, 2018).

323 **On the day the White House:** "Read the Powerhouse Politics Interview with Outgoing White House Lawyer Ty Cobb," ABC News, May 2, 2018.

323 **Later that same night:** Amber Phillips and Callum Borchers, "Rudy Giuliani's Revealing Interview with Sean Hannity, Annotated," *Washington Post,* May 3, 2018.

326 **At the *Times:*** Matt Apuzzo, "Jared Kushner Gets Security Clearance, Ending Swirl of Questions Over Delay," *New York Times,* May 23, 2018.

326 **That afternoon on CNN:** "Transcripts: Situation Room with Wolf Blitzer," CNN, May 23, 2018, us.cnn.com/TRANSCRIPTS/1903/01/cnr.05.html.

328 **shortly after 4:30 p.m.:** "Kim Kardashian West Goes to the White House to Talk Pardon with Trump," CNBC, May 31, 2018.

328 **she had insinuated her way:** Katie Rogers, "Trump Meets with Kim. Kim Kardashian West, That Is," *New York Times,* May 30, 2018.

328 **"Happy Birthday Alice Marie Johnson":** Kim Kardashian West (@KimKardashian), Twitter, May 30, 2018, 9:50 a.m., twitter.com/KimKardashian/status/1001823217219129344.

329 **President Clinton's pardon of Marc Rich:** David Johnston, "U.S. Is Beginning Criminal Inquiry in Pardon of Rich," *New York Times,* February 15, 2001.

329 **When President George W. Bush commuted:** Scott Shane and Neil A. Lewis, "Bush Commutes Libby Sentence, Saying 30 Months 'Is Excessive,'" *New York Times,* July 3, 2007.

329 **Instead of being wronged by the system:** Richard Pérez-Peña, "Former Arizona Sheriff Joe Arpaio Is Convicted of Criminal Contempt," *New York Times,* July 31, 2017.

331 **received a commutation of his sentence:** Mitch Smith, "President Commutes Sentence of Iowa Meatpacking Executive," *New York Times,* December 20, 2017.

331 **Trump pardoned a former sailor:** Matt Zapotosky, "Trump Pardons Former Navy Sailor Convicted of Retaining Submarine Pictures in Case That Drew Comparisons to Clinton," *Washington Post,* March 9, 2018.

331 **The following month:** Peter Baker, "Trump Pardons Scooter Libby in a Case That Mirrors His Own," *New York Times,* April 13, 2018.

331 **he issued a posthumous pardon:** John Eligon and Michael D. Shear, "Trump Pardons Jack Johnson, Heavyweight Boxing Champion," *New York Times,* May 24, 2018.

332 **"I would like to thank":** Kim Kardashian West (@KimKardashian), Twitter, May 30, 2018, 10:03 p.m., twitter.com/KimKardashian/status/1002007628501934083.

338 **"The White House counsel":** Michael S. Schmidt and Maggie Haberman, "White House Counsel, Don McGahn, Has Cooperated Extensively in Mueller Inquiry," *New York Times,* August 18, 2018.

339 **"I allowed White House Counsel":** Donald J. Trump (@realDonald Trump), Twitter, August 18, 2018, 6:12 p.m., twitter.com/realDonald Trump/status/1030940529037651968.

340 **We wrote that at the time:** Maggie Haberman and Michael S. Schmidt, "Trump Lawyers' Sudden Realization: They Don't Know What Don McGahn Told Mueller's Team," *New York Times,* August 18, 2018.

345 **McGahn had watched the testimony:** Carl Hulse, *Confirmation Bias: Inside Washington's War over the Supreme Court, from Scalia's Death to Justice Kavanaugh* (New York: Harper, 2019).

345 **"Did I tell you that":** Ibid.

348 **Bloomberg reported that Mueller:** Chris Strohm, Greg Farrell, and Shannon Pettypiece, "Mueller Ready to Deliver Key Findings in His Trump Probe, Sources Say," Bloomberg, October 17, 2018.

348 **NBC News reported that Mueller:** Pete Williams and Ken Dilanian, "Mueller May Submit Report to Attorney General as Soon as Mid-February, Say Sources," NBC News, December 20, 2018.

348 **CNN and NBC News reported:** Evan Perez, Laura Jarrett, and Katelyn Polantz, "Justice Department Preparing for Mueller Report as Early as Next Week," CNN, February 20, 2019.

348 **CBS News said the report:** Steven Portnoy (@stevenportnoy), Twitter, February 21, 2018, 7:33 a.m., twitter.com/stevenportnoy/status/1098561308142829568.

354 **At 4:00 p.m. that Friday:** Katie Rogers and Katie Benner, "Where's the Mueller Report? Washington Barely Handled the Anticipation," *New York Times,* March 22, 2019.

355 **"It was a complete and total exoneration":** Mark Mazzetti and

Katie Benner, "Mueller Finds No Trump-Russia Conspiracy, but Stops Short of Exonerating President on Obstruction," *New York Times,* March 24, 2019.

356 **"Up to the attorney general":** "Remarks by President Trump and Prime Minister Netanyahu of Israel After Bilateral Meeting," White House, March 25, 2019, www.whitehouse.gov/briefings-statements/remarks-president-trump-prime-minister-netanyahu-israel-bilateral-meeting-4/.

357 **Mueller sent a far more harshly worded letter:** Robert S. Mueller III, "Re: Report of the Special Counsel on the Investigation into Russian Interference in the 2016 Presidential Election and Obstruction of Justice (March 2019)," Special Counsel's Office, March 27, 2019.

358 **Barr thought the letter:** Peter Baker, "Barr Defends Handling of Mueller Report Against Withering Rebukes," *New York Times,* May 1, 2019.

359 **Barr later told Congress:** Isaac Stanley-Becker, " 'I Don't Know': Barr's Professed Ignorance Prompts Calls for His Resignation After Mueller Letter," *Washington Post,* May 1, 2019.

359 **"It was my baby":** Baker, "Barr Defends Handling of Mueller Report Against Withering Rebukes."

361 **"The Special Counsel found":** "Attorney General William P. Barr Delivers Remarks on the Release of the Report on the Investigation into Russian Interference in the 2016 Presidential Election," U.S. Department of Justice, April 18, 2019, www.justice.gov/opa/speech/attorney-general-william-p-barr-delivers-remarks-release-report-investigation-russian.

362 **the report contained stark new examples:** Special Counsel Robert S. Mueller III, "Report on the Investigation into Russian Interference in the 2016 Presidential Election," U.S. Department of Justice, March 2019.

363 **Out of the incidents:** Quinta Jurecic, "Obstruction of Justice in the Mueller Report: A Heat Map," *Lawfare,* April 21, 2019.

364 **In his testimony before the House:** "Transcript of Robert S. Mueller III's Testimony Before the House Intelligence Committee," *Washington Post,* July 24, 2019.

366 **"lying bastard":** Mueller, "Report on the Investigation into Russian Interference in the 2016 Presidential Election."

375 **"He is going to testify":** Adia Robinson, "Robert Mueller 'Is Going to Testify': Rep. Adam Schiff," ABC News, May 12, 2019.

375 **"And as set forth":** "Full Transcript of Mueller's Statement on Russia Investigation," *New York Times,* May 29, 2019, www.nytimes.com/2019/05/29/us/politics/mueller-transcript.html.

377 **It wasn't until June 25:** Nicholas Fandos, "Mueller to Testify to Congress, Setting Up a Political Spectacle," *New York Times,* June 25, 2019.

377 **There were small difficulties:** Matt Zapotosky and Rachel Bade,

"Mueller's Team Is Said to Have Told Congress His Acuity Was Not an Issue. Some Lawmakers Privately Worry It Was," *Washington Post,* July 27, 2019.

Epilogue: President Trump Finds His Roy Cohn

379 **On July 25, 2019:** "Memorandum of Telephone Conversation," White House, July 25, 2019, www.whitehouse.gov/wp-content/uploads/2019/09/Unclassified09.2019.pdf.

381 **Giuliani had discussed plans:** Kenneth P. Vogel, "Rudy Giuliani Plans Ukraine Trip to Push for Inquiries That Could Help Trump," *New York Times,* May 9, 2019.

388 **"does not appear to be consistent":** Alana Abramson, Brian Bennett, and John Walcott, "Whistleblower Found Trump Phone Call with Foreign Leader 'Troubling,' Official Says," *Time,* September 19, 2019.

389 **Nancy Pelosi stood firmly against:** John Bresnahan, Heather Caygle, and Kyle Cheney, "Pelosi Rebuffs Nadler on Impeachment After Mueller Flop," *Politico,* July 24, 2019.

392 **Eight days earlier:** Maggie Haberman, "John Bolton Will Speak in His Book, if Not at the Senate Trial," *New York Times,* January 15, 2020.

394 **"I think it's increasingly likely":** Michael D. Shear and Nicholas Fandos, "Bolton Revelations Anger Republicans, Fueling Push for Impeachment Witnesses," *New York Times,* January 27, 2020.

394 **we published a second story:** Michael S. Schmidt and Maggie Haberman, "Bolton Was Concerned That Trump Did Favors for Autocratic Leaders, Book Says," *New York Times,* January 27, 2020.

395 **According to Bolton:** Maggie Haberman and Michael S. Schmidt, "Trump Told Bolton to Help His Ukraine Pressure Campaign, Book Says," *New York Times,* January 31, 2020.

397 **In the fall of 2017:** Peter Baker, " 'Lock Her Up' Becomes More Than a Slogan," *New York Times,* November 14, 2017.

397 **Barr told a Senate Appropriations subcommittee:** Nicholas Fandos and Adam Goldman, "Barr Asserts Intelligence Agencies Spied on the Trump Campaign," *New York Times,* April 10, 2019.

397 **The next month:** Adam Goldman, Charlie Savage, and Michael S. Schmidt, "Barr Assigns U.S. Attorney in Connecticut to Review Origins of Russia Inquiry," *New York Times,* May 13, 2019.

397 **Two months later:** "Memorandum of Telephone Conversation," July 25, 2019.

397 **By October:** Anna Momigliano, "Italy Did Not Fuel U.S. Suspicion of Russian Meddling, Prime Minister Says," *New York Times,* October 23, 2019.

398 **Then, in February:** Eileen Sullivan and Michael D. Shear, "Trump

Praises Barr for Rejecting Punishment Recommended for Stone," *New York Times,* February 12, 2020.

398 **He decided the Justice Department:** Adam Goldman and Mark Mazzetti, "Trump White House Changes Its Story on Michael Flynn," *New York Times,* May 14, 2020.

Afterword

For this afterword, I reference speeches John Kelly delivered in 2019 in Redondo Beach, California, and in 2020 at the Lakeside School in Washington State. In addition, I reference the book *Frankly, We Did Win This Election* by Michael C. Bender; "John F. Kelly Says His Tenure as Trump's Chief of Staff Is Best Measured by What the President Did Not Do" by Molly O'Toole (*Los Angeles Times,* December 30, 2018); and "Trump: Americans Who Died in War Are 'Losers' and 'Suckers'" by Jeffrey Goldberg (*The Atlantic,* September 3, 2020). I also conducted dozens of interviews on background with former Trump administration officials and others who worked with Kelly.

INDEX

PHOTO: © SHARON SUH

MICHAEL S. SCHMIDT is a two-time Pulitzer Prize–winning Washington correspondent for *The New York Times.* Over his fifteen years at the *Times,* he has covered the investigations of the Trump presidency, the Pentagon, the FBI, the Department of Homeland Security, and the war in Iraq. He started his career at the *Times* as a clerk answering the phones on the foreign desk before becoming a sports reporter covering performance-enhancing drugs and legal issues. He is a graduate of Lafayette College.

Twitter: @nytmike

ABOUT THE TYPE

This book was set in Bembo, a typeface based on an old-style Roman face that was used for Cardinal) Pietro Bembo's tract *De Aetna* in 1495. Bembo was cut by Francesco Griffo (1450–1518) in the early sixteenth century for Italian Renaissance printer and publisher Aldus Manutius (1449–1515). The Lanston Monotype Company of Philadelphia brought the well-proportioned letterforms of Bembo to the United States in the 1930s.